Lit-Rock

Lit-Rock

Literary Capital in Popular Music

Edited by
Ryan Hibbett

BLOOMSBURY ACADEMIC
NEW YORK • LONDON • OXFORD • NEW DELHI • SYDNEY

BLOOMSBURY ACADEMIC
Bloomsbury Publishing Inc
1385 Broadway, New York, NY 10018, USA
50 Bedford Square, London, WC1B 3DP, UK
29 Earlsfort Terrace, Dublin 2, Ireland

BLOOMSBURY, BLOOMSBURY ACADEMIC and the Diana logo are trademarks
of Bloomsbury Publishing Plc

First published in the United States of America 2023
This paperback edition published 2024

Copyright © Ryan Hibbett, 2023
Each chapter copyright © by the contributor, 2023

For legal purposes the Acknowledgments on p. 241 constitute an extension of
this copyright page.

Cover design: Louise Dugdale
Cover image © Jean-Marie Périer/Photo12.

All rights reserved. No part of this publication may be reproduced or transmitted
in any form or by any means, electronic or mechanical, including photocopying,
recording, or any information storage or retrieval system, without prior
permission in writing from the publishers.

Bloomsbury Publishing Inc does not have any control over, or responsibility for, any
third-party websites referred to or in this book. All internet addresses given in this
book were correct at the time of going to press. The author and publisher regret any
inconvenience caused if addresses have changed or sites have ceased to exist,
but can accept no responsibility for any such changes.

Library of Congress Cataloguing-in-Publication Data
Names: Hibbett, Ryan, editor.
Title: Lit-rock: literary capital in popular music / edited by Ryan Hibbett.
Description: [1st.] | New York: Bloomsbury Academic, 2022. |
Includes bibliographical references and index. | Summary: "Discusses the
relationship between popular music and literature in conjunction with
the connection between high and low art"– Provided by publisher.
Identifiers: LCCN 2022009460 (print) | LCCN 2022009461 (ebook) |
ISBN 9781501354694 (hardback) | ISBN 9781501392856 (paperback) |
ISBN 9781501354700 (epub) | ISBN 9781501354717 (pdf) | ISBN 9781501354724
Subjects: LCSH: Music and literature. | Music and language. |
Popular music–History and criticism. | Popular music–Philosophy and aesthetics.
Classification: LCC ML3849 .L586 2022 (print) | LCC ML3849 (ebook) |
DDC 780/.08–dc23/eng/20220322
LC record available at https://lccn.loc.gov/2022009460
LC ebook record available at https://lccn.loc.gov/2022009461

ISBN: HB: 978-1-5013-5469-4
PB: 978-1-5013-9285-6
ePDF: 978-1-5013-5471-7
eBook: 978-1-5013-5470-0

Typeset by Deanta Global Publishing Services, Chennai, India

To find out more about our authors and books visit www.bloomsbury.com and
sign up for our newsletters.

To my brother David Brent Hibbett, through whose cassette-player and bedroom wall came all sorts of beguiling new sounds. And to my children, Jordan and Chase: You ignite and rejuvenate my interest in words and music, books and songs more than you know!

Contents

Introduction: Conspicuous Listening: Literature, Rock, and
the Pop Omnivore   1

Part I Authorship and Authenticity

1 David Bowie's *Diamond Dogs*, the Cut-Up, and Rock's Unfinished
Revolution *Barry J. Faulk*   35

2 Kurt, Kathleen 'n' Kathy: Cut-and-Paste and the Art of Being for
Real *Patricia Malone*   49

Part II Craft and Confession

3 Joni Mitchell and the Literature of Confession *David R. Shumway*   65

4 Pop Star vs. Harvard Professor: The "Amateur" Poetry of Taylor
Swift *Weishun Lu*   78

5 Personae Non Grata: Dramatic Monologue and Social Pathology in
Select Randy Newman Songs *John Kimsey*   91

Part III Aesthetics, Movements, Technology

6 New Wave, European Avant-Gardes, and the Unmaking of Rock
Music *Chris Mustazza*   109

7 Cycling on Acid: The Literariness of Altered Experiences in Psychedelic
Rock *Tymon Adamczewski*   120

Part IV Signs and Mediations

8 A Portrait of the Artist in a Pop Song: Images of James Joyce in Popular
Music *Kevin Farrell*   137

9 "Hand in Glove": Punk, Post-punk, and Poetry *Martin Malone*   152

Part V Nation and Narrative

10 Under an American Spell: U2's *The Joshua Tree* in the Shadow of
Flannery O'Connor *Scott Calhoun*   169

viii *Contents*

11 Rock, Hard-Boiled: The Mekons and American Crime Fiction
    Peter Hesseldenz   182
12 When Poetry Meets Popular Music: The Case of Polish Rock Artists in
    the Late Twentieth Century *Marek Jeziński*   196

Part VI Identity and Discourse

13 "It's Our Version of *Almost Famous*": Toward a Reimagined Canon of
    Rock Criticism *Kimberly Mack*   213
14 Limits of the Literary: Rethinking Allusions in Pop Music *Pat O'Grady* 227

Acknowledgments   241
List of Contributors   242
Index   245

Introduction

Conspicuous Listening: Literature, Rock, and the Pop Omnivore

Just when it had got rolling, rock music had a problem: it wanted to be art. When one considers that both the bubblegum and art-rock traditions are epitomized by the *very same* Beatles; that a great many rock bands, as Simon Frith and Howard Horn have shown, were the products of formal art school educations;[1] that MTV in its heyday devoted massive chunks of programming to "alternative" music;[2] and that the 2016 Nobel Prize in Literature was awarded to singer-songwriter legend Bob Dylan, one can begin to see the story of rock as the mainstreaming of the high/low binary itself. Far more relevant, in the rock era, than the split between classical and popular music is the latter's own, diversely manifested claims to seriousness, depth, and distinction. To put it another way, rock music very quickly became a space in which the *construct* of high and low, of the tasteful individual and the cultureless mass, was widely instituted and made functional through the resources, purchases, conversations, and experiences of everyday life; the trope of distinction was effectively loosened from simplistic class divisions and put to work—effectively and ineffectively, naively and skillfully—within communities who may have previously seen themselves as culturally homogenous. And though the new social currency meant opportunity for some previously excluded individuals, it was promptly invested in as well from above, and toward the emerging stock of the omnivore. Today, nearly every artist and fan has, in some way, shape, or form, a stake in the game, whose terminology, signs, and structures have been fully extrapolated into the globalized culture industry.

Literature has long provided a key resource in popular music's claim to prestige, as well as its role—across an ever-widening range of genres—in mediating the institutionalized, disproportionately accessible realm of high art. Some examples *not* accounted for in the chapters that follow? Steppenwolf, the Doors, and Soft Machine take their names, respectively, from books by Herman Hesse, Aldous Huxley, and William Burroughs; Beyoncé recites the poetry of Warsan Shire on her visual album *Lemonade*; progressive-rock gurus Rush, in addition to their tour de force "Tom Sawyer," engage works by Ayn Rand, Samuel Taylor Coleridge, Ernest Hemingway, Williams Faulkner, and David Foster Wallace; the teen-anthem-penning Beach Boys reproduce, as a kind of choral round on their beleaguered *Smile* project, William Wordsworth's paradox "the child is father of the man"; hip-hop artist Loyle Carner takes his album title "Not Waving, But Drowning" from poet Stevie Smith, whose recorded commentary he includes on the title track; Van Morrison found a signature litany song with "Rave on, John Donne"; William Basinski's ambient soundscapes include titles such as "Paradise Lost" (John Milton) and "For Whom the Bell Tolls" (Hemingway via Donne); Charles Mingus titled a 1959 record, which offers in fact no poems at all, *A Modern Jazz Symposium of Music and Poetry*; Johnny Cash's "The Man Comes Around" is chock-full of biblical references; and K-pop boyband BTS, celebrated both for their visual incorporations of classic art and uses of literary allusions, find material in works by Ursula Le Guin, Hesse, and Ovid. The list could go on indefinitely, sprawling well beyond the company of singer-songwriter elites, over the half-century-plus of rock music's evolution, and into a present in which the gestures and signs of artistic eccentricity and the effort to "be literary" are visible even among the pop kingdom's most commercially successful stars. And this is to say nothing of (equally eclectic) lists of pop performers who have actually published literary works (Jewel, John Lennon, Patti Smith, Gil Scott-Heron, Leonard Cohen, Bo Burnham, Halsey, Tupac Shakur, Scott Walker, Linton Kwesi Johnson, Lou Reed, Gulzar); assume more fully a bardic persona (Nick Cave, Sun Ra, Donovan, Moondog, the Incredible String Band, Bonnie Prince Billy, Tom T. Hall); pen lyrics that are conspicuously "poetic" in terms of technique or voice (Noname, David Berman, the Tragically Hip, Tasha, Tori Amos, Tom Waits, Paul Simon, Kendrick Lamar); or adapt—as do Jim Croce's "Gunga Din" (Rudyard Kipling), Iron Maiden's "Rime of the Ancient Mariner" (Coleridge), America's "Watership Down" (Richard Adams), the Cure's "Killing an Arab" (Albert Camus), Vikings Invasion's "The Love Song of J. Alfred Prufrock" (T. S. Eliot),[3] and A Winged Victory for the Sullen's *Invisible Cities* (Italo Calvino)[4]—particular literary works as lyrics, themes, or inspiration.

One objective of this book, then, is to give at least a precursory indication of just how widespread, diverse, and ongoing the uses of literature actually are across the pop music spectrum—something best achieved, I determined, by way of multiple authors and perspectives. What I did *not* aim to do was assemble together only the most heralded names in songwriting, or to isolate, brand, and define literary rock music as a subgenre or aesthetic; though these chapters offer close looks at particular artists and their creative practices, they keep a collective eye on the cultural, social, and historical significance of such practices—of the curious tensions, interconnections, and distances at work wherever literature is invoked in song. My inclination is to pick at rather than reinforce the hierarchies in play, though with an awareness that my own musical knowledge and preferences are largely a product of those hierarchies, and a trust that more would be lost than gained in trying to hedge contributors—whose international makeup and varied disciplines bring richness, I hope, to the conversation—within a singular ideological vision. I use the term "capital," furthermore, not to negate the realities of individual talent and creativity or to undermine the sheer pleasures of listening, but to emphasize, when it comes to literary references in pop contexts, the socially operative domain of *use*, *value*, and *circulation*—to show a high/low discourse at work, and to steal a glimpse at the typically invisible structures that guide, and are reinforced by, our seemingly personalized aesthetic experiences. Popular music in this respect is not literature's corporeal antithesis—a "crying out not to be written about,"

Introduction 3

as Hanif Kureishi puts it[5]—but its distributor and translator: a meta-medium of sorts, where literature is "made real" beyond the classroom.

There are, to be clear, some painful omissions: hip-hop may be, in its ear for cadence and syllabics, prizing of inventive and complex rhymes, and subjugation of the sung to the spoken lyric—in sum, its showcasing of the "music" of language itself—the genre most closely related to traditional poetry, and a form in which poetic expression continues to thrive. Tupac Shakur's 2017 Rock and Roll Hall of Fame induction and Kendrick Lamar's 2018 Pulitzer for *DAMN* but punctuate hip-hop's growing claim to artistic prestige (and, alternately, the cultural elite's investment in *it*): new generations of "hip-hop poets"—such as Sol, Naimo Yusuf, and others coming out of the University of Washington scene,[6] and Chicago's Noname (Fatimah Warner), Kevin Coval, and Ric Wilson—seem to bridge like their dub-poet forbearers[7] popular performance with academic culture, honoring the genre's stock practices even while stretching its subject matter and audience. "We are, at our foundation," Coval says of Chicagoan "breakbeats," "a generation of storytellers firmly rooted in the realist tradition of narrative, an extension of Gwendolyn Brooks and Carl Sandburg"[8]—a quotation to which David Browne adds: "As much as their rock predecessors, everyone from Kurtis Blow to Chuck D to Ice-T sounded like true modern bards, minus the literary self-importance."[9] Hip-hop possesses as well its own rich and provocative history of literary allusion, ranging, as Roy Christopher shows, from Dead Prez's retelling of *Animal Farm* and Emcee Killer Mike's incorporation of *Lord of the Flies* to its widespread engagement with the writings of Donald Goines.[10] Similar arguments—of literary merit within the "low" forms of oppressed communities—have been made regarding the blues, such as when Iain Lang, as early as 1943, pronounced it (in Frith's paraphrase) "music's most literary form," containing "the most sophisticated explorations of the rhythmic, metaphoric and playful possibilities of language itself."[11] "[I]f the blues are a form of poetry," Frith deduces, "then blues writers are poets, self-conscious, individual, more or less gifted in their uses of words."[12]

An easy out regarding hip-hop's (and other genres') absence here would be to point to the word *rock*, as used in my title, as genre-specific. Truthfully, however, I was open (as my subtitle indicates) to all forms of popular music, and hopeful of finding literature at work in some unexpected places. "Rock" here is foregrounded not for its aesthetic connotations (be it the four-dudes-with-guitars-and-drums prototype or something else) but as a pervasive and hegemonic discourse: rock, I suppose, in the Foucauldian sense, as a way of thinking and organizing, and as a concept whose power extends well beyond the demarcations of genre. Any attempt at setting aesthetic parameters crumbles regardless; in introducing his multi-dimensional concept of a "rock formation," Lawrence Grossberg observes that "there are, for all practical purposes, no musical limits on what can or cannot be rock"[13]—an ambiguity recognized as early as 1967 by Robert Christgau: "a term like 'rock' is impossibly vague; it denotes, if anything, something historical rather than aesthetic."[14] Indeed, basic rock instrumentation permeates as a privileged form all popular genres, including country and hip-hop, and has been parceled into the countless subcategories of soft-rock, post-rock, indie-rock, rockabilly, rocksteady, and so forth. Many rock bands qualify, based on airplay, chart success, and audience, as "pop," just as the majority of pop bands and solo-artists rely on basic rock instrumentation—a blurred reality evidenced by the two terms' frequent interchangeability, and in spite of their simultaneous manifestation as a contentious binary. Rock is in large part a *lyrical* phenomenon, a practice of self-referentiality, as reproduced endlessly (whether as verb or noun, music or lifestyle, sexual euphemism or battle-cry of independence) by titles like Bill Haley and His Comets' "Rock Around the Clock," Michael Jackson's "Rock with You," and Twisted Sister's "I Wanna Rock"; in nostalgia pieces such as Bob Segar's "Old Time Rock and Roll" and Billy Joel's "It's Still Rock and Roll to Me"; and drifting comfortably, if sometimes as a point of contention or contrast (e.g., DaBaby's "Rockstar," Alan Jackson's "Don't Rock the Jukebox"), into other genres.[15] The term enjoys, too, a rich life in everyday discourse. We identify and tip our caps, sincerely or begrudgingly, to the "rock star" colleagues and coworkers who outperform us. We play, whether as fanciful children or in actual garage bands, at being rock stars—a way of negotiating our desire to be apart from the crowd and gazed upon, rather than within it. We congratulate ourselves or others with having "rocked" an interview or test, or, if lucky, have our worlds "rocked" by some joyously upending revelation or lover. Even in colloquial expression, then, rock marries notions such as distinction, honor, exceptionalism, prestige, and recognition to a certain romantic sensibility, importing the idea of stardom metaphorically and within domains where it cannot literally exist. Thus Charles Baudelaire can be heralded as "France's first rock star," anticipating the tormented likes of Jimi Hendrix and Janice Joplin,[16] or Dylan Thomas as "the last rock-star poet," whose performances electrified audiences until "the *real* rock stars showed up."[17]

When "rock," like a hunk of glacier, first set itself adrift from its parent-term "rock and roll," it was accommodating already a need for seriousness and generational separation within what had largely been marketed and consumed as "kid's stuff." It was, to put it another way, a way to salvage the cool from the corny, but also a means to keeping the corny visible within what was more universally packaged as hip. This birth into self-consciousness is what Elijah Wald has in mind when titling his overview of American pop music *How the Beatles Destroyed Rock 'n' Roll*,[18] and what Michaelangelo Matos partially attributes—in "1966 vs. 1971: When 'Rock 'n' Roll' became 'Rock,' and What We Lost"—to the displacement of the 45 single with the LP as a privileged medium: "One of the key tenets of rock," he observes, "is that singles are kids' stuff while albums [*sic*] where the real meat is."[19] Indeed, the LP record brought a literariness to popular music in its potential for narrative arrangement and concept, as a platform for thoughtful and thorough artistry, and a form capacious enough to make "listening" an event of its own, promising, as does the novel, entrance into an alternative environment. It brought, too, in addition to more highly visible and elaborate artwork, the possibility of printed lyrics, the first instance of which is typically credited as the Beatles' *Sgt. Pepper's Lonely Hearts Club Band*. In this very material way, listeners became readers, songs became textual artifacts, music became literary. That album, released a meteoric four years after the band's bubblegummish debut *Please Please Me*, features famously a cut-out collage of celebrities, paying homage thereby to historical greatness and contemporary hipness alike, and including (in a now-glaringly all-white, all-male assemblage) authors Edgar Allan Poe, Dylan Thomas, Terry Southern, William Burroughs, H. G. Wells, James Joyce, Oscar Wilde, Stephen Crane, and Lewis Carroll. This cluster of greats, presented as something like a crude, DIY hodgepodge, represents rock's claim to literary ancestry while also exemplifying the ascendant value of cultural omnivorousness. "Reading [Peter] Blake's *Sergeant Pepper* sleeve—name the face, spot the cannabis, decode the lyrics," Frith and Horne reflect, "was like reading the underground press. This was a skill that could easily be acquired . . . but it was always constructed around a sense of difference from the 'mass' pop audience."[20] The cover also features the twinned images of the band themselves in their early suit-and-tie days versus their present-day psychedelic military regalia, which, coupled with the title and lyrics, seems to beat parody acts like the Rutles and the Residents to the punch. What better way to achieve godlike status in relation to a genre than to be at once its instigator and executioner, to embody and disclaim all in one breath?

This is all to account, however sinuously, for the hierarchies and exclusions within popular music criticism by connecting it to literature and literary culture—to position this study, essentially, in relation to the phenomenon of "rockism." Meant to call out an elitist and overly serious approach to music predicated on authenticity and knowledge, the term "rockism" is said to have been initially leveled at Americans by British performers favoring "irony, distance, and the pose."[21] It has since circulated, however, with its retaliatory term "poptimism," as a journalistic debate on both sides of the Atlantic—most notoriously, perhaps, in a pair of *New York Times* articles published ten years apart. In 2004's "The Rap Against Rockism," Kelefa Sanneh defines the term as a set of binary preferences—"idolizing the authentic old legend . . . while mocking the latest pop star; lionizing punk while barely tolerating disco; loving the live show and hating the music video; extolling the growling performer while hating the lip-syncher"—and questions why, given the rock canon's diminishing relevance, its ideology persists.[22] Sanneh calls rockism "imperial," guilty of claiming "the entire musical world as its own," and proffers that plenty of good music is created despite, and even because of, its corporate and commercial underpinnings.[23] He points out, too, the gendered framework and prejudices by which rockism tends to operate, pitting straight white men against the world, yet all the while owning the righteous position of the underdog: "the language of righteous struggle is the language of rockism itself."[24] Sanneh's op-ed contentions are more fully theorized by Miles Parks Grier, who, in "Said the Hooker to the Thief: 'Some Way Out' of Rockism," finds in rock's ethos of "not selling out" the gendered archetypes of the male cult artist and the prostitute, thus tracing "rock's identity-coded market moralities . . . to a longer line of anticommercial ideologies designed to preserve (or create) white male freedom."[25] Both Sanneh and Grier help to locate, beyond rockism's favoring of particular names and sounds (rock cred, Sanneh points out, may be earned by criticizing, not just lauding, one of its icons), its covert operations in sorting out people themselves. More at stake than the reputation of an established artist, after all, is the credibility of the fan: Who is in a position to make such claims in the first place? And who, when they venture to do so, is deemed worth listening to? Rock from this perspective becomes less about genre than discourse: the processes and dynamics of cultural distinction and social hierarchy, and the ways in which both formal criticism and the micropolitics of everyday interaction make felt a split between the mere consumer and the untouchable connoisseur. To delineate rockism, then, is to find something of the literary universe—its methods of ordering, its structurings of taste—fast at work: "From the start," Frith explains, "rock's claim to a superior pop status rested on the argument that rock songwriters . . . were, indeed, poets."[26]

Such are not the concerns of Saul Austerlitz's "The Pernicious Rise of Poptimism," a rebuttal to Sanneh and general lamentation for music criticism having, in an effort to atone for its "original sin" of cultural appropriation, "gone soft."[27] In a familiar kind of turf-defending, Austerlitz attributes the increased critical interest in mainstream pop stars to "party line" pressure—a superficial exercise of (market-driven) political correctness, to be resisted by the free-thinking critic.[28] Rock's age-old trope of mining for gems within a cultural landfill assumes here the image of a questing Sir Gawain: though plurality is nice, Austerlitz argues, the critic's imperative remains one of "hacking a path through the thicket of cultural abundance."[29] Austerlitz's diagnosis of an overbearing "poptimism" would seem to mark the apogee of what early Cultural Studies theorists most feared: a mass cultural stunting by way of popular texts: "Should gainfully employed adults whose job is to listen to music thoughtfully really agree so regularly," he questions, "with the taste of 13-year-olds?"[30] Both the generational narrative of taste—a trust that mainstream pop is squarely in the mature listener's rearview—as well as the binary of the "thoughtful"/active/responsible listener versus the thoughtless/passive/irresponsible fan are in play. Rather than grow up and into a mature relationship with music, Austerlitz worries, we appear even as critics to have entered, and remain contented by, an Orwellian Neverland of insipid pop.

Any number of observations complicate Austerlitz's critique, as well as the poptimist/rockist binary in general. One questions, for example, the reality (in practice, rather than as an operative, mythic construct) of a dominating wave of uncritical pop enthusiasts, out to police and reprimand anyone setting herself apart with obscure band names and aesthetic judgments. Are many critics, scholars, or even fans *really* arguing that Katie Perry is artistically superior to Joni Mitchell? That, when we hear Justin Bieber sing "Like baby, baby, baby no / Like baby, baby, baby oh / Thought you'd always be mine," we are encountering language as artful or observant as David Berman's "snowcloud shadowed interstates,"[31] or as eloquent and introspective as when Morrissey confides "a shyness that is criminally vulgar"?[32] Very little discussion takes place, I would venture, in the way of these kinds of direct lyrical contests, in part because many fans of pop's mega-stars are unlikely, within the channels of their socially produced *habitus*, to encounter the latter examples at all, or, if they do, to register them as up for grabs—that is, as socially useful—and not implicitly marked as someone else's property. Poptimism itself, from this perspective, could be seen as an extension or regeneration of its counterpart, the rift between them preserving at the same time a shared distance from those with no means of entering, or effectively entering, the conversation—a division, essentially, between cultural *participant*s and *non-participants*, which some researchers have found more indicative of class division than they do the genre-based distinctions of high and low taste.[33] Regardless, Austerlitz

Introduction 7

exemplifies in his defense what critics of rockism most wish to expose: the continued *use* of mainstream pop, *without* critical engagement, as a presumedly vapid, heavily feminized foil to "serious" music. Austerlitz does not have to engage in any specific way the songs or performances of the various mega-stars he names; rather, their names alone—the implied absurdity that they should be mentioned at all within a meaningful discussion or alongside "legitimate artists"—supply their own undoing: "Find Lady Gaga's bargain basement David Bowie routine a snooze? You, my friend, are fatally out of touch with the mainstream, with the pop idols of the present."[34] The contemporary pop star thus becomes a commercially cheapened rendition of the real thing, exemplifying the discourse by which artists are cast "as exemplary *characters* in cautionary tales about the market," and which generates profit by way of "moral distinctions between ascetic artists and debased whores."[35] In this book, where one finds a range of artists laying claim to seriousness by way of connections to literature, it is the final pairing of chapters that challenge rockism most directly: Kimberly Mack examines in "It's our version of *Almost Famous*" the strategic and influential, yet historically neglected, contributions of Black women writers to early rock journalism, while Pat O'Grady invites us, with his surprise example of the Bee Gees' "Islands in the Stream" in "Limits of the Literary," to consider the instances in which literary allusions do and do not convert to prestige, and to ask why.

The emergent challenge to rockism, seen by Austerlitz as a plague specific to music journalism, parallels certain developments in twentieth-century literary criticism, including its efforts to decenter the white male tradition and to expand the kinds of texts applicable for study. More specifically, rock's manifestations as a social rebellion or youth movement—its anti-establishment and therefore anti-literary identity—seems to have coincided early and awkwardly with its imported literary values of authenticity, hierarchy, and individual genius—criteria for engaging and sorting out pop that proved far more enduring and profitable than did wholescale rejections of the genre, be they those of high-art exclusivists for whom pop in all of its varieties translates as rubbish, or right-wing evangelicals who denounced and went to war against it as the devil's medium.

One fascinating example of this kind of negotiation, of attempting to get a handle on pop as a new and pervasive, yet potentially threatening, phenomenon, is the 1967 CBS special *Inside Pop: The Rock Revolution*, hosted by Leonard Bernstein.[36] Produced by classical musician and documentarian David Oppenheim, the show positions Bernstein as both cultural authority and relatable family man—a trusted, familiar face and mediator of sophisticated music in the way that Carl Sagan would soon become for science. He is both the irritated parent who resents "volume for its own sake" and "the way the words are often drowned out by drums and amplifiers," and the gentle, open-minded pedagogue who assures fellow adults that there is something of value present. Bernstein speaks at the outset of an "aching gap between generations," the need for adults to listen and try to understand, and goes on to sample and very eloquently discuss, describe, and explain the musical innovations within a number of pop tunes. Stationed casually at his grand piano, Bernstein becomes the entity through which the otherwise formless outpouring of pop is sifted and appraised; after delivering the poptimist hook to his opening monologue—"Why do adults resent [rock music] so? And why do *I* like it?"—he promptly qualifies his enthusiasm with a rockist metaphor: "Of course, what I like is maybe five percent of the whole output, which pours over this country like the two oceans from both coasts, and it's mostly trash." Bernstein thus fulfills even in his genuine curiosity the role of gatekeeper, letting his (presumed) audience mostly off the hook in their assumption that rock music is drivel, while also modeling a language and process by which to engage and transcribe it in small, sampled doses. The initial effort, as embodied by the "you/I" distinction in the hook above, is to curb the threat and messiness of pop with the ordering discourses of music education and criticism: the "gender breakdown" of high-pitched male vocals, for example—that "androgynous phenomenon of the pop scene that produces boys with long hair and ruffled shirts"—is safely (if rather romantically) recategorized as "a straining after falsetto dreams of glory." A large portion of the video consists of Bernstein's expressions and body language as he listens with the audience to these condensed and sequenced bits of music: he nods his head pleasurably to the beat, gazes up in analytic thought, oohs along to the Beatles "She Loves You," and so on. Through the filter of Bernstein, all of these moments become tame, sensible, and intriguing rather than wild, irreverent, or noisy; the skeptical viewer learns to locate the interesting but rare bits (e.g., the "one noteworthy musical twist" in the Monkees' "I'm a Believer," the "high Bach trumpet" in "Penny Lane") within songs that by the dictates of youth and commercialism possess "a highly limited musical vocabulary." But Bernstein—an author of multiple books, I should note, as well a conductor/composer who could comfortably shift from the high modernism of a Mahler symphony to the "middlebrow" scoring of *Westside Story*—also creates order by fitting these nuggets of pop invention into their respective genres and musical traditions; in addition to highlighting various time signature and key changes, for example, he locates respectively the "gospel shouting" and "old blues" roots of "I'm a Believer" and "Hanky Panky." In short, Bernstein models for mass viewership the emergent omnivore and pop connoisseur, affixing to the visceral, emotive reaction of the fan the metaphorical specifics of the rock journalist: "it *kills* me," he says of Janice Ian's "Society's Child," "that sassy retort of the organ at the end."

Bernstein does account, albeit more briefly, for the literary and not just the musical component of "good" popular music. As with his musical comparisons, however ("that could *almost* be by Schuman"), his examples of the poetic in pop are thoughtfully qualified: he finds in the best of pop lyrics "something bordering on poetry," or "beginning to sound like real poems." Even in singling out Bob Dylan, whose lyrics alone he says "would make a bombshell of a book *of social criticism*," Bernstein preserves distance from what we trust to be the real thing. Elite pop, then, is teased out not so much by its successful importation of literary language, but as a raw approximation of legitimate art—a form whose flirtations with literature or classical instrumentation demand scrutiny ("we *must* listen," Bernstein insists), but as a confused effort more so than an achievement, and whose obscure or inarticulate "message" is driven ultimately by an emotional discontent. Even with the show's second-half focus on hearing from rock musicians, fans, and protestors, the movement remains characterized (rather imperially, to be honest) as the ill-formed theatrics of children—a community struggling to articulate its own "message" ("I still don't get it . . . you've got to tell me better," Bernstein presses his interviewees), and who despite their passion and hopefulness, Bernstein concludes, "aren't [typically] swept up by anything more than the throb of a new beat they like, or the look of a new personality they love." When all is said and done, the topical and the social are mostly mitigated within a storyline of struggling youth and tone of parental condescension.

Though the program's various artists may seem eclectic, its argument for high pop is built fully around and upon the Beatles, whom Bernstein starts with and returns to, again and again, leaving a definite impression that there is the one band and then everyone else. Even as he turns specifically to lyrical artistry, it is the Beatles' "Paperback Writer"—whose lyrics bring directly to rock and roll the literary insignia of selling out, a cheapening of artistry through mass circulation—that provides his starting point. While expected names like Dylan and Paul Simon receive their due here, the narrative of the maturing pop star, whom we can see transcending the genre's "vocabulary," remains tantamount; perhaps the program's most enduring clip is that of a shaggy-headed Brian Wilson at the piano performing "Surf's Up"—a moment signifying in its visuals alone the introspective solo artist (and a kind of doppelganger for Bernstein himself), mature beyond his original, bass-strapped and stripe-shirted image. As part of the *Smile* album that would famously never arrive, the song's lyrics are penned by pop-surrealist Van Dyke Parks ("poetic, beautiful even in its obscurity," Bernstein remarks), a stark and sudden shift from the Beach Boys' previous and more conventional material. Though the project's failure is typically explained in terms of Wilson's mental breakdown, its acutely realized juxtaposition of aesthetic approaches—the drive for artistic experimentation clashing with the fear of alienating listeners—played no small role, culminating as legend has it in Beach Boy Mike Love demanding of Parks that he explain what his lyrics mean, and imploring Wilson to not "fuck with the formula."[37] What has since played out is a fascinating division, one with probable class implications, between devotees of Wilson as a musical genius and prodigy of studio production (whose tortured history and lost *magnum opus* only add to his appeal), and fans of Love's touring version of the Beach Boys, for whom Wilson's story is either unknown or not particularly relevant. The studio and the concert; the genius and the mercenary; the literary and the commercial—this anecdote alone is a concentrated version of the binaries that have come to dominate pop discourse and marketing, as well as an extension of literature's own, convoluted battle between artistic obscurity and simply "making sense."

Something of *Inside Pop*'s Bernsteinian presence—a position, historically entrusted of course to white males, whose desire to bring pop into sharper focus means invoking its legitimate other—has long governed the discourse of "rock as poetry." Through such discourse, we absorb not only the values of selectivity and obscurity but also learn to engage or frame pop ironically, to sense and respect the panoptical presence of those who "know better," and the shadowy backdrop of stuff we simply "don't get." Christgau's 1967 "Rock Lyrics are Poetry (Maybe)" seeks, far more than the parentheses of its title suggest, to enforce a boundary and to make any such argument or rocker's attempt at literariness a risky maneuver indeed; clipped truisms like "Poems are read or said.

Songs are sung" threaten to eclipse the entire discussion even as it unfolds.[38] What remains is largely an exercise in showing how even rock's most poetic lyricists sound silly on the page, and a kind of oxymoronic circle by which we learn that, in the end, it is the *absence* of literary signs or methods that allow for something genuinely poetic to emerge; charting his path through Dylan, Simon, and company, Christgau finds his way back at last to the Beatles and the unpretentiousness of "All You Need is Love": "[W]ritten in basic English . . . the song employs rock-and-roll—dominant music, big beat, repeated refrain, simple diction—and transforms it into something which, if not poetry, at least has a multifaceted poetic wholeness. I think it is rock poetry in the truest sense."[39] This is noticeably the same logic by which mid-century, anti-modernist authors, most prominently Philip Larkin, would find in a poet like Thomas Hardy a less overtly or self-consciously "literary" style, and therefore a beacon of authenticity.[40]

In the far more recent "Pop Star Poetics," David Browne similarly determines that rock lyrics are "generally only poetry when couched in song." The extent to which lyrics *do* succeed on paper or as recitation remains for Browne a historically frozen moment; reminiscing fondly on 1969's *The Poetry of Rock* anthology, he struggles to locate anything of similar poetic value in its contemporary equivalents, *The Spoken Word Revolution* and its *Redux* follow-up. While lamenting songwriting's generally "fallen" expectations, Browne finds in Jeff Buckley's tribute to Dylan the rare exception, and gestures back to 1967's *Songs of Leonard Cohen* as the unsurpassed "standard for the fusion of pop song and verse." One can begin to appreciate here the way in which rockism inhabits a literary mindset, but also provides a mechanism by which popular music is assimilated (Browne's piece is featured in *Poetry Foundation*) to the literary field and its institutional practices; in a firm but familiar distinction, Browne identifies "that far worse trend that still plagues us—rockers as poets. Those slim, forgettable volumes by Jewel and Alicia Keys and [Billy] Corgan himself, sharing bookshelf space with Wallace Stevens and Ginsberg at your local Borders." Such language threads directly back to Christgau—who sniffs out another would-be Borders resident, Jim Morrison, as an imposter dealing primarily in "histrionics" and a "nebulousness that passes for depth"—but finds contemporary equivalents (with something of Christgau's inverted authenticity test) in places such as Cameron Crowe's film dialogue: "Jim Morrison?," scoffs a character from *Almost Famous*: "He's a drunken buffoon posing as a poet. . . . Give me the Guess Who. They got the courage to be drunken buffoons, which makes them poetic."[41] Lurking behind such inversions, perhaps, is the intimation that pop stars are closer to poets in their original, bardic manifestation, rendering poetry of the contemporary era—that of classrooms and textbooks, silent reading and analysis—a suspicious intruder; poets and pop stars alike become weirdly susceptible to criticisms of being too "literary," and therefore must negotiate the claim to prestige with signs of the commonplace and a sense of humility.

What has largely eluded discussions of poetry and pop lyrics, with their trust in genres like "song" and "poem," in personae like "pop star" and "poet," as more or less distinct and self-dictating forms, is an appreciation for the fragmented and drifting nature of the language they mutually exploit; once we relax a text's claim to wholeness we can begin to appreciate the interplay of discourses—of linguistic "nuggets" that may

Introduction   11

invite recognition as poetic or plain, familiar or unfamiliar, stock or unique—both within and across its presumed boundaries. This heteroglossic approach helps, in turn, to unravel binary oppositions, offering instead the fluidity of an artistic spectrum—one on which artists and works might be positioned according to the ratio with which they pull from discernably "alternate" discourses, and which makes visible the investment in high and low—in negotiating the signs of seriousness and humility, the identities of artist and mere entertainer—shared by all. Such a model means acknowledging that "After I Made Love to You" by Bonnie Prince Billy—an indie-guru who has used D. H. Lawrence's poetry for lyrics, self-identified at one point as "Pushkin," and whose collective works Randall Roberts calls a "modern-day version of Walt Whitman's *Leaves of Grass*"[42]—shares verbal stock with songs by Engelbert Humperdinck ("After the Lovin'") and Alabama ("When We Make Love"). It means contextualizing an MFA-worthy gem like "We have to shout over the din of our Rice Krispies," courtesy of Sting, with the stock-couplet "Oh can't you see / You belong to me" of the same record, or appreciating how the half-vague phrase "that book by Nabokov" (Sting, again) at once interpolates and holds in abeyance the world of textbook literature. We might, by this same approach: find Nick Cave's professorial "lectures"[43] and symbolist metaphors curious companions to a chorus (in mainstream pop's epistolary tradition) like "Love letter love letter / go get her go get her"; suspect that Brian Eno's museum and poetic works[44] accrue prestige specifically *in relation to* his glam-rock foundations; ask whether Kristen Anderson-Lopez's Disney lyrics aren't every bit as witty and artful and those of Cole Porter; or investigate how a guitar-shredding superstar like Prince becomes not just a hieroglyph but (for analyst C. Liegh McInnis) a "musical poet, philosopher, and storyteller."[45] I think, finally, that the approach I am advocating for means reevaluating the cliché not simply as lousy or lazy writing, but as a formal convention that sets up, as does the metrical foot in poetry, instances of variation, and which maintains value as something anticipated, shared, unpretentious, and participatory. As Adam Bradley observes in *The Poetry of Pop*, "Sometimes lyrics consciously aspire to cliché," and "[s]ometimes, too, songwriters exploit the comforting space of the obvious to craft subtle subversions and strangeness."[46] Though commonplace criticisms like "trite," "clichéd," and "vapid" speak to a prevailing rubric, there is in lyrics and literature alike a dependent rather than purely hierarchical relation between generic and inventive, communal and individualized language.

The chapters in this book examine these kinds of exchanges, the fluid interplay of high and low, at the level of specific artists; one finds in their collective efforts, however, not simply the hybridized "master," but the great whirling pool of cultural and linguistic resources, of samples and signifiers, through which pop artists of all varieties drag their nets. Kevin Farrell explores, for example, how James Joyce and *Ulysses* are distributed through popular music, not only as co-opted signs of sophistication but also as symbols of pretentiousness or cultural authority from which the pop artist may contrive a self-authenticating distance; Martin Malone finds in punk and post-punk a resource to be "leached out" in formal poetry-writing, as exemplified not only by his own work but that of his former band-mate and Poet Laureate Simon Armitage; and Chris Mustazza, discovering in New Wave pop an unlikely ancestor to European avant-gardism, points to technological sampling itself as a practice in which "the totality of recorded music becomes an archive to be drawn from." What also arises, in these and other chapters alike, is the importance of overlapping fields, figures, and variables: mediating contexts that bridge and buttress, sometimes harmoniously, sometimes not, the worlds of literature and popular music. If for Mustazza the mutual context is that of technology, for Tymon Adamczewski it is the phenomenon of psychedelia, and not as mere stylistic trappings but as a shared interest in altered states and creative process that aligns authors like Aldous Huxley and Ken Kesey with Syd Barrett and the ensuing subgenre of "stoner rock." For John Kimsey, the bridging variable is that of form itself: the dramatic monologue made famous by Victorian poets finds use, as a vehicle for ironic social criticism, in the lyrics of Randy Newman. In other chapters, particular writing practices bridge the gap; William Burroughs's cut-up technique, in fact, emerges twice: in Patricia Malone's study of Kurt Cobain and Kathy Acker as a challenge to traditional authorship and deconstruction of the male body, and in Barry Faulk's chapter on David Bowie as a means to rekindling a stalled aesthetic revolution. For Peter Hesseldenz, Scott Calhoun, and Marek Jeziński, national identity comes to the forefront: we find, respectively, the prolific but obscure Mekons looking to American detective fiction as a lens for political struggle back in Britain; U2 similarly tapping Flannery O'Conner's fiction as a resource for artistic personae and a model for understanding good and evil; and various artists installing, in the transitional space of post-communist Poland and with impressive commercial success, formal poetry as lyrics. Finally, we have, in David Shumway's piece on Joni Mitchell and Weishun Lu's on Taylor Swift, the overlapping aesthetic of confessionalism, in the former as an inventive use of subjectivity in songwriting that remains distinct from the confessionalism of canonical poets, and in the latter as an audience-oriented technique whose poetic labor is undersold by the academically sponsored rubric of "craft."

To me, these case studies show something more strategic than random at work in pop's deployment of literature—less a leveling of distinctions than a persistent framing (the canonical author through the voice of the rambling balladeer, the platitude through the mic of the poet, etc.) of the high/low relation itself. So while it is tempting to find in this shared and shifting signage evidence of a "no-brow" pluralism, it remains, by my assessment, connected to the processes of social distinction and material gain. In recent decades, the distinction between those knowledgeable and ignorant, loquacious and silent in relation to culture has manifested as a renewed, if not uncontested, "hipsterism"—a "conversion of cool" into capital, as Michael Scott explains, by those skilled in "blending historical subcultural styles"[47] and occupying a class position not unlike Bourdieu's "new petite bourgeoisie."[48] There are, furthermore, as Alan Warde and his collaborating researchers conclude, "meaningful patterns" that emerge among taste-bearers, as well as "homologies between sub-fields."[49]

The example of beer commerce in today's booming "craft" market offers a telling analogue, I think, to the divisions that emerge among music listeners, as well as their traceability from the singular instance into larger social formations. Two men in a liquor store: one perusing the endless rows of artistically labeled craft beers, the other beelining directly to a case of Bud Light further down the aisle. Whether they wish

Introduction 13

it or not, there is a conspicuousness, an interpretable posture, in these behaviors: a picker and chooser, reading labels perhaps among the many styles and breweries, and a decisive, self-assured purchaser. It is a division (deliberately gendered here) fully borne out by the beer industry in its marketing, with either type (the pretentious, indecisive, and "girly" connoisseur; the tasteless, sheep-like consumer) an easy object of ridicule, and, at times, with the same macro-brewery working both angles.[50] If we were to survey such shoppers in high volume, correlations would likely emerge not only in things like clothing, cars, and musical preferences, but also education, political affiliation, and so forth. We should also note that both parties are beer drinkers, possibly with comparable incomes, and thus experiencing closer proximity than either would with a top-shelf wine drinker. Much like the pop omnivore in relation to the classical exclusivist, the beer-snob occupies an in-between position, an effort to fuse blue-collar credibility with high-class taste. His, like literary rock music, is a product that channels readily into discourse; which unites (in the case of the home-brewer) consumption with creation; and privileges, in keeping with Bourdieu's class model, form over function.

Does one enjoy more power and privilege than the other? Though the connoisseur may well, despite the consumer's conscious rejection of him, maintain the kind of class advantages Bourdieu correlated to cultural capital, I'd be reluctant to call his position hegemonic: there is simply too much friction, alternate and resisting forms of power, and shifting networks of participants. More accurately, we might suggest that both parties rely to some extent on their symbolic distance from the other, which they carry with them into like-minded, but equally competitive, social communities. Perhaps it is in these more homogeneous contexts, though with a keen trust in the cultureless other as found in the beer aisle, that *what* one likes becomes secondary to *how* one likes. How, and how convincingly, do we *wear* our music, so to speak? If not backed by other forms of capital, cultural gestures always entail risk. In his wonderful exploration of taste via Celine Dion, Carl Wilson reveals just how nuanced and contradictory, yet still socially relevant, the struggle for coolness-via-culture has become: "To ignore cool may mean risking downward mobility at a time when many people are falling out of the middle-class," he says, and yet "Even being *deliberately* uncool doesn't save you, as that's an attempt to flip the rules in your favor."[51] And so we learn, unequally perhaps, strategies for accommodating our musical preferences to the rather unforgiving circumstances of social integration and ascent, and in ways that allow the "kitsch connoisseur" to maintain a sense of distinction from the "doofus who just likes goofball stuff."[52]

What I'd like to do, then, in closing out this section is to position the genre-hopping, discourse-dipping omnivore in relation to social class more broadly. In their application of Pierre Bourdieu's theories to contemporary Britain, Tony Bennett et al. observe that, despite the clear emergence of the cultural omnivore, there remain entire genres whose boundaries are "rarely straddled":[53] classical music, for example, is wholly off-limits to certain demographics, country music categorically rejected by others, and so forth. This is consistent with Richard Peterson's and Roger Kern's study on the American omnivore, who, they determine, has displaced the traditional "snob," yet still actively "mark[s] symbolic boundaries."[54] The omnivore may, for example, champion the "low" forms of certain marginalized groups while "still holding commercial middlebrow forms in contempt."[55] Class, gender, and race are of course determining factors here, as is generational identity in its tension with the localized family unit—all parts of an individual's *habitus*, or environmental structures that mediate between subjective and objective experience, and therefore play a role in clearing some paths while camouflaging others. The simple anecdote of my music-obsessed teenage daughter, thoroughly insulated from anything *I* might happen to play, speaks to the explicitly social, yet subtly contentious, dimensions of taste; if my playlists span disparate genres and decades, offering any number of sonic curiosities and beloved hits, then *something* would *have* to catch her interest, right? Sheer musicality should, at some point, demand a second spin. But the potential for shared participation is circumscribed by a tacit sense of ownership—a silent contract that inscribes songs as "mine" or "not mine," which itself becomes absorbed into the acts of listening and interpretation.

This particular example could be dismissed of course as commonplace parent-child dynamics. Yet I suspect it translates in certain ways to taste as it functions beyond the family or the individual encounter. As Frith's early research, in which he attaches class connotations to synonyms such as "teenager" and "youth,"[56] seems to suggest, there are curiously functional ways in which social class is superimposed onto family or generation, and vice versa; just as one might temper, as does the *Inside Pop* special discussed above, a challenge to society's norms with the construct of the lost child and loving parent, we might find in a parent/child anecdote such as mine the signage and symbolism of class division. My daughter's disinterest in my music seems precisely that: not an aesthetic judgment or sneer, but a (mostly) respectful preservation of distance. And though there exists in such disengagement an element of resistance—a straightforward rejection of "taste" as represented by myself—even this seems testament to a joint understanding that I quietly hold most of the cards. In defending Bourdieu's work, Douglas Holt makes the important point that even a conscious dismissiveness of high art by the dominated classes does not mean its power over them, its superior status, is somehow lessened: "there is little evidence supporting the contention that the reproductive consequences of culture are weakened when dominated tastes oppose the dominant. Quite the opposite. Defiant tastes of dominated classes efficiently reproduce social potion while maintaining the ideology that tastes are elective and socially inconsequential."[57] How, then, might the presence of this "other" music, this "other" listener, affect my daughter's relation to what she deems rightfully hers? What factors might deter her from even trying to access it? To the extent that I force the issue, whether by engaging her music or pontificating on my own, there are no doubt elements of appropriation, realignment, and demonstrated authority at play: "dominant social classes," Holt concludes,

> reproduce the social structure in accord with their interests not because they impose a uniform conception of the world on the rest of society, but because they are able to articulate commonsensical ways of understanding class difference such that their potential antagonism is neutralized. Elites have the power to set the terms through which tastes are assigned moral and social value.

In terms of "lit-rock," I think there are signs at work, a specific form of cultural capital, by which artists and listeners can both compete and coalesce, align and stratify. "Do people in positions of power," Warde and his colleagues ask, "pick up from a relatively small proportion among all the myriad signs of cultural affiliation, which everybody displays, whether some individuals deserve more respect or better treatment than others? It seems that this is the case."[58] In the next section, I'll attempt to show how these systems of recognition and respect traffic in literary capital, specifically the cultural monolith that is Bob Dylan.

Where's Bob? Dylancentrism and Rock's Literary Structuring

He's so unhip that / When you say Dylan he thinks you're talkin' about Dylan Thomas[59]

—Paul Simon, "A Simple Desultory Philippic"

Yippee! I'm a poet, and I know it. / Hope I don't blow it.[60]

—Bob Dylan, "I Shall be Free No. 10"

As mentioned up front, it was not my objective with this collection to bind together an already-elite group of poetic songwriters, and so I have little problem not offering the obligatory chapter on Bob Dylan. Such a prerequisite hardly seems necessary, given the wealth of material—endless scholarship, connecting him internationally and across disciplines to all things literary, including of late his own Cambridge Companion (2009) and Simon and Shuster's thousand-page edited collection of lyrics (2014)— already in existence and showing no signs of slowing down. Of literary interest and acclaim early on, Dylan has become over the years not just a pop legend but a staple in the Study of American literature and culture. Indeed, he *is* his own field of study— the subject, as Kevin Dettmar reports, of entire courses at hundreds of colleges[61] as well as a university-housed research archive and museum in Oklahoma. Tended to by scrupulous networks of "Dylanologists" and "Dylanophiles," his late career finds him endowed with all the markers of cultural sainthood, including not just the infamous Nobel Prize, but a Presidential Medal of Freedom and, as of late 2021, a touring exhibition ("Retrospectrum") of his *visual* artwork. "His literary bona fides are unimpeachable," Adam Bradley affirms, noting that his Nobel Prize selection should, given this history, seem more "safe" than shocking.[62] And whereas Dettmar classifies Dylan not as a poet but as a "literary artist,"[63] the distinction for Bradley seems to collapse: "Dylan is now just as much a poet as he is a pop star,"[64] he concludes, though it is perhaps the mix of both, I'll add, that secure for him more than any of his pop *or* literary peers a position of untouchability. To doubt his influence would at this point be silly, to question his genius at least vaguely taboo.

And yet here I am devoting an entire section of my introduction to the man. While the bulk of Dylan scholarship has been focused on showcasing his achievements and defining the nature of his artistry, his relevance to this collection has to do with

16 *Lit-Rock*

the way that artistry and its reception reproduce and impose a specifically literary structuring onto popular music. This structure contains within it the notion of an artistic "alternative"—of a smaller-market body of artists and records that may, to the benefit of the proactive listener, be gleaned from the rest—which previously belonged to the realms of literary discourse and criticism, and that enacts (within pop culture itself) the "restricted"/"unrestricted" division Bourdieu correlates to high art verses pop in general.[65] It is a structure evident enough among literature's high Modernists, as when Ezra Pound raves upon *The Smart Set* magazine's drastic reduction in circulation as evidence of increased merit and literary value ("damning the public's eyes" as he puts it[66]), or when W. B. Yeats, in a private letter, devalues war-poet Wilfred Owen, whom he had willfully excluded as editor from his *Oxford Book of Modern Verse*, with the imagery of public pandering and commercialism: "When I excluded Wilfred Owen, whom I consider unworthy of the poets' corner of a country newspaper, I did not know I was excluding a revered sandwich-board Man of the revolution & that some body has put his worst & most famous poem in a glass-case in the British Museum. . . . He is all blood, dirt and sucked sugar stick."[67]

As with the "make-it-new" Modernists in relation to what they saw as emasculated coffee-table verse, with Dylan comes not just the conviction-cum-platitude "pop lyrics can have depth," but the more abstracted or pedagogical idea of discovery: the practices of foraging a cultural waste land for its hidden goodies, of being "turned on" to this or that artist by way of another's recommendation. This kind of pedagogical value depends on an intimation that Dylan exists beyond the ears (literally or in terms of comprehension) of most listeners, and despite the *actual* popularity that lands him smack between Def Leopard and Tupac Shakur at number forty-five on *Insider*'s best-selling-artists-of-all-time list,[68] and which translated in 1974, Dettmar reveals, to nearly 4 percent of the US population buying advanced concert tickets for his tour.[69] What I mean is, to claim Bob Dylan is to claim a certain "knowingness," to mark a symbolic distance from the "typical" listener, who is presumed to trust nonetheless, as an unread person might trust the literary sovereignty of Shakespeare, in his greatness and the structure that ensures it.

The idea here isn't to take shots at Dylan or his fans (I'm among them), but, rather, to account for this centrality beyond his personal artistry and achievements, and to recognize the monolithic, overshadowing nature of his place in rock history. I use the term "Dylancentrism" to mark the consensus of there being precisely "the one," a wizened old crow atop pop's sprawling conifer, to which all other artists ultimately lead and by which their value may be assessed. Given the extraordinary variety of talented, prolific, and creative musicians, Dylancentrism is hardly a logical phenomenon. Rather, it speaks to a preexisting structure, and carries with it, like the discipline of English itself, something of an imperial residue. It therefore seems reasonable to ask: If there was no Bob Dylan, would the void be sufficiently filled by someone else? Did the *structure* create Dylan more so than the other way around? As it is, his name has come to function ubiquitously as a touchstone among networks of taste-bearers, an essential piece of cultural capital and testament to the existence of "the good stuff" and of the people who know it when they hear it. It is a name that, compared to an *actually* obscure artist (Éliane Radigue, anyone?), can navigate meaningfully as capital the overlapping spaces of disparate social communities, and whose status is spread and reinforced through other textual forms. Invocations of Dylan appear not just in literature, as in the dedication to Joyce Carol Oates's "Where Are You Going, Where Have You Been?" or the many Dylan-inspired poems collected in the 2018 volume *Visiting Bob*,[70] but in the use of his music in a long list of films and television shows, many of which enjoy critical acclaim or subcultural credibility.[71] There is, in other words, a kind of symbiosis at work, in which "Bob Dylan" signifies depth, taste, and authenticity within the popular works that reference or incorporate his music, while those references function collectively to sustain his esteemed position.

Dylan's frequent cameos throughout these chapters testify to his centrality—the importance for others artists to establish proximity—when it comes to the relationship between popular song and literature. His most sustained appearances, however, occur in O'Grady's "Limits of the Literary," as the quintessential example of literary allusion converted into symbolic capital, and Faulk's "David Bowie's *Diamond Dogs*, the Cut-Up, and Rock's Unfinished Revolution," where we witness the strategic self-positioning of a major artist as Dylan's heir, and within a progressive narrative or lineage of rock. "Song for Bob Dylan," which Faulk locates as a "lyrical centerpiece" of 1971's *Hunky Dory*," is but one example of a widespread practice in which artists connect themselves to Dylan by way of song-covers, imagery, and lyrical allusions, contributing thereby to a sense that all things filter somehow through Bob.[72] It is a practice that extends from fellow luminaries (Syd Barrett, John Lennon, Paul Simon, the Who, Neil Young, Donovan, Nick Cave, etc.) and indie darlings (Wilco, Belle and Sebastian, Minutemen, Stephen Malkmus, T. Rex, etc.) to far more mainstream, pop connections. One finds, for example, in the late 1980s and early 1990s alone: Duran Duran's cover of "Lay Lady Lay"; Jesus Jones's lyric "Bob Dylan's didn't have this to sing about";[73] the Counting Crows' "I wanna be Bob Dylan" from the Dylan-alluding title "Mr. Jones";[74] and INXS's replication of Dylan's iconic, "Subterranean Homesick Blues" cue-cards (itself a widely borrowed trope[75]) in their video for "Mediate."

Clearly, there is ongoing and widespread value in referencing Bob Dylan, which, as these examples suggest, plays a role in balancing commercial success with artistic authenticity. Dylan very much becomes rock's laureate, making possible a narrative of rock music as poetry's descendant, if not its supplanter. Thus Bruce Springsteen, as Bohdan Szklarski points out, was "launched . . . to fame quite early" as "the 'new Dylan'";[76] Robert Plant humbles his own accomplishments before Dylan's unique gift of "seeing it all";[77] and deeply respected artists such as Chrissie Hynde, Rick Wagner, and Patti Smith continue to pay tribute by way of covering his songs. *Rolling Stone*'s minute-by-minute account of the "We are the World" session, at which Dylan's presence seems to have transformed his costars into awkwardly bedazzled fans, makes especially clear that even within such a diverse range of company there is Dylan and then there is everyone else.[78] Even the near-second tandem of Paul McCartney and John Lennon have consistently pointed back to Dylan as an inspirational hero who made possible their lyrical maturation. And if "the Beatles and Bob" operates to some extent as a single unit, representing rock in its fullest and most artful range, the relation still tips hierarchically toward the latter: Dylan preserves throughout the role of mentor, distanced as a solo artist from the Beatles boy-band origins and by his insular mystique from their unrivaled place in the limelight. The parent-child dynamic Dave Harker expounded in 1980, contrasting the individualistic and anti-hegemonic lyrics of "It Ain't Me Babe" to the social acquiescence and "adolescent sentiment" of "She Loves You,"[79] seems to persevere even in spite of Dylan's attempted tribute with 2012's "Roll on, John": "Lennon had to already be mythic," the *Atlantic* quibbles, "in order for Dylan to write a song about him."[80]

The phenomenon of Dylan-shadowing, pervasive not just among songwriting elites but within the broader field of popular music, is a hyper-condensed repeat of nineteenth- and twentieth-century authors' engagement of William Shakespeare. After their Romantic predecessors had soundly deified "The Bard"—testimony, it would seem, to his sheer poetic power and universal influence, yet also, scholars have shown, a practical means to "advance [one's] own political, artistic, or commercial interests"[81]— the "make-it-new" Modernists made textual interaction with Shakespeare an absolute must and a beacon of literary prestige: T. S. Eliot's "The Waste Land" and "The Love Song of J. Alfred Prufrock" make heavy use of both *Hamlet* and *The Tempest*; Auden's long-poem "The Sea and the Mirror" is, in the words of its subtitle, "A Commentary on Shakespeare's *The Tempest*"; Virginia Wolf, in addition to her feminist conjuring of "Shakespeare's sister" in *A Room of One's Own*, features Shakespeare regularly in her fiction; and D. H. Lawrence shares, in "When I Read Shakespeare," his "wonder" at "language so lovely" coming from such humble characters.[82] The list goes on and into subsequent generations, as evidenced by Sylvia Plath's *Ariel* and Derek Walcott's *Omeros*, and channeling rather forcefully, I would venture, into Bob Dylan himself.

Though Dylan's literary allusions are varied, Shakespeare no doubt serves him as a literary centerpiece. *Highway 61 Revisited* references *Twelfth Night* in its title track and *Hamlet* in the sprawling coda "Desolation Row"; Shakespeare appears as a character in "Stuck Inside of Mobile with the Memphis Blues Again"; *Time Out of Mind* takes its title from *Romeo and Juliet*, while *Tempest* alludes of course to Shakespeare's final play; "Pay in Blood" harkens *Julius Caesar* with the lyric "I come to bury, not to praise"[83]; and *Love and Theft* contains allusions to *As You Like It* and *Othello*. Dylan's use of Shakespeare, then—which ranges from character references ("Othello told Desdemona . . ."[84]) to fairly direct quotations ("I'm not even acquainted with mine own desires"[85]) to oblique allusions (e.g., "Dragon clouds so high above,"[86] as compared to "Sometimes we see a cloud that's dragonish")—has been a consistent practice, and always of the passing reference variety as opposed to fuller adaptations (writing a song or album based on one of Shakespeare's plays, for example). What is especially fascinating, however, is the way in which Dylan has magnified this connection on his most recent album and in the aftermath of his awkwardly (or is it coolly?) received Nobel Prize.

To the confusion of some, and perhaps the smirking delight of others, the Nobel Committee's selection was met initially by the singer with a week-long silence—a span sufficient enough for academy member Per Wastberg to deem the rock-star recipient "impolite and arrogant."[87] Dylan would, after apologetically passing on the formal ceremony (for which he supplied a thank-you letter, read at the event by US

Introduction 19

ambassador to Sweden Azita Raji), accept the prize belatedly at a private ceremony in Stockholm, and submit his formal lecture just before the June 10, 2017 deadline (which must be met, it is worth noting, in order to receive what amounted that year to $8.5 million in prize money). In that initial acceptance letter, couched in what I deem a sincere humility ("If someone had ever told me that I had the slightest chance of winning the Nobel Prize, I would have to think that I'd have about the same odds as standing on the moon"[88]), Dylan notes his familiarity with past recipients, listing specifically "Kipling, Shaw, Thomas Mann, Pearl Buck, Albert Camus, Hemingway."[89] He soon veers, however, toward a more focused comparison with none other than Shakespeare himself:

> The thought that he was writing literature couldn't have entered his head. His words were written for the stage. Meant to be spoken not read. When he was writing *Hamlet*, I'm sure he was thinking about a lot of different things: "Who're the right actors for these roles?" "How should this be staged?" "Do I really want to set this in Denmark?" His creative vision and ambitions were no doubt at the forefront of his mind, but there were also more mundane matters to consider and deal with. "Is the financing in place?" "Are there enough good seats for my patrons?" "Where am I going to get a human skull?" I would bet that the farthest thing from Shakespeare's mind was the question "Is this literature?"[90]

The connection here, even while unabashedly reaching for the greatest of all names in literature as a comparison, is curiously diffused of aesthetic values or notions of genius: Shakespeare is cast, instead, as a working man of material concerns and obligations, consumed with matters of production and consumption more so than language or prestige. It serves, in part, as an apology for what had been thought a snub, offering as an explanation that Dylan is above all else a performer with a busy schedule, who can only engage such formal rewards as a kind of afterthought. "Literature" as a category, as an honor, is fully someone else's concern: "But, like Shakespeare," he furthers the analogy,

> I too am often occupied with the pursuit of my creative endeavors and dealing with all aspects of life's mundane matters. "Who are the best musicians for these songs?" "Am I recording in the right studio?" "Is this song in the right key?" Some things never change, even in 400 years. Not once have I ever had the time to ask myself, "Are my songs literature?"[91]

Exactly paralleled in structure to Dylan's musings on Shakespeare, this quotation presents to us the rock star as workaholic, who must relentlessly continue to create, while cautiously avoiding the pitfalls of glamor and self-congratulation.

While Dylan's self-portrait in one sense demystifies the romantic and modernist versions of Shakespeare, inverting the illusion of the artist as beyond material and financial concerns, it manages to preserve him, and by extension Dylan himself, as wholly outside the realms of critical discourse, reward, and prestige. Anyone familiar with Dylan's history of interviews will recognize this willful evasiveness—a practice and persona manifesting what Bourdieu time and again, in characterizing his cultural elite, calls an "interest in disinterestedness," and which could well be added to the lists of attributes made by those ushering Dylan into the literary fold. Always one step ahead. Unpredictable. Alluringly enigmatic. Resistant to any and all labels and loyalties. This is Dylan mastering, at the resonantly symbolic level of the pop icon, Bourdieu's "cultural game": "He's legendary," Sir Paul McCartney states with confessed envy, "and doesn't give a shit."[92]

Like his direct allusions to literature, Dylan's elusive, detached persona is conducive to scholarship, especially that of an era in which "the author" has been theorized dead. We see this reflected in titles like Agnieszka Pantuchowicz's "Conspiring to be *Unknown*; or, Is a Bob Dylan There?"[93] and Jerzy Jarniewicz's "Bob Dylan—The *Unwilling* Icon of the Counterculture"[94] (italics mine in both). In his introduction to *Bob Dylan: The Essential Interviews*, Jonathan Cott links the Dylan persona specifically to certain literary figures, finding, for example, in Dylan's own statement—"I wake and I'm one person, and when I go to sleep I know for certain I'm somebody else"—a kinship with Virginia Woolf's many-selved Orlando.[95] The artist as chameleon. The "man of many hats." Such epithets extend of course well beyond Dylan, preceding him among the twentieth century's literary giants and the canonizing discourse that makes and maintains them as such. Compare, for example, Christophe Lebold's description of Dylan as "ever in search of a new 'mask' . . . a (non-) protest singer, a beat-like symbolist poet, an absurdist rocker with a touch of the Shakespearian clown, a country-music everyman in a bucolic fiction, a wounded man and lyrical poet in the early seventies, a Christian preacher announcing the apocalypse,"[96] with Tim Keane's assessment (following biographer Richard Ellman's lead) of W. B. Yeats as a donner of "many masks . . . from the punch-drunk dreamer of 'Lake Isle of Innisfree' (1893) to the doomed pilot in 'An Irish Airman Foresees His Death' (1917) to the inhibited aesthete of 'Among Schoolchildren' (1928) and the dying sage of 'The Tower' (1928)," or Meghan O'Rourke's description of W. H. Auden as the "endlessly evolving poet," who careened from "the private rhythms of Modernism" to an "accessible rhetoric" connecting "the individual to the public world."[97] Such discourse transitions readily not just to Dylan-types, but to pop luminaries such as Bowie and Madonna, the latter of which is deemed "as famous for changing her image as [for] her creative skills,"[98] the former lauded as art-rock's "ultimate chameleon."[99] Both legends receive the "many faces of" introduction one finds rangily applied (in musical anthologies, biographical pieces, etc.) to artists as diverse the Smiths, Eric Clapton, Metallica, and Daft Punk.

Dylan, however, adds to this criterion of shiftiness—to the persona of constant evolution, or even whimsical departure—a paradoxical rootedness. Since his notorious "betrayal" of acoustic folk, he has been unwaveringly committed to blues-rock composition and instrumentation. Electric guitars and drums, often with keyboard, remain his staples, producing songs that, for all their lyrical creativity, are determinedly distant from anything one would characterize as avant-garde. Verbally, too, be it through his early, nearly cartoonish folkisms or later lyrics like "I drive fast cars and I eat fast foods,"[100] "good old Bob" always seems present alongside the poetic sage;

Introduction   21

against the esoteric reader and cultural omnivore of "I Feel a Change Comin' On"—
"I'm hearing Billy Joe Shaver / And I'm reading James Joyce"[101]—is the songwriter's
folksy interview admission that he "couldn't make hide nor hair" of *Ulysses*.[102] There
is nothing of the cosmopolitan flamboyance of Bowie or Morrissey, or the romantic
anachronisms of, say, Nick Cave, in Dylan's persona and performances; every bit the
American "rockist" in this regard, he will not be found chatting up a crowd between
songs, and certainly won't be dancing or striking performative poses on stage. There is
then, in spite of Dylan's powerful persona and its down-to-earth elements, an ironically
text-centric, "it's about the music, period" disposition that whiffs distinctly of the New
Criticism that flourished even as he was growing his brand. Dylan's performative
model, appearing to grate uncomfortably against the star culture through which it is
dispersed, might well be compared to James Joyce's as articulated in *A Portrait of the
Artist as a Young Man*:

> The personality of the artist, at first a cry or a cadence or a mood and then a
> fluid and lambent narrative, finally refines itself out of existence, impersonalizes
> itself, so to speak. The esthetic images in the dramatic form is life purified in and
> reprojected from the human imagination. The mystery of esthetic, like that of
> material creation, is accomplished. The artist, like the God of the creation, remains
> within or behind or beyond or above his handiwork, invisible, refined out of
> existence, indifferent, paring his fingernails.[103]

What young Stephen Dedalus here lays out as an aesthetic philosophy (akin to both
Yeatsian "impersonality" and Eliot's fragmented poetic consciousness) is, in terms of
Bourdieu's framework, an argument for art as an autonomous field and experience—a
cultural positioning that, unlike the priesthood or the politics that likewise beckon
for Stephen's allegiance, enjoys a life free of commercial, economic, or political
determinants. While fostering the illusion of purity, however, artistic production in
fact satisfies what Leo Braudy describes as the "urge to fame," promising "a place where
private dreams of recognition triumphantly appear in public," allowing one "to stand
out of the crowd, but with the crowd's approval . . . to be an object of attention rather
than one of the mobs of attention payers."[104] When Dylan famously antagonizes *Time*
magazine's Horace Judson—"I got nothing to say about these things I write, I mean,
I just write them," "You'll probably call me a folk singer," and so on[105]—he is claiming
for his creative works, and with similar contentiousness, the autonomy asserted by the
likes of Ernest Hemingway ("The sea is the sea. The old man is an old man. The boy
is a boy and the fish is a fish."[106]) and Samuel Beckett ("[I]f by Godot I meant God I
would have said God."[107]). Such deliberate contrariness toward the world of readers
and critics, at times an attitude more so than an argument, has no doubt stockpiled for
Dylan over the years some serious rock cred.

But I'd like to reflect as well on the literariness of Dylan's actual lyrics, particularly
the panoramic, fragmented, allusion-heavy form that, while a persevering staple of
Dylan's repertoire, occurs also as a rarefied event among otherwise more succinct
and "standard" tunes. Thus the eleven-plus-minute "Desolation Row" caps off 1965's

Highway 61 Revisited, whose other tracks, with the exception of the six-minute, narrative opener "Like a Rolling Stone," are more conventional in length, and the seventeen-minute, Hamlet-titled epic "Murder Most Foul" closes out—as the full D-side on vinyl, the second disc on CD—2020's *Rough and Rowdy Ways*. It is in these types of songs, which always provide the title line as a culminating refrain, that Dylan seems to establish a larger-than-life persona, cataloging and shoring up as Eliot's natural decedent the disparate fragments of American experience and culture.

In the latter example, which at its outset appears to center narratively ("Twas a dark day in Dallas"[108]) on the assassination of President Kennedy, the lyrics veer, in the form of play-requests for Wolfman Jack, into an elegiac, celebratory catalog of songs and singers. Like Tiresias, whose prophetic vision, Eliot shares in his footnotes, presides over *The Waste Land* as the poem's unifying "substance,"[109] the disembodied singer lurks behind his images as an all-seeing, sifting and sorting presence; though the ugly and archetypal history of Kennedy's assassination does persist through the verses, winding piecemeal in and among Wolfman's delirious playlist, it seems to take a back seat to the cultural fragments through which it is buoyed and borne out. Another song on the album, "I Contain Multitudes," pushes this all-encompassing persona yet further; bringing, with its title/refrain, Walt Whitman and his bardic reveries into play, the song's "I" seems at once the eighty-year-old, gravel-throated Dylan, and the vast and varied landscape of American culture itself. Within its itemized cornucopia, William Blake, Edgar Allen Poe, and Anne Frank are juxtaposed with pop-culture references such as Indiana Jones and the Rolling Stones.

Belying the seeming all-inclusiveness and uncensored abundance of such lyrics—their assurance, through parallel, repeated structures like the former song's "play" or the latter's "I + verb," that all is accounted for—is their actual *selectivity* as lists. It is clear that Dylan wants popular culture, as experience, commerce, text, represented along with indicators of high art. It is also clear that "low" speech and forms—for example, "rub-a-dub-dub"[110]—are to offset the literary language and references they juxtapose. But it is notably an assemblage of "high" literature/art (Beethoven, Shakespeare, etc.) and a stream of classic Americana—infusing jazz, blues, country, and historic rock with emblems of vintage Hollywood—dispersed through the medium of Dylan's disc jockey. It is pop culture in black-and-white, so to speak, generally "rockist" in vision, and a textbook example of omnivorous capital on display. Toward this latter function, it displays in its selections an openness to mega-stars and the conventional representatives of "cool" so long as they are sufficiently distanced in time, and favors, when it does broach the contemporary, songwriting prowess over chops or stage performance. It surely means something, if you are Don Henley, Queen, or Billy Joel, to have made the cut on such a list, whereas entire planes of pop representation—genres such as heavy-metal and hip-hop, for example, pop legends like Whitney Houston or Michael Jackson, or even rivaling lit-rockers like Tom Waits and Leonard Cohen—are either a little too Dylanish themselves or else too broadly famous for consideration. There remains, then (though Dylan's choices are at least in part dictated by rhythm and rhyme), an organizing principle and canonicity at work. Like the elegiac tradition in poetry, as when Seamus Heaney honors Joseph Brodsky who had honored Auden who had honored Yeats, the lyrics serve both to consecrate past figures, bringing into relief a nameable lineage, and to secure the lyricist-at-hand within: it is notably Dylan's *own* title phrase, relieved of its original ownership yet harboring the ghost of a murdered father and king, which provides the song's concluding imperative: "play 'Murder Most Foul.'"[111]

Dylan in this way serves as a consecrator and guardian of important texts, and a stabilizer for society's trust in great art and its place in education. Both his work and reception suggest that America, or Americanness, may be defined by its cultural texts and artistry—a value that, much like everything else, has in recent years become more intensely and visibly contested; indeed, the back-to-back succession of the Obama and Trump presidencies appears to symbolize, at the highest and profoundly polarizing levels, Bourdieu's very model of *economic* versus *cultural* capital as the basis for contemporary class warfare. Obama, in fact, whose tastes in music and books circulate widely through social media, sought in Dylan (whose music would make the cut on his eclectic "favorites" list in 2020[112]) a key and galvanizing symbol, memorably hanging a Medal of Freedom around the evasive songwriter's neck in 2012, and articulating his cultural importance on various occasions.[113] It makes sense to me that Dylan would feature prominently at a time when left and right political positions are more pronouncedly seen as an educated vs. uneducated class war, though his unique connection to liberal education, Dettmar explains, was there from the beginning: "Dylan came to public prominence at precisely the moment that departments of English were seeking to break down traditional barriers between 'high' and 'low' culture, and his highly literate and literary popular songs provided the perfect texts for classroom use and scholarly analysis."[114] What was, however, within the walls of academia, a challenging of the status quo, could in the broader context of class struggle be seen as a replenishing of resources or "claim on pop" by the culturally advantaged. In any case, the literary culture that was poised to anoint Dylan upon his arrival has been comparatively stingy when it comes to making room for other lyricists and celebrities. Will Dylan hold his place as the academy's representative of literature-as-lyrics? Certainly, it will be interesting to see, in comparison with more conventional authors, how he fares amidst both internal efforts to decentralize curriculum and the external culture wars, as well as to observe how new generations of pop omnivores negotiate fame within his shadow or perhaps climb out from under it.

Weishun Lu's chapter on Taylor Swift strikes me as prescient in this regard. At the time Lu completed her analysis, Swift's most current release was 2017's *Reputation*, with its synthy production and two poems stashed within the liner material. Since then, Swift has undergone a more complete transformation, releasing first the more hushed and dreamy *Lover*, then the twin, Covid-era albums *Folklore* and *Evermore*. The latter pairing marks a pronounced departure from the pop aesthetic and into a folk music that reaches with one hand back to the esteemed singer-songwriter tradition of the 1960s and 1970s, while stretching the other toward a present-day, minimalist indie-rock. It represents, essentially, a culmination of the "mainstream alternative" or "high-pop" paradox I've been exploring throughout this introduction, though at perhaps an unprecedented level in terms of the mega-stardom Swift brings to the table. Contributions by producer Aaron

Dessner (The National, Big Red Machine), Justin Vernon (Bon Iver), and sister-trio Haim supply a direct infusion of indie cred and aesthetics, while the cover art displaces Swift's glamor with a woodsy plainness (on *Evermore*, she is plaid-coated with her back turned, a fellow-spectator and thinker rather than the sexualized object of our gaze). And the accompanying documentary *Folklore: The Long Pond Studio Sessions* seems to evidence the kind of artistic labor that, Lu demonstrates, is only selectively and with established biases awarded to pop stars. Already renowned as a genre-hopper, Swift, in this latest makeover, has landed with her massive and loyal fanbase a sense of poetic distinction, generating lists of allusions or "Easter eggs" to be found in her lyrics, boasts of her "alt-rock" chart domination, and fan essays such as blogger Roxanne Bingham's "Taylor Swift: The Poet of Our Generation." In that post, Bingham identifies in Swift's songs literary allusions to *Alice in Wonderland*, *Slaughterhouse Five*, *A Tale of Two Cities*, *The Great Gatsby*, *The Sun Also Rises*, and Robert Frost, as well as a string of "powerful lines" and "storytelling" tracks. Echoing Dettmar's claim for Dylan (via James Joyce) as "God's gift to English departments,"[115] the "all things bookish" blogger relishes *Folklore* in particular as "an English major's dream."[116] The album's bonus track, "The Lakes," was headlined by *Rolling Stone* as "Taylor Swift Channels Romantic-Era Poetry," and lists like BuzzFeed's ("Taylor Swift could have written *Romeo and Juliet*, but Shakespeare couldn't have written 'Blank Space'") circulate examples of her lyrics as "pure, unadulterated poetry."[117]

But the resistance to Swift-as-poet explored by Lu also persists: "Taylor Swift Could Use an Editor," Spencer Kornhaber titles his review of *Evermore* for the *Atlantic*. While complimentary toward Swift's songwriting in general and *Folklore* in particular, Kornhaber finds its "sister album" guilty of imprecise, self-indulgent metaphors, and mismatchings of lyrical and musical content. Its attempt at "gravity," he surmises, "lands on easy sentimentality, kind of like a pet photographer shooting in black and white." In short, the album (as Robert Christgau surmised of first-generation rock-poets[118]) is guilty of *trying to be*, rather than simply *being*, poetic: Swift dabbles rather than immerses. The review therefore functions, despite its specific examples, as a let's-not-get-carried-away refresher of boundaries, including restrictions on the kind of musical company a contemporary pop star can keep: whereas Swift's metaphorical ambiguity is evidence of poor writing, "A Case of You" by Joni Mitchell—whose landmark album *Blue* Swift calls her "favorite of all time"[119] and signals with her own title, 2012's *Red* —becomes for Kornhaber "a testament to . . . layered meaning."

Indeed, the Mitchell/Swift binary surfaces here, by way of confessionalism, in Lu's and David Shumway's respective chapters, both of which take into account the factors that elevate their subjects as generational, feminist icons and those that bar them from Dylanesque levels of respect. Mitchell herself has sought distance from the comparison; responding to the rumored possibility of Swift playing her character in the film version of *Girls Like Us*, the folk legend (who claims never to have heard Swift's music), explains why she "nixed" the project: "all you've got," she told its producer, "is a girl with high cheekbones."[120] As if to follow suit, Jessica Goldschmidt, writing for *Philadelphia* magazine, calls the possibility of Swift playing Mitchell a "travesty": "it's a sin and a shame that the girl who got famous off of the immortal complaint 'She wears short skirts / I wear t-shirts / She's cheer captain / And I'm on the bleachers' deserves to be mentioned in the same creative breath as she of 'All I really want our love to do / is to bring out the best in me and in you.'" Against Mitchell's "joyously wry poetry" is Swift's "saccharine diet of mixed literary metaphors" and "simplistic diary-transcript confessional pop." And what starts as a distinction between the authentic and the superficial artist becomes, with all of rockism's presumptuousness, a split between a small group of tasteful and intelligent listeners and the "barren musical lives" of those who just don't get it.

Would Swift's recent transformation satisfy the likes of Goldschmidt as evidence of artistic merit and growth, or simply be dismissed as a cheap rendition of the real thing? Readers will of course go their different directions as to whether Swift's literary uses are a kind of commercial ploy and superficial gesture, or part of a skilled artistry that, coming from a female pop star, teen idol, and sex symbol, are unlikely to be given a fair shake by the hands of legitimate culture. What we might agree on is that critics are unlikely to comb Dylan's literary moments for their inadequacies or bemoan his dependency on the pop tropes of relationships and romance as they currently do with Swift, and that the kind of teenage pandering Goldschmidt attributes to her could just as well be directed toward the Beatles. We might, furthermore, agree that her effort to enter this precariously male space, to convincingly and fully merge the pop superstar with singer-songwriter authenticity, is a fascinating experiment; certainly the (gendered) pop/art binary is one she consciously engages, be it through break-up lyrics like "And you would hide away and find your peace of mind / With some indie record that's much cooler than mine,"[121] or through her recent participation in the rockist tradition of the "stripped-down" production—a partnering of legendary artists with prestigious producers (e.g., Dylan's 1989 "comeback" record *Oh Mercy*, with Daniel Lanois at the soundboard) meant to retrieve or to illuminate their essence and best work. Dylan himself is cited as a direct influence on Swift's recent productions: for the song "Betty," Dessner explains, Swift specifically wanted "an early Bob Dylan" feel,[122] and the rubber bridge guitar that *Reverb* reports is "taking over indie music" can be heard on both *Folklore* and Dylan's *Rough and Rowdy Ways*.[123] Meanwhile, pop-star-poet Halsey, known for her elaborate incarnations as various male rock icons, furthers the idea of a Swift/Dylan fusion, telling *Advocate* that "Dylan was the reason that I picked up a guitar. I felt, as a 16-year old, I was equal parts Taylor Swift and equal parts Bob Dylan."[124]

As for Swift's chosen allusions? Though the high Modernists who inhabit Dylan's landscapes seem to have gone missing, she pulls with references to *Jane Eyre*, *The Sun Also Rises*, and *The Great Gatsby* from a similar canon of "classics." This last text in particular has emerged in recent lyrics by both songwriters, and as a symbol of nostalgic escape within an atmosphere of betrayal and corruption. In Dylan's "Summer Days," the charming yet naïve self-assurance of Gatsby himself enter anonymously as a (slightly altered) quotation: "You can't repeat the past? What do you mean you can't? Of course you can!"[125] The listener either knows the reference and therefore joins company with Bob, is educated regarding its source by a third party, or is simply left in the dark. Swift's *Gatsby*, on the other hand, in "This is Why We Can't Have Nice Things," is directly cited: "Bass beat rattling the chandelier / Feeling so Gatsby for that whole year."[126] Unlike Dylan's all-absorbing, disembodied persona, and in what may be indicative of rivaling interpretative strategies and communities, Swift *applies* the named text/character to a subjective emotional state and traceable narrative. Instead of the direct textual intrusion—ala Spencer, Baudelaire, etc. in Eliot's "The Waste Land"—we have the name-drop, albeit a highly recognized rather than obscure one. Such differences suggest that Dylan's elite place within the pop hierarchy has to do not simply with his literariness in general, but to his evocations of an academically privileged modernism, whereas the more common path for pop's entry into literature has been by way of its subordinated or even stigmatized schools (be it those of the confessionalists, the Beats, or something else). And yet some shared ground remains: the literary moment, like Gatsby's own fantasy, is in both songs unstainable, giving way for Dylan to a self-guardedness and bracing for heartbreak, and for Swift to the clichéd title line and finger-pointing revelations of the "diss track." As with Eliot's Prufrock, or, for that matter, the book-fortressed isolationist of Paul Simon's "I am a Rock," literature provides not a source of connection but a refuge for the socially defeated: a method by which the self is privately reconstituted, till "human voices wake us, and we drown."[127]

Notes

1 Simon Frith and Howard Horn, *Art into Pop* (New York: Methuen, 1987), 1.
2 *Postmodern MTV*, later rebranded *Alternative Nation*, aired daily from the late 1980s to 1997, while *120 Minutes*, recreated for MTV2 as *Subterranean*, ran initially from 1986 to 2000.
3 At least nine different pop artists, in fact, have recorded adaptations of this poem.
4 This instrumental album accompanied visual exhibits inspired by Calvino's imaginative book.
5 Hanif Kureishi, "That's How Good It Was," in *The Faber Book of Pop*, ed. Hanif Kureishi and Jon Savage (Boston: Gardners Books, 1995), xix.
6 Quinn Russell Brown, "With Spoken Word and Hip-Hip, a New Generation of Poets has Taken the Stage," *University of Washington Magazine*, March 2017, https://magazine.washington.edu/feature/poetry-hip-hop-spoken-word/.
7 I am thinking, for example, of Jean "Binta" Breeze and Linton Kwesi Johnson.
8 Kevin Coval, quoted by David Browne, "Pop Star Poetics," *Poetry Foundation*, May 29, 2007, https://www.poetryfoundation.org/articles/68884/pop-star-poetics.
9 Ibid.
10 Roy Christopher, "Literary Allusions Run Deep through the History of Hip-Hop," *Literary Hub*, March 18, 2019, https://lithub.com/literary-allusion-runs-deep-through-the-history-of-hip-hop/.
11 Simon Frith, "Why Do Songs Have Words?" *Sociological Review* 34, no. 1 (1986): 86.
12 Ibid.
13 Lawrence Grossberg, *We Gotta Get Out of This Place: Popular Conservatism and Postmodern Culture* (New York: Routledge, 1992), 131.
14 Robert Christgau, "Rock Lyrics are Poetry (Maybe)," *Cheetah*, December 1967, https://www.robertchristgau.com/xg/music/lyrics-che.php.

15 Other examples of "rock" titles in non-rock genres include Duke Ellington's "Rockin' in Rhythm" (jazz), Bob Marley's "Rock to the Rock" (reggae), and Adam Hambrick's "Rockin' All Night Long" (country).

16 Lara Marlowe, "How Charles Baudelaire became France's First Rock Star," *Irish Times*, August 30, 2017, https://www.irishtimes.com/news/world/europe/how-charles-baudelaire-became-france-s-first-rock-star-1.3202375.

17 James Parker, "The Last Rock-Star Poet," *Atlantic*, December 2014, https://www.theatlantic.com/magazine/archive/2014/12/the-last-rock-star-poet/382239/.

18 Elijah Wald, *How the Beatles Destroyed Rock 'n' Roll* (Oxford: Oxford University Press, 2011).

19 Michaelangelo Matos, "1966 vs. 1971: When 'Rock 'n' Roll' Became 'Rock,' and What We Lost," *The Record Music News from NPR*, September 22, 2016, https://www.npr.org/sections/therecord/2016/09/22/495021326/1966-vs-1971-when-rock-n-roll-became-rock-and-what-we-lost.

20 Frith and Horne, *Art into Pop*, 57–8.

21 Robert Christgau, "Decade: Rockism Faces the World," *Village Voice*, January 2, 1990, https://www.robertchristgau.com/xg/rock/decade-89.php.

22 Kelefa Sanneh, "The Rap against Rockism," *New York Times*, October 31, 2004, AR-1.

23 Ibid., AR-32.

24 Ibid.

25 Miles Parks Grier, "Said the Hooker to the Thief: 'Some Way Out' of Rockism," *Journal of Popular Music Studies* 25, no. 1 (2013): 32.

26 Frith, "Why Do Songs Have Words?" 87.

27 Saul Austerlitz, "The Pernicious Rise of Poptimism," *New York Times*, April 6, 2014, SM-48.

28 Ibid.

29 Ibid.

30 Ibid.

31 "All My Happiness is Gone," track 2 on Purple Mountains, *Purple Mountains*, Drag City, 2019.

32 "How Soon is Now?" track 6 on the Smiths, *Meat is Murder*, Rough Trade, 1985.

33 Alan Warde et al., "Cultural Taste and Participation in Britain," *Sociology of Consumption Working Group ESA 8th Conference*, September 2007, 21.

34 Austerlitz, "The Pernicious Rise of Poptimism."

35 Grier, "Said the Hooker to the Thief," 34.

36 Inside Pop: The Rock Revolution, CBS, 1967, Youtube, RareVideos@Random, 56:08, Jul 22, 2020, https://www.youtube.com/watch?v=vyiGFRj5b-k.

37 These accounts of the *Smile* sessions, to be clear, are both disputed and widely circulated.

38 Christgau, "Rock Lyrics are Poetry (Maybe)."

39 Ibid.

40 See, for example, Larkin's direct contrast of Hardy and Yeats in *Philip Larkin: Letters to Monica*, ed. Anthony Thwaite (London: Faber, 2010), 221.

41 Cameron Crowe, *Almost Famous*, directed by Cameron Crowe (2000: Warner Brothers, 2001), DVD.

42 Randall Roberts, "Out of the Fog: Will Oldham's Warm and Fuzzy Return as Bonnie 'Prince' Billy," *Riverfront Times*, April 8, 2009, https://www.riverfronttimes.com/

stlouis/out-of-the-fog-will-oldhams-warm-and-fuzzy-return-as-bonnie-prince-billy
/Content?oid=2453195.

43 Nick Cave, *The Secret Life of the Love Song and The Flesh Made Word: Two Lectures by Nick Cave* (London: Mute, 2000).

44 I am thinking, of course, of Eno's installation pieces when I reference museums. I add "literary" do to his musical collaborations with poet Rick Holland (*Drums Between the Bells, Panic of Looking*) and his production work on John Cale's "Dylan Thomas" album, *Words for the Dying.*

45 C. Liegh McInnis, *The Lyrics of Prince Rogers Nelson: A Literary Look at a Creative, Musical Poet, Philosopher, and Storyteller* (Clinton: Psychedelic Literature, 2009).

46 Adam Bradley, *The Poetry of Pop* (New Haven: Yale University Press), 248–9.

47 Michael Scott, "'Hipster Capitalism' in the Age of Austerity: Polanyi Meets Bourdieu's New Petite Bourgeoisie," *Cultural Sociology* 11, no. 1 (2017): 63.

48 Ibid., 64.

49 Warde et al., "Cultural Taste and Participation in Britain," 20–1.

50 Goose Island, for example, is owned by Anheuser-Busch, Blue Moon by MillerCoors, etc.

51 Carl Wilson, *Let's Talk about Love: A Journey to the End of Taste* (New York: Bloomsbury, 2007), 92.

52 Ibid.

53 Tony Bennett et al., *Culture, Class, Distinction* (New York: Routledge, 2009), 75.

54 Richard Peterson and Roger Kern, "Changing Highbrow Taste: From Snob to Omnivore," *American Sociological Review* 61, no. 5 (1996): 904.

55 Ibid., 901.

56 Simon Frith, *The Sociology of Rock* (London: Constable, 1978), 19. "Teenager," Frith says, is a working-class designation, whereas "youth" is a middle-class term.

57 Douglas B. Holt, "Distinction in America? Recovering Bourdieu's Theory of Tastes from Its Critics," *Poetics* 25 (1997): 95.

58 Warde et al., "Cultural Taste and Participation in Britain," 22.

59 "A Simple Desultory Philippic," track 9 on Simon and Garfunkel, *Parsley, Sage, Rosemary and Thyme*, Columbia, 1966.

60 "I Shall be Free No. 10," track 5 on Bob Dylan, *Another Side of Bob Dylan*, Columbia, 1964.

61 Kevin J. H. Dettmar, Introduction to *The Cambridge Companion to Bob Dylan*, ed. Kevin J. H. Dettmar (Cambridge: Cambridge University Press, 2009), 10–11.

62 Bradley, *The Poetry of Pop*, 20.

63 Dettmar, *The Cambridge Companion to Bob Dylan*, 3.

64 Bradley, *The Poetry of Pop*, 20.

65 Randal Johnson, Introduction to *The Field of Cultural Production: Essays on Art and Literature* by Pierre Bourdieu, ed. Randal Johnson (New York: Columbia University Press, 1993), 15.

66 Ezra Pound, quoted in David Early, *Re-Covering Modernism: Pulps, Paperbacks, and the Prejudice of Form* (New York: Ashgate, 2009), 24.

67 W. B. Yeats, *Letters on Poetry from W.B. Yeats to Dorothy Wellesley* (Oxford: Oxford University Press, 1964), 113.

68 John Lynch, "The 50 Best-Selling Music Artists of All Time," *Insider*, September 13, 2017, https://www.insider.com/best-selling-music-artists-of-all-time-2016-9.

69 Dettmar, *The Cambridge Companion to Bob Dylan*, 2.

Introduction 29

70 *Visiting Bob: Poems Inspired by the Life and Work of Bob Dylan*, eds. Thom Tammaro and Alan David (Moorhead: New Rivers, 2018).

71 Acclaimed shows and films that use Bob Dylan's music include *Easy Rider*, *High Fidelity*, *The Big Lebowski*, (Gregory Doran's) *Hamlet*, *The Walking Dead*, *Six Feet Under*, and *The End of the Fucking World*.

72 Eliott Grover, for example, argues that the "diss track" genre credited frequently to hip-hop is largely indebted to Bob Dylan. "Bob Dylan Belongs in the Diss Track Hall of Fame," *Inside Hook*, May 27, 2021, https://www.insidehook.com/article/music/bob-dylan-best-diss-tracks.

73 "Right Here, Right Now," track 5 on Jesus Jones, *Doubt*, SBK, 1991.

74 "Mr. Jones," track 3 on Counting Crows, *August and Everything After*, Geffen, 1993.

75 Other replications of Dylan's cue-cards include MaLLy and the Sundance Kid's tablet scrolling for "Heir Time," and even a Donald Trump campaign advertisement.

76 Bohdan Szklarski, "Dylan and Springsteen: Master and Follower," in *All Along Bob Dylan*, ed. Tymon Adamczewski (New York: Routledge, 2021), 127.

77 Robert Plant, "Digging Deep: The Robert Plant Podcast," Episode 19, YouTube, 18:02, June 6, 2021, https://www.youtube.com/watch?v=JaJmJCwWjmo&t=11s.

78 Gavin Edwards, "'We are the World': A Minute-by-Minute Breakdown," *Rolling Stone*, March 6, 2020, https://www.rollingstone.com/music/music-features/we-are-the-world-a-minute-by-minute-breakdown-54619/.

79 Dave Harker, quoted in Frith, "Why Do Songs Have Words?" 81.

80 Scott Beauchamp and Alex Shephard, "Bob Dylan and John Lennon's Weird, One-Sided Relationship," *Atlantic*, September 24, 2012, https://www.theatlantic.com/entertainment/archive/2012/09/bob-dylan-and-john-lennons-weird-one-sided-relationship/262680/.

81 Joseph M. Ortiz, Introduction to *Shakespeare and the Culture of Romanticism*, ed. Joseph Ortiz (Burlington: Ashgate, 2013), 2.

82 D. H. Lawrence, "When I Read Shakespeare," in *Pansies: Poems* (London: Martin Secker, 1929), 84.

83 "Pay in Blood," track 5 on Bob Dylan, *Tempest*, Columbia, 2012.

84 "Po' Boy," track 10 on Bob Dylan, *Love and Theft*, Columbia, 2001.

85 "Bye and Bye," track 4 on Bob Dylan, *Love and Theft*, Columbia, 2001.

86 "You're Gonna Make Me Lonesome When You Go," track 5 on Bob Dylan, *Blood on the Tracks*, Columbia, 1975.

87 "Bob Dylan Criticized as 'Impolite and Arrogant' by Nobel Academy Member," *Guardian*, October 21, 2016, https://www.theguardian.com/music/2016/oct/22/bob-dylan-criticised-as-impolite-and-arrogant-by-nobel-academy-member.

88 Dylan, Banquet Speech, *The Nobel Prize*, 2016, https://www.nobelprize.org/prizes/literature/2016/dylan/speech/.

89 Ibid.

90 Ibid.

91 Ibid.

92 Andrew Trendell, "Paul McCartney Recalls the First Time the Beatles Got Stoned with Bob Dylan," *NME*, April 15, 2021, https://www.nme.com/news/music/paul-mccartney-recalls-the-first-time-the-beatles-got-stoned-with-bob-dylan-2921282.

93 Agnieszka Pantuchowicz, "Conspiring to be *Unknown*; or, Is a Bob Dylan There," in *All Along Bob Dylan*, ed. Tymon Adamczewski (New York: Routledge, 2021), 71–81.

30   *Lit-Rock*

94   Jerzy Jarniewicz, "Bob Dylan—The *Unwilling* Icon of the Counterculture," in *All Along Bob Dylan*, ed. Tymon Adamczewski (New York: Routledge, 2021), 82–96.

95   Jonathan Cott, Introduction to *Bob Dylan: The Essential Interviews* (New York: Simon and Schuster, 2017), xi.

96   Chistopher Lebold, quoted in Agnieszka Pantuchowicz, "Conspiring to be Unknown," 78. See note 93.

97   Meghan O'Rourke, "The Many Faces of W.H. Auden," *Slate*, March 1, 2007, https://slate.com/culture/2007/03/the-many-faces-of-w-h-auden.html.

98   "The Many Faces of Madonna," *Sydney Morning Herald*, January 31, 2012, https://www.smh.com.au/entertainment/celebrity/the-many-faces-of-madonna-20120131-1qqac.html.

99   Trey Zenker, "Changes: The Many Faces of David Bowie," *Tidal*, December 26, 2016, https://tidal.com/magazine/article/changes-the-many-faces-of-david-bowie-best-of-2016/1-33825.

100   "I Contain Multitudes," track 1 on Bob Dylan, *Rough and Rowdy Ways*, Columbia, 2020.

101   "I Feel a Change Comin' On," track 9 on Bob Dylan, *Together Through Life*, Columbia, 2009.

102   Bob Dylan, quoted in Sean Sheehan, *Joyce's Ulysses* (London: Continuum, 2009), 10.

103   James Joyce, *A Portrait of the Artist as a Young Man* (New York: Penguin, 1916), 233.

104   Leo Braudy, *The Frenzy of Renown: Fame and Its History* (New York: Vintage, 1997), 6.

105   *Don't Look Back*, directed by D. A. Pennebaker (1967: Leacock-Pennebaker).

106   Ernest Hemingway, *Selected Letters 1917–1961*, ed. Carlos Baker (New York: Charles Scribner's Sons, 1959), 806.

107   Samuel Beckett, quoted in Philip Marchand, "Open Book: The Letters of Samuel Beckett 1941–1956," *National Post*, November 25, 2011, https://nationalpost.com/afterword/open-book-the-letters-of-samuel-beckett-1941-1956.

108   "Murder Most Foul," track 10 on Bob Dylan, *Rough and Rowdy Ways*, Columbia, 2020.

109   T. S. Eliot, "The Waste Land," in *Anthology of Twentieth-Century British and Irish Poetry*, ed. Keith Tuma (Oxford: Oxford University Press, 2001), 137.

110   "Murder Most Foul."

111   Ibid.

112   Daniel Kreps, "Barack Obama's Favorite Songs of 2020: Springsteen, Bad Bunny, Dua Lipa," *Rolling Stone*, December 19, 2020, https://www.rollingstone.com/music/music-news/barack-obama-favorite-songs-2020-springsteen-bad-bunny-phoebe-bridgers-dua-lipa-1106249/.

113   Obama expressed his deep appreciation for Dylan after his 2010 White House performance, upon his Medal of Freedom and Nobel Prize awards, and in a "surprise" video conversation with YouTube phenomes Fred and Tim Williams.

114   Dettmar, *The Cambridge Companion to Bob Dylan*, 10.

115   Ibid., 1.

116   Roxanne Bingham, "Taylor Swift—The Poet of Our Generation," *The Spellbinding Shelf* (blog), January 9, 2021, https://thespellbindingshelf.blog/2021/01/09/taylor-swift-the-poet-of-our-generation/.

Introduction

117 Andria Moore, "Taylor Swift is One of the Greatest Songwriters of Our Generation; Here are Her Best Lyrics," BuzzFeed, January 4, 2021, https://www.buzzfeed.com/andriamoore/taylor-swifts-most-poetic-lyrics.

118 See note 33.

119 Taylor Swift, "Taylor Swift Talks Joni Mitchell: On the Record," Napster, Youtube, 0:58, May 6, 2013, https://www.youtube.com/watch?v=vtQC8ILxHCs.

120 Joni Mitchell, quoted in Daniel Kreps, "Joni Mitchell Reveals Why She Nixed Taylor Swift-Starring Biopic," *Rolling Stone*, November 25, 2014, https://www.rollingstone.com/movies/movie-news/joni-mitchell-reveals-why-she-nixed-taylor-swift-starring-biopic-58131/.

121 "We are Never Ever Getting Back Together," track 8 on Taylor Swift, *Red*, Big Machine, 2012.

122 Aaron Dessner, "The Story behind Every Song on Taylor Swift's *folklore*," interview by Brady Gerber, *Vulture*, July 27, 2020, https://www.vulture.com/2020/07/taylor-swift-folklore-aaron-dessner-breaks-down-every-song.html.

123 Mario Shankweiler, "The Rubber Bridge Guitars Taking over Indie Music," *Reverb*, July 29, 2021, https://reverb.com/news/the-rubber-bridge-guitars-taking-over-indie-music.

124 Halsey, quoted in Tracy E. Gilchrist, "Halsey, the 'Poet' of Pop Music, Gender Bends Into Bowie and Bob Dylan," *Advocate*, January 21, 2020, https://www.advocate.com/exclusives/2020/1/21/halsey-transforms-bowie-jagger-hendrix-and-dylan-our-cover.

125 "Summer Days," track 3 on Bob Dylan, *Love and Theft*, Columbia, 2001.

126 "This is Why We Can't Have Nice Things," track 13 on Taylor Swift, *Reputation*, Big Machine, 2017.

127 T. S. Eliot, "The Love Song of J. Alfred Prufrock," in *Anthology of Twentieth-Century British and Irish Poetry*, ed. Keith Tuma (Oxford: Oxford University Press, 2001), 128.

Note on Uses and Organization

As you'll see in the table of contents, I've organized chapters in pairs and trios around various themes: Nation and Narrative, Craft and Confession, and so on. This of course is not the *only* way the book might have been assembled or that readers may wish to approach it: Martin Malone's ethnographic reflection on poetry-writing and punk, for example, which I've placed under "Signs and Mediations," could fit just as comfortably under "Authorship and Authenticity," while Patricia Malone's chapter on Kurt Cobain and the gendered body would pair productively with Kimberly Mack's exploration of gendered positionings in early rock journalism and groupie subcultures like the Plaster Casters. While reading the book in its entirety will most effectively showcase the range of literary rock music and challenge traditional understandings of the high/low binary, there are, I think, opportunities for readers to selectively mix and match, or to apply chapters individually within the classroom: instructors of James Joyce or Flannery O'Connor, for example, may find in Kevin Farrell's and Scott Calhoun's respective chapters an opportunity to showcase how these authors are mediated, engaged, and sustained through popular culture. Certainly, my own awareness of literature in pop music has been expanded and enriched by the work of each contributor to this collection.

Part I

Authorship and Authenticity

1

David Bowie's *Diamond Dogs*, the Cut-Up, and Rock's Unfinished Revolution

Barry J. Faulk

The "David Bowie Is" exhibit, which despite modest expectations attracted millions of visitors over its international, five-year run, is a staunch indicator of the posthumously renewed and widespread interest in the singer's musical and cultural legacy. Within this wellspring of posthumous interest (Bowie died in 2016, two years before the exhibit wrapped up at Brooklyn Museum) is an increased attention to the singer's dialog with the American writer William S. Burroughs, as reported by Craig Copetas and published in *Rolling Stone* magazine in 1974.

That the meeting of the two men has become a trope of Bowie Studies is partly explained by its spectacular optics. There are the iconic photographs of the two men taken by Terry O'Neill, whom Bowie would continue to work with and commission for the singer's last photoshoot. A legendary fashion chameleon, Bowie was a man of many looks. O'Neill's photos capture Bowie in his *Aladdin Sane* period; with his thin frame, dyed red hair, and Alex the droog t-shirt, the singer looks like he beamed in from some indeterminate time in the future. Meanwhile, Burroughs's reputation as a writer of notoriously explicit scenes of queer sex, violence, and drug use in his fiction are comically at odds with the elegant, middle-aged man in the photos. By the 1990s, the tension between Burroughs's writing and his formal attire had become an in-joke for alternative rock musicians and audiences; the video for Ministry's "Just One Fix" (1992), for example, randomly insert images of Burroughs in a suit and tie amidst footage of explosions, tornadoes, and desperate young junkies on the street hoping to score.

The symbolism of the meeting was equally important. David Bowie had rocketed to fame in the UK playing the role of Ziggy Stardust, a visitor from another planet who hooks up with a rock band and becomes a legend, singing songs about the imminent end of the world. The role threatened to swallow Bowie whole in the minds of his most devoted young fans. Although Bowie at this point was eager to grow his fan base in the United States, the meeting with Burroughs suggests an even stronger desire to be taken seriously as an artist, as well as an eagerness to incorporate (or appropriate) avant-garde ideas in his own work.

Burroughs also had something to gain from the encounter: greater access to the younger audience that read *Rolling Stone*. The writer had been courting the attention of a younger readership since 1966 when he published "The Invisible Generation" in the *International Times*, London's major underground newspaper. The short manifesto is a concise critique of technology as a means to social control, as well as an instructional manual on how to use the (newly invented) tape recorder to subvert media messages. Burroughs even references the Beatles' latest single, "Yellow Submarine," as if to seal the deal with his "hip," young audience.

The dialog begins tentatively, with both men reluctant to make any personal disclosures. However, their conversation becomes animated when they discover their mutual distrust of received ideas, or, what amounts to the same thing, their shared interest in ideas, topics, and practices either ignored or deemed dangerous by the establishment. These included science fiction (then still on the margins of literature), UFOs, pornography (both were fascinated by the new gay porn houses in New York's Times Square), meditation, and even recent efforts by the military to weaponize sound frequencies.

As Casey Rae observes in *William Burroughs and the Cult of Rock 'n' Roll*, the meeting intrigued Burroughs but was transformative for Bowie. By the time the two men met in 1973, Bowie was committed to role-playing as a primary means of self-exploration, having already concluded, in Rae's words, that identity was merely "a series of manufactured illusions."[1] Burroughs's work provided Bowie with an example of an even more radical take on identity than his own. Character is inherently unstable in Burroughs's fiction; it mutates rather than evolves as is typical in realist fiction. By Bowie's own admission, he had not read anything by Burroughs before the *Rolling Stone* interview; his literary tastes ran instead to the ecstatic, visionary prose of Burroughs's lifelong friend, Jack Kerouac. At Copetas's urging, however, Bowie would read *Nova Express* (1964), in which the agents of Control are literally viruses, programmed, as Rae puts it, "to infect reality with the Control agenda."[2]

Inspired by Burroughs's radical take on the subject, Bowie would drastically alter his own approach to songwriting. He was especially fascinated with the "cut-up" technique that Burroughs had utilized to construct *Nova Express*, which involved literally cutting up a pre-existing written text into segments that are rearranged and printed in random order. After the meeting, Bowie would cut up his own song lyrics, a practice he would continue to use for the rest of his life.

All this is noted in Casey Rae's in-depth account of the Bowie-Burroughs interview. Interestingly, Rae also hints that Bowie was as stressed by meeting the writer as he was artistically stimulated. In Rae's words, Bowie struggles in the interview to present himself "as a sophisticated student of letters."[3] Copetas also provided Burroughs with a reading assignment before the interview: selected song lyrics from Bowie. At one point in the interview, Burroughs compares one of Bowie's (unspecified) lyrics to T. S. Eliot's verse, to which Bowie briskly responds, "never read him."[4]

My aim in revisiting this connection is not to reclaim Bowie for the English major. However, I will attempt to make the case here that Bowie's meeting with Burroughs inaugurated the most self-consciously "literary" period of his career. *Diamond Dogs*, released in May 1974, is Bowie's first post-Burroughs recording, and, not coincidentally, the artist's most comprehensive attempt to engage with literary texts and infuse so-called literary values into his work. Yet Bowie's new venture is inspired less by literature as such than it is by his new awareness that literature is, before it is anything else, a medium. Bowie's meeting with Burroughs seems to have confirmed Bowie's intuition that literature needed an upgrade in order to reach an audience whose perceptions were already being transformed through their interactions with new media. In *Diamond Dogs*, Bowie redefines the literary to accommodate the emerging information society.

Appropriately enough for such a contrary artist, Bowie's literary turn is full of paradoxes. There is the initial contradiction of utilizing the cut-up—a device initially intended to be used as a weapon against the idea of "literature"—for stylistic reasons. As Burroughs acknowledges in his first written account of the technique, the procedure originated in Dadaist Tristan Tzara's practice of taking a scissor to "hard copies" of his poems, placing the fragments in a hat, and picking them up at random.[5] The Dadaists were the first in a long line of experimental artists in the twentieth century who hoped to undermine the very idea of art, a notion they believed was fatally compromised by its bourgeois audience. The cut-up was initially developed by poets and writers who refused to separate artistic language from social life. Yet while the technique denied the autonomy of literature, it affirmed the magic power of language because words themselves were magic.

Before I turn fully to Bowie's new relation to the literary, I wish to triangulate my topic: while it is important to understand how Burroughs altered Bowie's songwriting process, it is also valuable to understand why Bowie was so eager to adopt the technique. That answer requires a detour into rock history. Bowie's artistic practice was informed by his own highly sophisticated understanding of that history. Well before meeting Burroughs, the singer was already convinced that rock music as an art form was at an impasse. Although the cut-up provided Bowie with the formal means to take what I would call his "literary turn," Bowie's notion of literature was largely informed by a musician whose words challenged the idea that "literature" could only be found in books: Bob Dylan. Before Bowie learned to consider literature itself as media, Dylan had provided Bowie with the chief example of how literary values could be integrated within rock music. As Nduka Otiono and Josh Toth argue, from the very beginning of his career, Dylan's work has "[engaged and provoked an] odd anxiety about the nature, or finite boundaries, of the literary."[6] Well before Dylan won the Nobel Prize in Literature in 2016, his songwriting provoked doubts that literature was contained by the written word.

Dylan's revolutionary approach to rock lyrics profoundly affected Bowie, partly because he grasped, perhaps more than any of his peers in the field, the unfinished aspect of Dylan's revolution in songwriting. As I discuss below, Bowie's "Song for Bob Dylan" characterizes the folk-rock singer as a revolutionary leader who has abandoned the struggle. Dylan fundamentally reshaped songwriting in the rock field: but revolutions are often as hard to perpetuate as they are to establish. Bowie's career in the early 1970s is characterized by a restless eclecticism that I argue is a conscious response to both Dylan's achievement in the 1960s and that singer's retreat from the "front lines" of rock music. This achievement was of existential import to any rock musician interested in the artistic aspect of rock and roll, as was Bowie. Ironically, Burroughs's cut-up method, aimed at unsettling conventional ideas about form, inspired Bowie to think more creatively about form in songwriting. The technique provided the singer with the last piece of the puzzle, allowing him to overcome the crisis in art-rock brought on by the astonishing work that Bob Dylan produced in the mid-1960s.

"If you don't want to do it, I will":[7] Bowie and the Authentic Folk Singer

I found myself writing this song, this story, this long piece of vomit about twenty pages long, and out of it I took "Like a Rolling Stone" and made it as a single. I'd never written anything like that before, and it suddenly came to me that this is what I should do. Nobody had ever done that before. . . . Because it was a whole new category. I mean, nobody's ever written songs before, really.[8]

—Bob Dylan

It is a commonplace of rock history to note that rock musicians became more self-conscious about their identity as artists and the possibilities of the art form in the mid-1960s. The Beatles and the Beach Boys expressed this new self-consciousness by embracing the process and possibilities of studio recording. In contrast, Dylan's audience has always regarded his innovative songwriting, particularly his lyrics, as the core of his artistry; as Anthony DeCurtis puts it, Bob Dylan's songs "are the very heart of the matter—the foundation on which his aesthetic reputation rests."[9] Like many of Dylan's admirers, DeCurtis is quick to dismiss the role that studio recording might play in Dylan's creativity; still, his statement perfectly captures the idealistic way in which Dylan's songwriting was received in the 1960s and beyond: as an artistic achievement that somehow exists outside the recording process.

Dylan's continuing commitment to lyric writing when he moved from folk music to rock transformed the latter genre. It is one thing for folk singers to emphasize the words that they sing or incorporate poetic imagery in their song lyrics: but presenting literary elements in a rock song is a game changer. In particular, Dylan challenged received ideas about the appropriate scale of the rock song. He released two full-length albums in 1965. The first of these, *Bringing it all Back Home,* was also his first recording with a backing band. The album was divided into an acoustic and an electric side, respectively; the second, acoustic side includes several songs with surreal imagery that are over five minutes long. Dylan's first full-fledged rock album, *Highway 61 Revisited,* closes with an acoustic song, "Desolation Row," that is almost twelve minutes long, suggesting that Dylan's eagerness to test the limits of the song form and his audience's attention span did not end with his shift into rock and roll.

By 1966, with the release of *Blonde on Blonde,* Dylan's (and one of rock music's) first double record sets, the songwriter's ambitions had reached new heights; the question now was whether rock music could accommodate the massive amount of new material that Dylan brought to the form. *Blonde on Blonde* is a record virtually exploding with words, stories, characters, and concepts. As Michael Coyle and Debra Rae Cohen put it, Dylan's lyrical surrealism at this stage "begins to assume new functions."[10] In songs like "Stuck Inside of Mobile," an expanding list of images "aim to conceal rather than reveal" the song's meaning.[11]

"Stuck Inside of Mobile" also plays an important role in Brian McHale's account of postmodern literature, which pinpoints 1966 as the movement's "Big Bang": "Abrupt career changes, impasses and renunciations, interruptions and breakdowns, crashes literal and figurative, and endings and beginnings are the hallmarks of the year 1966 at the cutting edge of culture."[12] Dylan's *Blonde on Blonde* checks all these boxes. Like most of the "cutting edge culture" that McHale surveys, Dylan's "Stuck Inside of Mobile" is an extended meditation on "being at an impasse": a situation that would seem to be at odds with the reality of a singer who released three albums in little over a year while also touring worldwide. For McHale, the song suggests that Dylan was haunted by the sense of an ending even as he reached a creative peak. And no wonder: the long-form songs on *Blonde on Blonde* carried with them the very real threat of implosion. With a single song, "Sad Eyed Lady of the Lowlands," covering an entire album side, the scale and breadth of *Blonde on Blonde* suggested a terminal moment for the form as much as it did a new beginning. How could anyone, including Dylan, follow this high-wire act?

Rather than try, Dylan attempted to escape the rock world altogether. After *Blonde on Blonde*, Dylan would go underground; as McHale observes, it will remain a mystery whether the songwriter was forced to do so because of serious injuries that he sustained in a motorcycle accident in the summer of 1966, or whether the accident was used as a pretext for dropping out of sight.[13] Although Dylan wouldn't release another record officially until December 1967, it would later become known that he had never stopped writing. The songs that Dylan wrote and recorded in the basement studio of the Band, his touring group and near neighbors in Woodstock, New York, continued his characteristic surreal imagery and wordplay. But this time Dylan's surrealism was more playful than portentous, veering in "Odds and Ends" and "Million Dollar Bash" into the realm of nonsense. Dylan made yet another new start with the songs that he recorded on *John Wesley Harding*, an album generally darker than most of the songs that Dylan would write in 1967, but which, like *The Basement Tapes*, reveals a "sparer, more severe songwriter" than before.[14] With the exception of the nearly-six-minute "The Ballad of Frankie Lee and Judas Priest," Dylan's *Harding* songs bear little in common with the epic, sprawling songs of *Blonde on Blonde*. On "I'll Be Your Baby Tonight," Dylan even welcomes back the rhymes that he had once tried to banish from pop music: "That big fat moon," he sings without a hint of irony, "is gonna shine like a spoon."[15]

Both Dylan's achievement and subsequent retreat leave their mark on David Bowie's *Hunky Dory*, released nearly five years after *Blonde on Blonde*, in December 1971. With the exception of "Queen Bitch," Bowie's musical homage to *Loaded*-era Velvet Underground, *Hunky Dory* is not a rock record. The album is predominantly acoustic, with strong, accessible melodies, a hard left turn away from the proto-heavy metal album that preceded it, *The Man Who Sold the World*. On the surface, *Hunky Dory* resembles the many classic singer-songwriter records released in that year, including Joni Mitchell's *Blue* and Carole King's *Tapestry*. These artists, too, were engaging Dylan's legacy, wrestling with "the image of a solo artist with a guitar and harmonica" that he had made "an indelible symbol of authenticity."[16] In stark contrast, however, with these other singer-songwriters, the Bowie of *Hunky Dory* has no truck with ideas of authenticity or originality; nor does he seem much interested in romance or relationships, the typical subject matter of the era's singer-songwriter genre. Bowie is preoccupied instead with a big idea: the disintegration of the rock counterculture. The premise of *Hunky Dory* is that rock culture has collapsed in on itself in the aftermath of the Beatles' breakup and Dylan's return to conventional songwriting. The album's opening song, "Changes," sets the stage, challenging the authority of the rock star who, he warns, will soon "get older" and become culturally irrelevant.[17] Of course, the song also underscores the temporary and tenuous nature of the singer's own claims to authority: rock authenticity, it seems to say, is a dead letter.

Bowie's rejection of rock authenticity might make *Hunky Dory* the first "post-rock" record. In the absence of any coherent center for the rock community, Bowie alternately pays homage to his art heroes past and present or else contemplates—as in "Oh! You Pretty Things," a chilling song that re-imagines the hippies as a new "master" race banishing their elders—an apocalyptic future. The protagonists in "Kooks" and "Fill Your Heart" (by Biff Rose) find pleasure in being an outsider, but the pastoral moments on the album are sharply juxtaposed by songs ("The Bewlay Brothers" and "Quicksand") that explore madness and psychic turmoil.

"Song for Bob Dylan," with its vision of the songwriter in retreat along with his audience, is arguably *Hunky Dory*'s lyrical centerpiece. It's a far more pedestrian melody and performance than both "Andy Warhol," which precedes it, and "Queen Bitch," which follows. In "Song for Bob Dylan," Bowie addresses the Dylan of his day, urging the singer to return to the creative experiments of his past. The song expresses a frank, unironic nostalgia for the world of rock gods. Bowie romanticizes Dylan as a voice from the margins, who "sat behind a million pair of eyes / and told them how they saw."[18] Bowie makes an impassioned plea for Dylan to write songs using words of "truthful vengeance" as he once did, and "to give us back our unity / and give us back our family." It is hard to reconcile the writer of this plea with the composer of the rest of *Hunky Dory*, where the current culture of fragmentation seems necessary to establish the future. Moreover, the chorus, the most vital part of the song, is also the most troubling. Here Bowie introduces a new, shady character: the "same old painted lady," who will "scratch this world to pieces / as she comes on like a friend." Luckily for the singer, "(just) a couple of songs from your old scrapbook / could send her home again." These images, which seem drawn from the 19th century, recall the cultural stereotypes analyzed by Andreas Huyssen, specifically the notion that "mass culture is somehow associated with women while real, authentic culture remains the prerogative of men."[19] Dylan's songs here represent the masculine front line capable of holding back the advance of a "feminized" rock culture in decline. On the positive side, Bowie also provides a powerful view of the contemporary rock audience, who he imagines is as preoccupied with the disintegration of the counterculture as is the songwriter himself: "Then we lost your train of thought / the paintings are all your own / While troubles are rising we'd rather be scared / together than alone."[20]

Bowie followed *Hunky Dory* with the landmark album *The Rise and Fall of Ziggy Stardust*. The singer's transformation into the Ziggy avatar resulted in his meteoric rise to fame in the UK, but it merely sidelined rather than resolved the aesthetic and existential problems posed on *Hunky Dory*; Bowie would quickly tire of "the spaceman schtick," as Casey Rae calls it.[21] Through a serendipitous meeting, William Burroughs would help Bowie resolve the problem of rock songwriting that had preoccupied him in the wake of Bob Dylan's retreat from the rock-art pinnacle.

Diamond Dogs and the Cut-Up

From Dylan to Bowie, by way of Burroughs: a circuitous path in some respects, and yet necessary in order to grasp the full significance of David Bowie's 1974 recording, *Diamond Dogs*. As we will see, the cut-up method provided Bowie with a way to both incorporate and move beyond Dylan's songwriting legacy. At the same time—as *Cracked Actor*, Alan Yentob's 1974 documentary on Bowie, hints—the singer was also attracted to the cut-up for personal reasons. He had faith that the technique provided a glimpse into the future: no small matter for a supremely ambitious performer on the verge of breaking out of his niche, "cult" following and reaching a broader audience. Yentob's film includes a memorable scene of the musician creating his own cut-ups backstage before performing at the Universal Amphitheater in Los Angeles.[22] Bowie admits to applying the cut-up technique to his own diaries as well as his song lyrics, touting the method as a pathway to enlightenment: "I've tried doing it with diaries and things, and I was finding out lots of amazing things about me and what I've done and where I was going."[23] He goes on to compare the cut-up to "a kind of Western tarot,"[24] another emblem of late 1960s Western counterculture.

There are many indications in the Burroughs dialog, too, that Bowie's search for a new approach to making music heightened his interest in the cut-up. The singer declares at one point: "Songwriting as an art is a bit archaic now. Just writing a song is not good enough."[25] In a similar vein, he complains that songs themselves are no longer "good enough": "I'm just not content writing songs, I want to make it three-dimensional. . . . A song has to take on character, body and influence people to an extent that they use it for their own devices. It must affect them not just as a song, but as a lifestyle."[26] As we saw, the implosion of the counterculture is a major theme of *Hunky Dory*, and Bowie seems to have concluded that the singer-songwriter tradition that he inherited from Dylan was part of the problem. Contrary to the egalitarian ideals of the counterculture, the singer-songwriter ethos set the performer above the audience and put a premium on authenticity and originality, notions that for Bowie had become suspect. The cut-up does away with all this ideological baggage, along with the idea of art as mere self-expression.

42   Lit-Rock

As mentioned earlier, Bowie and Burroughs quickly established a rapport once it became clear to both men that they shared many common ideas about the 1960s counterculture. Marshall McLuhan's argument about the central role of media in shaping the age was an important part of that culture; his 1964 book *Understanding Media* was popular among counterculture intellectuals who shared his belief that media was expanding human consciousness and would henceforth play a primary role in shaping social relations. Among other things, McLuhan argued that the era was defined by a transition from print culture to a new information society that traded in the circulation of images, confirming the intuition of counterculture intellectuals that they inhabited a completely different world from the one their parents knew.[27]

As the interview proves, both Bowie and Burroughs shared a McLuhan-esque fascination bordering on obsession with new audio and visual technologies.[28] Burroughs's interest in media theory is well documented; he published an essay collection on what he called "the electronic revolution" three years before he met with Bowie, offering instructions for scrambling, by means of the cassette player, mass-media messages, and worked throughout the 1960s with various collaborators, including Ian Sommerville and Antony Balch, to apply the cut-up method to media beyond the novel. Bowie reveals his own passion for new media and its potential to alter consciousness several times during the *Rolling Stone* interview. In a fascinating aside, Bowie relates the sci-fi backstory of his song "All the Young Dudes" with a macabre twist; the unmarked narrator of the song, he discloses, turns out to be the alien Ziggy Stardust, compelled to break the news to his young fans that there will no longer be any news. The buoyant chorus of the song, proclaiming that young men "carry the news," turns out to be an updated version of the blues "death letter": "Ziggy was in a rock and roll band and the kids no longer want rock and roll. There's no electricity to play it. Ziggy's adviser tells him to collect the news and say it, 'cause there is no news. So Ziggy does this and there is terrible news. 'All the Young Dudes' is a song about this news. It is no hymn to youth as people thought. It is completely the opposite."[29]

Bowie's revelation about his song also sheds light on his core beliefs at the time: namely, that a world without electricity is tantamount to the apocalypse. Throughout the *Rolling Stone* interview, Bowie declares his wish to accelerate the new media revolution through the process of immersion. At one point the singer declares outright, "The media is either our salvation or our death. I'd like to think of it as our salvation."[30] Elsewhere Bowie claims that the freedom to consume the visual culture of one's choice is an essential human right: "Libraries of video cassettes should be developed to their fullest during the interim. You can't video enough good material for your own TV. I want to have my own choice of programs. There has to be the necessary software available." (Not to be outdone, Burroughs replies, "I audio-record everything I can.") Bowie also declares a preference for television over cinema because the former allows the viewer to immerse oneself in images in privacy: "People having to go out to the cinema is really archaic. I'd much rather sit at home."[31]

Bowie's stated preferences suggest his willingness to integrate the electronic revolution described by Burroughs and McLuhan into every aspect of his life, including his music. There were obvious aesthetic reasons to include rock within the media revolution. Just a few years before the Bowie/Burroughs exchange, the San Francisco Digger and sci-fi writer Chester Anderson claimed that McLuhan's description of the new media culture perfectly described "pop, op, and camp . . . and especially what we will keep calling rock and roll until we can find some more appropriate name for it."[32] Despite their ostensible differences, these movements share key features and highly specific modes of reception, including "synthesis and synesthesia; non-typographic, non-linear . . . mythic modes of participation; involvement of the whole sensorium; . . . participation in depth; extended awareness; preoccupation with textures, with tactility, with multi-sensory experiences."[33] Bowie's adoption of the cut-up method should be understood as a move within this larger context, as an expression of his commitment to explore the radical potential of new media. In the context of the ongoing electronic revolution, the cut-up seemed like futuristic instructions on how to utilize the literary in a new multimedia world. As such it served as the ideal bridge between the old world of culture and the futurescape that both Bowie and Burroughs believed was imminent.

The strongest case for reading *Diamond Dogs* in relation to Bowie's new media-consciousness is found in the album itself—an effort that Shelton Waldrep nominates as Bowie's first, fully successful concept album: "perhaps for the first time in his career, the songs really do have an existence mainly together, in their relationship with each other."[34] While the "concept album" designation is not inaccurate, Marshall McLuhan's brief account of early twentieth-century Cubist painting provides a more precise description. By providing "the inside and outside, top, bottom, back, and front and the rest in two dimensions," McLuhan writes, Cubism "drops the illusion of perspective in favor of instant sensory awareness of the whole."[35] *Diamond Dogs* is best understood as a post-Cubist text in this sense, striving to attain the conditions of simultaneity that McLuhan prophesied would be a key feature of cultural production in the future.

Bowie's growing awareness of literature as media can be seen in the new way he treats the various sources for the *Diamond Dogs* album. With references to George Orwell's *1984*, Burroughs's *The Wild Boys* (1972), J. G. Ballard's *Crash*, and Anthony Burgess' *A Clockwork Orange* (1962), *Diamond Dogs* brings "the literary allusions that permeate the trilogy [of Bowie's glam-rock era albums] to a head."[36] One might add to these the literary songwriting of Dylan himself, whose sprawling epics like "Desolation Row"—in which Ophelia, Ezra Pound, and T. S. Eliot make guest appearances—are invoked by *Diamond Dogs'* terse, rapid-fire mode of reference. Like Dylan, Bowie utilizes literary references more for their textures than for plot or story. Yet there are also differences: in "Desolation Row," Dylan's literary name-dropping works to a singular, totalizing effect, underscoring the carnivalesque aspect of the song. In contrast, the literary allusions in *Diamond Dogs* render its individual reference points even more abstract. Like the Cubist paintings that Marshall McLuhan describes as the precursor to the electronic media text, the album's swarm of stylistic references visualize different orders of meaning simultaneously, gesturing to several narratives all at once.

As early as 1972, Bowie had the idea of writing a full-scale rock opera based on *1984*, but Orwell's widow refused to give him permission to adapt the text. In this regard, the meeting with Burroughs seems fortuitous: the cut-up provided Bowie with an alternative way to utilize the Orwell source text. Rather than adapt Orwell's novel,

Bowie fragments it, reassembling bits and pieces of the book along with elements taken from the previously named dystopian fiction writers, and including Stanley Kubrick's film adaptation of Burgess's novel. Bowie's later explanation of his project emphasizes the important role that cut-up style fragmentation plays in his new sense of narrative: "I had in mind this kind of half *Wild Boys, Nineteen Eighty-Four* world . . . and they were these ragamuffins. . . . I guess they staggered through from *A Clockwork Orange* too."[37] The *Diamond Dogs* story is literally a mash-up of its source texts, anticipating the efforts of 1970s industrial music pioneers Throbbing Gristle, also inspired by Burroughs, to apply the cut-up to music, reassembling the bits and pieces of various sonic sources—tape loops, pre-recorded tapes—to create a new, compound sound. In the case of both Bowie and Throbbing Gristle, the musical results are not formless but rather take on their own unique and hybrid forms.

There is nothing as aggressive as Throbbing Gristle's tape loops to be heard on *Diamond Dogs*: yet there are many musical approximations to the cut-up effect. Many songs are sequenced in a way that deliberately, and disorientingly, heighten their sonic differences. The "Sweet Thing-Reprise" is taken over by a heavily distorted, screeching guitar sound that is suddenly interrupted by the sharp, precise metallic guitar riff of "Rebel Rebel." And as the final piano notes of "We Are the Dead" recede, they are quickly replaced by "1984," a song with a radically different arrangement from what preceded it, and indeed from every other track on the record. The swelling strings and syncopated guitar, bass, and drums recall the contemporary "Philly Soul" sound created by writer/producers Kenny Gamble and Leon Huff. "1984" is sonically distinct from the rest of the songs on the album, many of which feature Bowie's rudimentary rhythm guitar.

Of course, it is impossible to absorb a whole album as uniformly and succinctly as one might take in a painting. Nevertheless, the idea that the text is connecting with the listener on multiple levels simultaneously is part of *Diamond Dogs'* own unique brand of textuality. Perhaps the most striking example of Bowie's conscious manipulation of time frames is evident in "Rebel Rebel," which closes side "A" of the album. Preceded by "Sweet Thing-Reprise," the song is used to suggest a cut-up within the story's temporal frame. The function of "Sweet Thing" in its second appearance on the album is both to advance the story and provide narrative continuity; it serves as a musical cue that Halloween Jack, the album's central character, is once again prowling the city streets with his "wild boys." The song's lyrics express an urgent hedonism and gender confusion fully appropriate to the futuristic world in which the album is set. In contrast, "Rebel Rebel" breaks with the idea of narrative continuity, evoking instead the preapocalyptic past, a time outside the diegesis of the album. The conceit, as Waldrep puts it, is that the song "arises out of a jukebox that in this barren city landscape has been made to play again, the song seeming to start up like an old 45-rpm single that is slowly chugging to life."[38] In the context of the album, "Rebel Rebel" performs the most dramatic cut-up on the album, the past abruptly slicing into the *Diamond Dogs* futurescape. While lyrically provocative, musically "Rebel Rebel" is a conventional hard rock song. By means of these careful juxtapositions, Bowie also daringly points out the formulaic aspects of the song, suggesting both the anachronistic nature of the song and of rock music itself.

Bowie's bold play with the temporal frame of the *Diamond Dogs* story here suggests the full extent of his engagement with Burroughs's technique. We saw that Bowie applied the cut-up to his own diaries, with results that he believed both illuminated the past and somehow forecast the future. Burroughs also insisted on the power of the cut-up to operate on time as well as words. "When you experiment with cut-ups over a period of time," the writer proclaims, "you find that some of the cut-ups in re-arranged texts seem to refer to future events. . . . We had no explanation for this at the time, it just suggested that when you cut into the Present the Future leaks out."[39] "Rebel Rebel" evokes the past in the context of the *Diamond Dogs* album, but it could also be read in reverse: the present moment of the song already contains the future world that the album represents.

Bowie's next step would be to go beyond the mere juxtaposition of different sounds on the record and normalize the practice of integrating different musical genres. The live footage of "Sweet Thing" in the Yentob documentary illustrates how adroit Bowie and his backing group became at incorporating rock and soul music.[40] I use the word "incorporating" advisedly; Bowie's glam-rock period came to a surprising end with the release of *Young Americans* (1975), a conscious attempt to remake the singer as an American-style Soul artist. However, the music that Bowie and his band initially made on the American tour to promote the record is different from the carefully crafted, meticulously arranged rhythm-and-blues songs on his next recording. Like *Young Americans*, *Diamond Dogs* as performed borrows from both rock and soul music; but unlike that record, the music Bowie and his band played live highlights these sonic elements without integrating them. The different musical sounds are not harmonized; instead—in a manner perhaps reflective of Bertolt Brecht's "epic theater"—they are set apart from each other: an extended rock guitar solo here, a jazzy piano fill, or an R&B sax solo there. In Bowie's live performances from that year, one hears the sounds of different kinds of music appear and then disappear, without coalescing into a uniform style.

As a literary device uniquely suited to a post-literary world, the cut-up provided Bowie with a way out of what he perceived to be rock's artistic impasse. *Diamond Dogs* represents the culmination of Bowie's specific literary ambitions within rock and roll. The concert shows that Bowie created to promote the record was one of the most ambitious and extravagant of its type ever conceived by a rock artist.[41] The urban wasteland of the future suggested by the *Diamond Dogs* scenario was given a literal presentation by means of an elaborate and expensive set design, including a model skyscraper and bridge. Unsurprisingly, the singer's ambitious new aesthetic ideas were not sustainable, and he was forced to scrap his multimedia extravaganza mid-tour. Yet the record's true legacy lies elsewhere. *Diamond Dogs*-era Bowie would inspire many of the singer's younger fans in northern England to form their own rock bands in the mid- to late 1970s. The future members of Sheffield groups like Cabaret Voltaire and the Human League believed they already lived in the grim cityscapes of filth, pollution, and decayed high-rise apartment blocks that Bowie projected onto the future, and they set out to make music that evoked the desolate urban environments in which they grew up. Ian Curtis and Mark Stewart, the front men for Manchester's Joy Division and Bristol's the Pop Group, respectively, were not just Bowie fans, but passionate autodidacts like Bowie himself. Curtis and Stewart eagerly read books by Ballard and Burroughs because Bowie referenced these writers in his interviews. And the Bowie of *Diamond Dogs* became, in turn, a point of reference for a legion of rock groups in the late 1970s who, as Simon Reynolds eloquently observes, "grew up in cities, physically and spiritually scarred by the violent nineteenth-century transition between rural folkways and the unnatural rhythms of industrial life," and were searching for ways they might "aestheticize their panoramas of decay."[42]

Although the futurescape of *Diamond Dogs* seems far removed from Bob Dylan and the folk revolution, I have tried to indicate here how Bowie effectively absorbs and brings into view Dylan's mid-1960s epic expansion of the rock song. For listeners like Ian Curtis and Mark Stewart, however, eager to create a musical world beyond the scope of "classic rock," such historical contextualizing was beside the point; the record made visceral sense on its own terms. These aficionados regarded *Diamond Dogs* as more than a concept album about a dystopian future as viewed from the present day; it was itself a message from the future, a representation of the hyper-mediated society now at hand.

Notes

1   Casey Rae, *William S. Burroughs and the Cult of Rock 'n' Roll* (Austin: University of Texas Press, 2019), 111.
2   Ibid., 112.
3   Ibid., 121.
4   Craig Copetas, "Beat Godfather Meets Glitter Mainman: Burroughs and David Bowie," in *The Rolling Stone Book of the Beats*, ed. Holly George-Warren (New York: Hyperion, 1997), 198.
5   William Burroughs, "The Cut Up Method," in *The Moderns: An Anthology of New Writing in America*, ed. Leroi Jones (New York: Corinth, 1963), 345–8.
6   Josh Toth and Nduka Otiono, "Introduction: The Foreign Sounds of Dylan's Literary Art," in *Polyvocal Bob Dylan*, ed. Josh Toth and Nduka Otiono (New York: Palgrave, 2019), 2.
7   David Bowie, interview by Robert Hilburn, *Melody Maker*, February 28, 1976.
8   Bob Dylan, quoted in Robert Polito, "*Highway 61 Revisited*," in *Cambridge Companion to Bob Dylan*, ed. Kevin J. H. Dettmar (Cambridge: Cambridge University Press, 2009), 141. Italics added.
9   Anthony DeCurtis, "Bob Dylan as Songwriter," in *Cambridge Companion to Bob Dylan*, ed. Kevin J. H. Dettmar (Cambridge: Cambridge University Press, 2009), 42.
10   Michael Coyle and Debra Rae Cohen, "Blonde on Blonde," in *Cambridge Companion to Bob Dylan*, ed. Kevin J. H. Dettmar (Cambridge: Cambridge University Press, 2009), 146.
11   Ibid.
12   Brian McHale, *Cambridge Introduction to Postmodernism* (Cambridge: Cambridge University Press, 2015), 24–5.
13   Ibid., 23.

14 Ibid.

15 "I'll Be Your Baby Tonight," track 12 on Bob Dylan, *John Wesley Harding*, Columbia, 1967.

16 DeCurtis, "Bob Dylan as Songwriter," 52.

17 "Changes," track 1 on David Bowie, *Hunky Dory*, RCA, 1971.

18 "Song for Bob Dylan," track 9 on David Bowie, *Hunky Dory*, RCA, 1971.

19 Andreas Huyssen, *After the Great Divide: Modernism, Mass Culture, Postmodernism* (Bloomington: Indiana University Press, 1986), 45–6.

20 "Song for Bob Dylan," track 9 on David Bowie, *Hunky Dory*, RCA, 1971.

21 Rae, *William S. Burroughs and the Cult of Rock 'n' Roll*, 114.

22 See Ibid., 109. As Rae notes, Bowie's lucid explanation belies his noticeably unhealthy appearance: lines of cocaine are clearly visible on the table alongside the fragments of paper.

23 Bowie, quoted in Rae, *William S. Burroughs and the Cult of Rock 'n' Roll*, 109.

24 Ibid.

25 Ibid., quoted in Copetas, "Beat Godfather Meets Glitter Mainman," 196.

26 Ibid.

27 McLuhan advanced the argument that media should be studied in terms of its various structures rather than its content in his breakthrough book, *Understanding Media: The Extension of Man* (New York: McGraw-Hill, 1964).

28 The affinity of both artists with media and technology has something to do with their complicated but nevertheless deeply rooted commitment to modernist art. As Arjun Mulder notes, modernity and technology are closely intertwined: "If one wants to be modern, and preferably as modern as possible, one can do nothing else but allow one's worldview to be defined by the newest medium and technology, for only media and technologies change and can therefore be modern"; *Understanding Media Theory* (Rotterdam: V2_NAi, 2004), 17–18. For more on Burroughs's agonistic relation to modernism, see Timothy S. Murphy, *Wising Up the Marks: The Amodern William Burroughs* (Berkeley: University of California Press, 1997). For more on Bowie's rock modernism, see David Baker, "Bowie's Covers: The Artist as Modernist," in *Enchanting David Bowie: Space/Time/Body/Memory*, ed. Toija Cinque, Christopher Moore, and Sean Redmond (New York: Bloomsbury Academic, 2015).

29 Copetas, "Beat Godfather Meets Glitter Mainman," 195.

30 Ibid., 201.

31 Ibid., 200. In "Drive-In Saturday," also recorded in 1973, Bowie imagines a future world where TV sex substitutes for the physical act. Bowie's tele-philia makes an interesting contrast with Jonathan Crary's description of television as a "dress rehearsal" for the advanced techniques of state and corporate power to normalize a 24/7 routine for working and shopping; *24/7: Late Capitalism and the Ends of Sleep* (New York City: Verso, 2014).

32 Chester Anderson, "Rock and the Counterculture," in *Rock History Reader*, ed. Theo Cateforis (New York: Routledge, 2007), 125.

33 Ibid.

34 Shelton Waldrep, *Future Nostalgia: Performing David Bowie* (New York: Bloomsbury, 2016), 8.

35 McLuhan, *Understanding Media*, 13.

36 Waldrep, *Future Nostalgia*, 147.

37 Bowie, quoted in Ibid., 151.

38 Waldrep, *Future Nostalgia*, 8.
39 William Burroughs, "Cut-Ups." Quedear, 3:13, YouTube video, May 21, 2011. https://www.youtube.com/watch?v=Rc2yU7OUMcI&featur.e=emb_logo.
40 The live performance of "Sweet Thing" begins around the fourteen-minute mark in *Cracked Actor*. Yentob superimposes images of cut-up lyrics from the song onto Bowie as he performs.
41 Waldrep, *Future Nostalgia*, 149.
42 Simon Reynolds, *Rip It Up and Start Again: Postpunk 1978–1984* (New York: Penguin, 2005), 103.

2

Kurt, Kathleen 'n' Kathy

Cut-and-Paste and the Art of Being for Real

Patricia Malone

In what follows, there are a number of references to the concept of "woman," "women," and femininity as associated with a particular uterine discourse. These categorizations are not intended to be exclusionary and should be read as used within the context of historically and contextually specific critical and cultural attitudes.

Public confusion over the question of authenticity perhaps reached its nadir in the 1990s. The rise of televisual culture, often seen since its introduction as a force or influence slowly deforming public life in America, was reframed in 1992 with the introduction of MTV's *The Real World*, which had its genesis in a 1973 show called *The American Family*.[1] Laurie Ouellette marks this as the beginning of what she calls "lifestyle TV"—a form of broadcasting that aligns with, promotes, and even shapes the neoliberalized framing of the self as an enterprise.[2] *The Real World* is of particular interest because it marks the beginning of a televisual lifestyle which, in tandem with the rise of social media, has seen the incursion of sociality into elements of life where previously it did not exist. In this metastasized celebrity culture, exposure—self-display, particularly of suffering—becomes a primary form of public currency.

Kurt Cobain has been, to some degree, the poster boy for this moment of cultural shift. As an artist as well known for his drug addiction and eventual suicide as for his music (which often featured references to both addiction and self-loathing), Cobain and his partner, Courtney Love, seem to exist at the tipping point of celebrity culture, firmly in the crosshairs of the authenticity war that continues to rage in an ever-more virtualized present. It is to this Mark Fisher was referring to when he coined the term "precorporation," signifying the totality of culture-as-product (in fact, life-as-product), and marking the end of "the old struggle between *détournement* and recuperation."[3] This points to the end of any potential subversive element to counter or alternative cultures and their total subsumption into the logic of capital.[4] In the 1990s, and in the punk scene that Nirvana came from, there was a much simpler term for this: selling out.

In the parlance of punk, selling out can be understood at its most basic level to mean signing to a major record label. The pejorative sense of the term comes from the tacit understanding that such a move means handing creative control over to the "men in suits," the business-end of the record industry who are seen to have little to no interest in creativity or artistry (even, perhaps, in music). An important part of the concept stems from the idea that punk *networks*, as much as punk art, might function to disrupt or counter dominant capitalist networks of exchange and in so doing disrupt the ideology of value. This was the ethos of Dischord, the DC record label that acted as a locus point for the 1980s hardcore scene in America, from which elements of the grunge scene emerged. Founded by Ian McKaye and Jeff Nelson, the label sought to press and distribute records without the support of major labels, keeping prices for recorded music and live performances to a cost-covering minimum. This distribution model has also been used by literature described as "punk," as both William Burroughs and Kathy Acker sought, from design and necessity, publication in "alternative" presses or even to self-publish.[5] The relationship between punk and commerce is an important one here, sitting close to the heart of the question of authenticity, the use of the cut-up form, and the alternative networks of exchange at work in and around America's Pacific North West during the early days of Nirvana and of riot grrrl—a "punk feminist" community and ethos comprised of a (very) loosely allied group of artists, musicians, and other engaged parties.[6]

"I Went to School in Olympia":[7] The DIY Ethos and Community as Praxis

Kurt Cobain and Kathleen Hanna (the performer often, and erroneously, referred to as the "leader" or "founder" of riot grrrl) both existed within the orbit of Olympia, a college town in Washington State. Hanna attended Evergreen College; Cobain drove down from his native Aberdeen to spend time around the town's burgeoning music scene.[8] Central to this scene was K Records, founded by Calvin Johnson, a member of the lo-fi band Beat Happening. Johnson's band and label were widely considered the crux of a particular type of naïve indie-pop, owing to the childish nature of their lyrical subject matter, their kitsch performances, and (a controversial point) their amateurish musicianship. The Olympia ethos borrowed much from the UK indie scene, and bands like the Pastels and the Vaselines would see this acknowledged in Cobain's frequent and fervent public declarations of fandom following his own ascension to taste-maker status.[9] The naïve aesthetic and the attachment to a curated form of childishness are both useful in thinking through the question of authenticity beyond a "simple" punk form (where punk is simply shorthand for nihilism or aggression) and in understanding how Cobain's work, particularly *In Utero*, might be read in the context of feminist praxis.

In writing on the collage technique in the work of Burroughs and Acker, Rob Latham has drawn attention to the childishness or apparent naivety of the form itself.[10] Although

Burroughs's proto-deconstructionism enacts a sophisticated attack on the linearity of discourse and those modes of power that are sustained by it, the process itself might take the practitioner back to the days of childhood, to pots of glue and safety scissors. Latham frames a number of other ways that the "collage technique" connects to ideas of childishness or childhood, including his description of "promiscuous" authorship, which holds particular significance for anti-Oedipal readings of such texts.[11] This has been noted by a number of critics writing on Acker, too; Georgina Colby in *Kathy Acker: Writing the Impossible* (2016) marks this disruption as requisite a mode of literary self-fashioning for "woman," writing in a language from which she is and must always be categorically excluded.[12] One begins already to suspect how such praxis might have significance for an album titled *In Utero*, conceived in part as a commentary on the nature of authentic appearance in an age of hyper-celebrity. Further, for Acker as for those involved in the praxis of riot grrrl, the faux-naïve aesthetic acted as a way to reveal the insidious distortions of female sexuality and bodily autonomy emerging in the wake of second-wave feminism and against the Reagan administration's persistent calls for return to "family values."

Acker's influence on riot grrrl is as well documented as Burroughs's influence on Cobain: several of the works cited so far make reference to the wonderfully direct instruction given by Acker to Kathleen Hanna, to start a band rather than pursuing a literary career because musicians enjoyed more of a "community."[13] This concept of community is central to the questions of authenticity with which Cobain wrestled in his art, and to his fandom of Burroughs and other countercultural figures. Greil Marcus describes Cobain as "infected with the folk virus . . . a belief in the existence and transcendentally moral state of a small, localized, culturally and commercially isolated, like-minded and homogenous community in which artist and audience are indistinguishable."[14] The flipside to such belief is the conclusion that a popular—that is, widespread and commercially successful—form of public discourse must be "false, dishonest, cheap, shallow, meaningless, and corrupt—and corrupting."[15] Thus the problem of fame is not simply the demands of existing in the public eye, though these may be intolerably stressful and unwanted. It is the fact that the attainment of success in this forum, that is, the attainment of commercial success and mass audience, is in fact the proof of *failure*, the proof of the corruption and venality of the artist's output (and, by extension, of the artist themselves, if one believes the two are inextricable). In such a position one could not sell out, as such, because one would already *be sold out*: precorporated by the banality of dissent in an (alleged) age of total irony.

Kathy Acker never quite attained this measure of success in her lifetime, becoming instead a countercultural figure for whom commercial success always seemed to lie just beyond reach—although Acker, like Burroughs, was not shy about her need for money and her hope that her art might also afford her a way to make a living.[16] For Acker, too, writing was about community, about finding an audience who would be bound together in some way by her work. Lee Konstantinou has suggested that what Acker wanted was "production and circulation without consumption," thus capturing the dilemma faced by artists who self-consciously strive to interrupt dominant cultural modes while still relying on the systems of commerce that structure those modes.[17] Although the question of whether or not Kurt Cobain was actually engaged in such a project in the same self-consciously political fashion as Acker is muddy, it seems entirely fair to read his frequent eviscerations of mainstream American culture in *Journals* and elsewhere as a legitimate statement of intent, and a desire to elude consumption equivalent to Marcus's "folk virus." What is of note here is that riot grrrl might actually be considered as just such a "transcendentally moral state" of "homogenous community," patently evident in the extreme reluctance with which practitioners engaged with the media, including a total media block in 1992.[18] Indeed, it is likely that riot grrrl may have generated too homogenous a community: the inability of white participants to confront issues of systemic and personal racism is and was a persistent problem.[19] However, without understating the serious and endemic blind spots of riot grrrl practitioners, I want to draw attention to the way in which riot grrrl putatively worked as a spontaneous, self-generating, and DIY community—in short, the sort of audience that Cobain apparently sought above all else. This is also connected to the thematic preoccupations and discursive strategies of riot grrrl, which evolved, as we will see shortly, beyond those of the earlier DIY networks, and drew extensively from the literary practice of the "cut-up."

Televisual Imaginations?: Gysin, Burroughs, Acker

The rise of reality in the 1990s might be tied to the expansion of the televisual mode or the extension of image culture. This extension has historically been understood in terms of postmodernism, gesturing not just to the period after (literary) modernism, but also to works of art that share certain thematic and aesthetic preoccupations and techniques. Although I would prefer to avoid the term altogether with reference to both Burroughs and Acker, I must acknowledge its utility in describing a certain strain of cultural imagination that was by the 1990s marked as a strain of exhaustion. This exhaustion has been connected to an overweening mode of ironic discourse that came, as Konstantinou deftly shows in *Cool Characters*, to permeate cultural "common sense" in the United States. In attempting to distance Burroughs's work from the postmodern appellation, I am seeking to recognize its distinctiveness, both in its form and content.[20] The cut-up technique—and particularly its *practice*—is essential to understand this distinctiveness and properly contextualize Cobain's artistic engagement with Burroughs and his authorial practice.

It was Burroughs's friend Brion Gysin who developed the cut-up technique, and it was his collaboration with Burroughs, *The Third Mind* (1977), that Acker would later use to "teach" herself how to write.[21] In a 1965 interview with *The Paris Review,* Burroughs discussed Gysin's influence while acknowledging a longer and more diverse history of cut-up that he himself had not fully understood when coming to the technique, invoking the works of the Romanian poet Tristan Tzara, novelist John Roderigo Dos Passos, and even T. S. Eliot's modernist urtext, "The Waste Land." The cut-up technique emerges from within the field of visual art, where collage had long been employed as a methodology and form.[22] Cut-up, then, is a deliberate process whereby one text is undone—literally cut up—and its pieces re-formed—collaged—to make another, where different syntactical, grammatical, and thematic relationships emerge between words and sentences.[23] This can be directly connected to the sensorial bombardment of mass media associated with the ascendance of television and particularly with the commercial aspect of televisual culture; the cut-up style (though not the method) was famously deployed by J. G. Ballard in *The Atrocity Exhibition* (1970) to make just this point.[24]

Ballard's refusal of the method is also related to his claims, from the same text, regarding the "death of affect," a desensitization to and of the world at large.[25] In contrast, Burroughs saw the practice of the method as key to producing the quality so deeply fetishized by the Beats: spontaneity. The eruption of spontaneity disrupts the reification of language and (in theory, at least) of experience itself (the experience of using and engaging with language, even). Anticipating the do-it-yourself ethos of the punk movement, Burroughs insisted, "Cut-ups are for everyone."[26] This egalitarian commitment comes under serious strain when read against the author's persistent misogyny (rather grimly), dismissed by Wayne Pounds as "too well known for me to need to discuss it."[27] This misogyny emerges in the unthinkable difference of women in Burroughs's writing, in which the move toward utopian imaginaries is predicated on the total exclusion of the female, even as a matter of reproductive necessity. There is, then, an important distinction to be made here between the Burroughsian discourse of the bodily grotesque and the figuration employed by Cobain in his lyrics and visual art—one that may be traced to Acker's work and to its "trickle-down" influence through riot grrrl praxis.

Girls Are Gross: Assholes, Uteri, and Other Permeable Passages

Burroughs's breakthrough work, *Junky* (1953), was published and marketed as "pure" autobiography. Later work saw Burroughs move away from this genre, although he still drew largely on his own life experiences and those of others he knew. This is documented by Oliver Harris in his introduction to *Junky*, where Harris offers a brief sketch of how *Junky* might be understood within the field of autobiography, connected to the text's wider position as an addiction or illness narrative operating within the confessional mode. These terms gesture toward the discursive practices of riot grrrl, particularly in zine culture, and make plain the through-line that exists between "sickness" and "authenticity," discussed by Jessica L. Wood in her work on Cobain.[28] Wood's discussion looks at the figuration of the sick body within Cobain's multimedia oeuvre, suggesting that Cobain's aesthetic of disgust functioned "as a means to signal the 'realness' of his art."[29] I borrow the phrase "aesthetic of disgust" here from Konstantinou, finding it more apt a term than the grotesque when exploring what Wood describes as Cobain's "eviscerating vocals and unintelligible lyrics" as well as "scatological imagery."[30] The stress on both vocal performance and unintelligibility presents an immediate challenge to any simple categorization of the embodied grotesque as concrete aesthetic here, although I am less convinced by the singular emphasis on the scatological aspect of Cobain's work that forms the crux of Wood's discussion.

Indeed, Wood opens her discussion with an anecdote involving Cobain's interpretation of tour-mate Tad Doyle's daily vomiting as "a work of art."[31] Doyle's affliction stemmed from a chronic gastrointestinal problem that Cobain may very well have identified with, given his own lengthy history of stomach problems (material in *Journals* and elsewhere reveals these problems as the source of his decision to start using, or "self-medicating" with, heroin, though the truth of this is far from settled). The particular site of Cobain's suffering, its concentration in his stomach, points to a particularly feminized form of pain: menstrual cramps, or even pregnancy itself. Cobain's feelings toward his own body, as described in *Journals* and by a number of the critics cited above, were usually expressed as self-loathing: his extreme thinness, a result of his stomach problems and later of his heroin use, was a persistent mark of "unmanliness" that he worried about throughout his life. Wood addresses this in her discussion of Cobain's "marginal body," where she offers a close reading of a cartoon of Cobain's "rock star" face drawn by another artist, under which Cobain has drawn a diminutive torso for himself.[32] Of interest in tracing the musician's literary influences is the scrap pasted above the image, an excerpt from a poem by Alicia Ostriker:

> Passing that firey tree—if only she could
> Be making love,
> Be making poetry,
> Be exploding, by speeding through the univer[letters cut off]
>
> Like a photon, like a shower
> Of yellow blazes -[33]

The lines are taken from "A Young Woman, A Tree," in which Ostriker compares the life of a woman to that of a maple tree. One might, without straining too much, see something tree-like in the sinewy trunk Cobain sketches for himself on that page. There is something recognizable, too, in the woman's discovery, late on, that "*The desire / To burn is already a burning!*"[34] As for the tree, its very survival is due to its taste for the toxic, "to its uniquely / Mutant appetite for pollutants." Ostriker's poem moves toward not a straightforwardly affirmative image of the natural world and its cycles but instead closes by looking at what lies beneath, the tree's thoughts turning toward "the sewage pipes' / Cold slime," an image that must surely have spoken to Cobain's aesthetic of disgust, the tree's wretched appetites recalling the "meat-eating orchids" of *In Utero's* "Heart Shaped Box."[35] The purpose of these forays into poetry is to explain that while Cobain may have had a frequently scatological imagination in the style associated with Burroughs and his notorious anal fixation, he also explored and identified with a mode of abjection that can best be described as feminine. When Pounds discusses the "postmodern anus" in Burroughs's work (focusing on the talking asshole of *Naked Lunch*), he situates that work in a long tradition of modernist "body writing," citing Ezra Pound, James Joyce, George Bataille, and looking to Burroughs as an inheritor of Mikhail Bahktin's work on degradation. Of this, Bahktin wrote:

> To degrade means to concern oneself with the lower stratum of the body, the life of the belly and the reproductive organs; it therefore relates to acts of defecation and copulation, conception, pregnancy, and birth. Degradation digs a bodily grave for a new birth; it has not only a destructive, negative aspect, but also a regenerating one. . . . Grotesque realism knows no other level; it is the fruitful earth and the womb. It is always conceiving.[36]

What Cobain essentially grasped, and where his work sits closer to Acker's than to Burroughs's, is the generative possibility in the discourse of degradation as situated at the level of embodiment: the abjection of the (female or feminized) body is not reviled but celebrated in Cobain's work. This is apparent in the artwork Cobain made and used as the album sleeve for *In Utero*. The front cover was designed by Robert Fisher and features the instantly recognizable image of the female Transparent Anatomical Mannikin with added wings. The back cover of the record was an artwork of Cobain's own making, a mixed media collage that featured anatomical models of fetuses in utero, broken bones, dying flowers, and a range of other items that feature in the album's lyrics. The very obviousness of the images here and elsewhere runs the risk of banality: a sort of naïve faux-bohemian comment on birth, death, and decay, with no clear oppositional stance or overtly political comment. However, given the theoretical background outlined above, it seems fair to suggest that the image—like the album itself—is designed to provoke and to *disappoint*. That is, to move Cobain and the band closer to that "folk"-type community, where you had to "get it" to get in. As if to prove this point, the album was censored by chain stores such as Walmart and Kmart, who objected to the collage and to the title of the album's fourth song, "Rape Me."

This sort of censorship is relatively mild compared to that faced by Burroughs, or that which Acker saw during her efforts to publish the text that would finally be *Blood and Guts in High School*. Here, Acker's take on the cut-up text saw the incorporation of visual and textual materials with which Cobain's work on *In Utero* shares a number of thematic preoccupations, although Acker's theoretical background—and her political position—were much more clearly developed. Her textual assemblage, as it's been called, set the tone for the faux-naïve aesthetic of riot grrrl that Cobain borrowed heavily from for *In Utero*. This borrowing emerged, as stated, from a desire to disappoint those drawn to his music by its "dumb jock" elements; that is, the "pop" container that curbed the darker edges of the music and in so doing was supposed to imbue it with a sense of irony, but instead only ensured its chart-topping status. For all Cobain's efforts to disgust, his music, like his much-discussed heartthrob appearance, remained too "pretty." Like Acker and those involved in riot grrrl, Cobain sought to find a way to reroute this "prettiness" into something more vital and disturbing. This was largely based on his own non-identification with the patriarchal discourse of masculinism embedded in American culture and can be recognized as a nascent,

56   *Lit-Rock*

if not fully, political mode of expression.[37] This is connected to the mode of political discourse propagated within Acker's work and adopted by practitioners of riot grrrl.

See Me Suffer: Celebrity, Authenticity, and Making Yourself Up

In her work on riot grrrl and pop-feminism, Emily Spiers is at pains to draw attention to the genre-spanning forms of riot grrrl zines, which she (and others) have marked as the primary locus of the spontaneously generated community. Emphasizing the "self-reflexive" nature of zine output, Spiers vehemently insists on the constructed nature of the zine text:

> In general, riot-grrrl texts connote performances that cannot be read at face value but as modes of politicized self-fashioning. They deconstruct but also construct the creator's identity. The confessional passages pick apart layers of social conditioning, encompassing privilege-checking and public self-shaming, as well as traumatic and oppressive experiences, but the *act* of zine construction, of creating a multimedia, self-reflexively composed narrative constitutes a strategy of collaborative identity construction which ... was threatened not only by conventional patriarchal forces but by strands of pervasive critical theory.[38]

This self-reflexivity can be seen as an expression of the heightened self-awareness attributed to Gen Xers, as Cobain's peer group were known, and is also associated with the literary style of postmodernism: this is the "pervasive" theory Spiers refers to, encapsulating the deconstructive practices most commonly associated with Jacques Derrida, though Judith Butler's hugely influential *Gender Trouble* (1990) was a major touchstone for those rethinking gender during the 1990s. Cobain too displays an incipient awareness of these ideas, not least in his sketch of a seahorse bearing the words, "the MALe Seahorse carries the children and gives them Birth."[39] This is significant when considering the way in which Cobain inhabits a female consciousness for much of *In Utero*; the speaker on "Pennyroyal Tea," for example, sips an abortifacient to "distil the life inside" of him.[40]

Such reflexivity has been marked as a feature of Cobain's writing and lyrical style; Duane Fish writes, "Attempting to do a thematic analysis of the songs of Kurt Cobain is extremely difficult. The lyrics of the songs reflect the fragmentation that is indicative of postmodernity: the songs are not narratives that follow an easily understood story to make a point."[41] I draw on Fish's rather thin reading here because of his use of the term "fragmentation," which also occurs as a critique of the impact of postmodern theory on the formation of personal subjectivity in Spiers's work, by way of Kathleen Hanna's "When the Words that once Liberated You."[42] Wood also notes this reflexive tendency and very nearly connects it to the revelatory function of Cobain's journal writing when she draws attention to the performative aspect of this writing. Drawing on evidence from Charles Cross's biography of Cobain, *Heavier Than Heaven* (2001), she writes:

"Cobain often showed his writings to friends and . . . his journals would frequently lie open around the apartment [that he shared with Courtney Love]."[43] Wood also notes Cobain's habit of addressing his writing to an unknown (even nonexistent) recipient, frequently adopting the epistolary mode that often marked riot grrrl zines. This functions somewhat differently in riot grrrl zines if or when we think of them as instruments for building and maintaining a "folk community," to return to that term. In such an instance the (imagined) addressee is a fellow riot grrrl and the address may function as a form of interpellation as well as a gesture of solidarity.

Such a reading should not suggest that the diaristic or epistolary mode of riot grrrl zines was without its own set of conventions or tropes, however. Spier, following the work of Mimi Thi Nguyen, points to the interconnected "commodification of crazy" and the reification of suffering that occurred within the punk framework of oppression as cache.[44] Ramdasha Bikceem, the author of the zine *GUNK*, directly used the phrase "COMMODITY OF CRAZINESS" in recognizing the way that a performative display of transgressive otherness became enshrined in riot grrrl zine culture.[45] While there is much to be said on the coincidence of this model and the rise of therapeutic discourse as a form of public discourse throughout the 1990s, there is too little space here to give this full voice.[46] Instead, I want to tie this practice back to the emergent culture of exposure that developed in conjunction with the rise of the "reality genre," discussed at the beginning of this chapter. There are, as ever, much longer roots to the culture of confession, but the particular practice of self-disclosure as a mode of authentic revelation that was instantiated by the form of reality television is a distinct one, tied to developments in both media technology and generational shifts in media consumption (a shorthand for this might be the "MTV effect"). With regards to Cobain's work, in both songwriting and performance, the presence of pain is often described as a key marker of his output and persona, a sort of existential suffering that is apparently at once depressive and disaffected (despite the difference in these two states). In centering such suffering as a core component of Cobain's artistic practice, commentators often locate a sort of primal pain at the heart of this work—a negative rendering of Walt Whitman's barbaric yawp emerging from the throat of a tousle-headed angel whose undeniable working-class credentials served to anoint him as another in that lineage of democratic practitioners. Again, and in closing, I want to modify or even expand this reading, to push the limitations it imposes on the more radical aspects of Cobain's work, most particularly his pointedly empathetic practice.[47] Where I have noted that the cut-up technique in the work of authors such as Ballard has been linked to the widespread desensitization occurring through the sensory impact of televisual media, it is clear, as discussed above, that for writers such as Burroughs and Acker, the possibility of spontaneity inherent in the technique is also a way *out of* language, which is also to say a way out of the (reified) self.[48] This method exceeds Cobain's rather more obviously constructed image as the heroin-using-punk-rock-superstar and returns again to the question of artistic practice as a generative form of community-building beyond the structural determinations of patriarchal, racist, and heterosexist power. Seth Kahn discusses Cobain's work in the context of a struggle between alienation and agency, but to my mind this is too simple a rendering, failing to account for Cobain's

58   *Lit-Rock*

clear awareness of the riot grrrl politics of intimacy, as Nguyen has it, as well as the theoretical significance of cut-up practice.[49]

Rather than suggesting that Cobain was torn between selling out or standing up (and by doing so, potentially fucking up his superstardom), I have posited here that Cobain sought to conduct a form of artistic practice that would function as a site of spontaneously generated community in the same way the work of Acker and Burroughs did for other writers and creators. Acker herself described Burroughs's writing as "immediate," claiming kinship with it and with what she called "the nonacceptable literary tradition."[50] The purpose of this tradition, according to Acker, is to "present the human heart naked so that our world, for a second, explodes into flames."[51] She continues, "This human heart is not only the individual heart: the American literary tradition of Thoreau, Emerson, even Miller, presents the individual and communal heart as a unity. Any appearance of the individual heart," according to Acker, "is a political occurrence."[52] While it is impossible not to notice the imbalance in this tradition (fairly typical of Acker's self-constructed lineage, in which she seemed unreceptive to comparisons with female writers), it is my explicit contestation that Cobain's efforts at deconstructive self-fashioning, as revealed and self-consciously enacted in the literary experiments of his journals, owe a crucial debt to Burroughs via Acker via riot grrrl practice. "Rape Me" is perhaps the apex of this practice: the song's ambiguous perspective allows it to give ironized voice to the appetite for other-pain, addressing oppression not known to the singer without appropriating the pain such oppression causes. Rather than "exposing" his own pain in a representative mode, Cobain's work satirized the appetite for such revelation, though its efficacy was directly undermined by the corporate machinations of the music industry during the predigital period. It is tempting to speculate on the way that the opportunities offered by the peer-to-peer model of sharing ushered in by the current age of internet use might have affected Cobain's artistic practice and allowed the expansion of the cut-up technique. As it is, we can only recognize the radical impulse behind his body of work and acknowledge his efforts to engage with the politics of intimacy in such a way as to position his work in that same "nonacceptable tradition" Acker claimed for herself. Complicating meaning through an embryonic aleatory practice, Cobain's work has a feminist core that is as yet under-appreciated. If Cobain smelled like Teen Spirit, remember that he got it from Kathleen Hanna; riot grrrl, after Acker, was written all over Kurt.

Notes

1   Laurie Oullette, *Lifestyle TV* (New York: Routledge, 2016), 8.
2   Lois McNay, "Self as Enterprise: Dilemmas of Control and Resistance in Foucault's *The Birth of Biopolitics*," *Theory, Culture and Society* 26, no. 6 (2009): 55–77.
3   Mark Fisher, *Capitalist Realism* (London: Zero Books, 2009), 13.
4   One may suggest that this is precisely what Walter Benjamin, Guy Debord, and other earlier theorists had in mind in their critique of culture or the society of the

spectacle: that each generation thinks itself uniquely placed at the end of history is hardly surprising, and indeed this particular perception of "Gen X" has significant resonance here. However, the 1990s mark the emergence of a set of technologies that *literally* virtualize life. The uptake of these technologies has occurred at a level on par with the introduction of televisions into US households, perhaps even exceeding it, if one considers the individual ownership of handheld devices such as smartphones, and so on.

5 Of the two, it is Acker who is associated with self-publication; Burroughs's economic imperative for publication has been well documented in discussion of the difficulties of publishing and marketing his work; see, for instance, Oliver Harris's introduction to *Junky* (London: Penguin, 2002), ix–xxv.

6 It seems to me less useful to think of riot grrrl as a "scene" or "movement" and more fruitful to conceive of it as a mode of praxis. This also allows the term to more easily accommodate the contradictions and disagreements regarding its precise type or kind of feminism.

7 This is the opening line of the Hole song "Rock Star" (a mislabelling: the original title was simply "Olympia"), the final track on 1994's *Live Through This*.

8 See Kurt Cobain, *Journals* (New York: Riverhead, 2003), 67, for an account of one such visit (and a rather sceptical reading of the "cute, innocent and clean" image of Olympia).

9 For a brief but comprehensive account of "indie" history, see Nitsuh Abebe, "Twee as Fuck: The Story of Indie Pop," *Pitchfork*, October 24, 2005, https://pitchfork.com/features/article/6176-twee-as-fuck/.

10 Rob Latham, "Collage as Critique and Invention in the Fiction of William S. Burroughs and Kathy Acker," *Journal of the Fantastic in the Arts* 5, no. 3 (1993): 46–57.

11 Ibid., 50.

12 This follows Acker's engagement with the "French feminists": Luce Irigary, Helene Cixous, Julia Kristeva. Georgina Colby discusses this in greater detail in *Kathy Acker: Writing the Impossible* (Edinburgh: Edinburgh University Press, 2016), 69 in particular.

13 My preferred source for this oft-told tale is Sara Marcus, *Girls to the Front: The True Story of the Riot Grrrl Revolution* (New York: HarperCollins, 2010). Speculation on just how charitable Acker's motives were, I will leave to the reader. Burroughs's relationship with Cobain enjoyed a similarly uncertain dynamic, although the writer seemed willing to treat the musician as a creative peer in their collaborative piece, "The Priest, They Called Him," one of the more unlikely Christmas singles of the twentieth century.

14 Greil Marcus, "Comment on Mark Mazullo, 'The Man Whom the World Sold,'" *Musical Quarterly* 84, no. 4 (2000): 750.

15 Ibid., 751.

16 For Acker this was true on two levels, where "making a living" refers both to the material necessity of getting money (openly acknowledged by Burroughs as a motivating force) but also in that the practice of writing—the physical act of sitting down and writing—was an essential part of Acker's effort to construct and live within a life she found bearable within the confines of capitalist patriarchy.

17 Lee Konstantinou, *Cool Characters* (Cambridge: Harvard University Press, 2016), 139.

18 Marcus, "Comment on Mark Mazullo," 750. It's unclear if this is the "media blackout" Cobain refers to on pages 210 and 211 of *Journals*, though the lyrics under

60 *Lit-Rock*

construction do appear to be those from songs on *In Utero*, which would fit the timeframe.

19 Mimi Thi Nguyen discusses this most illuminatingly in "Riot Grrrl, Race and Revival," *Women & Performance: A Journal of Feminist Theory* 22, no. 2/3 (2012): 173–96.

20 For the purposes of this discussion, I will treat *Junky* (1953) and *Naked Lunch* (1959) as the exemplary Burroughs texts, although it is his later trilogy that is usually regarded as cut-up "proper"; for Acker, *Blood and Guts in High School* will serve as a primary point of reference for her work. These respective texts constitute the most commercially successful works of each author, which is important in this context.

21 Peter Wollen, "Death (and Life) of the Author," *London Review of Books*, February 5, 1998, 20: 3.

22 This codicil is also useful in loosely categorizing the work of both Burroughs and Acker; I would suggest their output may best be understood as "conceptual writing," as described in the 2012 collection *I'll Drown My Book*, ed. Caroline Bervall et al. (L.A.: Les Figues). Again, this is particularly applicable to Acker's work, which is more directly engaged with theory-as-practice than is Burroughs's.

23 These differences do not always make the meaning of the cut-up entirely new, as William Burroughs has noted. See "2 Notes on Vaudeville Voices and The Cut-up Method," in *The Moderns: An Anthology of New Writing in America*, ed. Leroi Jones (New York: Corinth, 1963), 345–8. The cut-up he offers here rather proves his point.

24 Ballard too has often acknowledged his debt to Burroughs, who contributed the foreword to *The Atrocity Exhibition*. Ballard and Acker also shared mutual respect— admiration, even—with each citing the other as one of the few contemporary authors they would deign to read.

25 This is a vastly simplified gloss on the term; nevertheless, it will suffice here.

26 Burroughs, "2 Notes on Vaudeville Voices and The Cut-up Method," 346. See note 23.

27 Wayne Pounds, "The Postmodern Anus: Parody and Utopia in Two Recent Novels by William Burroughs," *Poetics Today* 8, no. 3/4 (1987): 620.

28 Jessica L. Wood, "Pained Expression: Metaphors of Sickness and Signs of 'Authenticity' in Kurt Cobain's *Journals*," *Popular Music* 30, no. 3 (2011): 331–49.

29 Ibid., 331.

30 Ibid.

31 Ibid.

32 Ibid., 337–8.

33 Alicia Ostriker, *Poetry* 50, no. 6 (1987): 331–4. The scrap used by Cobain, however, is inconsistent with this version.

34 Ostriker has also commented on Cobain's use of her work, as reported by Tim Appelo in "Desire to Burn?," *Poetry Foundation*, April 10, 2006, https://www .poetryfoundation.org/articles/68518/desire-to-burn.

35 *Les fleurs du mal* indeed.

36 Mikhail Bahktin, *Rabelais and His World* (Bloomington: Indiana University Press, 1984), 22.

37 There is evidence in *Journals* (177–80) to suggest that Cobain associated this system of patriarchy with wider systems of oppression including homophobia, classism, and racism.

38 Emily Spiers, *Pop-Feminist Narratives* (Oxford: Oxford University Press, 2018), 111.
39 Cobain, *Journals*, 272. The phrasing here—"gives them Birth," rather than "gives birth to them"—is noteworthy. The act is shifted toward a generative gift rather than a bodily action, signaling Cobain's awe in the face of the creation of life, which he frequently mentioned when writing about the birth of his daughter. This phrasing is deconstructive, too, in the additional signification it gives to the standard expression.
40 Kurt Cobain, "Pennyroyal Tea," track 9 on Nirvana, *In Utero*, DGC, 1993.
41 Duane R. Fish, "Serving the Servants: An Analysis of the Music of Kurt Cobain," *Popular Music and Society* 19, no. 2 (1995): 89.
42 See Spiers, *Pop-Feminist Narratives*, 106, where Hanna is directly quoted decrying the detrimental effects of deconstructionist theory at its most unsubtle (or even misapplied).
43 Charles Cross, *Heavier Than Heaven: The Biography of Kurt Cobain* (London: Sceptre, 2001), 165.
44 Nguyen draws in turn on Daniel Traber's work, which usefully unpacks the fetishization of alterity that haunts the valorization of "authenticity" within punk communities and is a particular problem when it comes to recognizing and deconstructing individual imbrication within systemically racist modes of thought and practice. See *Whiteness, Otherness, and the Individualism Paradox from Huck to Puck* (London: Palgrave Macmillan, 2007).
45 Bikceem's work is quoted in both Spiers's monograph and Nguyen's article.
46 Eva Illouz's work is a useful starting place for this topic.
47 There is certainly evidence that such practice shifted at various points throughout Cobain's career; it does not seem to me an overstatement to acknowledge that his relationship with Courtney Love also saw him take up a more "traditional" mantel of masculinity, which worked as a balm to some of his deeply ingrained discomfort with such discourse.
48 This is a broadly Wittgensteinian rendering of the problem of other minds, also associated with David Foster Wallace's work. Colby discusses Wittgenstein in relation to Acker's writing in *Writing the Impossible* (see note 12).
49 Seth Kahn, "Kurt Cobain, Martyrdom, and the Problem of Agency," *Studies in Popular Culture* 22, no. 3 (2000): 83–96. There is more to be said here too on the gendered construction of the slacker figure and its relative unevenness despite the enshrinement of the character as emblematic of the post-Boomer generation.
50 Kathy Acker, *Bodies of Work* (London: Serpent's Tail, 1997), 6.
51 Ibid., 7.
52 Ibid.

Part II

Craft and Confession

3

Joni Mitchell and the Literature of Confession

David R. Shumway

Around 1970, a new genre of music emerged that was sometimes mistaken for folk, but which was actually an element of rock and roll and included the music of the singer-songwriters James Taylor, Carole King, Carly Simon, and Jackson Brown.[1] Joni Mitchell would become the most important contributor to this genre, both because of the longevity of her career and aesthetic achievement. The new music was connected to folk in the sense that some of its most important performers, including Mitchell, had begun their careers in the folk scene. And, since the music was less raucous and softer than what had been typical of rock, the mistake is understandable. But the differences are more significant. While folk music generally made use only of acoustic instruments, these singer-songwriters were often backed by rock bands, including drum kits and electric guitars. The music usually did not sound traditional; it bore the influence of numerous kinds of popular music, and often, as was the case with both Taylor and Mitchell, involved significant musical innovations. Most important, where folk had been public music that celebrated the people and their traditional forms, these singer-songwriters wrote about their private experiences. As this suggests, confessionalism was central to this new genre. When the confessional songs of Mitchell and Taylor first appeared, they were likened to the confessional poetry of Robert Lowell, Sylvia Plath, and others that had emerged around 1960. I want to explore in this essay not only this connection but also the larger literary and cultural confessionalism that developed in the 1960s and became even more significant in the 1970s. Putting the work of Mitchell and the other singer-songwriters in the context of the larger confessionalism of the period helps us understand why it emerged and what it meant, but it is also vital to understanding how the confessional mode differs from medium to medium. Confessionalism in songwriting is not the same as confessionalism in poetry, just as confessionalism in fiction isn't the same as confessionalism in cinema.

When people hear a work of art called "confessional," they often assume that the term primarily refers to the truth of its representation of the author's own life. But that is not how the literary critics who first identified confessional poetry understood the term. The key issue for M. L. Rosenthal is the way that the self is presented in the poems, the poet appearing as him- or herself and not in the convention of an invented "speaker."[2] As another literary critic explained after Rosenthal's term had gained wide currency, "A confessional poem would seem to be one in which the writer speaks *to* the reader, telling him, without the mediating presence of imagined event or *persona*, something about his life. . . . The sense of direct speech addressed to an audience is central to confessional writing."[3] In my book *Rock Star: The Making of Cultural Icons from Elvis to Springsteen*, I argue that if we understand *confessional* in this way, then Joni Mitchell's songs seem to fit better than most of the poems that have been called confessional.[4] That's because many of Mitchell's songs and those of other singer-songwriters are even more direct in their address than are most confessional poems.

To limit the discussion of the "confessional" to poetry, however, is to ignore the fact of a much broader movement of confessional art in the 1960s and 1970s. In 1979, Christopher Lasch published a best-selling book called *The Culture of Narcissism* in which he devotes some pages to confessional writing, none of it poetry. His examples include Norman Mailer's *The Armies of the Night: History as a Novel/The Novel as History*, Phillip Roth's *Portnoy's Complaint*, and several novels by Erica Jong.[5] To those works Lasch cites, one should also add the films of such directors like Woody Allen and Paul Mazursky, the movement called the "New Journalism," associated with Joan Didion, Tom Wolfe, and Hunter Thompson, and, more recently, the growing popularity of the memoir. All of these forms represent the increased importance of the self and its subjective perspective in the culture, and together with singer-songwriter music should be understood as a significant cultural movement.

Formally, what these various instances of the confession share is the effect of direct address, the convention that the "author" is speaking in an unmediated way to us as an audience. In novels, that can be a first-person narrator, a fictional "author," like Roth's Portnoy, or it can be the actual author representing him or herself as a character, something Mailer does in *Armies*. Lasch observes of the confessional mode an "increasing interpenetration of fiction, journalism, and autobiography."[6] *Portnoy's Complaint* is literally a confession, as the novel is told to the narrator's psychoanalyst, but Portnoy is not Roth, and this novel makes no claim to be telling the truth about the author's life. When Mailer labeled *Armies* a "nonfiction novel," however, he was asserting the factual character of his reporting while drawing on the formal devices usually reserved for fictional narrative. There are two cultural developments entailed here. One is that an author is interesting enough to be a protagonist of his own novel. While the first generation of literary celebrities such as F. Scott Fitzgerald and Ernest Hemingway were known for various extraliterary exploits, they did not make themselves the main characters of their own fiction, but that is exactly what Mailer does in *Armies* and several books that follow it. Mailer had pioneered more open forms of self-promotion and had titled an earlier book, a collection of fiction, nonfiction, and poetry, *Advertisements for Myself*. Paradoxically, *Armies* is written in the third person, so the author speaks of himself as "Mailer." The confessional character of the work comes from the frequent focus on Mailer's inner states and the author's frank appraisals of celebrities who turned up at the anti-Vietnam-War protest in Washington, which is the novel's central event. The increased interest in authors' extraliterary lives is one of the conditions for the emergence of the singer-songwriter.

The second cultural development is the increased recognition of subjectivity in genres where objectivity had previously been assumed as the norm. *Armies* won the Pulitzer Prize for nonfiction and the National Book Award in arts and letters, indicating that it was not understood primarily as a novel. Indeed, the book is often regarded as a chief instance of the New Journalism, a trend usually traced to Truman Capote's *In Cold Blood*, of which the term "nonfiction novel" was first used. Capote used novelistic techniques, but *In Cold Blood* is narrated in the third person by a seemingly omniscient narrator. The pattern in the New Journalism, as illustrated by Hunter Thompson's *Hell's Angels* and Tom Wolfe's *The Electric Kool-Aid Acid Test*, however, was for first-person narration in which the subjective state and impressions of that narrator are part of what is reported. Joan Didion's essays, collected in *Slouching Toward Bethlehem* and *The White Album*, involved significant personal revelation and a subjective approach. *The White Album*, similar to much confessional poetry, discusses in detail her nervous breakdown. In these texts, the author is not a character as in Mailer but expresses subjectivity openly as a participant in the events being described. The assumption here seems to be similar to the credo of cinema verité, which was that the presence of the camera needed to be acknowledged in order not to falsify the event being recorded. In New Journalism, the presence and perspective of the author likewise must be openly represented, avoiding a claim to reportorial disinterest.

By the time Lasch published *The Culture of Narcissism,* he could also have used film to support his observation of the widespread presence of the confessional mode. Two influential examples are Paul Mazursky's *Blume in Love* and Woody Allen's *Annie Hall*. These films mirror the different approaches of Roth and Mailer, in that *Blume* is a film about a fictional character confessing, while *Annie Hall*, because its director and writer is also the film's male lead, seems to be the author's own confession. Mazursky's film was described by Pauline Kael as "a hip updating of *The Awful Truth*," Leo McCarey's 1937 screwball comedy, both films beginning with a divorce and ending with a reconciliation. But while McCarey's film is conventionally "narrated" by the camera, *Blume*, played by George Segal, narrates much of his story in voice-over. That Blume is unhappy and still in love with the wife who left him after he cheated on her makes the character of that narration confessional. *Annie Hall* begins with Woody Allen addressing the camera directly, making the entire film the confession, not literally of Allen, but of the character he plays, Alvy Singer. Yet because Allen was known as a standup comedian, the film's opening invites the audience to ignore the distinction. Like confessional prose and poetry, *Annie Hall* produces a powerful sense of direct address which seems to give the audience access to the artist's inner life. This confessional mode of cinema would be one to which Allen repeatedly returns from the late 1970s through the 1990s, and can be found in different forms and in different degrees in other "relationship stories" of the period, such as *When Harry Met Sally* and *High Fidelity*.[7] The genre of "relationship story" is especially relevant because the analysis of love, courtship, and marriage found there is the same kind of activity Joni Mitchell pursues in many of her songs.

The confessionalism of the nonfiction novel and of film was predated by confessionalism in poetry, which is in many respects more similar to song lyrics.

Lowell's *Life Studies* is the work around which the concept of confessional poetry was first developed. Rosenthal was the first to use the term in a review of the book, and he later developed the concept at greater length in his book *The Modern Poets*. Besides Lowell, prominent poets associated with confessionalism include three who studied with him—Plath, W. D. Snodgrass, and Anne Sexton—as well as John Berryman. As I have noted, confessional poetry is defined by the treatment of the self in the poems, the poet speaking as him or herself without the mediation of a fictional "speaker." This distinguished confessional poetry from the high modernism of Yeats, Pound, and Eliot, who were associated with Eliot's dictum that "poetry is an escape from personality." Confessional poems are not necessarily literal in their direct address; Berryman's *Dream Songs*, for instance, are about a character named Henry whom the poet described as his alter ego. However, even though Henry is not the same as the poet, we read him as revealing the poet's self; confessional poetry is about the poet regardless of the literal subject. Many of the poems in *Life Studies* are focused on Lowell's parents, but the context makes clear that it is their relation to the poet that matters. Confessional poetry was associated with particular kinds of revelations, things that one would be more inclined to confess rather than those about which one would be likely to brag. Problems of mental illness are a frequent topic, as are alcoholism, sexual indiscretions, marital difficulties, and so on. The threat of and even the desire for suicide may be the most shocking of confessional poetry's revelations, one that is reinforced by the fact that Plath, Berryman, and Sexton did take their own lives. Rosenthal asserts,

> Confessional poetry is a poetry of suffering. The suffering is generally "unbearable" because the poetry so often projects breakdown and paranoia. Indeed, the psychological condition of most of the confessional poets has long been the subject of common literary discussion—one cannot say gossip exactly, for their problems and confinements in hospitals are quite often the specific subjects of the poems.[8]

While confessional prose is sometimes seen as produced for the purpose of self-promotion—even when the works describe behavior that is less than admirable—confessional poetry was described by Rosenthal as "self-therapeutic" in motive, the poet seeking to get well by writing about his or her problems and their sources. This implies that the poems are not some sort of pure emotional outpouring, but rather a distanced reconsideration of past experience. Lowell's poems all fit that description, even if the events and emotions described are raw and undisguised and may therefore shock. There are poems by Plath and Sexton which seem more like primal-scream therapy than psychoanalysis, but that doesn't mean these poems were not intended as self-therapy. Rosenthal places the poets on a sort of scale of "intellectual objectivity," with Lowell at one end as the most "objective," and Plath and Sexton, having less distance between poetic expression and subjective experience, at the other.[9] Of course, the work of all of the confessional poets I've mentioned here is finely wrought verse. So even those poems that express extreme emotions do so in language that one recognizes as art.

Joni Mitchell and the Literature of Confession

Lasch identifies a therapeutic character in confessional prose, but for him this is evidence of the general narcissism his book is critiquing. Therapeutic prose is contrasted with socially critical writing, the former being self-indulgent and uninterested in the larger world. Confessional poetry, however, was from Rosenthal's initial description of it always associated with social critique. He reads Lowell's poems in *Life Studies* not as self-absorbed but as revealing "the whole maggoty character" of American culture, "which [the poet] feels he carries about in his own person" and is thus looking "at the culture through the window of psychological breakdown."[10] Elsewhere, Rosenthal contrasts the poetry of Lowell and Plath with that of other poets whose work seems to amount to mere "private notations."[11] Lowell and Plath succeed in representing their individual suffering in a way that transforms it into cultural critique, putting the poet "at the center of the poem in such a way as to make his [or her] psychological vulnerability and shame an embodiment of [their] civilization."[12] It is important to keep in mind that when these poets were writing the poems in question, the late 1950s in Lowell's case and the early 1960s in Plath's, critique was not commonly associated with poetry, which was generally approached under the doctrine of art for art's sake. Moreover, the civil rights, women's, and anti-war movements were either in their infancy or waiting to be born. Lowell would go on to emerge as a poet strongly identified with the anti-war movement and social justice, while Plath would be regarded as an essential voice by second-wave feminism, but both articulated their critique in advance of the movements with which they were associated.

One reason that Plath's poems resonated so powerfully with the women's movement is that they illustrated one of its most influential slogans, "the personal is the political." That they did resonate is demonstrated by Elaine Showalter in the second issue of the feminist theory journal, *Signs,* where she observes, "A relatively tiny group of women writers has engaged the attention of critics so persistently over the past five years that they could be said to constitute a new 'great tradition.' While the current interest in women writers encompasses a number of familiar names, the work on Charlotte Brontë, George Eliot, Virginia Woolf, Doris Lessing, and Sylvia Plath predominates."[13] Plath is the only poet mentioned and Lessing one of only two contemporary writers. Plath was recognized for giving expression to the suffering caused by patriarchal domination in the 1950s before the emergence of second-wave feminism. Showalter notes that "her suicide, in conjunction with the suicides of Virginia Woolf and Anne Sexton, has made her a tragic heroine."[14] Because the autobiographical stance of the poems creates an "identification of Plath the sufferer with Plath the creator," this heroic status must be a part of the poems' meaning.[15]

This is not to say that there was unanimity in women's judgment of Plath, nor that she was herself understood as a feminist. Jane Marcus asserts that "Plath was not a feminist; her novels and poems were not feminist."[16] Rather, in Marcus's view, Plath's work expresses an "obscene" hatred of men, and she finds "the hatred in the poems is enhanced by the elegance of form, the strength of line, irony, wit, and control," producing an aestheticization of "death as revenge" that the critic likens to the fascism and anti-Semitism of Yeats and Pound.[17] Marcus's pointed feminist critique echoes that made by other critics who observed that Plath's use of the Holocaust to express her personal suffering is unjustified. Irving Howe, for example, criticized Plath for the way she, in "Lady Lazarus," "enlarge[s] the magnitude of her [suicide attempt] through illegitimate comparisons with the Holocaust" and for "a willed hysteric tone, the forcing of language to make up for an inability to develop the matter."[18] Joni Mitchell's own critique of Plath and Sexton is less pointed, but not inconsistent with these judgments. As interviewer Stephen Holden reports,

> she heatedly rejects any comparisons of her work to that of women like Sylvia Plath and Anne Sexton. "The only poets who influenced me were Leonard Cohen and Bob Dylan," she insisted. "What always bugged me about poetry in school was the artifice of it. When Dylan wrote, 'You've got a lot of nerve to say you are my friend,' as an opening line [of "Positively Fourth Street"], the language was direct and undeniable. As for Plath and Sexton, I'm sorry, but I smell a rat. There was a lot of guile in the work, a lot of posturing. It didn't really get down to the nitty-gritty of the human condition. And there was the suicide-chic aspect."[19]

As I have argued elsewhere, Mitchell's rejection of confessional poetry as an influence does not negate the importance of that body of work for the reception of hers and others' confessional songs of the period.[20] Indeed, Mitchell herself did not always reject the connection. In a 1979 interview, she said she "became a confessional poet" because her fans' adoration was "too much to live up to. I thought, 'You don't even know who I am. You want to worship me?' . . . I thought, 'You better know who you're applauding up here.' It was a compulsion, to be honest with my audience."[21] Note that what Mitchell is claiming for Dylan and, by implication, herself is an even more direct address than that of the confessional poets. I believe she is correct in this judgment.

Confessionalism in popular music was first popularized, not by Mitchell, but by James Taylor in the form of his 1970 hit single, "Fire and Rain," and Taylor's first two albums have more in common with confessional poetry than do Mitchell's songs or those of most other singer-songwriters. Like the most important confessional poets, Taylor's self-titled first album dealt, in "Knocking Around the Zoo," with his experience of confinement in a mental hospital. The self-therapeutic character of the album was noted by Jon Landau in his *Rolling Stone* review: "Mr. Taylor is not kicking out any jams. He seems more interested in soothing his troubled mind."[22] *James Taylor* did not reach a wide audience on its release, but *Sweet Baby James* (1970) did. While this album is less specific about the singer's problems, it is even more starkly an instance of direct expression. The album's hit, "Fire and Rain," produces a powerful autobiographical effect through lyrics, music, and production. The song begins, "Just yesterday morning," making it the revelation of a particular loss, one so devastating that the singer "can't remember who to send" his response to.[23] This kind of suffering was not the usual subject of popular songs, which conventionally deal with lost love rather than lost lives. While the song is based on events and conditions of Taylor's personal life, the lyrics are not explicit enough to allow the specifics to be easily grasped. The song works not because we know the references, but because we feel the singer's pain.

Joni Mitchell's first confessional songs may be found on *Ladies of the Canyon* (1970). Her earlier recordings were more folk in style, and she was originally marketed as a folk performer. *Ladies* combines impersonal songs like "Circle Game," "Woodstock," and "Big Yellow Taxi" with songs like "Willy," which begins, "Willy is my child, he is my father."[24] "Willy" is a love song, but one that analyzes as well as celebrates a relationship. It is confessional in the sense that the singer is revealing something about a particular relationship rather than discussing love in general. This gives the song an autobiographical cast whether or not listeners were aware that the song was written about Graham Nash, with whom she had lived in Laurel Canyon. Because popular music celebrities are the subject of more published gossip than poets, such information would have been available to Joni's fans, but there is no evidence that such knowledge was for most listeners significant in their appreciation of the song. Indeed, before David Yaffe's recent biography, *Reckless Daughter*, in which Yaffe confidently asserts their identities, the men Joni wrote about in her songs remained, as an earlier biography attests,[25] a matter of speculation. What is most significant about Willy is not its source but its analytic stance, something that would be the hallmark of Mitchell's later confessional songs.

Blue (1971) was Mitchell's first album to fully exhibit the characteristics of the new genre; it was her breakthrough recording and it remains her greatest achievement. All of the tracks are confessional, and none of them sound a bit like folk music. Indeed, reviews considered whether it might be best understood as a collection of art songs (Dan Heckman) or of cabaret music (*Stereo Review* called the songs "torch songs").[26] The confessional character of *Blue* did not, for the most part, lie in its apparent simplicity, although most tracks feature relatively sparse arrangements, often with only piano accompaniment. The songs themselves are complex musically, while the lyrics, while not in general obscure, are complex in the ideas they present and in their form, which often ignores typical pop patterns. "Blue," for example, dispenses with the usual form of the pop song in favor of something much more like free verse, using rhyming triplets but not in any regular pattern. The song is addressed to Blue, but it's not clear whether Blue is a person or a mental state:

> Blue, here is a song for you
> Ink of a pin
> Underneath the skin
> An empty place to fill in[27]

The confessionalism of *Blue's* songs has been most often illustrated by lines from "River," to which Mitchell herself has called attention: "I have, on occasion, sacrificed myself and my own emotional makeup, . . . singing 'I'm selfish and I'm sad,' for instance. We all suffer for our loneliness, but at the time of *Blue*, our pop stars never admitted these things."[28] "I'm selfish and I'm sad" is a frank admission in the plainest of language, and Mitchell describes it as a sacrifice, suggesting that writing or even singing the song was a sort of ordeal, perhaps as much because of having abandoned the usual social mask as of the feelings expressed. The song does express suffering, but, unlike "Fire and Rain," it seems less like a cry for help than a piece of self-analysis, which is a good description of the project of the album as a whole.

72 *Lit-Rock*

There is, of course, a self-analytic dimension to the confessional mode in general, and Lasch observed that self-disclosure allows writers "to achieve a critical distance from the self" and that "confessional writers walk a fine line between self-analysis and self-indulgence."[29] But Mitchell's songs on *Blue* and her other confessional albums are more analytic than most confessional prose or poetry. Like most of Mitchell's confessional albums, *Blue*'s focus is on relationships, and the singer's attitude toward them is repeatedly presented as ambivalence. "All I Want," for example, reveals the emotional waffling and exacting dualities that can accompany the quest for self-knowledge; traveling "a lonely road" and "looking for something," the singer vacillates: "Oh I hate you some, I hate you some / I love you some / Oh I love you when I forget about me."[30] "A Case of You" begins by saying that love has been lost, but the chorus proclaims that the singer could still drink a case of the apparently former lover. Like the characters in many films, Mitchell seems to be describing over and over the experience of being caught in a double-bind of the desire for intimacy and the desire for freedom. Many of the songs are about travel, both the singer's and her partner's, which represents both freedom and loneliness. The songs offer no solution to the conflicting desires they express, suggesting that the best we can do is to live with them. In that regard, the songs are similar to most of the relationship stories, but while those films have mainly male protagonists, Mitchell represents a woman's experience. That a woman could articulate the same ambivalence about love as men have long done was unusual in 1971.

On *Blue*, the language that Mitchell uses might be best described as conversational, not only because of her choice of words but also because her lines sometimes do not obey a regular rhythm or make use of a consistent pattern of rhyme. "River" uses mainly off or half-rhymes, and the lack of rhyme on the chorus is especially notable. "A Case of You" contains lines that run much longer than the song's rhythm should permit. This is done in part to enable the song to include pieces of remembered conversation—a technique found also in "The Last Time I Saw Richard"—and both songs retell in some detail what seem to be particular incidents in the singer's life. That specificity is a feature of confessional songwriting as well as much confessional poetry. But while a remembered conversation is an element of many of the poems in *Life Studies*, Lowell's conversations take place farther in the past and involve his parents and grandparents. Mitchell seems to be reporting much more recent incidents, and her family history is not her subject here or elsewhere.

Prior to writing these songs, Mitchell had rejected Graham Nash's marriage proposal—even as she called him the love of her life—because she feared having to sacrifice her artistic goals to play the role of helpmeet and homemaker. This is the context for "My Old Man," which proclaims that the singer and her man don't need to be married, while "The Last Time I Saw Richard" seems to present both Richard and his bride as shadow figures—people the singer refused to become.

Richard got married to a figure skater and he bought her a dishwasher and a coffee percolator and he drinks at home now most nights with the TV on and all the house lights left up bright[31]

Joni Mitchell and the Literature of Confession 73

The fact that Mitchell chose not to marry in order to pursue her career represents a central biographical difference between her and the poets Plath and Sexton. Their coming of age in the 1950s in upper-middle-class households meant that they could only imagine themselves as wives and mothers whatever else they might do. This is largely the substance of Plath's unhappiness, and, as we saw, why she was both attractive to feminists and not understood to be one of them. Born more than ten years later and not bound by expectations of academic achievement or class status, Joan Anderson experienced the struggle and the freedom to define her own identity. She married Chuck Mitchell, a fellow folksinger, after giving birth to another man's child in the hopes of providing her with a father. She decided, however, to give the baby up for adoption, and the marriage lasted less than two years. According to Yaffe, Joni called Chuck "my first major exploiter, a complete asshole," but Chuck did help Joni set up her own publishing company.[32] That Joni was able to leave and go on to make her art central in her life made her an unusual woman even in the 1960s. The fact that she would retain control of the publishing rights to her songs and that she has had complete artistic control of her albums distinguishes her not just from most women in the music industry, but from most men as well.[33]

The song on *Blue* that might be closest to confessional poetry is "Little Green," which is now known to be about the child Mitchell gave up for adoption. It is paradoxical that while the events behind the song are traditionally the stuff of confession, the song's reference to them is obscure. This obscurity itself makes it more like the poetry, and less like the direct address of many other confessional songs. Critics did not get the title reference until Mitchell herself explained the song when she and her daughter were reunited in 1997. The song itself begins ambiguously, referring to a "her" whom we should call "green," but not letting us in on who she is. The chorus refers to "a little green,"[34] and gives us a series of hopeful images, but ends with the prediction that there will sometimes be sorrow. The last verse describes the adoption decision obliquely as signing papers but asserts that the emotions accompanying the decision do not include shame. The refusal to be ashamed should be read as a statement of strength, something that cuts against the vulnerability often expressed elsewhere on the album.

Mitchell's confessions, then, are those of a woman who has already come to consciousness, but who did not need the women's movement to do it. This may account for her rejection of the label "feminist," which she asserted in 1991 was "too divisional for me."[35] It may also account for why her songs are less angry than the poems of Plath and Sexton. Of course, there are other explanations that should not be excluded, especially that the two poets seem to have suffered more severely than Mitchell from mental illness. Mitchell did suffer from depression, something that might have been gathered from listening to *Blue* had the disease acquired the currency in 1971 that it would have by the 1990s. After recording that album, she went to live in the wilderness of northwest Canada where she claims to have read every work of psychology in the library in an attempt to figure out her own unhappiness. That struggle yielded *For the Roses* (1972), a record that is more angry but less sad than *Blue*. Where *Blue* tends to make the singer the cause of her own unhappiness, *For the Roses* accuses men of failing her. "Blonde in the Bleachers" says of the unfaithful man to whom the song is addressed, "'Cause it seems like you've got to give up / Such a piece of your soul / When you give up the chase." Yet, the songs here seem to render the singer more the victim than do those on *Blue*, presenting her as more willing to accept mistreatment.

Another way that confessional songwriting differs from confessional poetry is that popular songs are typically less dark in tone. This is doubtless in part a necessity of selling songs that will be listened to for entertainment, often in social settings, rather than pondered over by lone readers. It is in part an effect of the music, which is not funereal, even when it is somewhat sad. And even the darkest songs, like "Fire and Rain," contain hopeful lines. *Blue* is not, as one critic asserted, "doleful"; the singer of these songs is not wallowing in self-pity or contemplating suicide.[36] Rather, she is trying to think her way out of contradictions of self and to comprehend the minds of others. And if the emotional tone of "River" is made darker by the minor key and slower tempo, other cuts on the album are musically upbeat even if the lyrics are not. "All I Want," for example, is jaunty, even though it verbalizes the singer's loneliness and is addressed to someone she both loves and hates. "California," similarly, is an infectious ode to the place where the singer wants to return despite bad news and loneliness. The songs "Carey" and "My Old Man" are more upbeat in both music and lyrics, even though both express a degree of dissatisfaction or unhappiness. Rather than presenting us with unbearable suffering, these songs give us a life in which the blues are frequent, but exist in tension with hope and joy. *For the Roses* included Mitchell's first hit single, "You Turn Me On I'm a Radio," which Ellen Willis describes as "an irresistible tour de force, a metaphysical poem . . . based on the crucial technological metaphor for rock and roll. Witty, playful, gently self-mocking, it explores the lighthearted surface that half covers and half exposes Mitchell's passionate fatalism (or fatalistic passion)."[37] The song is infectious with a great hook, but it is also the confession of a woman who will put up with a man who often makes her unhappy.

The project of self-analysis and the related project of an analysis of love in contemporary culture reaches its culmination in *Court and Spark* (1974). The songs here are more distanced from particular events in the singer's life, but still seem to be serious, witty ruminations on the difficulty of relationships, placing the singer at the center of most of them. There are two songs, however, "Free Man in Paris" and "Raised on Robbery," which clearly are not sung from the songwriter's perspective. The former is a confession of a man who laments the earlier freedom he had in Paris but has given up for his career in the music industry, a song usually said to be about David Geffen, whose home Mitchell platonically shared for a time. The latter is about a woman trawling a bar for a man to take her home and pay her for the privilege. The character evoked has little to do with Mitchell's persona, making the song among the least confessional of her work during this period. Even the songs focused on the "I" who is singing are less direct, in part because the events described are often depicted as patterns rather than single events. This is someone who has a sense of how she is and how things are, and has accepted these conditions. This makes the songs on *Court and Spark* more like popular songs in general, even though their analytic look at relationships remains unusual.

Analysis of love and sex is what all of the songs on *Court and Spark* have in common. Just as the relationship stories then emerging in cinema are not love stories—*Annie Hall* is a comedy about a failed relationship—but stories about love, *Court and Spark* contains, as Loraine Alterman said in reviewing the album, not love songs but "songs about love."[38] And, while most relationship stories were told from a male perspective and all of them were directed by men, Mitchell gives us a woman's perspective on love. The attitude conveyed on tracks such as "Car on a Hill" or "People's Parties" is self-reflection, the singer musing on the state of her own life and emotions and comparing them to those of others. Where *Blue* had located the source of the singer's unhappiness mainly in herself, *For the Roses* mainly in the men who let her down, here the source seems to be in relationships, in the patterns of interaction between lovers. The singular relationships depicted on *Blue* have given way to "The Same Situation," repeated over many years, of love not turning out to be what romance had promised. Yet the singer of these songs cannot give up on relationships, either. As "Help Me" reveals, she still falls in love too fast; the singer, like the man to whom the song is addressed, loves her loving but loves her freedom more. There is in these lines a sense that Mitchell is now identifying with men like those whose hands she says, in "Blonde in the Bleachers," could not be held for very long. The strong implication of "Court and Spark" is that there is no moving beyond this contradiction that we want to love but that it will not be enough.

One wonders why Joni Mitchell has not become the feminist heroine that Plath and Sexton became. Is it because the experience of unbearable but unresolvable oppression is more politically useful than the example of triumph in the face of oppression? Is Mitchell's example not relevant because it suggested that women could achieve equality if they only were willing to make the necessary sacrifices? Or is it merely that she is a singer-songwriter and a popular musician, making her work low culture? The controversy over Bob Dylan's being awarded the Nobel Prize for Literature suggests that this cultural divide is still very much with us. While I would argue that Mitchell's songs are aesthetically superior, the Nobel was awarded, one assumes, because of Dylan's cultural impact. There are ways in which Dylan's example prepared the way for Mitchell, and she has acknowledged his influence; his impact, however, was also a function of his gender as has been the greater seriousness with which his work has been treated.

Joni Mitchell's songs expand our conception of the confessional mode. While critics of the confessionalism of the singer-songwriters often associated it with narcissism and self-absorption, it is better understood as self-analysis and social critique. The issue is not a matter of explicitly political positions staked out by the singer-songwriters, but rather of the songs, like the poems, illustrating that individual lives matter. This is a political position, one often associated with the right; but second-wave feminism challenged that by starting with the lives of individual women as the basis for its campaign for gender equality. The point, of course, is that the individual life is always also a social life, and its meaning is never merely private. Neither the poets' nor Mitchell's use of autobiography was an exercise in self-absorption: it was the bridge by which they sought to understand the larger world.

Notes

1 David R. Shumway, "The Emergence of the Singer-Songwriter," in *Cambridge Companion to the Singer-Songwriter*, ed. Katherine Williams and Justin A. Williams (Cambridge: Cambridge University Press, 2016), 11–20.

2 M. L. Rosenthal, *The Modern Poets: A Critical Introduction* (New York: Oxford University Press, 1960), 226.

3 Irving Howe, "The Plath Celebration: A Partial Dissent," in *The Critical Point: On Literature and Culture* (New York: Dell, 1973), 167.

4 David R. Shumway, *Rock Star: The Making of Musical Icons from Elvis to Springsteen* (Baltimore: Johns Hopkins University Press, 2014), 159.

5 Christopher Lasch, *The Culture of Narcissism: American Life in an Age of Diminishing Expectations* (New York: Warner, 1979), 47–61.

6 Ibid., 49.

7 On the new genre of the "relationship story," see David R. Shumway, *Modern Love: Romance, Intimacy, and the Marriage Crisis* (New York: Oxford University Press, 2003), 157–87.

8 M. L. Rosenthal, *The New Poets: American and British Poetry Since World War II* (London: Oxford University Press, 1967), 130.

9 Ibid., 82.

10 Rosenthal, *The Modern Poets*, 233.

11 Rosenthal, *The New Poets*, 81.

12 Ibid., 79.

13 Elaine Showalter, "Literary Criticism," *Signs* 1, no. 2 (Winter 1975): 439.

14 Ibid., 441.

15 Marilyn R. Farwell, "Feminist Criticism and the Concept of the Poetic Persona," *Bucknell Review* 24, no. 1 (Spring 1978): 151.

16 Jane Marcus, "Nostalgia is Not Enough: Why Elizabeth Hardwick Misreads Ibsen, Plath, and Woolf," *Bucknell Review* 24, no. 1 (Spring 1978): 172.

17 Ibid., 171–2.

18 Howe, "The Plath Celebration," 163–4.

19 Stephen Holden, "The Ambivalent Hall of Famer," *New York Times*, December 1, 1996, http://www.nytimes.com/1996/12/01/arts/the-ambivalent-hall-of-famer.html?scp=4&sq=Joni+Mitchell&st=nyt.

20 Shumway, *Rock Star*, 156.

21 Joni Mitchell, "The *Rolling Stone* Interview," by Cameron Crowe, *Rolling Stone*, July 26, 1979, 49.

22 Jon Landau, review of *James Taylor*, *Rolling Stone*, April 19, 1969, 28.

23 "Fire and Rain," track 7 on James Taylor, *Sweet Baby James*, Warner Brothers, 1970.

24 "Willy," track 5 on Joni Mitchell, *Ladies of the Canyon*, A&M, 1970.

25 Karen O'Brien, *Joni Mitchell: Shadows and Light* (London: Virgin, 2002); David Yaffe, *Reckless Daughter: A Portrait of Joni Mitchell* (New York: Sarah Crichton, 2017).

26 Dan Heckman, "Pop: Jim Morrison at the End, Joni at a Crossroads," review of *Blue*, by Joni Mitchell, *New York Times*, August 8, 1971: D15; Peter Reilly, review of *Blue*, by Joni Mitchell, *Stereo Review*, October 1971, rpt. in *The Joni Mitchell Companion*, 41.

27 "Blue," track 5 on Joni Mitchell, *Blue*, A&M, 1971.

28 Joni Mitchell, quoted in Timothy White, "A Portrait of the Artist," *Billboard*, December 9, 1995, 15.

Joni Mitchell and the Literature of Confession

29 Lasch, *The Culture of Narcissism,* 48, 50.

30 "All I Want," track 1 on Joni Mitchell, *Blue.*

31 "The Last Time I Saw Richard," track 10 on Joni Mitchell, *Blue.*

32 Yaffe, *Reckless Daughter,* 38, 37.

33 Ani DiFranco, "Ani DiFranco Chats with the Iconic Joni Mitchell," *Los Angeles Times,* September 20, 1998, 20.

34 "Little Green," track 3 on Joni Mitchell, *Blue.*

35 David Wild, "A Conversation with Joni Mitchell," *Rolling Stone,* May 30, 1991, 64.

36 Timothy White, "A Portrait of the Artist," *Billboard,* December 9, 1995, 15.

37 Ellen Willis, "Joni Mitchell: Still Travelling," in *Out of the Vinyl Deeps: Ellen Willis on Rock Music,* ed. Nona Willis Aronowitz (Minneapolis: University of Minnesota Press, 2011), 141.

38 Loraine Alterman, "Joni's Songs Are for Everyone," *New York Times,* January 6, 1974, 127.

4

Pop Star vs. Harvard Professor

The "Amateur" Poetry of Taylor Swift

Weishun Lu

Pop artists' forays into capital-L Literature are, as if by default, occasions for skepticism. Taylor Swift's is no exception. Swift's sixth album *Reputation* (2017) includes not only songs but also—to the surprise of her fans and critics—two poems. These poems—printed on the last pages of her album booklets and resembling, by way of a pressed-flower décor and light mustard yellow background, a faded diary entry—stand in awkward contrast to the album's overall fiery tone and themes of self-reclamation and reinvention. In her song "Look What You Made Me Do," for example, Swift enacts a melodramatic and symbolic rebirth by killing off her previous incarnations: "the old Taylor can't come to the phone right now . . . cause she's dead."[1] Her poems, on the other hand, convey something quite different. In an album filled with motifs about loss, death, and revenge, the poems "Why She Disappeared" and "If You're Anything Like Me" look back to an innocent, younger self and serve as a sentimental reminder of the wide-eyed country girl Swift symbolized early in her career.

It is no surprise that literary critics would find Swift's poems inadequate. In a *Cosmopolitan* interview, Stephanie Burt, a Harvard poet and professor, dissects Swift's work. Burt is known to be a generous and open-minded reader and, true to her nature, tries to offer some measured feedback, prefacing her review, for example, by complimenting the sonic quality of Swift's writing. Nevertheless, Burt feels that Swift's poems are, in the end, song lyrics posing as poetry and therefore undeserving of the term: not *bad*, per se, but necessitating a gentle nudge to the periphery from which they came. While many of Swift's fans would no doubt be comfortable pronouncing her a "poet" or "artist" in the most hallowed sense of the word, it remains important for the audience represented here by Burt to deny her legitimacy. Whether her attempted entry into "legitimate" culture is forbidden from the outset based on her superstardom is hard to say.

Burt's mixed review of Swift's work creates an opportunity to interrogate the vocabulary and frameworks used to assess commercial, "amateur" poems—poems whose target audience goes well beyond the bubble of professional poets and literary critics. This chapter ultimately addresses the clash between popular poetry and academic culture more so than any particular literary critic's response to Swift's writing. Burt's response is convenient, however, as she provides a rare and somewhat detailed analysis as to why Swift's poetry "doesn't work."[2] In this chapter, Burt figures as representative of the literary critic in order to show how the collision between Swift and Burt is not just a confrontation between two individuals; instead, it stands for an encounter between popular commercial poetry and the academy itself, and an example of how these two "fields" feed off of each other.

Concerns about whether Swift's poetry is "good" or if it is poetry at all reveal deeply ingrained assumptions of what poetry should do and how poetry should be consumed. Burt's disavowal of the poeticity of Swift's work reflects a certain impulse to analyze writing through the lens of genre and to judge poetry by institutionalized standards of craft. The next section of this chapter examines how Burt's analysis sheds light on existing scholarship on poetic discourse and academized understanding of craft, while the final section presents Swift's poems as a contemporary, amateur poet's reinvention of the confessionalist mode. Unlike early confessionalist poetry, known for its revealing, taboo subject matter, this new wave of confessionalism focuses on a "relatable" speaker or figure created and sustained by the author. What I want to draw attention to is that certain modes of reading and analytic frameworks might lead to an oversight of how poems born outside academic fields may register the afterglow of past literary movements, and how popular verse reinvents otherwise canonical modes of writing. Moreover, reading Swift as the new confessional poet helps to broaden the conventional conception of "craft." This is important because it makes legible the labor done by amateur poets, and emphasizes, against more elitist traditions, a democratic approach to poetry and poetic identity.

Swift Appraisals: Amateur Verse, Poetic Discourse, and the Lens of Craft

It is easy to assume that Swift's poetry is not legitimate since she does not have the ethos of an academic poet; she writes without a degree in creative writing and has not published a collection of poetry or a portfolio. Having acknowledged the pleasing auditory quality in Swift's writing, Burt offers backhandedly that the poems are "good in the way that songwriting is good."[3] She further elaborates that poetry should be distinguished from lyrics because poems "do what they do just with the words, and usually they do what they do if you just read them and hear them aloud in your head." Underlying this disavowal of poetic quality, then, is the belief that song lyrics and poetry are mutually exclusive. Song lyrics as a distinctly lesser genre has to some extent been a defining stigma all along, with scholars operating on the assumption that "pop lyrics were illiterate."[4] In short, popular lyricists' writing were the opposite of "literary," sometimes supplying academic poetry—as it does in Burt's treatment of Swift—a means of contrast by which to assert its own value.

Burt's evaluation of Swift's poems reveals an age-old question about the place of poetic language in relation to other discourses. One might argue that high poetry gains its special status from an accumulation of cultural capital and institutional endorsements. Nonetheless, cultural studies scholars have increasingly argued to broaden the scope of poetry studies to include amateur poetry and commercial verse, going against traditional tendencies to privilege some verse forms over others. Resisting the tradition that puts poetry on the pedestal, some scholars propose that poetry should be studied not in canonical isolation but as a part of "culture" or cultural production. For example, Rei Terada proposes to "let 'lyric' dissolve into literature and 'literature' into culture."[5] One problem faced by scholars who wish to broaden the scope of poetic discourse, however, is a dearth of critical language with which to evaluate extra-canonical verse. To address this problem, Maria Damon proposes the label "micropoetry," which refers to amateur verses that are "raw material left raw" found in the everyday, for the study of quasi-poetic texts that are not yet recognized as poetry, thereby destabilizing the border between poetry and other verse forms.[6] Equally relevant to this discussion is Adam Bradley's work on popular artists. In *The Poetry of Pop*, Bradley examines the "aesthetic labors of language and performance" in popular lyrics and compositions, arguing that popular music can be read as poetic acts as it often exudes literary and sonic qualities commonly associated with poetry.[7] Regarding Swift specifically, BuzzFeed writer Stephen LaConte goes so far as to offer a quiz testing whether readers can differentiate the pop star's lyrics from lines by "history's greatest poets," his selections showing not only the use of "ordinary," pop-transferrable language by poets like Maya Angelou and Robert Louis Stevenson, but some strikingly poetic moments from Swift.[8] Joking aside, there is an increasingly strong sense that although poetry may be perceived as a distinct genre in the classroom, poetics can be located in even the most commercial categories of texts.

A counter-tendency is to argue that poetry should be strictly set apart from other types of utterances; indeed, that this "setting apart"—be it semantically and/or socially—is what defines it as such. In the twentieth century alone, the question regarding the "specialness" of poetic discourse sparked lively discussions among linguists, philosophers, and literary critics. Roman Jakobson, Mikhail Bakhtin, and Julia Kristeva, among others, have examined how poetry is distinct from other speech genres.[9] By blending aesthetic and economic analyses, Pierre Bourdieu suggests that the perceived separation between highbrow genres (such as poetry) and commercial genres (such as commercial fiction) is not simply a matter of aesthetic judgment or linguistic debate, but a legitimacy conflict. In his paradigm, the kind of poetic Burt defends would be securely located in the "subfield of restricted production" due to its limited audience and its association with aesthetic revolutions.[10] Consistent with this model, though applied specifically to American poetry and culture, is Marjorie Perloff's assertion that critics begin to consider experimental poetry as a discourse that resists commodification and consumerism. In Perloff's words, "the most interesting poetic and artistic compositions of our time do position themselves, consciously or unconsciously, against the languages of TV and advertising."[11] Popular verses that deploy accessible language, such as Swift's poems—texts garnering attention by way of a highly visible "star power," yet whose potential influence and power for change (Swift's increasingly outspoken political activism, for example) far outweigh its counterpart—have become perhaps from the academic or avant-garde perspectives a lamentable phenomenon, if not a nightmare.

The belief that poetry should radically depart from commercial or everyday discourse might explain Burt's discontent with the transparency of Swift's poems, which, she says, "don't do some other things that poems do that make [her] want to re-read them."[12] Interestingly, in her book *Don't Read Poetry*, Burt herself admits that "poetry" as a category has been fetishized and argues that we are "caught in a myth about what counts as poetry and how we might learn to enjoy and to read it."[13] Her critique of Swift, then, which ends up delineating what is poetic and what is not, lends testament to just how difficult it is to escape the "myths" and mindsets by which we are accustomed to operating and making judgments, which includes an unconscious and profound desire to treat poetry as a genre that hovers above what Fredric Jameson would call postmodern "aesthetic populism." Although Jameson claims that there is an "effacement . . . of the older (essentially high-modernist) frontier between high culture and so-called mass or commercial culture," a strand of literary elitism that privileges *difficult* texts over accessible writing seems to have replaced high culture.[14]

Poets who come from creative writing programs and workshops would presumably be more skilled at managing the dynamic between opacity and transparency. As a result, they are more competent at demonstrating their "craft" and establishing their ethos as poets. Thus the question of poetic discourse in contemporary literature is often intertwined with the question of craft, or more precisely, what practicing poets and creative writing instructors perceive as craft. To better understand the institutionalized emphasis on craft, one must understand the professionalization of creative writing in post-war American literature. In *The Program Era*, Mark McGurl suggests that "craft" is an important part of the holy trinity of creative writing ("experience," "creativity," and "craft") in post-war America; in particular, "[c]raft—also called 'technique'— adds the elements of acquired skill and mental effort of the process, and is strongly associated with professional pride and the lessons or 'lore' of literary tradition."[15] Put another way, "craft" is a catchall term for deliberate, or, as Timothy Yu puts it, "self-conscious work."[16]

However, craft is not just about honing skills as an individual author. Tim Mayers approaches the question of craft by examining different manuals and "textbooks" on craft by authors and creative writing instructors. Having looked at different creative writing instructors' recommendations, he notices that the notion of craft has to do with an author's ability to negotiate standards set by practicing writers and leaders in the field. There are critics who try to destabilize the status quo, but in general, craft is determined by whether a writer has worked hard enough to apply "the institutional-conventional wisdom of creative writing."[17] By implication, craft signals that a poet has put in work that is legible as work by academic standards. Poets who build their careers on new media platforms or in popular presses instead of creative writing programs might appear to lack craft, and find their works rejected by editors operating on a traditional sense of craft as a criterion.[18]

In assessing the poeticity of Swift's writing, Burt implicitly performs *craft criticism*. Mayers defines craft criticism as "critical prose written by self or institutionally identified 'creative writers,'" and in which "a concern with textual production takes precedence over any concern with textual interpretation."[19] He further explains that craft criticism has "pedagogical" and "evaluative" elements. By implication, craft criticism serves a different function from that of "close reading" as experienced in a literature class: craft criticism aims to foster and produce texts that would earn recognition from other artists, gatekeepers, and agents of consecration in the field. Burt does not use the word "craft" probably because she intuits that a *Cosmopolitan* interview is not the typical setting for craft criticism. But her remark, which implies that Swift's writing is not polished or sufficiently worked over, leads me to believe that she is looking at the poems through such a lens. While she does not explicitly say that Swift's writing is undercrafted, she relies heavily on the word "clichéd," which implies that Swift's work is lazy or insufficiently polished.

During the *Cosmopolitan* interview Burt looks, for example, at a stanza in Swift's "Why She Disappeared":

When she finally rose, she rose slowly
Avoiding old haunts and sidestepping shiny pennies
Wary of phone calls and promises,
Charmers, dandies and get-love-quick-schemes.

Burt asks, "Why do the pennies need to be shiny? Does Taylor step on pennies that are dulled with time?" These rhetorical questions are Burt's way of saying that Swift's word choice seems arbitrary. However, one can argue that the word "shiny" is used intentionally to enhance the sibilance in "sidestepping shiny pennies," which creates a series of soft sounds to complement the idea that she takes caution in her slow, quiet recovery from failure. In addition, "sidestepping shinny pennies" can be read as a figurative expression of the speaker's distrust of all things with a temptingly slick façade: there may be value in the familiarity of "shiny" and its suggestiveness of the cliché "shiny and new." What I want to show is that Burt's criticism—especially the reconstituting of the poet's language in terms of intention and craft—is not the be-all-end-all of interpretation. How might we create space for exploring the appeal of Swift's voice, and be less quick to dismiss its resonance with millions of listeners? How can we situate it in a broader literary tradition and cultural history?

Swift as the New Confessionalist

Swift's writing falls well short of literary critics' and academic poets' criteria of craft. Perhaps what "works" in Swift's poems, however, is precisely their ostensible lack of craft, which creates—among her many followers—the impression of authenticity. I propose that Swift's work captures the resonances, without the institutional credibility, of confessional poetry and that the invocation of an unpolished, authentic autoethnographic subject is key to the effect and affect of her writing. The affinity between Swift's style and confessional poetics has not gone unnoticed—for example, Rachel Greenhaus calls Swift "1989's confessional poet" in a 2015 *JSTOR Daily* post, and in a 2017 *Independent* article, Eleanor Spencer-Regan crowns Swift "the new Sylvia Plath."[20] These articles either draw on Swift's references to autobiographical details or focus on the similarity between Swift and a particular poet. Diverging from these approaches, the remainder of this chapter explores the ways Swift reinvents confessionalist poetics.

The "confessional" mode, as coined by M. L. Rosenthal in 1959, refers to writing that reveals the author's personal experiences and emotions in relation to private and sensitive topics. Among the most well-known "confessionalists" are Robert Lowell, Sylvia Plath, and Anne Sexton—poets whose individual statures, one might argue, depended on critics' success in extracting their talents and voices from the potential stigma of the label. Confessional poetry fell under criticism primarily for two reasons. First, its discussion of taboo subjects was considered inappropriate; Lowell's *Life Studies* was flagged early on, for example, for revealing "shameful" information about his family dysfunction.[21] (Certainly, this view is largely forgotten now as an increasing number of critics find confessional poets' attention to the private sphere formally and politically groundbreaking.[22]) Second, confessional poetry was ridiculed for self-indulgence and excessiveness, associated increasingly, Jo Gill explains, "with an authorial self-absorption verging on narcissism."[23] For these two reasons, early confessional poets faced mixed reviews and struggled to equal or supplant in terms of prestige their modernist forebearers.

What literary history tends to forget is that confessionalism was also frowned upon by critics for edging too closely to everyday language and appearing to lack formal innovation. Laurence Lerner claimed that the chief characteristics of confession were "factual accuracy of remembering, self-centeredness, and self-abasement expressed in clichés."[24] The implication here is that confessional poetry, by relying on a direct expression of the subjective, the "unpleasantly egocentric," the naked "personality" (in a way modernist poets like W. B. Yeats and T. S. Eliot so stridently resisted), ceases to be poetry at all.[25] In a way, Burt's criticism of Swift's "clichéd" verse echoes Lerner's concern about early confessional poets. One may argue that authors of popular verse have replaced the mid-twentieth-century confessionalists as the new target in cultural elites' aversion toward the clichéd. Indeed, pop poets like Swift would seem to fit the stigma once applied to purely literary figures, and as discussed by Miranda Sherwin and Alan Williamson: "[B]ecause confessional poetry continues to be associated with private, self-revelatory impulses that are insufficiently and transparently transformed into art," they write, "it is frequently understood in opposition to literary movements that underscore formal and linguistic innovation."[26] In opposition to a perceived "lack of craft," confessionalist poets offered the shock of private revelation. One wonders, however, the extent to which such revelations, having lost the potential to surprise, no longer seem progressive, or can carry over without a heightened skepticism to the realm of the superstar; Swift's deliberate tending to the demarcations of, and tensions between, her privately and publicly constructed selves, may well seem—from the perspective of one who recognizes the formula—conformist, naïve, or trite. Swift's position in this regard becomes reminiscent of what Perloff calls a poetic of "strenuous authenticity" specific to the sixties,[27] and risks unintentionally serving the function of distinguishing a "real" poetics of maturity and taste.

Swift, far removed not only in fame but in generation, place, and upbringing from canonical confessionalists, shares nonetheless the appeal of a sincere and subjective voice that shares "real" and personal narratives. While she is not divulging "inappropriate" material or unleashing the closeted skeletons of a dark and sinister past, she certainly stakes and profits from a position as "oversharer" of information—a foot-in-mouth persona that seems more taunting than apologetic, and, true to the pop tradition, focuses heavily on romance and break-ups. The general perception is that most of Swift's love ballads are alluding to her ex-boyfriends and past relationships. "Back to December" is presumed to be about Taylor Lautner, "Dear John" is believed to be a letter to John Mayer, and the timing of the release of "I Knew You Were Trouble" suggests that it was directed at Harry Styles. Swift's aesthetic, then, is not quite that of an open book, but, rather, one that self-consciously plants "Easter eggs," thereby positioning the eager fan in the role of detective and as assimilator of biography to the lyric. It is also worth noting that Swift has deliberately used lyric poetry as a substitute for other confessional discourses; in 2017, she turned down *Vogue UK*'s invitation to give an interview, offering a poem instead. This seems like an odd decision since a poem opens more room for misinterpretation than does the forward-driving, dialectical form of an interview. But it seems that Swift prefers the expressive, open-ended potential offered by lyric poetry, and perhaps seeks to develop a new audience for poetry, which is often perceived as the property of an intellectual and condescending elite.

This is not to assert that Swift deliberately inserts herself in the tradition of confessionalism. But I do think that her writing registers the ripple effect of a confessionalist poetic, which has spread profusely from the ivory tower to the mainstream. Because the style of confessionalism is very much present in the cultural air, one does not need to read Robert Lowell or Anne Sexton specifically to understand it. As Sherwin argues, "The widespread appeal of confessional poetry, tell-all memoirs, and reality television is rooted in the idea that these works are able to cut through the pretensions, obfuscations, and devices of high-brow art and deliver the unadorned truth."[28] This is to say that, while the popularity of confessional poetry declines in the academy, the confessionalist mode becomes increasingly widespread in mainstream media. Again, Swift may not be deliberately participating in this poetic tradition, but her writing should be considered in the genealogy of confessionalism because it captures some of the key characteristics of the confessional mode: it discloses, that is, potentially shameful information in a seemingly unfiltered manner and indulges in self-melodramatization.

"If You're Anything Like Me," in which Swift reveals and wrestles with her own insecurities, is a choice example of the confessionalist mode at work. Behind the cover flap of the booklet containing this poem, Swift leaves the following message: "Don't read the last page" (on which "If You're Anything Like Me" is printed). This warning dramatizes the poet's ambivalence towards disclosing confidences to a

Pop Star vs. Harvard Professor 85

public audience, while also betraying this very dynamic—the thrill of disclosure—as a conscientious tactic. The speaker in this case presents herself as someone who has been hurt in her past relationships, and as a result, is paranoid, guarded, and bitter. She addresses the reader directly, stating that "if [they're] anything like [her]," they would be ultra-superstitious and be disappointed by the person they have become. Many of us may find gestures such as "knock[ing] on wood" and "wish[ing] on lucky numbers and eyelashes" relatable.[29] The poem's refrain of "if you're anything like me" might seem fully within the realm of the banal pop lyric. However, as Bradley reminds us, poetry and song craft are not necessarily separate.[30] In this case, the repetition of direct address not only creates a rhythm, but also enacts a gentle yet persistent hailing. Evan Watkins compares celebrities' and stars' adoption of direct address to capture their fans' attention to Louis Althusser's analysis of ideology, which is epitomized by the policeman's hail ("Hey, you there!").[31] Certainly, there is a tonal difference between the policeman's order and Swift's modest opening: the conditional mode in the latter sounds considerably more tentative. In contrast, too, with the interpolations of advice-driven pop lyrics—Billy Joel's "Listen boy" imperatives in "Tell Her About It" come to mind—Swift allows for the possibility that interpellation could fail. Rather than demanding full identification from the reader, the speaker opens a tentative space for connection, inviting the reader to relate to bits and pieces of her experiences: something of a balancing act between the personal and the shared experience emerges.

Crafting a relatable text requires more than capturing the reader's attention, especially since, as Watkins points out, attention is produced rather than residing "out there" as an available resource.[32] Swift, like many other successful creators of relatable content, contributes to the production of a new class of literate subjects who are trained to expend affective labor in their reading process. To maintain an intimate bond with her emotionally invested readers, Swift changes the role of the speaker as the poem progresses. At the outset, Swift positions herself near her reader as a fellow sufferer: they both have difficult relationships in the past that lead to an anxious personality and an over-reliance on superstitions. However, in the end, she rises above and becomes the consoler: "If you're anything like me, / I'm sorry. // But Darling, it's going to be okay." Though she sounds broken and insecure in the beginning, she appears calm and self-assured in the end—a trajectory much more in line with the tropes of pop than with the nearly mandatory, sustained privileging of strong passions associated with classical art. By addressing her readers with a folksy word, "Darling," Swift gestures to her humble beginning as a country singer and, more importantly, highlights a close bond between the speaker and the reader—a bond akin to the intimate relation between lovers or between a mother and her child. We get the impression here that the speaker not only requests attention *from* the reader, but she also pays attention *to* the reader. This reciprocal power relation between the author and the reader is not unique to Swift's work, but her performance of care stands out in its candor.

This author-reader relation is different from that of traditional confessional poems, in which the constructed persona demonstrates "the inability to project [the] self into a recognizable milieu of other independent Human agents," and whose poetic identity "tends to remain isolated."[33] Lowell certainly did not expect his readers to relate to the affairs of his dysfunctional Mayflower family, and Plath most likely did not expect her readers to identify with her depressed, suicidal state of mind. However, the twenty-first-century iteration of the confessional voice yearns for some degree of identification. In sum, not only does Swift's poem have the self-therapeutic function that Rosenthal[34] and Gabriel Pearson[35] observed in traditional confessional poetry such as *Life Studies*, but it also exemplifies a new modality of confessionalism that is less concerned with demonstrations of linguistic precision or invention and becomes therapeutic for the poet and the reader alike.

In contrast, the other poem in *Reputation*, "Why She Disappeared," does not immediately strike us as confessional, since the lyric "I" is replaced by a third person "she." At first glance, this piece resembles Instagram's notorious "she poems."[36] However, even though Swift is not using the pronoun "I," we can read this as an illeist monologue where the confessing subject distances herself linguistically from her confession. Not all "she poems" are confessional, but in this case, the similarity between the narrative in the poem and Swift's life—which fans are likely to ascertain—invites readers to approach her work as such. Writing about oneself through a third-person persona allows a paradoxical engagement with selfhood as it affords both detachment and dramatization. According to Marcus Nordlund, who studies the mode of illeist address in Shakespearean plays, illeism functions to portray dramatized "mental detachment."[37] To put it another way, illeism offers an exploration of personality in a depersonalized way, or, rather, an exploration of interiority under the disguise of critical distance.

The tension between intimacy and distance is certainly present in "Why She Disappeared." The poem opens with a reflection on a misstep—a fall that is both literal and metaphorical. From the outset, the speaker sounds dramatic as she connects the experience of falling on the sidewalk to the dissolution of childhood dreams.

> When she fell, she fell apart.
> Cracked her bones on the pavement she once decorated
> as a child with sidewalk chalk
> When she crashed, her clothes disintegrated and blew away
> with the winds that took all of her fair-weather friends[38]

The first line registers a shift from an impersonal observation ("she fell") to a personal exploration of feelings of injury ("she fell apart"). What begins as a bland, objective description is merely a springboard to an examination of the subject's formation. The feeling of "falling apart" is then literalized as a physical fall in the next line, as we learn that the persona's bones are broken as a result. Not only does she fall hard, but she also falls alone, since her "fair-weather friends" have left. These experiences of falling apart and falling out, while told as a personal story, rely on a set of generalized images instead of specific references to someone's life.

The speaker's struggle to find love is likewise conveyed through vague and wistful imagery, which draws the reader to a scene rather than a person. The scenes of romantic promises play out like a movie trailer. Its establishing shot shows a heroine lying "on the ground," dreaming of avenging her broken heart by hopping on "time machines" and reworking her past. In this dreamscape, Swift pits the idea of love against the reality of love. The persona claims to be nostalgic for a love that is "really something" rather than "the idea of something." And yet, the image she summons is of someone "standing broad-shouldered"—standard rom-com affair to say the least. The line between the real and the ideal, the private and the generic, becomes blurred, as her personal attachment to love is mediated and expressed through popular figures and images of romance. By deploying generalized images, Swift taps into affective circuits in what Lauren Berlant would call the "intimate public sphere," where "the personal is refracted through the general" and the generic feels oddly personal.[39] In this case, what hails the reader is not a specific figure or narrative, but the way Swift's persona draws on a shared storehouse of the commercial.

The struggle for the persona arises when she has let go of her attachment to what life should look like. In the last stanza, the self-melodramatic subject has to reckon with the fragility of her reputation. Swift declares: "And in the death of her reputation, / She felt truly alive." This triumphant conclusion does not offer clues about how exactly she came to terms with loss but rewards us with its confessionalist movement "from necessity and entrapment to qualified liberation."[40] Thus, even though the shift from the theme of love to that of rebirth seems abrupt, it taps into the confessional sentiments of liberation and individual agency. Certainly, it may seem disingenuous for someone as famous and beloved as Swift to pronounce her reputation dead and to demand some sort of resurrection, but this is where her use of illeism comes in handy: the displacement of the "I" effectively tamps down the poem's self-indulgence.

On the whole, Swift shows that to craft a relatable confession requires more than straightforward self-disclosure. The material arrangement of her poems further sheds light on Swift's strategy: she obscures as much as she reveals, and the pairing of the two poems examined above show not a singular and static mode of composition, but, rather, an openness to experimentation and a subtle negotiation of the personal with the impersonal, the generic with the particular. The album booklet containing her poems—the cover layout for which blends, in an explosion of sensational "headline" texts around an airbrushed Swift, the tabloid with the fashion magazine—is part of a self-mythologizing project in which the singer orchestrates confessions to construct truths and half-truths about herself. In doing so, Swift blends together two audiences—those who love her and those who love to hate on her. While the diaristic pages where her poems are printed suggest a dissolution between the private and the public, the generalized and evasive language in her poems, which might strike us as "clichéd," protects her from total exposure. Her confessionalist voice grants us permission to identify with her feelings even as we learn little, amidst the vague and often abstract language of her poetry, of a specific nature. She secures at the same time the valued attributes of relatability and mysteriousness, familiarity and unpredictability.

Conclusion: "Is it cool that I said all that?"

Maybe Swift's poetry "doesn't work" as professional poetry. It seems to lack the semantic density and formal innovativeness one would expect in properly "crafted" writing by institutionally sanctioned poets. Meanwhile, it is true to much mainstream pop in its saccharine and melodramatic revelations of feelings. However, Swift's writing is a useful case study for literary and cultural critics because it epitomizes a new culture of confessionalism. She represents a generation of "amateur" poets who turn a mode that is centered around the revelation of the private into a self-dramatizing form of writing that invites identification. Her works, and those like them, serve as a testament to the enduring appeal of confessionalism, which speaks to our desire to make distinctions between the authentic and the artificial, the "real thing" and the conceit. Amateur poets may not be consciously building on literary tradition, but literary tradition may influence cultural production through circuitous routes and reappear in a refracted light. By positioning Swift's work in the genealogy of confessional writing, we may begin to see ways in which it is innovative, even if it seems to exist outside of academia. Such a reading also requires us to broaden the notion of craft and to bring ourselves to recognize the otherwise illegible labor exerted by the author. Though our aesthetic presumptions may or may not budge as a result of such an analysis, it remains important to reach beyond the parameters of conventional criteria as we attempt to locate art within—and high/low exchanges among—mainstream and mass culture practices.

Notes

1 "Look What You Made Me Do," track 6 on Taylor Swift, *Reputation*, Big Machine, 2007.

2 Patti Grecco, "A Harvard Professor Critiques Taylor Swift's New Poems," *Cosmopolitan*, November 13, 2017, https://www.cosmopolitan.com/entertainment/celebs/a13528212/taylor-swift-poetry-harvard-professor-review/.

3 Ibid.

4 Richard Goldstein, *The Poetry of Rock* (Toronto: New York, Bantam, 1969), xi.

5 Qtd. in Dorothy J. Wang, *Thinking Its Presence: Form, Race, and Subjectivity in Contemporary Asian American Poetry* (Stanford: Stanford University Press, 2014), 2.

6 Maria Damon, *Postliterary America: From Bagel Shop Jazz to Micropoetries* (Iowa City: University of Iowa Press, 2011), 194.

7 Adam Bradley, *The Poetry of Pop* (New Haven: Yale University Press, 2017), 5.

8 Stephen LaConte, "Do You Actually Know the Difference between Taylor Swift and History's Greatest Poets?" *BuzzFeed*, August 30, 2019, https://www.buzzfeed.com/stephenlaconte/taylor-swift-lyrics-famous-poets-quiz.

9 Jakobson, as Linda R. Waugh explains, argues that the poetic function of language foregrounds "the linguistic sign as a sign" and brings about a "divorce of the sign from its referent"; "The Poetic Function in the Theory of Roman Jakobson," *Poetics Today* 2, no. 1a (1980): 69. Bakhtin pits poetry against novels and argues that poetic discourse negates the plurality of voices of everyday life in favor of "a tense

discursive unity"; *The Dialogic Imagination* (Austin: University of Texas Press, 2002), 111. Unlike Bakhtin, Kristeva views poetic language as a negation of univocal speech and finds that "poetry and maternity represent privileged practices within paternally sanctioned culture which permit a nonpsychotic experience of the heterogeneity and dependency characteristic of the maternal terrain"; see Judith Butler, "The Body Politics of Julia Kristeva," *Hypatia* 3, no. 3 (1988): 110.

10 Pierre Bourdieu, *The Field of Cultural Production* (New York: Columbia University Press, 1993), 51–3.

11 Marjorie Perloff, *Radical Artifice: Writing Poetry in the Age of Media* (Chicago: University of Chicago Press, 1991), 19.

12 Grecco, "A Harvard Professor Critiques Taylor Swift's New Poems."

13 Stephanie Burt, *Don't Read Poetry* (New York: Basic Books, 2019), 6.

14 Fredric Jameson, *Postmodernism, Or, The Cultural Logic of Late Capitalism* (Durham: Duke University Press, 1991), 54.

15 Mark McGurl, *The Program Era* (Cambridge: Harvard University Press, 2009), 23.

16 Timothy Yu, "Instagram Poetry and Our Poetry Worlds," *Poetry Foundation*, April 24, 2019, https://www.poetryfoundation.org/harriet/2019/04/instagram-poetry-and -our-poetry-worlds.

17 Tim Mayers, *(Re)Writing Craft: Composition, Creative Writing, and the Future of English Studies* (Pittsburg: University of Pittsburgh Press, 2005), 63.

18 See Kazim Ali, "On Instafame and Reading Rupi Kaur," *Poetry Foundation*, October 23, 2017, https://www.poetryfoundation.org/harriet/2017/10/on-rupi-kaur. Ali, for instance, criticizes Instapoet Rupi Kaur for her lack of craft: "the real difference [between professional poets and Kaur] here is not about intention or focus or subject matter but about craft."

19 Mayers, *(Re)Writing Craft*, 34.

20 Rachel Greenhaus, "Taylor Swift: 1989's Confessional Poet," *JSTOR Daily*, September 23, 2015, https://daily.jstor.org/taylor-swift-confessional-poet/; Eleanor Spencer-Regan, "Here's Why Taylor Swift is the New Sylvia Plath," *Independent*, September 20, 2017, https://www.independent.co.uk/voices/taylor-swift-look-what-you-made -me-do-sylvia-plath-poet-songwriter-lyrics-singer-a7957011.html.

21 M. L. Rosenthal, "Poetry as Confession," in *Our Life in Poetry: Selected Essays and Reviews*, ed. Macha Louis (New York: Persea, 1991), 109.

22 John Thompson wrote that Lowell's disregard for propriety "[had] won a major expansion of the territory of poetry"; "Two Poets," *Kenyon Review* 21 (1959): 483. More famously, Deborah Nelson argued that Lowell's self-disclosure was progressive as it "create[ed] social and poetic informality in formal terms"; *Pursuing Privacy in Cold War America* (New York: Columbia University Press, 2002), 45.

23 Jo Gill, "Textual Confessions: Narcissism in Anne Sexton's Early Poetry," *Twentieth Century Literature* 50, no. 1 (2004): 60.

24 Laurence Lerner, "What is Confessional Poetry?" *Critical Quarterly* 29, no. 2 (1987): 52.

25 M. L. Rosenthal, *The Modern Poets* (New York: Oxford University Press, 1965), 231. Modernist aesthetics differ markedly from those of confessionalism. T. S. Eliot, for instance, championed "the process of depersonalization" in poetry, while W. B. Yeats strived for an "impersonal beauty." See Eliot's "Tradition and the Individual Talent," in *Selected Essays*, (London: Faber, 1999), 17, and Yeats's "The Tree of Life," in *The Collected Works in Verse and Prose of William Butler Yeats,*

Vol. 8 (Project Gutenberg, 2015), 16, https://www.gutenberg.org/files/49615/49615 -h/49615-h.htm.

26 Miranda Sherwin, *"Confessional" Writing and the Twentieth-Century Literary Imagination* (New York: Palgrave Macmillan, 2011), 15.

27 Perloff, *Radical Artifice*, 20.

28 Sherwin, *"Confessional" Writing and the Twentieth-Century Literary Imagination*, 5.

29 Taylor Swift, "If You're Anything Like Me," from liner material for *Reputation* (Special Edition Vol. 2), Universal, 2017.

30 Bradley, *The Poetry of Pop*, 23.

31 Evan Watkins, *Literacy Work in the Reign of Human Capital* (New York: Fordham University Press), 105.

32 Ibid.

33 Steven K. Hoffman, "Impersonal Personalism: The Making of a Confessional Poetic," *ELH* 45, no. 4 (1978): 703–4.

34 Rosenthal, "Poetry as Confession," 109.

35 Gabriel Pearson, "Robert Lowell: The Middle Years," in *Contemporary Poetry in America*, ed. Robert Boyers (New York: Schocken, 1974), 53.

36 "She poems" refer to a popular category of poetry, most commonly found on Instagram, that focuses on an anonymous female persona. It has been criticized for being formulaic and simplistic.

37 Marcus Nordlund, *The Shakespearean Inside* (Edinburgh: Edinburgh University Press, 2017), 130–3.

38 Swift, "Why She Disappeared," from liner material for *Reputation* (Special Edition Vol.1), Universal.

39 Lauren Berlant, *The Female Complaint* (Durham: Duke University Press, 2008), viii.

40 Hoffman, "Impersonal Personalism," 702. Though Swift's concluding lines are of course more abstract and less threatening than, say, Sylvia Plath's notorious conclusion to "Lady Lazarus," one can find—here, and in other works by the two writers—a parallel formula.

5

Personae Non Grata

Dramatic Monologue and Social Pathology in Select Randy Newman Songs

John Kimsey

"On the edge." "In your face." "Dark." If we had a nickel for every time a rock connoisseur has used terms like these to talk about music, we could retire in style. Usually, such talkers are referring to a figure like Iggy Pop or Johnny Rotten—some sacred bad boy seen to embody rock's romantic fantasy of the noble savage. Seldom do they have in mind someone like Randy Newman, an affluent, affable resident of suburban L. A. whose bread and butter has for many years been composing scores for the likes of *Toy Story*. And yet Randy Newman has written and recorded some of the edgiest, most confrontational, and uncompromising pop music of the last fifty-some years. Though music alone can and does play a role in his achieving these effects, his approach to lyric writing is key, and demonstrates two important traits that qualify it as "literary": (1) Newman almost always writes in the voice of a character, such that his lyrics are comparable to persona poems; and (2) the character in question often reveals himself through his discourse to be somehow suspect, unsavory, or unreliable in terms of his implied values, choices, and/or perspective. This second feature recalls a celebrated sub-category of persona poetry, the dramatic monologue. In her 1992 essay, "Randy Newman and the Extraordinary Moral Position," Sara Dunne foregrounds the similarity of Newman's lyrics to this poetic form, focusing especially on Robert Browning's "My Last Duchess" and "Porphyria's Lover"[1] and (applying Robert Langbaum's term from his pioneering 1957 study of dramatic monologue) their "reprehensible narrators."[2] Using this lens, Dunne examines a set of Newman songs, dividing the speakers into those who manifest (a) insanity; (b) political insanity; (c) hopeless self-involvement; and (d) criminal insanity.[3] In this chapter, I hope to further Dunne's work by comparing Newman's songs to dramatic monologues of this shocking type, which populate (but do not exhaust) Browning's *oeuvre*; however, both my choice of songs (with one exception) and their respective headings will be different. What I am concerned with are lyrics that use personae to address three familiar yet still-fraught realms of oppression in US society: race, gender, and class, particularly as these tie in with privileged, white masculinity. While in no way discounting Dunne's

92   *Lit-Rock*

analysis, I submit that a notable portion of Newman's work goes beyond individualistic categories such as "insanity," even though the songs in question center on individual characters. In her comprehensive 2003 study, *Dramatic Monologue*, Glennis Byron asserts that "[w]ith its dynamic of self and context, the dramatic monologue is a particularly appropriate form for the purposes of social critique."[4] Turning Byron's lens on popular music, I submit that Newman's songs speak, in their oblique way, about social pathologies which transcend the personae voiced in them.

   Newman is well-read, and in interviews has spoken of his fondness, as a songwriter, for the literary device of "the untrustworthy narrator."[5] In his book-length survey of Newman's career, Kevin Courrier explores Newman's penchant for "the mask,"[6] and even draws on Herman Melville's satire *The Confidence Man*, with its nested tales of money-mad Americans, as a kind of precursor to Newman's treatment of characters.[7] While I agree that Newman's writing is literary, I, like Dunne, see poetry's dramatic monologue as a more apt literary analogue than the unreliable narrator associated with prose fictions such as *One Flew Over the Cuckoo's Nest*. This is because Newman's characters do not appear within an explicit story, nor are they necessarily telling one in any developed sense; they are, instead, soliloquizing. In addition, and in formal terms, the song lyric is more akin to poetry than to prose in that it typically entails both strophic forms and rhyme schemes. Moreover, like the three-minute pop song, poems often privilege an economy of words. And yet a number of Newman lyrics, despite their brevity, involve a measured unveiling of something initially obscure; what is revealed, though, is less a story than the habitus of the persona. As Monique Morgan has pointed out, both Langbaum and his critical antagonist James Phelan agree that "revelation of character" is "the purpose of dramatic monologue"[8] such that, in Phelan's words, "events typically are present, but not because they are essential to the progression of a story of change but because they are an effective means to reveal character. Change is not present, because [such poems are] focused on depicting a character at a particular moment or a particular phase of life that we understand as ongoing."[9] Anatomizing the dramatic monologue in poetry, M. H. Abrams notes three distinctive features: The first is that the poem consists solely of the words of a speaker who is clearly not the poet and who utters the words in a "specific situation." The second is that this speaker addresses "one or more other people," though readers know of the "presence" of such "auditors" (and any response they may make) only from "clues in the discourse of the . . . speaker." The third and final feature is that the speaker's words are intended, as emphasized above, "to reveal to the reader . . . the speaker's temperament and character."[10]

Dramatic Monologue and Popular Song

The peak period of Newman's solo output is 1968–83 and, in the early years of that span, musical-dramatic monologues were peculiar stuff for pop-rock. In the late 1960s, prevailing canons of authenticity affirmed singing as autobiography and songwriting as window-on-the-soul. Of course, in musical theatre, persona songs have remained the prevailing currency. And in other genres of twentieth-century popular music, the dramatic monologue's uses of irony and persona are less hard to come by, often taking the form of the revelatory lyric. Bob Russell's lyric to Duke Ellington's "Do Nothing Till You Hear From Me," for example, gives the song a surprise twist when its persona, who is assuring his betrothed, in form of a love letter, that she should pay no attention to mean-spirited gossip, concludes:

> Some kiss may cloud my memory
> And other arms may hold a thrill
> But just do nothing till you hear it from me
> *And you never will.*[11]

In Nashville-style country, one finds songs like "Miller's Cave" (a hit for Bobby Bare in 1964) in which Jack Clement's lyric, related in the voice of a spurned lover, slowly reveals its persona to be not only the murderer of his love object and her partner, but also a madman who will never be apprehended because he's "lost" in the song's titular cave.[12] And in blues songwriting, the classic example of such a device is Mose Allison's 1957 "Parchman Farm." As a nameless prisoner incarcerated at the infamous Mississippi State Penitentiary, the song's speaker stoically catalogs the abuses he's compelled to endure, gaining the listener's sympathy by contrasting heavy punishment with a light crime: "I'm sittin' over her on number nine / And all I did was drink my wine." So it goes until the end when the singer twice avers that he is sentenced to life; then, in a third iteration, the listener is confronted with "I'm a-gonna be here for the rest of my life / And all I did was shoot my wife."[13] Even 1960s rock finds some room, albeit scarce, for persona-writing. The singer in the Kinks' 1966 hit "Sunny Afternoon" is clearly not Ray Davies himself but a profligate upper-class playboy; and, inspired by Davies, the Who's Pete Townshend often wrote in character as well.[14] But these persona songs typically lack the twist—a revelation, by the end, that the persona and/ or his account is somehow dubious or mortifying—that characterizes the dramatic monologue of the "Porphyria's Lover" sort.

Newman began his solo career at a moment when, for most rock listeners, identifying the singer with the song and its subject had become common sense, "confessional" songwriting having by then become a hippie pop trend.[15] Part of what such music was supposed to be about was the singer sharing with listeners some deeply personal truth about her/his life. It was not always thus, of course; prior to the Beatles and Bob Dylan, no one expected pop or rock songwriting to feature riveting self-revelation. Part of what was revolutionary about Lennon-McCartney and Dylan was that they established writing one's own material as the norm in rock circles. And by the time the confessional trend got underway at the turn of the decade, the assumption was that a writer/performer such as Joni Mitchell or David Crosby was opening up, for a mass audience, the musical equivalent of an intimate diary.[16]

This assumption is well captured in Crosby's spoken introduction to the song "Triad" on Crosby, Stills, Nash & Young's 1971 live album *Four Way Street*: "We write a lot of our songs just right out of what goes on, you know—to us. About the people that we love and stuff and things that happen to us, you know, 'cause like that's what you have to write about if you're gonna get down to stuff that means anything to you."[17] Under the heading "Genres: History: the Singer/Songwriter," the BMI website articulates the confessional ethos as follows:

> When a song is both written and performed by the same person, audiences assume that the material comes from the heart; that it emerges from the person's own experience. A certain transparence is inferred such that the audience believes a singer/songwriter has cast aside any impediments to their thoughts and feelings and put into words their honest and authentic point of view.[18]

This was never Newman's way. In the words of Lenny Waronker, Newman's best friend since childhood and closest musical collaborator, "He never could understand why other songwriters didn't work in character. For him, it just made sense. He felt he couldn't be as interesting as his characters. . . . The problem is that he's *so* good at getting inside these characters that listeners frequently confuse him with the subjects of his songs."[19]

Robert Christgau once noted that Newman virtually never uses metaphor in his lyrics.[20] Moreover, if we go by the number of words per song, Newman stacks up as the anti-Bob Dylan. And yet despite this lack of figuration and lyrical prolixity, Newman is a master of verbal artifice, thanks largely to his practice of never approaching a subject directly, but always through the medium of character. But then, Randy Newman has always had difficulty looking at things straight on. In the words of Waronker: "Oh, he always had these eye problems—crossed eyes—which I think really affected him, his appearance and the way he looked and did certain things. He was always kind of sloppy and didn't have a good fix on himself. But I think he found ways of overcoming that."[21] The connection is intriguing: this songwriter, whose specialty is adopting the viewpoint of the other, felt the need, since childhood, to literally deflect his gaze when looking at someone else. Interviewers have long noted Newman's tendency to avoid direct eye contact—a holdover, it would seem, from the days before his "eye malady" was corrected. Waronker says that being unable to read people's faces to any great extent, Newman became instead an expert listener to their voices.[22]

Newman's family history and early career play important roles here as well, each bit of his experience furthering—both within and in the face of pop music's "look at me" tendencies—his ventriloquistic, impersonal approach: a sense of "writing others" more so than the self. On his father's side, Newman comes from a musical family— if not musical royalty—of a particularly Hollywood sort. His uncles Alfred, Lionel, and Emil Newman were all film composers, each with an impressive resumé of movie scores.[23] Randy himself came late to scoring films, years after doing his landmark singer-songwriter work. His first major score was for 1981's *Ragtime*. And since doing the score and songs for 1995's *Toy Story*, composing music for Pixar productions has been his prime source of income.[24] Given such family connections to the film industry, it's no surprise that Newman grew up in Los Angeles. But his mother was from New Orleans, and the childhood summers he spent there left him with an abiding respect for the city's musicality: "It's like the whole populace has a casual talent for it," he observed in a 2012 interview.[25] Though not a permanent resident of the Crescent City, Newman has been influenced by its music, particularly its 1950s-era brand of piano-based rhythm-and-blues and rock-and-roll.[26] Then there is the sound of Newman's singing voice which, unlike his personae, remains the same throughout most of his songs. His delivery and pronunciation have a slightly mushed-mouth quality and more than a hint of a Louisiana drawl.[27] Though the point is purely speculative, it may be that, residing part-time in New Orleans, the young Newman absorbed something of the city's oft-remarked "outsider" status relative to the rest of North America; if so, he may have identified not just with the city's music, but with its otherness too, including perhaps its carnivalesque culture of masking.

Newman studied composition at UCLA, but always retained an interest in radio pop, and by 1962 was employed as a staff songwriter for Metric Music.[28] He even released a solo single, 1962's "Golden Gridiron Boy," which went nowhere.[29] By the mid-1960s and into the 1970s he was known, at least within the industry, as a writer of hits or signature songs for artists such as Judy Collins ("I Think It's Going to Rain Today"), Alan Price ("Simon Smith and the Amazing Dancing Bear"), Three Dog Night ("Mama Told Me Not Come"), Ringo Starr ("Have You Seen My Baby"), Bonnie Raitt ("Guilty"), and Joe Cocker and Tom Jones ("You Can Leave Your Hat On").

Newman's own career as a recording artist began with the 1968 LP *Randy Newman Creates Something New Under the Sun*, produced by simpatico pianist/composer/arranger/ironist Van Dyke Parks. Unlike his subsequent solo albums, this debut featured an orchestra, scored and conducted by Newman himself, as the primary accompaniment to every song. It was the moment of *Sgt. Pepper's* and the beginnings of art-pop, and Newman, like the Beatles and Brian Wilson (another Parks collaborator), was interested in exploring new possibilities for orchestral accompaniment in pop music.[30] Though admired by a discerning few, the album flopped commercially. His next album, 1970s *12 Songs*, did away with the orchestra and replaced it with an L. A. roots-rock ensemble featuring Ry Cooder and Clarence White on guitars, and centered around Newman's own piano and vocals. This collection received much more attention and acclaim; indeed, Christgau proclaimed it "the finest record of the year."[31] Then came 1972's *Sail Away*, another masterwork which retained the L. A. rhythm section while reinserting dollops of orchestra, and which contained some of Newman's most enduring numbers ("Political Science," an American idiot's complaint about foreign relations which concludes "Let's drop the big one now"; "Lonely at the Top," sung from the viewpoint of Frank Sinatra; and "Burn On," a cockeyed tribute to Americana's "big river" trope, the river in this case being the Cuyahoga, which had become so polluted that it occasionally caught fire).[32] This was followed in 1974 by the startling and controversial *Good Old Boys*, an album whose sides featured two separate song cycles about the American South—one centering on a self-described "redneck" and reprobate whom Newman initially named Johnny Cutler, and the other on Louisiana's legendary governor and economic populist presidential candidate, Huey P. Long.[33] This was followed by *Little Criminals* (1977), *Born Again* (1979), and *Trouble in Paradise* (1983). As we shall see from the range of songs examined below, Newman's use of personae, of "American grotesques,"[34] of sophisticated irony and/or low comedy does not abate through this string of albums; nor does his periodic use of the dramatic monologue with its surprise, slow motion reveals about the repugnant character delivering the words.

"Charleston Bay": Social Pathology and Race

The melody, chords, and orchestration of 1972's "Sail Away" create a sense of ease and nostalgia.[35] The gently rendered major pentatonic melody, whose words wax dreamily about an apparently faraway place called "America," is set to chords Stephen Foster might have employed.[36] And the refrain, keynoted by the repeated phrase "sail away," evokes in its dramatic amen-like cadences the sound of nineteenth-century Protestant hymnody. It's difficult not to find this subtly soaring chorus moving; majestic, even.

Thus does Newman set his trap. Upon closer inspection of the sparse lyric, the listener begins to sense something rotten amidst the praiseful sonorities. As is typical, there is no omniscient authorial voice present. Instead, the singer begins: "In America, you get food to eat / Won't have to run through the jungle and scuff up your feet." The auditor is further informed "You'll just drink wine and sing about Jesus all day," and by the time we arrive at "Climb aboard, little wog, sail away with me," it's clear that the speaker is white and either European or American and the addressee a resident of colonialism's heart of darkness. The twist is underscored in the refrain when the singer intones, following two noble-sounding entreaties to sail away, "We will cross the mighty ocean into Charleston Bay."[37] No further clues about the place are provided, and yet the historically astute listener may recall that Charleston, South Carolina was, for the thirteen colonies and then the United States, the foremost center of the slave trade, and the place where enormous numbers of newly enslaved subjects first set foot in the New World.[38]

Sail away indeed. The lyric never mentions Africa, let alone the slave trade, but the singer's words subtly betray his occupation as a human trafficker. Moreover, it's clear from the ironic contrast between the churchlike music and the few-but-telling racist locutions, that the character either views his vocation as charitable (lifting savages out of their savagery per imperialist ideology) or, more cynically, is framing the voyage as something romantic so as to seduce his auditor into climbing aboard. "Sail Away" is smooth and pretty on the surface, with something monstrous lurking just below. This is an American anthem of a brutally honest sort—one saluting, from the speaker's perspective, the crime against humanity on which the country's wealth was founded.

This theme of Newman's work and concerns is thrown into high relief by the 1974 LP *Good Old Boys*. The opening song, "Rednecks," sets against its jaunty, laid-back shuffle the following words:

We talk real funny down here
We drink too much and we laugh too loud

We're too dumb to make it in no Northern town
And we're keeping the n*****s down[39]

This was shocking to listeners in 1974 (and remains eyebrow-raising even today), and not only because it made emphatic use of America's most charged racial epithet. There was also the matter of the song's attitude—the fact that it seemed, at first glance anyway, to sympathize with the white bigots of the title, down in Dixie doing the yeoman's work of white supremacy. A prelude to the song notes that "last night" the character saw segregationist Georgia Governor "Lester Maddox on a TV show with some smart-ass New York Jew" and "the Jew" simply laughed at the segregationist politician, as did the audience.[40] "Well he may be a fool but he's our fool / If they think they're better than him they're wrong," says the character, and that, he confides, is why he "made this song."[41] What follows is the verse quoted above, along with a comic catalog of buffoonish Southern white stereotypes. But then in the last verse, the character begins to catalog something quite different: all the ghettos (called "cages") in metropolises above the Mason–Dixon line—Detroit, Chicago, Cleveland, Los Angeles and, yes, New York—where "the North has set the n****r free."[42] Parodying the voice of an angry, working-class Southern white, Newman is able to simultaneously express a modicum of sympathy; he generates comedy at the persona's expense but then allows him to point out the hypocrisy of supposedly tolerant Northern white liberals, ultimately recalling Malcolm X's observation that if a Black person is south of the "Canadian Border," she or he "is in the South."[43] In the words of Byron, "The tendency of dramatic monologues, no matter what their particular focus, always appears to be to question rather than to confirm. From the very start, the dramatic monologue worked to disrupt rather than consolidate authority, drawing upon speakers who are in some way alienated from, rather than representative of, their particular societies."[44]

Songs such as "Sail Away" and "Rednecks" show Newman to be intricately attuned to and adept at working with the multiplicity of registers from which songs are made. His is an aesthetic of contrast and disjunction—between what the lyrics say and the song-form encodes; between the persona of the singer and the author of the song; between our desire for "the authentic" in songs and the dizzying possibilities of artifice in both performance and life. In the words of racial formation theorists Michael Omi and Howard Winant, "To study race in the United States is to enter a world of paradox, irony and danger."[45] This is partly because, in their view, "race is a matter of both social structure and cultural representation."[46] By this they mean that, on one hand, race is a social construction, not a biological essence. However, in a society founded on white supremacy, this discursive construct is taken as natural fact and thus shapes the way the society is both organized and stratified. Pop's supreme ironist finds in both the discursive trope of race and the very worldly phenomenon of white supremacy topics well-suited to his formal skills and inclinations. Indeed, Newman is one of the few pop composers to write in ethically conscious ways about prejudice and racism without simply hurling curses or spouting pieties. And again, this is a function of his use of personae, a practice which allows him to show, rather than tell about, intolerance and injustice from, as it were, the inside.

Of course race in relation to masks in American cultural history is itself a sizeable, fraught, and complex topic, ranging as it does from the literal and figurative resonances of blackface minstrelsy to African American poet Paul Laurence Dunbar's penetrating *crie de coeur* of 1895, "We Wear the Mask."[47] White rock has often been analogized to minstrelsy,[48] but as Courrier and Dave Laing note, Newman's own relation to/ impersonation of musical "blackness" departs, in typical Newman fashion, from the genre's norm.[49]

Then, too, in more psychological terms, there is the power of masking to release or allow exploration of what Carl Jung called "the shadow"—the ill-favored, potentially threatening and value-inverting counterpart, in the unconscious, of the conscious ego.[50] In Jung's paradigm, Newman's personae become nothing less than the collective shadow of white male America, which by necessity must be honestly engaged with in order to heal and to unify.

"She turns on easy": Social Pathology and Gender

Newman has an additional set of songs about men behaving badly toward women, the most written about being 1970's "Suzanne," with its sexually predatory male speaker and deliberate upending of the bohemian dream-woman trope evoked by Leonard Cohen's song of the same name. But several of Newman's men are more subtle in conveying their misogyny or exploitative relationships to women. In 1983's "Real Emotional Girl," the male persona expresses his affection for the "girl" in the title, who "wears her heart on her sleeve" such that "every little thing you tell her / She'll believe / She really will." It's that last line, with its double-insistence, that provides the first clue to the narrator's attitude to this extraordinary *inamorata*: As if impressed, or as if *to* impress his auditor, he discloses a number of her unique, inward-turning behaviors. Gradually it becomes clear that he prizes her vulnerability not because it marks her as sensitive, but because, to the male gaze, it objectifies her as a curiosity:

> lives down deep inside of herself
> She turns on easy
> It's like a hurricane
> You would not believe it.[51]

And suddenly listeners find themselves in the realm of too much information. This guy, who sounded at first like a lovestruck admirer of the title character, is actually a creep, turning intimate facts about this absent woman into boorish barroom boasts. As Morgan notes, "All dramatic monologues reveal the speaker's character to the reader gradually, in stages," and some make "a previously unveiled trait so extreme that it seems to differ in kind (rather than merely in degree) from our previous conception of it."[52] Newman's formula here is indeed consistent with that of Browning, whose narcissistic, bride-seeking Duke in "My Last Duchess" has not only (the reader gradually learns) killed his former bride for failing to properly feed his ego, but enjoys the full control he now has over her curtained portrait. It is a gender critique by way of the dramatic monologue that Charlotte Mew took up in the twentieth century with poems like "The Farmer's Bride" ("Oh! My God! the down, / the soft young down of her," yearns the poem's rejected speaker and the girl's imprisoner[53]), and which runs straight through to UK Poet Laureate Carol Ann Duffy: "I don't talk much," Duffy writes in "Pyschopath": "I swing up beside them and do it / with my eyes. Brando. She was clean. I could smell her."[54]

Such leering male fetishism can likewise be found in 1972's "You Can Leave Your Hat On," whose speaker dictates to a female precisely how she should perform a striptease so as to give him "reason to live."[55] As noted earlier, this song has been covered by ecstatic sounding, macho-voiced singers Tom Jones and Joe Cocker; singers whom Newman has indicated don't get the joke that the speaker is a "wimpy" fantasist.[56] The song means to deflate the cock-rock ethos, not participate in it. "I would never think all that was a good thing, ordering someone around," he told an interviewer in 1998.[57]

The fact that, from Newman's viewpoint, such interpreters misread his songs (according to Marcus, another clueless rendition is Linda Ronstadt's seemingly straight-faced version of "Sail Away"[58]) is worth pausing over. At least in the cases of Jones and Cocker, it's quite possible they *do* get the joke and have simply chosen to make an interpretive swerve. But this phenomenon points up the potentially precarious effects of employing irony in the way Newman typically does. The music to which the words of "You Can Leave Your Hat On" are set—a pounding, bluesy piano drone driven by a four-on-the-floor drum groove—arguably conveys no sense of irony about the song's macho-seeming male-female dynamic; quite the contrary, given the stock semiotic codes of rock instrumental performance. Listeners are free to privilege that hard rocking, purely musical register of meaning if they wish and, like any author, Newman cannot control audience responses. His work departs from poetry proper in this respect precisely because it signifies through music and not just words alone. In his groundbreaking 1975 chapter on Newman, Marcus was already lamenting the loss, on the part of rock listeners, of the ability to read lyrics in terms of fictional personae (something they were perfectly capable of doing, he observes, when Dylan came on the scene).[59] This may mean that the rock audience has, from a cultural literacy standpoint, been dumbed down over the years, an assessment that would effectively place Newman's work under the sign of high, as opposed to popular, culture. This may be what long kept Newman the solo artist from mainstream pop success (something he finally achieved with 1978's "Short People"), while also flattering his fans for their ability to "get" what seemingly eludes the masses. Indeed, a dichotomy of "getting" and "not getting"—of irony as a basis for assembling educated audiences around the pop song, as opposed to a performance-driven ethos valuing sincerity and raw passion—seems to have become a standard part of the Newman experience. Even the aforementioned "Short People," despite its hit status and seemingly transparent (if not over-the-top) portrayal of a witless bigot, resulted in some "little people throwing eggs" at the singer.[60] While Newman shrugged off that particular response, he has said, regarding "Rednecks"—with its speaker's blatant use of the N-word—that performing the piece makes him "nervous," given its use of "one of the ugliest words in the language" and the possibility of misinterpretation.[61] Newman's work sits challengingly, then, at least in its use of irony, at the intersection of "high" and "low" aesthetics and in terms of how audiences register offensiveness; the satire may well be missed altogether, as the isolated utterance—*sans* persona—takes precedence. Notably, a sizeable section of the Victorian audience responded in a similar fashion to Browning's early dramatic monologues.[62]

"They're trying to wash us away": Social Pathology and Class

"Louisiana 1927" keynotes *Good Old Boys*' song cycle about Huey Long. Addressing the great Mississippi flood of 1927, which chronicler John Barry has called "the greatest natural disaster [the United States had] ever known" until Katrina,[63] the song positions its speaker as a working-class individual displaced by the disaster. And yet, as Barry explains, it was not the *natural* disaster that left "six feet of water in the streets of Evangeline,"[64] but rather a manmade scheme in which members of "The Club," a congeries of New Orleans' business and political elite, deliberately blew up the Caernarvon levee 13 miles south of New Orleans to relieve pressure on the down-flowing deluge before it could inundate the state's most prosperous commercial hub. This scheme entailed the deliberate destruction of lower-class parishes St. Bernard and Plaquemines, something to which the powers-that-be persuaded the inhabitants to literally sign-off on, with the promise that they would be remunerated by the government for their losses. The remuneration never came, and this is one of the abuses of power about which Long campaigned in his first, successful bid for the governorship.[65] The words of the refrain could hardly be more stark, and they are set, like "Sail Away," against a blend of what Peter Winkler describes as Newman's penchant for both barbershop harmony and the orchestral vocabulary developed by Aaron Copland to signify Americana[66]:

> Louisiana
> Louisiana
> They're trying to wash us away
> They're trying to wash us away.[67]

Verses of the song speak of condescending consolations from "President Coolidge" about what "the river has done to this poor cracker's land,"[68] but the third-person plural pronoun in "They're trying to wash us away" indicates the speaker's sense that it's not the river that actually menaces him and his lower-class peers. However, the ultimate surprise animating *this* Newman song concerns not the fictive speaker from 1927, but rather how New Orleans singers have adapted and recontextualized this 1972 composition *post*-Katrina. Singers such as John Boutté changed the lyrics to address government neglect during the 2005 catastrophe so that President Coolidge becomes "President stand-by Bush," and "this cracker's land" becomes "this Creole's land."[69] In the new iteration, "They're trying to wash us away" is the refrain of the African American "Lower Nine," and the words have, according to many singers and listeners, never sounded more poignant.[70] Here, the toxic intersection of race and class in a profoundly unequal society is captured in one plaintive, six-word refrain. This particular appropriation of a Newman song stands in stark contrast to the hyper-masculine interpretations of "You Can Leave Your Hat On" discussed earlier. For here, the interpretation works on behalf of the oppressed as opposed to participating in a dominant ideology that is the source of oppression.

Inequality in interpersonal relations, enabled by economic deprivation, is the subtext of "Davy the Fat Boy," the 1968 song with which Newman practically began his solo career. Musically speaking, the song is through-composed except for the refrain, and the orchestra is employed to take listeners on an emotional roller coaster in just under three minutes. Melancholy and slightly dissonant sonorities at the beginning surround a plangent vocal which, unusually for Newman, is over- rather than understated. Perhaps straining to convince himself, the speaker notes that he and Davy have been friends since infancy; how he was "a comfort to his mother and a pal to his dad"; and how, anticipating their own demise one day, the parents implored, "Please take care of our Davy / You may be the only friend he ever will have."[71]

Then a perky eighth-note figure on the tonic sends the pathos packing: "Davy the fat boy, Davy the fat boy / Isn't he round? Isn't he round?" And suddenly we gather that the speaker's "care" entails promoting his "best friend" as a sideshow freak. The friend-turned-huckster goes on to pitch the Davy experience, exhorting the spectators to guess Davy's weight—wherein the prize for accuracy is—that's right, you heard right—a "teddy bear"! As if this weren't humiliating enough, Davy's "friend" wheedles him into doing "the famous fat boy dance" for the audience, and the drama becomes nonverbal as slow-moving, awkward-sounding orchestral chords signify that obscure but disturbing slice of showbiz. Apparently guileless, the "friend" ends the song with the refrain: "Isn't he, isn't he round?" Pathos, grotesque humor, and nausea, all in 2:47 and, again, another persona who is not, by the end, what he seemed at the beginning. Through the microcosm of one character, Newman elucidates the sickness of a society built on exploitation.

Coda: "My life is good"

The class hierarchies that inform popular music itself do not escape Newman's attention. The "authentic" self-expression valorized by the singer-songwriter genre— BMI's transparent "music . . . from the heart"—is itself highly fictive and, in its refusal to acknowledge that truth, amounts to what Roland Barthes calls "depoliticized speech,"[72] passing off the cultural as the natural. But needless to say, the truth doesn't rhyme and, as Simon Frith has argued, 1960s rock culture's definition of "the authentic," while drawing on that concept's meaning as defined by twentieth-century folklorists, was always disconnected from any actual community of "folk" as defined by measurable, anthropologic criteria.[73] Instead, authenticity in 1960s-style rock typically consists of a set of gestures—for example, rough-hewn and/or aggressive-sounding vocal textures and "dirty" guitar tones. Rock listeners then infer from this set of musical signs that the musician is a member of, and is communicating sincerely with, the rock "community." But, says Frith, this puts the musical cart before the sociological horse since, on one hand, anyone can adopt such musical rhetoric, and, on the other, the rock community does not (again, in any sociological sense) exist prior to the music. Instead, the existence of the community is inferred from the predetermined stylistic markers.[74] By troubling these ideological waters, Newman is doing something bold, valuable, and, in its quiet way, outrageous.

Newman has expressed both admiration and unease regarding rock legend Bruce Springsteen,[75] who, though he writes the occasional persona song, has advanced his career through the cultivation of a no-fooling ethos—the sense that a flannel-shirted everyman is present, giving us the straight lowdown, minus any mediation or artifice. This is the version of rock authenticity that Frith critiques, and which Keir Keightley has identified with the strong Romantic strain in rock culture.[76] This "Bruce Springsteen" is, of course, a highly artificial construction, one whose power has been sufficient at times to obscure the songwriter's own cultural criticisms.[77]

In 1982's "My Life Is Good," Newman makes Springsteen a character in an anecdote told by a supremely affluent, aggressively narcissistic music industry star—one who, for once, invites us to imagine a version of Newman himself. After cataloging various "first-world," 90210-style problems that his privilege makes him plague to, the speaker recounts a meeting at his son's private school with a teacher who has had the temerity to tell him his obnoxious son needs disciplining. The speaker's response? "My life is good, you old bag"[78]—because, according to the values of the new, Reaganomic American dream, it is. But there's more: The speaker proceeds to harangue the teacher about a visit, paid earlier in the day, by the speaker and his wife to a posh Beverly Hills Hotel "Where a very good friend of ours happens to be staying / . . . Mr. Bruce Springsteen." Then, after a tedious account of their shoptalk, the speaker suddenly avers, "And you know what he said to me . . . / He said, 'Rand, I'm tired / How would you like to be the Boss for a while?'" "Well yeah," replies the speaker, whose "Blow, big man, blow" cues a Clarence Clemons-style sax fanfare.[79]

By placing rock stardom—its most "authentic" and "artificial" exponents, respectively—under the sign of economics, by outing both Springsteen and himself as members of rock's monied elite, Newman does "something new under the sun." As so often before, Newman dons a mask—in this case, that of a bullying Beverly Hills plutocrat—so as to expose through artifice something that haunts the social realm. But this time he doesn't stop at the Boss or the Big Man as objects of ridicule: he implicates himself as well. This fits with Frederic Bogel's notion that satire is never fully and safely isolated from its targets.[80] Rather, it contains within itself some trace of what it finds disgusting in the world and then projects that outward for criticism. As the adage goes, it takes one to know one. Robert Browning might not put the point so baldly, but Randy Newman has set it to music.

Notes

1 Sara Dunne, "Randy Newman and the Extraordinary Moral Position," *Popular Music and Society* 16, no. 2 (1992): 53–61.

2 Robert Langbaum, *The Poetry of Experience: The Dramatic Monologue in Modern Literary Tradition* (New York: Random House, 1957), quoted in Dunne, "Randy Newman and the Extraordinary Moral Position," 54.

3 Dunne, "Randy Newman and the Extraordinary Moral Position," 54.

4 Glennis Byron, *Dramatic Monologue* (New York: Routledge, 2003), 100.

5 Paul Zollo, *Songwriters on Songwriting* (New York: Da Capo, 1997), 269.

6 Kevin Courrier, *Randy Newman's American Dreams* (Toronto: ECW, 2005), 1; 250. Courrier takes inspiration from Greil Marcus's 1975 chapter, "Randy Newman: Every Man Is Free," in Marcus's book *Mystery Train: Images of America in Rock 'n' Roll Music* (New York: Penguin, 2015), 90–112.

7 Ibid., 5; 12–16.

8 Monique Morgan, *Narrative Means, Lyric Ends: Temporality in the Nineteenth-Century Long Poem* (Columbus: Ohio State University Press, 2009), 158.

9 James Phelan, *Experiencing Fiction: Judgments, Progressions, and the Rhetorical Theory of Narrative* (Columbus: Ohio State University Press, 2007), 153, qtd. in Morgan, *Narrative Means, Lyric Ends*, 160.

10 M. H. Abrams, *A Glossary of Literary Terms* (Boston: Thomson Wadsworth, 2005), 70–1.

11 "Do Nothing Till You Hear From Me," track 8 on Duke Ellington and his Orchestra, *The Popular Duke Ellington*, Sony, 2017. Italics mine.

12 "Miller's Cave," track 5 on Jack Clement, *For Once and For All*, IRS Nashville, 2014.

13 "Parchman Farm," track 2 on Mose Allison, *Local Color*, Prestige, 1958. For more on Allison and this song, see John Kimsey, "One Parchman Farm or Another: Mose Allison, Irony, and Racial Formation," *Journal of Popular Music Studies* 17, no. 2 (2005): 105–32.

14 "Sunny Afternoon," track 13 on The Kinks, *Face to Face*, Reprise, 1966. Newman has expressed admiration for Townshend's use of the stuttering mod persona at the center of "My Generation." See Zollo, *Songwriters on Songwriting*, 282.

15 Cameron Crowe, "Joni Mitchell Defends Herself," *Rolling Stone*, July 26, 1979, https://www.rollingstone.com/music/music-news/joni-mitchell-defends-herself-61890/.

16 See John Kimsey, "Beatles Unplugged: The White Album in the Shadow of Rishikesh," in *The Beatles through a Glass Onion: Reconsidering the White Album*, ed. Mark Osteen (Ann Arbor: University of Michigan Press, 2019), 72–90.

17 "Triad," track 4 on Crosby, Stills, Nash and Young, *4 Way Street*, Atlantic, 1971.

18 "History: The Singer/Songwriter," *BMI*, October 15, 2020, https://www.bmi.com/genres/entry/history_the_singer_songwriter.

19 Lenny Waronker, "The Man," in *Guilty: 30 Years of Randy Newman* (Rhino Warner Archives, 1998), 7–9. Liner notes. Italics in original.

20 Robert Christgau, review of "Randy Newman: *12 Songs*," October 15, 2020, https://www.robertchristgau.com/get_artist.php?name=Randy+Newman.

21 Waronker, quoted in Timothy White, "Bet No One Ever Hurt This Bad: The Importance of Being Randy Newman," in *Guilty: 30 Years of Randy Newman* (Rhino Warner Archives, 1998), 24. Liner notes.

22 Ibid., 38.

23 White, "Bet No One Ever Hurt This Bad," 28. See note 21.

24 For information on Newman's lengthy Pixar career, see Courrier's two final chapters, note 6.

25 Randy Newman, quote in Siobhan Kane, "Surviving with a Sense of Humor," *Irish Times*, March 1, 2012, https://www.irishtimes.com/culture/music/2.681/surviving -with-a-sense-of-humour-1.472941.

26 Scott Jordan, "Randy Newman," *Offbeat*, November 1, 1998, https://www.offbeat.com /articles/randy-newman/.

27 Newman's vocal delivery reminds me of celebrated white R&B songster Robert Guidry (aka Bobby Charles) of Lake Charles, Louisiana.

28 White, "Bet No One Ever Hurt This Bad," 27.

29 Ibid.

30 Zollo, *Songwriters on Songwriting*, 268.

31 Christgau, "Consumer Guide 9," October 15, 2020, https://www.robertchristgau.com /xg/cg/cg9.php.

32 "Political Science," track 7; "Lonely at the Top," track 2; "Burn On," track 8 on Randy Newman, *Sail Away*, Reprise, 1972.

33 Waronker, "The Man," 13.

34 See note 28.

35 Both Marcus and Courier treat this song at length, not only because of its quality, but because of its connection to American history and culture, "America" being the lens through which both view Newman's work.

36 Peter Winkler, "Randy Newman's Americana," in *Reading Pop: Approaches to Textual Analysis in Popular Music*, ed. Richard Middleton (Oxford: Oxford UP, 2000), 27–57; 32–3; 46–50.

37 "Sail Away," track 1 on Randy Newman, *Sail Away*, Reprise, 1972.

38 Hicks, Brian, "Slavery in Charleston: A Chronicle of Human Bondage in the Holy City," in *The Post and Courier*, April 9, 2011, postandcourier.com.

39 "Rednecks," track 1 on Randy Newman, *Good Old Boys*, Reprise, 1972.

40 Ibid. Newman himself witnessed this actual TV scene when Maddox was a guest on the *Dick Cavett Show* in 1970. See Jordan, note 26. The irony of the lyric is intensified when we note that Newman is himself Jewish, while Cavett is not.

41 Ibid.

42 Ibid.

43 "Black Nationalism Can Set Us Free," *Malcolm X Reference Archive*, https://www .marxists.org/reference/archive/malcolm-x/index.htm.

44 Byron, *Dramatic Monologue*, 100.

45 Michael Omi and Howard Winant, *Racial Formation in the United States: From the 1960s to the 1990s* (New York: Routledge, 1994), xi.

46 Ibid., 68.

47 Paul Laurence Dunbar, "We Wear the Mask," *Poetry Foundation*, https://www .poetryfoundation.org/poems/44203/we-wear-the-mask.

48 Discussions of minstrelsy in relation to rock are widespread. Penetrating analyses often center on the figure of Elvis Presley, and these include Marcus, "Presliad," in *Mystery Train*, 113–66 (see note 6); Alice Walker, "Nineteen Fifty-five," *You Can't Keep A Good Woman Down* (New York: Harcourt, 1981), 3–20; and Michael J. Bertrand, *Race, Rock and Elvis* (Champaign: University of Illinois Press, 2005). On

the overall phenomenon and its conventional framing, the writings of Michael Jarrett are instructive and thought-provoking. See, e.g., "On the Progress of Rock and Roll," a page on the author's website at http://www2.york.psu.edu/~jmj3/saq.htm, and his book *Sound Tracks: A Musical ABC, Volumes 1–3* (Philadelphia: Temple University Press, 1998). For an analysis of minstrelsy in relation to pre-rock American popular music, see Linda Williams, *Playing the Race Card: Melodramas of Black and White from Uncle Tom to O. J. Simpson* (Princeton: Princeton University Press, 2001), 136–86.

49 Courrier quotes Dave Laing on page 9: "Many white singers are attracted to black . . . styles because of the impression of authenticity . . . such styles can convey. . . . Newman seems to be appropriating [them] for the opposite reason: to intensify a sense of alienation, [that is] the gap between himself and the characters. . . . He is laughing at his own blackface act."

50 John A. Sanford, *Evil: The Shadow Side of Reality* (New York: Crossroad, 1986), 60–1.

51 "Real Emotional Girl," track 8 on Randy Newman, *Trouble in Paradise*, Reprise, 1983.

52 Morgan, *Narrative Means, Lyric Ends*, 94.

53 Charlotte Mew, "The Farmer's Bride," in *Anthology of Twentieth-Century British and Irish Poetry*, ed. Keith Tuma (New York: Oxford University Press, 2001), 61.

54 Carol Ann Duffy, "Psychopath," in *Anthology of Twentieth-Century British and Irish Poetry*, ed. Keith Tuma (New York: Oxford University Press, 2001), 852.

55 "You Can Leave Your Hat On," track 11 on Randy Newman, *Sail Away*, Reprise, 1972.

56 Keith Spera, "Singer, Composer Randy Newman Knows the Big Easy Well," *The Times-Picayune*, October 3, 2003, https://www.nola.com/entertainment_life/music/article_5b00fb4d-335a-5097-8edf-7d396f574262.html.

57 Jordan, "Randy Newman."

58 Marcus, "Presliad," 301.

59 Ibid., 98.

60 Roberta G. Wax. "Hit Song 'Short People' Ignites Tall Controversy," *Boca Raton News*, January 25, 1978, 3A.

61 Jordan, "Randy Newman."

62 Melissa Valiska Gregory, "Robert Browning and the Lure of the Violent Lyric Voice: Domestic Violence and the Dramatic Monologue," *Victorian Poetry*, 38, no. 4 (Winter 2000): 491.

63 John Barry, *Rising Tide: The Great Mississippi Flood of 1927 and How It Changed America* (New York: Simon & Schuster, 1998).

64 "Louisiana 1927," track 6 on Randy Newman, *Good Old Boys*, Reprise, 1974.

65 Jim Bradshaw, "Great Flood of 1927," *64 Parishes*, October 15, 2020. https://64parishes.org/entry/great-flood-of-1927.

66 "Randy Newman's Americana," 32–3; 51–5.

67 See note 63.

68 Ibid.

69 "A Monday Night Between Friends—Louisiana 1927," 7:12, YouTube Video, posted by chinolaproductions, November 25, 2006, https://www.youtube.com/watch?v=OxF7AoN6Y9s.

70 Geoffrey Himes, "A Flood of Emotion in Song," *New York Times*, April 27, 2008, https://www.nytimes.com/2008/04/27/arts/music/27hime.html.

106   *Lit-Rock*

71   "Davy the Fat Boy," track 11 on Randy Newman, *Randy Newman Creates Something New Under the Sun*, Reprise, 1968.

72   Roland Barthes, *Mythologies*, trans. Annette Lavers (New York: Hill and Wang, 1972), 142.

73   Simon Frith, "'The Magic that Can Set You Free': The Ideology of the Folk and the Myth of the Rock Community," *Popular Music* 1, no. 1 (1981): 159–60.

74   Ibid., 166–7.

75   Zollo, *Songwriters on Songwriting*, 282. Dunne also writes about this song, though she takes a different tack.

76   Keir Keightley, "Reconsidering Rock," in *The Cambridge Companion to Pop and Rock*, ed. Simon Frith, Will Straw, and John Street (Cambridge: Cambridge University Press, 2001), 133–6.

77   Consider, for instance, Springsteen's persona song "Born in the USA," whose lyrics, read closely, present a critique of US involvement in the Vietnam War, which was used by Ronald Reagan as a campaign song in the 1984 presidential race.

78   "My Life Is Good," track 6 on Randy Newman, *Trouble in Paradise*, Reprise, 1983.

79   Dunne, "Randy Newman and the Extraordinary Moral Position," 57, observes that the sax plays the theme from *The High and the Mighty*. See note 1.

80   Frederic Bogel, *The Difference Satire Makes: Rhetoric and Reading from Johnson to Byron* (Ithaca: Cornell University Press, 2001), 42.

Part III

Aesthetics, Movements, Technology

6

New Wave, European Avant-Gardes, and the Unmaking of Rock Music

Chris Mustazza

Introduction (to De[con]struction)

"*i. Nous voulons chanter l'amour du danger, l'habitude de l'énergie et de la témerité*" ("We choose to sing the love of danger, the life of energy and audacity"):[1] an odd sentiment to be printed in clean font on the front page of Paris's conservative newspaper *Le Figaro* in 1909. Such was the first tenet of F. T. Marinetti's "Futurist Manifesto," his paean to technology and attack on the totality of history, art, and human knowledge. "Put fire to the libraries' shelves! Divert the canals to flood the museums' hoard! . . . Oh! Let the glorious canvases float and bob! Take up your picks and hammers! . . . Compromise the foundations of venerable cities!":[2] Marinetti saw a world so enamored by the old masters, so sedimented with outdated logic and mores that there was only one solution, to burn it all down and start anew. The Manifesto detailed how Futurist art should be made, and that process involved first forgetting everything the artist knew, letting the technologies of the day shape the art. This machine-centric process of creation is a poetics of tinkering, an homage to the bricoleur, in that it derives from a keen knowledge of how machines operate and how they might be hacked to function outside of their intended outputs. By embracing the technologies of the day and seeing them as intrinsic dimensions of formal innovation, adherents to *Il Futurismo* sought to hack their way out of the known human sensorium into a space that could be called posthuman, or perhaps bionic—using technology as a way to extend the human body in search of an expanded experience.

In the same manner that Dada aesthetics reemerged, as Greil Marcus argues,[3] with a new look and sound in 1980s New Wave, so too did the technics of the Italian Futurists in bands like Art of Noise and works like Paul Hardcastle's "19." Taking its name from Luigi Russolo's eponymous text, Art of Noise distributed its work on bandmember Trevor Horn's Zang Tumb Tumb (ZTT) record label, named after a Marinetti poem, which was itself modeled on the onomatopoetic sound of machine gun fire. What did it mean for Horn, J. J. Jeczalik, Gary Langan, Anne Dudley, and Paul Morely to revivify the Italian Futurists in 1983? The Futurists' stock wasn't exactly at its high point given the movement's entanglement with Italian fascism. Without such a direct naming of Marinetti's gang, one might listen to tracks like "Peter Gunn" and "Kiss" and only hear the musical détournement that Marcus traces to the Situationists. But the invocation of Russolo and Marinetti make audible a different dimension: the same technological, tinkerer dynamics that drove Russolo's invention of sound machines and his desire to replace "pure sound" with machinic hums, pulses, and vibrations were present in the synthesizer programming work done by Jeczalik and fellow New Wave artists. Traditional rock and roll was being deconstructed and reassembled as sound collages in a manner akin to the Dadaists, yes, but the methodology employed was distinctly Futurist. The 1980s Futurist renaissance in popular music is rarely discussed, yet it provides a new understanding of this vexed avant-garde, a parallax view that is difficult or impossible to obtain when conversations are confined to the domain of print, visual poetics, and so-called experimental music, as is usually the case with Il Futurismo.

These experimental movements of the early twentieth century—Italian and Russian Futurisms, Surrealism, and various strains of Dada—can be usefully disambiguated to delineate New Wave's literary-aesthetic lineage. For example, the Zurich Dada made so famous by Hugo Ball and directly channeled by the Talking Heads in "I Zimbra" is very different from the linguistic deformations of Kurt Schwitters's Hanover Dada, which was not interested in mockery but rather in a kind of affective linguistic research. "I Zimbra," a reworking of Hugo Ball's Dadaist "Gadji Beri Bimba," draws from the Cheshire-Cat grinning deconstruction of the Zurich Dadaists. Conversely, the audio deformations in Paul Hardcastle's "19" connect more with the Schwitters school of Dada, in that the disintegration of language into its particulate matter is meant to draw attention to how sound shapes meaning. All in all, the late Cold War years created the ideal conditions for the return of the aesthetics of Weimar, Germany, post-Risorgimento Italy, and the anything-goes variety shows of Zurich's Cabaret Voltaire. In other words, when the logics of the day became untenable, the only way forward was to "stop making sense," and New Wave's citations to the early twentieth-century avant-gardes provide a coherent roadmap to the genre's incoherence.

That said, the songs discussed in this chapter do not always sit comfortably alongside their aesthetic forebears. The New Wave artists seem to embrace and reject their influences simultaneously, a dynamic similar to what Tracie Morris terms "handholding" (a term I will come back to in my conclusion). Art of Noise and ZTT go so far as to craft their identities based on the Futurists, while at the same time eschewing core tenets of Futurist poetics. Such a contradiction is generative in that it highlights the limits of influence and defines a space of uneasy acceptance of the past, rather than an easy symbiosis. This chapter takes up these agreements and disagreements, moving between discussions of literature and music, to reveal in New Wave aesthetics— most specifically its engagement with technology, the disordering of dominant language structures, and sensitivity to voice—the revisitation, reconceptualizing, and popularization of what had been largely (and often remains historically fixed as) a literary, "high art" phenomenon.

New Wave, Avant-Gardes, & the Unmaking of Rock Music 111

The Martial Machinery of Sound

In 1913, Futurist painter, inventor, and sonic tinkerer Luigi Russolo wrote a letter to Francesco Balilla Pratella that would become his manifesto "The Art of Noise." The letter begins with a curious historical observation:

> Life in antiquity was all silence. In the nineteenth century, with the invention of machinery, Noise was born. Today, Noise triumphs and reigns supreme over men's sensoria. For many centuries, life went on in silence, or at least quietly. Any noises that interrupted this silence were neither loud, nor prolonged, nor varied. If we set aside exceptional natural occurrences like earthquakes, hurricanes, storms, avalanches, and waterfalls, nature is silent.[4]

Russolo raises here the now-famous noise-sound dichotomy: what precisely is the difference, he incites us to ask, between the two? Rather than a value judgment about which organization of frequencies rises to the level of music, Russolo locates sound in the intentional, the measured, and the hieratic. Noise was something else, something altogether outside the desire to harmonize or praise. Most importantly, it was the byproduct of machinery: the drone of engines, the buzz of electricity, and the clash of construction equipment (sounds that would become central to genres like ambient and industrial music[5]). He contrasted these "noise-sounds" with "pure sounds," the particular frequencies that follow from Western, Pythagorean musical intervals. If music was locked into a finite set of sonic frequencies that correlated to musical notes, how could anything new be created? At best, music could be a finite set of sonic permutations shaped by genre. The question then becomes how an artist can escape this sensorium, find new sonic landscapes, and create new realities through new aesthetics.

Russolo is not calling for a Cagean, aleatory composition. Far from the idea, as with Cage's "4'33," that ambient sounds are not only part of the *werktreue*[6] but can indeed compose it, Russolo is interested specifically in the newfound timbres of machinic sounds as elements of intentional composition. He prescribes that "[w]e want to key and regulate harmonically and rhythmically these very varied noises. Keying the noises is not to say that we should excise all of the temporal and dynamic irregularities from them, but rather that we should give a tone to the strongest of these vibrations."[7] Russolo wanted to score these sonic byproducts "without losing [their] peculiarity, which is to say the timbre that distinguishes [them]."[8] For example, if we take the musical note A and consider its one-lined octave to be 440 hertz, we necessarily privilege this arbitrary frequency and its harmonics by returning to it as a quilting point of measure/reason. Machinic sounds are composed of frequencies that don't map easily onto preexisting, named notes. They could be at any frequency because the engine of a bulldozer, for example, was not designed for its sonorous qualities—this doesn't mean, however, that the sound of the machine is anesthetic; Russolo suggests appropriating this sound and deploying it in a work of artifice. It's precisely because the designers of the machine did not seek to make its sound musical that Russolo sees it as a way to access new terrain in the human sensorium.

What better way to think about the advent of the synthesizer era and the rise of the music programmer than through this Futurist lens? It almost sounds like Russolo is predicting Horn, Jeczalik, et al., as well as the advent of the synthesizer, when he muses: "The variety of noises is infinite. If today, when we have perhaps a thousand different machines we're able to generate a thousand different noises, tomorrow, with the proliferation of new machinery, we will be able to generate ten, twenty, or thirty thousand different noises, not simply simulate them, but combine them limited only by our imaginations."[9] When N. King Adkins describes Art of Noise, he could easily be describing Russolo's vision from his eponymous manifesto: "[the group] wasn't made up of musicians but rather sound engineers and producers working to some extent with electronic instruments, but more often using the production studio itself, its computers, and recording technologies to produce sound."[10]

What does it mean for Adkins to contrast "musicians" with "sound engineers"? In one sense it implies an alignment between musicians and traditional instrumentation and "sound engineers" with technological artifice, which speaks directly to Russolo's differentiation between sound and noise. Of course, many of the greatest rock record producers were themselves accomplished musicians (e.g., consider producers like Phil Spector or, later, Butch Vig). But in the era of New Wave, the frame of discussion moved from the ability to manipulate an instrument to the ability to manipulate an environment. The production studio morphs from a voyeuristic space meant to represent a performance that took place within it to an instrument in and of itself. Phil Spector's "Wall of Sound"—his term for audio production that saturated the frequency spectrum in order to give 1960s pop the impact of a Wagnerian opera—included multi-tracking vocals, uses of physical echo chambers, and other sonic manipulations to make recordings sound much more forceful than the original performance.[11] New Wave's unmaking of rock and pop used the same tools, but the difference was that producers underscored the artifice rather than naturalizing it as part of an "original" recording session. New Wave's postmodernity, its acknowledgment of its own artifice, contributed to claims that it was somehow less natural than rock, demoting the artist from musician to mere sound engineer.

While the use of synthesizers to generate unique tones and the use of the studio as an instrument connect Art of Noise and Horn's ZTT to their Futurist namesakes, certain aspects of their work do run countercurrent to Futurist principles. One example is the use of sampling, or in Situationist parlance, *détournement* (an act of quotation that resituates the original sample within a new context and thus imbues it with a new meaning). With the practice of sampling, the totality of recorded music becomes an archive to be drawn from, which is a far cry from Marinetti's reference to accumulated and stored knowledge as a "cemetery." In other words, a direct invocation with the Futurists might sound like the new tones and timbres of the synthesizer that Russolo predicted, but would not seek a referentiality/intertextuality with prior music, as does "Peter Gunn."[12] Instead, the archive would be discarded, eschewed, and denigrated. Here is the flex point between Dada's collage aesthetics and the Futurists' desire for

New Wave, Avant-Gardes, & the Unmaking of Rock Music   113

invention. The practice of sampling is a paean to the archives that Marinetti sought to burn, but the manner of deployment of the samples, with a kind of ironic, tongue-in-cheek redirection, makes Art of Noise's *détournement* less an instance of authorial citation than a new way of seeing the present through the past and vice versa. Put another way, the reuse of materials and their processing by the sound engineers in the studio allowed the original materials to become new. At the same time, this new context rewrote the archive, forcing listeners to encounter the originals on different ground, a process the Russian Futurists would call defamiliarization. If, for Marinetti, the archive was a cemetery, then New Wave resurrected the dead to forever haunt the original contexts from which they came.

Recordings of Marinetti himself help to illustrate the difference in form between the Futurists and the New Wavers. In his reading of "Definizione di Futurismo," recorded in 1924, fifteen years after the publication of the Manifesto, we can hear the aggressive voicing that listeners might attribute to another strongman leader of the time, Benito Mussolini.[13] As I've argued elsewhere, poetic form can be modeled on apposite vocal genres,[14] and the Marinetti-Mussolini connection is a prime example of the political speech shaping a poetic work. A listener can hear *Il Futurismo's* descent into *Il Fascismo* in the voices attempting to shout down alterity—an alterity that would threaten the uniform binding that is etymologically present in "fascism" (recall that the party's symbol, the fasces, was a bundle of uniform sticks fastened together). Marinetti's voice is projected as if boomed over a densely populated piazza of adherents, synchronizing them in his prosodic rhythms. He does not sound like he wants to "discuss," as his metaphoric cyclists did, anything: he aims to dictate. He performs his authority by controlling the tempo of speech and using the volume of his voice to drown out any other sounds.

Though this formal strongman act is nowhere to be found in New Wave music (if anything it has more resonances with certain strains of industrial music), there is something of a shared fixation on masculinity between *il duce dei Futuristi* and ZTT records—a fixation abundantly present in the lyrics of the label's most prominent signing, Frankie Goes to Hollywood. The band's biggest hit, "Relax," is a lightly encrypted bro-joke about premature ejaculation,[15] while "Welcome to the Pleasuredome" riffs on Samuel Taylor Coleridge's "Kubla Kahn," changing the opening line, "In Xanadu did Kubla Kahn / A stately pleasure-dome decree" to "a pleasuredome erect."[16] One hears, furthermore, in the "hit me with your laser beams" of "Relax" the shooting off of Marinetti's "Zang Tumb Tumb" machine guns. In fact, "The Futurist Manifesto" *begins* with a kind of male climax, where Marinetti crashes his car into a *maternel fossé* (maternal ditch).[17] What brought about this premature ending? An encounter with the status quo: bicyclists, agents of an older, preengine technology that served as obstructions to his unbridled progress: "swerving before me like two equally persuasive and yet contradictory arguments. Their stupid undulations enunciated in my way . . . Ugh, so boring! . . . They cut me off, and to my disgust, I crashed into a ditch."[18] The lack of a combustion engine makes the bicyclists obsolete and marks them as feminine, impeding the speaker's aggressive drive forward. Though their playful irony perhaps separates the lines of "Relax" from the earnest and egocentric contours

114   *Lit-Rock*

of their label's namesake, they maintain a hyper-sexualized connection between masculinity and new technologies.

Perhaps a more perfect application of the techno-martial poetics of Il Futurismo is Paul Hardcastle's "19,"[19] which, much like Art of Noise's work, is shaped around a sound sample. The primary sample in "19" is taken from the audio of *Vietnam Requiem*, a film about the psychological effects of the Vietnam War on its veterans.[20] The authoritative voice of Peter Thomas, who did the voice-over work for many documentaries, declares: "In 1965, Vietnam seemed like just another foreign war. But it wasn't. It was always different in many ways. And so were those who did the fighting. In World War II, the average age of the combat soldier was twenty-six. In Vietnam, it was nineteen."[21] The age of the young people sent to die in Vietnam becomes emphasized through repetition and sonic distortion of the audio sample. The archive from which the sample is drawn becomes, in the manner discussed by Lisa Samuels and Jerome McGann's,[22] deformed, thus enacting the deformed morality of war. War and (audio) technology, here, are intertwined.

"19"'s emphasis on a sample from the archive, its focus on war and masculinity, and its use of sonic manipulation make it the perfect Futurist anti-Futurist work. Rather than "singing the love of danger," as Marinetti had done, Hardcastle uses technology to focus on the persistent horrors of war. "19" reminds the listener that "[a]lmost eight-hundred-thousand men are still fighting the Vietnam War" due to the then newly named Post Traumatic Stress Disorder (PTSD). Hardcastle differentiates Vietnam from the Second World War to speak to futurity that might learn from its pasts. The sonic disintegration of words like "destruction" and "nineteen" in the song use the sound technologies of the day as mimetic of the age of machine warfare, which began with the Great War. Technological processes were making all kinds of new things possible, from the mechanized efficiency of death through the very song the listener was hearing. There was a continuum of composition between art and war, the same one Marinetti identified and pushed toward its collapse into Italian fascism.

A particularly fascinating aspect of the song is its use of female voices to sing counterpoint harmonies. Evocative of a 1960s Brill Building girl group arrangement, as used in songs written by Jeff Bruce and Ellie Greenwich and songs produced by Jerry Lieber and Mike Stoller, these sections of the song present a devastating irony. What does it mean to use the tone of a song like "Da Doo Ron Ron" within a song about mass casualties and irreparable psychological harm from the horrors of war? Listeners are reminded that they are being entertained by, and finding pleasure in, the sounds of a song about these topics. The sweet, harmonic tones of the voices become almost pathological, suggesting that listeners need to inhabit the discomfort of the world they have created even while seeking an alternative to it. The voices are not meant to temper the masculinist aggression "19" grapples with, but instead to make the topics more troubling by connecting them to the poppy mundanity of the music of the previous era, the music that bore less and less of a connection to contemporary realities.

The tone of "19" is also distinctly Futurist in its direct and oppositional mode. One does not find the mocking tone of the Dadaists here, only an overt political engagement devoid of playful irony. In many ways, the samples are not *detourned* but rather returned as citations to works that would otherwise be relegated to the category of documentary edutainment through their generic markers. By taking the deep, authoritative voice of Peter Thomas, which listeners would understand generically as "documentary voice," and placing it against a synthesizer-generated background, the domain of information becomes explicitly aestheticized while still moored to the sonic markers of "truth" and historicity. In other words, listeners of the time (and now), even if they could not name Peter Thomas, would recognize his voice as didactic, implicitly built upon evidence and research. The sample comes to stand in for a contemporary understated version of Marinetti's booming dictatorial voice, which beckoned adherents through its self-assured bombast. If in the contemporary moment, an understated voice has come to connote intellectualism, as discussed in Marit MacArthur's work on academic poetry readings and so-called "poet voice,"[23] Thomas's voice invokes such a genre while retaining the traditional markers of authority: a deep voice, declamatory phrasing (rather than intonations that would belie doubt or the possibility of multiplicity, cf. "uptalk"), and so on. Marinetti was thus deformed and detourned through Hardcastle's sampling, though in a manner of historical anti-citation that Marinetti himself might have employed.

One of the formal musical innovations of "19" was the use of audio technology to create repetitive sound structures in keywords like "nineteen" and "destruction." This lingual deformation returns us to the particular mélange of Dadaist and Futurist (in this case both Italian and Russian Futurist) aesthetics that came together to fuel New Wave's resistance to traditional musical modes of sentimentality. Having a sense of these variant strains will highlight the complex interaction between variants of New Wave, including Hardcastle's sampling of bellicosity and the Talking Heads' desire to stop making sense. Here, in the space of sound abstracted from lexical referentiality, we can hear the echoes of some of the more important poets of the early twentieth century, including Hugo Ball, Kurt Schwitters, and Velimir Khlebnikov.

Before returning to "19," let's contrast it with a couple of other examples, the first being the Talking Heads' adaptation of Hugo Ball's great Dadaist sound poem "Gadji Beri Bimba" in "I Zimbra."[24] Even though it was eventually printed in *De Stijl*, "Gadji Beri Bimba" was written for poetic performance in the Cabaret Voltaire. In true Dadaist style, Ball satirized the sacrosanct nature of public address through a costume evocative of a bishop and a kind of incantation that relates to the speaking of the Catholic mass in Latin. By refusing traditional denotation through modeling the poem on the cadences of speech, Ball allowed the audience to tarry with the sonic contours of speech sounds without the weight of traditional semantics, to hear a foregrounded prosody as mellifluous without the burden of "content." As when listening to a language one does not understand, listening to the poem allows the listener to focus just on the sounds of the words. Or, alternatively, the experience of listening might mimic hearing muffled voices behind a door (or the tromboney "voice" of Charlie Brown's teacher), where the feeling of speech allows us to table the specific meaning while retaining its sense.

"I Zimbra," via "Gadji Beri Bimba," is marked by one strain of Dadaist thought— that which burlesques the status quo through spectacle and mockery. Another kind of Dada, the work of Kurt Schwitters, presents an alternative experimental mode. Schwitters's *Ursonate*,[25] one of the greatest experimental works of the twentieth century, renders speech sounds as a musical composition. It would be too simplistic to fold *Ursonate* in with "Gadji Beri Bimba" just because they both sound like "made-up languages." Schwitters's aim in his sonata is to access a prelingual sound symbolism, to connect with the affective response latent in phonemes and spoken prosodies.[26] Like Ball's work, it also reaches back, but not back into the past in search of something more visceral; Schwitters's work reaches back to when a child first begins to acquire language. Put another way, the sheer sounds of speech, devoid of denotative meaning, can have an emotional effect on the listener. This effect may be from the style of voicing (the voice may remind us of someone we do or do not like), or it could be from particular word sounds. The kind of Dada that Marcus discusses, that which was passed to us through the Situationists, owes more to the Ball school than to Schwitters's school, but both can be found in the genre.

In "19," the transformation of the speaking voice to sound mechanical or computer generated serves a modernist aim of dampening overt sentimentality with detachment. And while the repetitions and deformations of language in the song certainly bear the connotation of glitch/mechanical failure (a skipping record) that enacts a broken societal system, they also serve to make us aware of language's particulate matter. As the word "in" is both truncated and repeated, the listener becomes attuned to the sonic contours of the word rather than its referential meaning or syntactical function as a preposition.[27] By slotting it into the synthesizer-generated beat, the word's simple prosody makes it a rhythmical sixteenth note rather than a word. It thus sits as the intersection of a linguistic focus on the sound of the word and a kind of onomatopoetic enactment of the machinery of war, a la "Zang Tumb Tumb." This is popular music ("19" reached number one on the UK singles chart in 1985) enacting the fragmented, hyper-self-referential approach to sound and language most typically associated with early twentieth-century avant-garde poets.

Returning to Russolo's dichotomy of sound-to-noise, the scored sound of this piece gives way to noise, the deformed language. Looking at Schwitters's work, the opposite is true: from a scored arrangement of guttural and glottal emanations meant to transcend language, recognizable speech arises. Is this just the way abstraction works—that onto ostensible disorder the mind imposes an order—or is it impossible to render even made-up sounds outside the bounds of one's linguistic conditioning? Hard to say, but listeners familiar with the German language will most certainly hear in *Ursonate* ostensible words reaching up out of the viscus, primordial material. For example, Schwitters performs a phrase that sounds like *rakete bebe* ("rocket to vibrate," or "missile to shake"). These lines obviously conjure the era of modern warfare that shook Europe during the Great War, but they are presented as a linguistic abstraction. Tracie Morris's incredible recreation of *Ursonate* uses a kind of sonic transliteration, or perhaps homophonic translation (cf. Louis Zukofsky's homophonic translations of Catullus) to render the word "baby" from these lines, a word that will be audible to English speakers. The influence of Schwitters's *Ursonate* on "19" is audible through this inversion. While Schwitters attempted a Futurist endeavor of creating from a tabula rasa, to make a language that was disconnected from the history of linguistic morphology, Hardcastle starts at the other end of the spectrum and tries to defamiliarize the known—in terms of language, in terms of music, and in terms of samples from the archive, all as a martial assault on the idea of war. The song is unironic, it is unequivocal, and its mode of engagement is head-on.

Between Art of Noise and Paul Hardcastle an expansive range of artists populates the New Wave genre, from those that employed "the self-conscious 'art' posturing of . . . New York bands of the period such as Television or Talking Heads"[28] through those whose approach was perhaps more conducive to mainstream marketing and youthful fans. Bands like Duran Duran, Joy Division, and Blondie, for example, while classified typically as New Wave, extended the generation-long reliance on a singular front-person who exuded sexuality and confidence. Others, like Art of Noise, however, backgrounded the individual in favor of the collective. Bands like Wham! seem to usher in a gleeful "poptimism" while others, like Bauhaus and Romeo Void, extend the sneering iconoclasm of punk. Across this eclectic range is audible many of the agons that animated the culture of the early twentieth century: self vs. collective, human vs. machine, irony vs. sincerity, and absorption vs. distance. All of these artists respond to their aesthetic forebears differently and have extended literary history into music, which is now extending back into literature.

Conclusion: Handholding the Futurists

Influence is not always agreement. In her collection *handholding: 5 kinds*,[29] Tracie Morris introduces the term "handholding" to describe a complex engagement with an influence, an engagement that can exist in the space between respect, resentment, and reckoning. Handholding can connote affection or care; it can serve as a guiding or stabilizing force; it can be an act of aggression or defense. In her handholding with—or sampling of—Gertrude Stein, Morris tarries with problematic inheritances. She finds Stein to be an important aesthetic precursor to her own work, but must also accept that some of Stein's work, particularly "Melanctha" from *Three Lives*, is hurtful and harmful. A similar dynamic can be said to unfold with the influence of the Futurists on New Wave. Even groups like Art of Noise and others signed to ZTT who willfully connected with Marinetti's appetite for destruction must also accept that, much like familial descent, aesthetic descent is not always without its faults. We might say that Trevor Horn, Paul Hardcastle, David Byrne, and others of this era were, much like Morris, creating handholdings, with the full range of connotations that come with that term. It's not enough to say that the Italian Futurists and various strains of Dada were an influence on New Wave. In each case, the manner of that influence is complex and varied, and each artist grappled with the problems of inheritance in a different way. In short, these dialogic encounters are not for the explicit purpose of establishing literary capital; some of them may even be forms of attempted divestiture.

118   *Lit-Rock*

Of course, New Wave is a kind of catchall generic term, but however one prefers to define its boundaries, it is clear that the varying experimental art forms of the early twentieth century and so-called Interwar period were heavily present in popular music of the late 1970s through the 1980s. I provide a number of examples here for the sake of discussion, but there are many others one could point to. For example, "Mittageisen" ("Metal Postcard")—Siouxsie and the Banshees' musical ekphrasis of John Heartfield's photocollage "Hurrah, die butter ist Allah!," whose host album takes its name from Edvard Munch's impressionistic paragon *The Scream*—brings together tenets of Zurich Dada, Italian Futurism, and Surrealism into a bitter kind of Juvenalian satire. And Devo's comically futuristic look and reframing of elevator music in *E-Z Listening* seem befitting of the Cabaret Voltaire or Chicago's Dill Pickle Club (where many American modernist poets performed spectacles of literature). Perhaps this proliferation of handholdings can be attributed to an impending dread of mutually assured nuclear destruction, a shared sense of malaise that had precedent in the Interwar period. If, by applying Paul Saint-Amour's concept of a pre-traumatic stress disorder that stems from a perpetual interwar period,[30] New Wave can be said to connect with its modernist forebears, it makes all the sense in the world that these artists would come to redeploy, reimagine, and at times redirect back, the political-aesthetic poetics of the previous interwar.

In our current moment, we are seeing a resurgence of interest in New Wave. Whether Depeche Mode's induction into the Rock-and-Roll Hall of Fame signifies that the band has been appropriated by the mainstream music it sought to resist is an open question. But there is no denying that the music of the period integrated the technology-fueled dreams of Russolo into the common vernacular and serves as the precedent to genres like ambient music, industrial, and perhaps even vaporwave (though the latter is animated more by nostalgia for primitive technologies, produced with modern technologies). And so, even if they are not named or referenced as in the 1980s, Ball, Schwitters, Russolo, Marinetti, and many others continue to reverberate through popular music. We would do well to ask ourselves why. What affinities does the current moment of Covid-19 lockdowns, deep political discord, and perpetual anticipation of disaster have to the era of the AIDS crisis, mutually assured destruction, and trickle-down economics, as well as to the Interwar, Depression-Era world that trailed the Industrial Revolution? And, more importantly, how can the legacy of these persistent aesthetics inform the ways we cope, resist, and coexist? In other words, how can we filter out the sound to hear the noise?

Notes

1 F. T. Marinetti, "Le Futurisme," *Le Figaro* (Paris), February 20, 1909, https://gallica .bnf.fr/ark:/12148/bpt6k2883730. All translations are my own.
2 Ibid., 1.
3 Greil Marcus, *Lipstick Traces: A Secret History of the Twentieth Century* (Cambridge: Belknap, 1989).

New Wave, Avant-Gardes, & the Unmaking of Rock Music　　　119

4　Luigi Russolo, *L'Arte Dei Rumori* (Milan: Edizioni Futuriste di "Poesia," 1916), 9.
5　See Jason James Hanley, "Metal Machine Music: Technology, Noise, and Modernism in Industrial Music 1975–1996" (doctoral dissertation, Stony Brook University, 2011).
6　Lydia Goehr argues that the musical work emerged as a standalone object, rather than as background for other arts, in the late eighteenth century. Lydia Goehr, "Being True to the Work," *The Journal of Aesthetics and Art Criticism* 47, no. 1 (1989): 55–67.
7　Russolo, *L'Arte Dei Rumori*, 14.
8　Ibid.
9　Ibid., 16.
10　M. King Adkins, *New Wave: Image is Everything* (New York: Palgrave Macmillan, 2015), 102–3.
11　Mick Brown, *Tearing Down the Wall of Sound: The Rise and Fall of Phil Spector* (New York: Vintage, 2007), 115.
12　Art of Noise, "Peter Gunn," track 8 on *In Visible Silence*, China Records, 1986.
13　F. T. Marinetti, "Definizione di Futurismo," track 1 on PennSound, 1924, https://writing.upenn.edu/pennsound/x/Marinetti.php.
14　Chris Mustazza, "Processing Poets' Voices: Machine(-Aided) Listening and the Poetry Archive" (invited lecture, UC San Diego, October 10, 2019), https://library.ucsd.edu/news-events/events/processing-poets-voices/.
15　Frankie Goes to Hollywood, "Relax," track 3 on *Welcome to the Pleasuredome*, ZTT Records, 1984.
16　Ibid., "Welcome to the Pleasuredome," track 2 on *Welcome to the Pleasuredome*, ZTT Records, 1984.
17　Marinetti, "Le Futurisme," 1.
18　Ibid.
19　Paul Hardcastle, "19," track 2 on *Paul Hardcastle*, Chrysalis, 1985.
20　*Vietnam Requiem*, directed by Bill Couturié (1982; New York: ABC News, 1984).
21　Hardcastle, "19."
22　Jerome McGann and Lisa Samuels, "Deformance and Interpretation," in *Radiant Textuality: Literary Studies after the World Wide Web*, ed. Jerome McGann (New York: Palgrave, 2001), 105–36.
23　Marit MacArthur, "Monotony, the Churches of Poetry Reading, and Sound Studies," *PMLA* 131, no. 1 (2016): 38–63.
24　The Talking Heads, "I Zimbra," track 1 on *Fear of Music*, Sire, 1979.
25　Kurt Schwitters, *Ursonate*, tracks 1 and 2 on PennSound Kurt Schwitters, PennSound, 1924–32, https://writing.upenn.edu/pennsound/x/Schwitters.php.
26　For more on Cognitive Poetics and the how the brain treats poetic language, see Reuven Tsur, *What Makes Sound Patterns Expressive?* (Durham: Duke University Press, 1992).
27　The song's use of glitched repetitions parallels, for example, the activity of repeating the same word over and over until it begins to sound strange and foreign.
28　Brown, *Tearing Down the Wall of Sound*, 306.
29　Tracie Morris, *Handholding: 5 Kinds* (Tucson: Kore, 2016).
30　Paul K. Saint-Amour, *Tense Future: Modernism, Total War, Encyclopedic Form* (Oxford: Oxford University Press, 2015).

7

Cycling on Acid

The Literariness of Altered Experiences in Psychedelic Rock

Tymon Adamczewski

Thinking about rock's reliance on literature brings to mind disparate forms of experimentation in the 1960s, with artists like Bob Dylan or the Beatles serving perhaps as the most obvious practitioners. This can hardly be surprising, as their lasting contribution to complicating the form and content of what was then known as the "pop song" certainly invites a literary perspective. In these examples, it is primarily the lyrics—which readily lend themselves to the study of poetics and metaphors, or encourage investigations of intertextuality—that constitute the relationship and most common point of interest. But lyrics are not the sole nodal point between music and literature: psychedelia—the decade's endemic, hallucinogenic-inspired cultural trend—intriguingly bridges the two art forms in terms of inspiration and process rather than through the end-products of written and recorded texts.

Most accounts of the psychedelic phenomenon focus on the interplay between the auditory and the visual as rooted in drug-inspired sensations. However, since both music and literature can be seen as modes of registering and translating experience into a different medium, it makes sense to look at psychedelia and its musical production in the context of literature-like practice, or even to see it *as* literature. This approach becomes particularly salient if literature is seen as a discourse with the potential to transgress its own formal or thematic limitations,[1] or when we recognize that the protean qualities of psychedelia can be regarded as performative manifestations of perceived reality. Above all, artistic production of this sort can be viewed as a text intended to affect the listener and to instigate transformations in the audience. In this sense, the genre's immersive qualities echo Nicholas Royle's understanding of literary texts as "veering,"[2] or typified by a certain push-pull dynamic transcending the very form of their medium.

The discussion in this chapter is based on thinking about psychedelia in terms drawn from musical and sociological discourses, but it goes beyond identifying merely stylistic features. It is premised on Scott B. Montgomery's proposition that psychedelia (in music and other media) be perceived in plural terms as "an approach" or "an ethos," as "different and distinct formulations of the psychedelic intent and spirit around the world," and thereby as "a cognitive/philosophical endeavor."[3] Psychedelia can also be seen as a discourse attempting to explore both the self and the language, or signifying practices in general, used to represent such an exercise. To see the importance of literature through the LSD-colored haze is to view it as a textual form capable of both recording and producing (altered) experiences—a potential shared with psychedelic music. This capacity does not stem simply from the particular stylistics employed in a given text, be they intertextual features or a reliance on particularly literary poetics. While traits like these should not be ignored, this chapter addresses psychedelia's affinity with literature as stemming from the very constitution of both of these discourses and their propensity for effecting immersion. It also frames psychedelic stylistics in the context of selected tenets of modernist literary practices to argue that the early manifestations of the genre's literary roots (Syd Barrett's Pink Floyd) and their more recent offshoots (Sleep) can be seen as two versions of modernistic-like experimentation and filtering of experience; although articulated in distinct poetics, they share a reliance on altered states of mind and an emphasis on evoking a synaesthetic dimension in their compositions.

Reading Psychedelia

Despite the customary difficulties with the genre's definition, the literary aspects of psychedelia and the music generally classified as such rarely receive more than a passing mention. Instead, the literary component is often downplayed within a taxonomy of historically specific artistic trends, which stress the importance of drug-induced experiences, or, alternatively, a sociological focus on spirituality, experimentation, or escapism. Paul Hegarty and Martin Halliwell, to give one example, see psychedelia as an iconic 1960s "self-referential cultural mode," whose celebration of "the experience of sensual absorption" and potential for audience immersion come "at the expense of the contemplative and cerebral spaces that would characterize progressive rock."[4] It thus seems that the literary connections of psychedelic music are much more difficult to illustrate than, say, those of prog—a genre that was much more open to using literature as an underlying narrative for music production.

As is the case with most attempts at providing a definition, looking for psychedelia's particular features requires an essentialist perspective that views the phenomenon as a style rather than an experience.[5] For many listeners, such music simply cannot exist without a corresponding hallucinogenic dimension, whether in the very recording of altered sensations or by producing them in the audience. Such associations of the drug-driven stylistic are pretty well established within the field of music and have become synonymous with what might be called fluid poetics. Unconstrained musical structure, extended duration of the composition's elements, odd time signatures, emphasis on improvisation, experimentation in sound processing, the introduction of non-Western tonal variations and instrumentation—traits like these have morphed into the now-familiar idiom which Sheila Whitely classifies as "psychedelic coding."[6]

Musical poetics of this sort may also develop forms of sensory synaesthesia, expressed through the instrumental parts of tracks being as important as the whole. In this case, emphasis is placed on the present moment and on the extended duration of the passing of time, which contributes to the oneiric and magical atmosphere, aptly termed by Russel Reising as the "melting clocks" and "the hallways of always."[7]

From a broader (experiential) point of view, however, psychedelic art does not necessarily have to be about drug use at all, but "can include any form of art or practice explicitly concerned with the expansion and exploration of consciousness."[8] This may be especially true once we recall the Greek etymology of the term (Gr. *psyche, delein*), which signifies mind-manifesting. Psychedelic forms of expression can thus be synonymous with various types of art ("cosmic," "transcendental," or "visionary"), particularly when they are "indebted to the modern movements of abstraction and surrealism."[9] W. B. Yeats, for instance, provides an easy example of an artist attempting to tap into the unconscious without any extensive aid of drugs. Similarly, recording artists like Robert Fripp, Frank Zappa, and Steven Wilson publicly admitted to being sober, despite creating music that could easily fill any psychedelic bingo card.

At first glance, literature's underlying role in psychedelic stylistics and musical production is not specifically pivotal. Although it seems subservient to the musical modes of expression, on closer inspection both discourses overlap significantly. The psychedelic coding in a song or a composition can not only add to the exploration of the subconscious but also encourage the perception of these texts as constructs with their own peculiar story-world(s). Similarly, even the most bizarre and mind-bending poetics operate within a self-contained dimension activated by the hazy bracketing of reality that psychedelic art offers. Musically, such compositions may reach out to the listener through flowing, unsteady structures or tonal coloring. This gradual unfolding or progression brings to mind narrative terms, even though the tendency in analyses of musical tales (tonal and post-tonal) seems to privilege lyrical discourse at the expense of story.[10] We expect a classic like the Beatles' "Tomorrow Never Knows," for instance, to be described in multi-sensory terms indicative of the synergy between the lyrics and physical or emotional sensations: "Severing and swooping through the sound mix, the overdubs captured the ebbs and flows, zaps and zings of LSD's perceptual overload, while the overall drone—established on the final version by the opening tambour—harmonized with the synaesthetic lyrics: 'Listen to the color of your dreams.'" No wonder, then, the song was felt to have positively shattered pop's linear time, or perceived simply as a simulation of the acid trip.[11]

While there is nothing terribly wrong with seeking literature's role in psychedelic rock through the medium of the lyrics, such practice excludes nontextual aspects of artistic communication, like the commodification that accompanies music's growing popularity. This process could already be seen in the genre's heyday and in the hallmarks of popular poetics of the time, which were quickly absorbed by the mainstream and applied to numerous psyched-up, yet otherwise distinctly *pop*, songs (e.g., "Eight Miles High and" "I Just Dropped in [To See What My Condition was In]") or employed by such artists like the Yardbirds, the 13th Floor Elevators, the Amboy Dukes, and Donovan). In fact, the stylistic combination of sights and sounds proved to be so widespread and effective that "by 1966 people who never had a psychedelic experience *thought* they had a fairly good idea what one was like" just by listening to the records.[12] Literary history, whose substance-experimenting authors include, but are not limited to, Charles Baudelaire and Edgar Allen Poe, might also be said to have provided new and distinct relations as commodities by way of cheaper, mass-produced paperbacks and contemporary cover art, and as a textual resource for progressive rock artists. The focus on lyrics, however, has obscured the context in which such experiences were recorded and the framing used for channeling hallucinogenic sensations into cultural texts or their receptions.

Seemingly detached from any literary roots, the cultural distribution of psychedelics was in fact quite paradoxical. The post-war era saw the spread of drugs as invariably tied to *both* mainstream and alternative cultural production, and was advanced via such disparate cultural channels as psychiatry and the military. If the roots of psychedelic art lie in writing down one's sensory experiences, then in the case of 1960s psychedelia the filtering of the popularity of drugs, LSD in particular, indeed owes a lot to artists and people of letters. While this does not mean that drug experiences were only given their cultural impetus through the likes of Aldous Huxley's drug memoir *The Doors of Perception* (1953)—a title supplying Jim Morrison and company with their band name and thereby broadening the circulation of psychedelia as a musical-verbal experience—drugs became an element of a cultural zeitgeist at a time when literature still could provide important forms of shared artistic, intellectual, and emotional experience.[13] Literary works would also supply drug advocates with the conceptual and symbolic language to express characteristic ideals of the time: a sense of collectiveness, an urge to explore the self or to provoke civil dissent and subversion. Huxley, referencing William Blake, was only one of several important figures connected with the written word who spearheaded the process of promoting psychedelics within the globalizing Anglophone culture of the 1960s. Others, like Ken Kesey, were also writers or, like Timothy Leary, drew heavily on literary production despite being trained in a different field. The fact that these key personages offered contrasting models of spreading the word about LSD does not significantly change the overall picture; Huxley's heights of culture, top-down approach, and Leary's seemingly all-American, democratic thinking about the psychedelic experience can be similarly situated in relation to literature and its cultural role at the time.

The "acid pope," as Leary was dubbed, modeled his countercultural perceptions of drugs and many of his activities on the work of the Beat poets and the Eastern mysticism of the *Tibetan Book of the Dead*. Despite its countercultural allure, his famous slogan "Turn on, tune in, drop out" should not be dismissed as mere drug-infused escapism.[14] Instead, it should be seen as a direct reference to the veering effect of psychedelia in general. Leary's maxim, which became a 1960s leitmotif and an invitation to let go and open one's mind to both an exploration of the individual psyche and participation in a shared unconsciousness, also served to de-regulate the senses of the listening public— very much in the same way as the sound of the guitar, the Hammond organ, or the slowdown in music contributed to the immersion offered by psychedelia. In this way,

124   *Lit-Rock*

the turning (on) evoked by the catchphrase links directly with the perpetual dynamics emanating from literature.

In fact, Nicholas Royle's proposition[15]—that literature be understood as a shape-shifting and reality-changing discourse—seems premised on objectives similar to those informing psychedelia. The critic's deconstructive conceptualization of *veering*, as simultaneously a noun and a verb, points to everything that is equivocal about texts and suggests multiple contexts or dimensions of reading. While the French root of the word (*virer*) calls upon the activities of turning and spinning, it may also mean swerving or changing direction, which corresponds to the rapid changes in meaning or sense-making as one's eyes run through sentences on a page. Yet, the veering spiral movement evoked by the term represents more than the push-pull dynamics of forces stemming from interacting with a text; the critic recognizes such cognates as *re*volution or en*vir*onment—terms particularly handy in describing the 1960s and its cultural soundtrack. This relationship was most pronounced in the decade's endemic format: the LP, with its 33 1/3 *revolutions* per minute (RPM), from which the fusion of words and music recorded on vinyl effectively emanated. In this sense, Dylan's protest songs (or, for that matter, those that more outwardly reference drugs, like "Mr. Tambourine Man" or "Rainy Day Women #12 and 35") were not revolutionary simply by way of their content but also because they made their audiences veer, instigating, in turn, the transformation of their social, cultural, and political surroundings. This also corresponds to the paradoxical perception of the mid-1960s understanding of pop, which "was no longer simple commerce, teen romance or good times but something else: a total immersive experience, the popular form that, out of all the arts truly reflected contemporary life."[16]

While seemingly detached from the toils of life and often seen as merely playful, psychedelic distancing managed to achieve an important thing: it exposed the veiled strangeness of the surrounding world. Idiosyncratic multimedia stylistics were hence more readily employed in making words, the building blocks of literature, into items of secondary importance. Curiously enough, the genre's synesthetic stylistics, which privileged the visual and the auditory over verbal expression, were recognized as part of a long-established, often ritualistic, cultural tradition. Although there have been some attempts at tapping into this tradition by way of parallels between psychedelia and poetry,[17] applying the concept of veering onto a broader field of cultural texts, including musical pieces, is instrumental in pushing beyond lyrics. Instead of focusing on verbal literariness, Royle's proposition can help to recognize the musical text's immersive potential, its positioning and dislocation of audiences within an ever-widening, dazzling spin:

> The age of space is moving us outward . . . the age of drugs in moving us inward. And the age of new mass arts is moving us upward, inward, outward, and forward. In this era of exploration, there are many breeds of navigators, but few more daring than the poet-musicians who are leading our pop music in new directions.[18]

Music, in this description of cultural "veering," seems to be taken over by poetry and poets, but despite the elitism and a sense of cultural prestige, viewing psychedelia in this way usefully links it to the performative. This does not mean simply pointing to the hazy-colored stylistics that the decade is typically associated with, but emphasizing such activities as a countercultural theatrical performance or the period's burgeoning processual understanding of art.[19] Importantly, all of these aspects echoed a modernist-derived interest in the estrangement of the everyday and a striving for altered means of perception.

Psychedelia's Modernism

One such artistically estranged everyday object was certainly the bicycle. In fact, it was the experience of riding a bike after taking LSD that was to prefigure the recording of altered states of mind. What seemed like an ordinary situation involving a mundane object occasioned a full-blown acid trip, which contributed to a major change in contemporary culture. Albert Hofmann, the Swiss chemist who on April 16, 1943, accidentally ingested LSD and then cycled home is reported to have perceived on his way "an uninterrupted stream of fantastic pictures, extraordinary shapes with intense, kaleidoscopic play of colors."[20] Although not literary in themselves, experiences like these were subsequently conceptualized in a literary language, serving as inspiration for several psychedelic tracks. Even the accounts of events related to this celebrated bike ride would employ literary allusions. For example, Jim DeRogatis reports that the son of Hofmann's boss, Dr. Werner Stoll, "found himself swept away" after taking the drug "by images of Edgar Allan Poe's maelstrom."[21] As if to channel these earlier testimonies into the world of 1960s pop, songs like Tomorrow's "My White Bicycle" and Pink Floyd's "Bike" would create their own bike-inspired psychedelia.

The first of these almost openly references Hofmann's acid ride. Beyond the sonic effects typical for the genre (echo, clangy guitar, phasing, whispering, and reverse playback), however, its fundamental structure remains fairly traditional. It is made up of the usual structural items (verse, chorus, etc.) through which altered experiences are merely referenced. While the hazy states provide a recognizable stylistic call-out, they are neither challenged nor particularly probed within the musical form. The song offers a psyched-up recording of cycling as an experience, describing the individual sensations of speeding past people (including the obligatory policeman as an authority figure) or feeling gusts of wind and rain falling on one's face. In acknowledgment of the track's (and the bike's) cultural relevance, Joe Boyd quite recently used this song for the title of his own book on 1960s music-making, which begins by both recognizing its power in live performance and classifying the track as "a tribute to the free transport provided by Amsterdam's revolutionary *provos*."[22] That said, the song never ventures musically beyond the customary limits of a popular ditty, and fits ultimately into a strand of psychedelic songs like "Shapes of Things" (Yardbirds) and "Eight Miles High" (the Byrds), which attempt to negotiate hints of psychedelia within the standard pop tune.

If the psychedelic coding in Tomorrow's number existed mostly in the lyrics in tandem with a smattering of conventional sound effects, and perhaps its fetishization of the eponymous object, Pink Floyd's "Bike" offers something radically different. Here, the pharmacist's ride is only alluded to, in a more convoluted fashion, with the vehicle becoming a stepping-stone to what sounds like an auditory exploration of outer space. Although both tracks are similar in length, almost half of Floyd's composition is taken up by the seemingly incoherent sonic experiments that follow the vocal part, which ends halfway through the song. This obviously recalls the Beatles' classic "Strawberry Fields Forever," released earlier the same year, yet represents a lengthier and more speculative approach to the very nature and fabric of sound. The Fab Four's psychedelic coding, at least at that stage, was steeped in nostalgia and, like its sister song "Penny Lane," thematizes the past and ambience of particular places.[23] English psychedelia was in this sense different from its American counterpart—it explored the universe of childhood, with its tradition of nursery rhymes filtered through nonsense poetics of the likes of Lewis Carroll, while simultaneously merging its backward-looking tendencies with the melting-pot atmosphere and cutting-edge vivacity of Swinging London. This is perhaps most evident in Syd Barrett's early work with Pink Floyd as registered on the band's first two singles ("Arnold Lane," "See Emily Play"—both from 1967), which portray eccentric and imaginative individuals whose bizarre, personal inner worlds are populated by an intertextual array of characters.

The most complete, literary-derived artistic statement in this respect, however, is *The Piper at the Gates of Dawn* (1967), on which the previously discussed "Bike" appears as a closing track. Using the familiar imagery and setting of an English pastoral landscape (a barley field with a scarecrow), the album reveals an eerie underside filtered through a disturbed psyche, only to take these fragmented elements on an intergalactic space trip ("Interstellar Overdrive").[24] The explicit and tacit range of literary references here includes J. R. R. Tolkien ("The Gnome") and children's literature ("Mathilda Mother"), with Kenneth Grahame's *Wind in the Willows* furnishing the overarching intertext, and rounded out with echoes of Poe and Jules Verne.

Even in such a context, however, "Bike" itself presents a weird sort of love song. The singer's detailed description of this otherwise ordinary object seems to trigger an enumeration of properties that might win the affection of the song's presumably female addressee. As the lyrics progress, so the bike—described with a kind of monomaniac concentration—turns out to be only one of several things identified by the singer (cape, mouse, gingerbread men), conceptualized either as offerings to the potential partner or as items somehow significant for the protagonist. Accompanied by disturbing, carnival-like piano sounds, the recurrent chorus highlights the singer's subjective world, into which he believes the girl would fit. As is typical of Barrett's poetics, this romantic build-up is continually deconstructed through the detached and needlessly detailed focus on selected parts of the bike (a basket, a bell, "things to make it look good"[25]). Interestingly, the preoccupation quickly dissolves (at the end of the first verse) when it turns out that it is *borrowed*. Barrett's stylized vocal delivery suggests alienation from the lyrics themselves and corresponds to the strange atmosphere of this bizarre serenade: an invitation to the singer's possibly deranged story-world in which adult implications are articulated by means of an infantile poetics. The lyrical style, that is, evokes the poetics of nursery rhymes, suggesting an underdeveloped or child-like psyche indicative of an insular psychological world, made even more disturbing not only through the deadpan delivery but by the lyric's sexual implications.

Cycling on Acid   127

The meticulous focus on an object's details, together with a particular sense of estrangement, very much recalls the ambitions and strategies of literary modernism; a similar filtering of individual objects through a character's psyche marks the works of T. S. Eliot, James Joyce, Virginia Woolf, and William Carlos Williams. In its stitching of disparate images toward an overarching emotion (Eliot's "objective correlative") and explorations of the relationship between artistic imagism and material meaning, literary modernism surely exceeded Williams's privileging of "things" over "ideas," and, like psychedelics, worked to "strip away the crust of habit" in seeing things, thinking about them, and, above all, experiencing them.[26] A similar rootedness in material things can be seen in Sylvia Plath's works including "Daddy" (written in the early 1960s), which not only zooms in on an everyday object (a shoe) but also filters it (in a nursery-rhyme cadence, no less) into a personalized form that "shifts backwards and forwards in time in a hallucinatory motion which takes the poem away from the more documentary mode . . . into the realm of the abstract."[27] While not necessarily psychedelic, the disturbing description of an everyday object that we find in Plath's poem shares much with a drug-induced experience because, just like Floyd's bike, it echoes a seemingly innocent perception of things: "As adults we don't see a chair with the same intensity with which we examined one when we were children."[28]

It is tempting to view the psychedelia of records such as *Piper at the Gates of Dawn* as a direct channeling of avant-garde poetics. If modernism is associated with a commitment to experimentation and radical shock tactics, the album seems to offer at least something of a comparable formula; although the forms of experimentation are perhaps probed more extensively and subtly in modernist literary texts, the album shares at the very least an impulse to contrast the realist mainstream. *Piper* may also be construed as resting on the very avant-garde contention "that the relationship between the artistic materials and meanings was, like power relations in the society, ultimately arbitrary and therefore open to change and improvement."[29] However, as an exercise in a somewhat elitist poetics of psychedelic pop, the project remains hard to see as containing an "implicit political critique of society at that moment"—hard to see, that is, as a direct or outwardly focused political radicalism—even if the authors would likely subscribe to the modernistic rejection of "the current state of things in favor of the new, the different and the radical."[30]

Still, *Piper at the Gates of Dawn* drew on literature and modernism in some specific ways, including its reliance on imagism, or, more specifically, a surreal perception of reality as mediated through the fragmented subjectivity of the author. Coupled with intertextual references, such expressive strategies as wordplay, obliqueness, and paradoxical juxtaposition (reminiscent of Lear or Carroll) in Barrett's lyrics illustrate language bursting the seams of signification. Incidentally, 1967 was also the year of the simultaneous publication of Jacques Derrida's seminal deconstructive works. While it is highly unlikely that the artist was familiar with the philosopher's works, many of Barrett's writings evoke a deconstructive understating of language. From the recognition that "words have different meanings" ("Matilda Mother")[31] to the ultimate estrangement from the authored text in the later "Jugband Blues" ("I'm wondering who could be writing this song"[32]), one senses that writing and language are a space for the enactment of the play of meanings, which takes the place of authorial control. Musically speaking, psychedelic sound seems to perfectly reflect the aporetic language of the lyrics, with many of the deceptively simple songs being undermined or destabilized—carried onwards into stellar regions—via the dreamy and flowing atmosphere. The excessive fragmentation of meaning affected by this form of psychedelia would reverberate across subsequent decades, lending Barrett the cult status of a "dark rock poet"—an immensely creative and sensitive artist whose childhood readings of sinister Victorian fairy tales would crop up in his very own "dark nursery rhymes," turning "sardonic and more abstract."[33] This was due not only to the artist's own damaged personal life but also to those aspects of musical and literary experimentation reminiscent of a bad trip: shadowy experiences that would be expressed in his solo recordings' more ominous-sounding juxtaposition of lyrical fragmentation and quasi avant-garde concrete music.

If lyrics in psychedelic music were initially seen as secondary in terms of their role in the musical psychedelic experience, Barrett's songwriting and overall approach to music demonstrate a conceptual creative process that overlapped the media of words and sounds with visual thinking. In his excellent biography, Rob Chapman not only points out the literary roots and references of the artist's work but also notes that the creative impulse behind the formation of the band and its music sprang precisely from "cubism, surrealism and pop art," and that Barrett as a consequence regarded "playing *as* literature": "Syd merely adapted the collaging of image and textures and applied it to text."[34] In this sense, Barrett's work not only exhibits a modernist search for "making it new" but constitutes a veering-like, psychedelic merger of text, sound, and vision. In this amalgam, the notion of play not only signified psychedelia's attempt at a return to the state of childhood but also meant literally losing one's mind "at play" (e.g., "See Emily Play"). By following the explorations of the very limits of signification and language, listeners could also participate in this process.

Despite its subversive traits, *Piper at the Gates of Dawn* evolved out of the "smart end of pop" epitomized by 1960s heavyweights such as the Beatles and the Rolling Stones, who at the time were enjoying a life of privilege: "arty, drugged, closed to the general public."[35] Suffused with pop aesthetics, with which Barrett was himself clearly familiar, it drew on the raw materials of commercial mass culture for its form and content but defied full alignment with commercial expectations of the time. The record can thus serve as a case study in the limits of distinctions between the alternative and mainstream, or underground and official. The version of psychedelia it represents problematizes the negotiations between the modernist search for new languages and the importance of images, or visual culture in general, while still coming from the privileged background of Cambridge, which made the grade by speaking the here-and-now language of Swinging London.

Cycling beyond Acid

The psychedelia rooted in the bike rides mentioned above would continue to spiral and spread across the decades and through various artistic forms, hitting wider audiences initially through Ken Kesey's acid gang before it was more fully absorbed by 1960s pop. Guided by the notorious author of *One Flew Over the Cuckoo's Nest*, the Merry Pranksters would, in the mid-1960s, purposefully try to evoke the feeling of sensation overload as a part of their (in)famous Acid Tests, that is, LSD "initiation ceremonies." Sure enough, at least one of these events was successful at getting close to the "intended maelstrom" of "lights, film, swirling sound recorded and instantly played back."[36]

Seemingly lost in this process may be the importance of the bicycle itself, but the fact is that its prominence never went away; it was simply displaced. So much more than a mere prop on the road to the altered experience, the bicycle may well be understood as "a rolling signifier": "from its earliest incarnations [it] was embraced as a technological marvel associated with newfound mental and physical freedoms."[37] With its fluid list of cultural connotations ("from being a marker of modernity to one of antiquity and from signifying wealth to signifying working-class status"[38]), it is interesting how the perception-bending qualities of psychedelia coincide with the contrasting dichotomies the bike points to, especially in the case of the expansion and constriction of space it permitted for its users. The independence it suggests as a nonindustrial object might, furthermore, explain why many literary authors expressed their love of the bike and included it in their works. On the other hand, its shifting cultural significance may be the reason why modernist-driven estrangement, when filtered through the already commercialized pop psychedelia of early Pink Floyd, was fundamentally at odds with the more democratic impulses behind psychedelic bike trips. Despite the renewed perception and the propaganda of heightened awareness, the use of drugs like LSD, too, had an elitist resonance. Already in 1966, the year of pronounced warnings about drugs, acid was described as "particularly attractive to students" because of its "intellectual snob value," and seen "as something to be appreciated by writers, artists and serious thinkers but not by the masses"; nonetheless, the actual drug users of the time included groups as diverse as "college and high school students as well as advertising men, housewives and ministers."[39] The psychedelic maelstrom was thus in full swing.

Riding a bike could offer a similar experience to the psychedelic voyage, but it was probably the device's usefulness as a means of travel that made it truly roll for the writers, musicians, and "the regular people." Acid, too, can take you for a ride, but it is the combination of sound and mind-altering substances that really does the synesthetic trick: "together, psychedelics and music achieve a stunning synergy because music, too, is felt as something very near to us and at the same time as a world that is quite distinct from the world mapped by vision and touch."[40] Despite this literary-like propensity for textual (musical) immersion, the cultural importance of psychedelia seemed to gradually wane—especially when the rock star's drugs of choice changed—but it never went completely away. Although the language of 1960s pop, which attempted to fuse modernistic experimentation with sites of cultural prestige, seems to be relegated to the past, psychedelic poetics were kept alive and were particularly pronounced in other musical genres.

One of these is stoner rock, which just like psychedelia evokes lexical difficulties and definition problems. While in popular representations, the term may evoke the continually stoned, spaced-out pot-heads depicted in several Hollywood renderings

130   *Lit-Rock*

of high-school life, on musical ground "stoner" refers to a genre created in North America in the 1990s as a creative fusion of the gritty heaviness of Black Sabbath with the psychedelic, flowy textures of early Pink Floyd.[41] Also referred to, in recognition of its California origins, as desert rock, the genre's sonic makeup conjures vast landscapes filled with oneiric auditory storytelling, mixing heavy riffs, escapism, and drug-affected vision. Notwithstanding the differences between individual exponents (e.g., Kyuss, Fu Manchu, Queens of the Stone Age, and many more), stoner's key stylistic traits encompass various forms of iconography and symbolism related less to LSD than to cannabis. Both of these, however, are often directly derived from the 1960s conceptualization of the relationship between mind expansion and smoking pot, including the disparate artistic, mystical, and political dimensions of drug taking, and a degree of escapism connected to Jamaican Rasta culture and the search for heightened sensual pleasures.[42] The record cover iconography and the imagery within the lyrics are accompanied musically by de-tuned, fuzzed guitars, slow-paced tempos, or trans-like repetitiveness and a loose approach to musical composition. Such psychedelic coding of the musical production resulted from a particular countercultural economy, similar to that of the 1960s, connected geographically to the California landscape of Joshua Tree National Park but implicating a whole sub-culture of mixed media and artistic activities: visual arts, printing, sketches, and independent filmmaking.[43] The general psychedelic feel of the music in this case, however, is filtered through later musical developments such as punk and grunge and positioned to contrast the highly trained, academic virtuosity or bombastic pretense of, say, progressive rock. Whereas the mixture of musical stylistics and general heaviness of sound among stoner bands (doom, sludge, metal) might cause generic confusion, it is united by a willingness to deflect signs of elitism with ambience, volume, and sonic saturation.

As with psychedelia, the literary links of stoner rock are not its dominant features, especially insofar as many bands distance themselves from the broadly understood mainstream, which connotes forms of elitism and canonization. The themes explored by a wide range of (mostly) California bands range from skate culture (Fu Manchu) and esoteric mysticism (Monster Magnet) to desert landscapes (Kyuss, All Them Witches) and sorcery (Electric Wizard), to intergalactic travel (Sleep) and retro modes that revive psychedelia (Dead Meadow) or employ B-movie horror stylistics (Uncle Acid, Kadavar). The unifying and abiding trait which gives the genre its name, however, is a commitment to the language and instruments of mind-bending: LSD and other hallucinogens, mushrooms, and cannabis. In this sense, stoner rock constitutes another attempt to render the acid trip in musical form, often characterized by the staple musical slowdown and evoking the typical 1960s theme of travel. Traditional literary traits are also present, if one looks deep enough, although in many cases they take the form of isolated name-dropping or references drawn from science fiction, heroic fantasy, or alternative mythology (H. P. Lovecraft, for example). The literary basis for the music, in this case, expresses itself rather in the artistic mode of filtering altered experience more than any customary literariness of the lyrical form. Like the imagistic approach seen in Barrett's work, it is the fusion of music and words, rather than a fixed list of traits, that manifests the veering and immersive aspects of the musical text.

Cycling on Acid

While Kyuss, whose name comes from a book in one of the Dungeons and Dragons series, *Deities and Demigods*,[44] is often regarded as one of the early and prominent exponents of stoner rock, it is the Californian band Sleep that represents the most daring connection between the 1960s psychedelic impulses and the modernist-like intent on experimentation. As a perfect example of the claim that lyrics alone do not account for any exceptional psychedelic literariness, the heavy metal trio achieves its most powerful effects with relatively little help from words. The band's first full-scale outing, *Sleep's Holy Mountain* (1992), like many other musical texts within the genre, is rather vague when it comes to formulating a coherent or intellectually stimulating narrative. Musically rooted in a fascination with the sound of Black Sabbath's or Saint Vitus's doom metal, the lyrics rely foremost on images conventional of the genre. The title track, for instance, speaks of a dreamer waking up to the red sunrise (an invocation of the magic caravan and a blurring of the field of vision are a must here) and centralizes the album's themes: intergalactic journeys featuring magical creatures ("Dragonaut"); evil powers and meditation ("Druid"); or general escapism phrased in terms of magic villages, castles, or mythological civilizations such as Atlantis ("Evil Gypsy/Solomon's Theme"), which lead the stoner caravan onwards "[i]nside the sun" and beyond.

This is the scope of the now-familiar symbolism the band would continue exploring in their brief but intensive career, most intriguingly elaborated in their *magnum opus*: the almost hour-long composition *Dopesmoker* (2003), originally entitled *Jerusalem*. The single, album-filling track constitutes a pinnacle of stoner fascination with the motif of travel and oneiric sonic voyages. It is based on a single hypnotic and repetitive guitar riff and accompanied by lyrics rooted in a biblically phrased cannabis journey—that is, a "stoner caravan" transporting "Weedians," who are on a pilgrimage through the insurmountable desert landscape, to the holy mountain and Jerusalem-like, "riffed-filled" land. The lyrical incorporation of biblical symbolism (the Jordan River, the Son of the God of Israel, etc.) is certainly the most evident literary layer here. However, it is only together with the composition's reliance on the performative enactment of the musical slowdown, the perception of time-stretching within the psychedelic experience, that the work reveals its immersive dimension. Its very length and sluggish tempo, emphasized by the droning vocal delivery alongside the mercilessly paced guitar riff and tantric drumbeat, effectively connote the slow yet powerful ambience of the psychedelic trip. The composition's overall complexity and running-time gesture, of course, against popular commodification, positioning it within a counterculture ethos of alternative impulses and modernistic experimentation, and additionally building upon the idea of circularity present in non-Western (Hindu, Indian, Tibetan) cultures.[45] Several elements of the composition—from the referencing of a 1960s-like reverence surrounding the holy weed to the hypnotic, chant-like delivery—undermine the dominant assumption that a song's overall "message" hinges on a precise grasp of its lyrics. Above all, it illustrates the workings of the psychedelic form of veering, combining sounds and words in a way that simultaneously lengthens and unravels, builds and traverses, the musical text itself.

Conclusion

When it comes to psychedelic rock, literariness is more than a discursive form of artistic expression; thinking about the overlapping ground of these two seemingly different forms enables one to move beyond the understanding of a mere stylistic formation. Following Royle's proposition that literature be understood as veering invites a view of psychedelia as a similar mode of recording and instigating altered, synesthetic experiences—more of a collectively produced emotional departure than an isolated look at lyrics or particular sound effects. Additionally, these experiences seem to share features with the modernist conception of literariness, especially in their estrangement of everyday objects or challenge to conventional, especially realistic, modes of artistic expression. Psychedelic production, however, as a popular music genre, enjoys a greater freedom from accusations of elitism than do most classic modernist texts.

As illustrated by the examples from Syd Barrett's early work with Pink Floyd, the verbal dimension of songs can certainly contribute to immersive qualities associated with literature. The band's work from around the time of their first album, *Piper at the Gates of Dawn*, displays the propensity of psychedelic music for both employing and deconstructing literary references, or, more generally, for probing the limits of language and signification. This form of quasi-literary, psychedelic music seems to encourage the listener's participation in the very process of seeking meaning, without indicating that any final stage can be ever reached.

If late 1960s psychedelic pop, despite its subversive and surrealist features, might be seen as a somewhat commodified version of high modernism, Sleep's stoner rock seems to (less-commercially) rekindle or extend the modernistic attributes of 1960s psychedelic experience and drug use. It also demonstrates a challenging way of recording and expressing this experience through music, which may align it more closely with modernism's search for new means of expression. While literature, or the lyrical engagement with mystical and biblical imagery, renders a reverential approach to cannabis, the music's immersive features generate much more than the escapism stereotypically attributed to psychedelia. Sleep's *Dopesmoker* in particular stands out among other stoner works because, despite its reliance on common weed-related iconography, the musical effort registers an almost avant-garde, modernist-like attempt at challenging the dominant modes of musical representation. The very length and crawling pace of this intriguing composition boldly reject the tenets of commercialized pop, offering a programatic immersion that mirrors the veering that takes place in literature and that can be associated with the expanded awareness of psychedelic experience.

Notes

1   Jonathan Culler, *Literary Theory: A Very Short Introduction* (Oxford: Oxford University Press, 2000), 40.
2   Nicholas Royle, *Veering: A Theory of Literature* (Edinburgh: Edinburgh University Press, 2011).

Cycling on Acid 133

3 Scott B. Montgomery, "Italian Progressive Rock as Indigenous Psychedelia," *Rock Music Studies* 5, no. 3 (2018): 292.

4 Paul Hegarty and Martin Halliwell, *Beyond and Before: Progressive Rock since the 1960s* (New York: Continuum, 2011), 34.

5 William Echard, *Psychedelic Popular Music: A History through Musical Topical Theory* (Bloomington: Indiana University Press, 2017): 11.

6 Sheila Whiteley, *The Space between the Notes: Rock and the Counter-Culture* (New York: Routledge, 2005), 8 *et passim*.

7 Russel Reising, "Melting Clocks and the Hallways of Always: Time in Psychedelic Music," *Popular Music and Society* 32, no. 4 (2009): 523–47.

8 Echard, *Psychedelic Popular Music*, 11.

9 Stanley Krippner, "Ecstatic Landscapes: The Manifestation of Psychedelic Art," *Journal of Humanistic Psychology* 57, no. 4 (2016): 416.

10 Michael Leslie Klein, "Musical Story," in *Music and Narrative since 1900*, ed. Michael L. Klein and Nicholas Reyland (Bloomington: Indiana University Press, 2013), 3–28.

11 Jon Savage, *1966: The Year the Decade Exploded* (London: Faber and Faber, 2016), 132.

12 Jim DeRogatis, *Turn On Your Mind: Four Decades of Great Psychedelic Rock* (New York: Hall Leonard, 2003), 10.

13 Simon Warner, *Text and Drugs and Rock 'n' Roll: The Beats and Rock Culture* (New York: Bloomsbury, 2013).

14 Scott B. Montgomery, by contrast, views Leary's approach somewhat reductively, placing it within an Apollonian framework in which it appears as "a kind of transcendent enlightenment rather than an immersive, sensorial experience." 293. See note 3.

15 Royle, *Veering*.

16 Savage, *1966*, vii–viii.

17 See, for example, R. A. Durr, *Poetic Vision and the Psychedelic Experience* (New York: Syracuse University Press, 1970).

18 Royle, quoted in Savage, *1966*, viii.

19 See Anthony Ashbolt, "'Go Ask Alice': Remembering the Summer of Love Forty Years On," *Australasian Journal of American Studies* 26, no. 2 (2007): 42. See also Lucy Lippard's claim about the "dematerialization of arts" as "a shift in interest from art as object or product to art as idea, to art based on the thinking process prior to its physical execution," in *The Fontana Dictionary of Modern Thought*, ed. Allan Bullock, Oliver Stallybrass, and Stephen Trombley (London: Fontana, 1978), 161.

20 Albert Hofman, quoted in DeRogatis, *Turn On Your Mind*, 3.

21 Ibid., 4.

22 Joe Boyd, *White Bicycles: Making Music in the 1960s* (London: Serpent's Tail, 2009), 11.

23 David Rassent, *Rock Psychédéliqie: Un Voyage en 150 Albums* (Marseille: Le Mot et Le Reste, 2017), 31.

24 Ibid., 72–3.

25 Syd Barrett, "Bike," track 11 on *The Piper at the Gates of Dawn*, EMI Columbia, 1967.

26 Nick Bromell, *Tomorrow Never Knows: Rock and Psychedelics in the 1960s* (Chicago: The University of Chicago Press, 2002), 71.

27 Jo Gill, *The Cambridge Introduction to Sylvia Plath* (Cambridge: Cambridge University Press, 2008), 62.

28 Bromell, *Tomorrow Never Knows*, 71.
29 Keir Keightley, "Reconsidering Rock," in *The Cambridge Companion to Pop and Rock*, ed. Simon Frith, Will Straw, and John Street (Cambridge: Cambridge University Press, 2001), 136.
30 Ibid.
31 Syd Barrett, "Matilda Mother," track 3 on *The Piper at the Gates of Dawn*, EMI Columbia, 1967.
32 Syd Barrett, "Jugband Blues," track 3 on Pink Floyd, *A Saucerful of Secrets*, EMI Columbia, 1968.
33 Rob Chapman, *A Very Irregular Head: The Life of Syd Barrett* (Cambridge: Da Capo, 2010), 185, 195.
34 Ibid., 53.
35 Savage, *1966*, 409.
36 Ibid., 118.
37 Jeremy Withers and Daniel P. Shea, introduction to *Culture on Two Wheels: The Bicycle in Literature and Film*, ed. Jeremy Withers and Daniel P. Shea (Lincoln: University of Nebraska Press, 2016), 37.
38 Ibid., 37–8.
39 Savage, *1966*, 133.
40 Bromell, *Tomorrow Never Knows*, 72.
41 Jean-Charles Desgroux, *Stoner: Blues for the Red Sun* (Marseilles: Le Mot et Le Reste, 2019), 9 *et passim*.
42 Ibid., 23.
43 Ibid.
44 DeRogatis, *Turn On Your Mind*, 547.
45 See Tymon Adamczewski, "(Re)Constructing the Sixties: On Psychedelic Experience in Sleep's *Dopesmoker*," in *Memory, Identity and Cognition: Explorations in Culture and Communication*, ed. Jacek Mianowski, Michal Borodo, and Pawel Schreiber (Cham: Springer Nature, 2019), 103–13.

Part IV

Signs and Mediations

8

A Portrait of the Artist in a Pop Song

Images of James Joyce in Popular Music

Kevin Farrell

In 2016, *The Wall Street Journal* published a picture of Patti Smith's copy of *Finnegans Wake* as part of its "Favorite Things" feature. The photograph, taken by Steven Sebring, displays a number of objects placed on and around a writing desk, with the book set in the center of the frame and open roughly to the middle. Smith herself is credited with the accompanying paragraph, which explains the objects she has selected for reasons both personal and aesthetic. Several of these objects are included, at least in part, for their literary value: a *carte de visite* of Baudelaire, a coffee cup purchased at the Charles Dickens Museum in London, a set of pencils ("the most humble tools of the writer"), and even her reading glasses ("books are central to my life, and I couldn't read them without my glasses!"[1]). As for her copy of the *Wake*, Smith identifies it as an autographed first edition. "The book is almost unreadable," Smith writes, "but as an object it's beautiful."[2]

Smith's comment speaks to popular culture's oft-superficial relationship with James Joyce, a relationship that can seem defined more by Joyce's reputation than by his actual work. While Smith's affinity for Joyce is surely genuine, and her own literary bona fides are strong—the so-called "Poet Laureate of Punk Rock" is herself a published poet and a National Book Award Winner—her inclusion of Joyce's book treats it as something of a prop, an object for display that represents (for anyone even vaguely familiar with the author's name and book titles) a heightened form of artistry, intellectualism, and prestige.[3] It offers, that is to say, a kind of shorthand for literary brilliance, to which Smith, by association, lays claim.

Claims of this sort are typical enough in popular music, wherein artists often define themselves—whether through cover songs, fashion choices, or lyrical and musical allusions—in reference to their influences. Smith's chosen objects, the *Wake* included, are comparable to the LPs surrounding Bob Dylan on the cover of *Bringing it All Back Home,* or the various cut-outs surrounding the Beatles on *Sgt. Pepper's Lonely Hearts Club Band.*[4] As for Joyce himself, he has long been construed in symbolic terms across a broad array of cultural fora, including everything from television to comic strips to political rhetoric. We often find such treatment of Joyce in popular music,

138 *Lit-Rock*

an arena wherein the author becomes a sign of one's literariness that requires little engagement with the literature itself. Given Joyce's reputation as an experimental genius and academy darling, allusions to him or his works can be seen as statements of artistic kinship and tacit claims to serious literary artistry. References to Joyce are not uncommon in lyrics and music criticism, with the author's name typically serving as a synecdoche for intellectualism, libertinism, and avant-garde experimentation.[5] As such, Joyce and Joycean things hold capital for artists seeking academic, intellectual, or literary credibility; however, that capital is generally derived more from reputation than from exegesis of the author's works. In popular music, then, Joyce is often more important as a symbol than he is as a lyrical or musical influence.

Derek Pyle, Krzysztof Bartnicki, and Tess Brewer have compiled an impressive timeline of musical references to Joyce on the website for "Waywords and Meansigns," itself an ambitious attempt to set *Finnegans Wake* to music. This timeline charts everything from Frank Bridge's 1925 adaptation of "Golden Hair" to independent Polish artist M8N's *The ULSSS*, a 2018 album based on *Ulysses*.[6] Across the near-century between the former and the latter, Pyle, Bartnicki, and Brewer identify hundreds of references to Joyce and Joyce's works from a wide array of musicians representing a wide variety of musical genres. Among the entries that might be broadly termed "popular music," one finds both obscure (independent and DIY) artists, whose work appears on social media platforms and websites like Bandcamp, and world-famous rock stars, including several Rock and Roll Hall of Fame inductees. While the content and delivery of these allusions vary as much as the music itself, a few patterns can be discerned by studying the list. First, allusions to Joyce himself are far less common than allusions to his works and characters. Second, among those allusions to Joyce's writing, Joyce's most "challenging" works receive markedly more mentions than his more "accessible" fiction; indeed, *Finnegans Wake* is the most commonly referenced of Joyce's books, followed by *Ulysses*, with *Dubliners* and *A Portrait of the Artist as a Young Man* both receiving far less attention. Joyce's two volumes of poetry, though less significant to literary scholars than his fiction, receive considerable attention from musicians, while his lone play, *Exiles*, has been altogether ignored. This seemingly disproportionate emphasis upon *Finnegans Wake* suggests that the Joyce celebrated, and sometimes mocked, by musicians is the experimental Joyce, the avant-garde artist who recreated language as he recreated fiction. Other aspects of Joyce and his work—his political views, his Aristotelian and Thomist philosophy, his complex attitudes toward Ireland and Roman Catholicism—are, for musicians who reference him, generally less significant.

This study considers a selection of allusions to, and appropriations of, James Joyce and his works in popular music, arguing that Joyce's (academically constructed) position as the quintessential modernist writer renders him (in popular culture) a convenient symbol of high art. I argue, furthermore, that such references are often based upon an essentialized version of Joyce and his novels, rather than the actual themes, plots, or characters of his texts; rather ironically, the notion of avant-gardism, of an artist notorious for his inaccessibility, carries more value in popular music than does Joyce's actual and (in the case of *Dubliners*, at least) accessible work. For some artists—Kate

Bush, Syd Barrett, Jefferson Airplane, Sleepytime Gorilla Museum—the symbolic Joyce is an aspirational peer; for others—Allan Sherman, Therapy?, and Black 47—Joyce becomes an object of ridicule. An allusion to Joyce, then, is essentially a means of self-identification, a rhetorical tool by which artists can lay claim to the mantle of "serious art," or else distance themselves (as authentic artists) from artistic pretentiousness or academic conceit. The implications of such self-identification extend beyond one's affinity, or lack thereof, for Joyce's works: invocations of Joyce speak to popular music's tenuous relationship with literature and the academy, negotiating with their respective audiences, and sometimes ambivalently, the seriousness with which lyrics and lyricists should be taken. While recognizing the often-tenuous relation between Joyce's work and allusions to it in popular song, I hope nonetheless to discourage easy dismissals—on the grounds of superficiality—of this practice; the examples I focus on show considerable diversity both in *how* they use Joyce and toward what ends, and open space, I hope, for reimagining the concepts of authorship and intertextuality.

Inevitably, to study the place of Joyce in popular culture is to wrestle with two largely unanswerable questions: who is the "real" James Joyce, and to whom does he belong? The Joyce of popular music often appears as a distortion of the Joyce who wrote *Dubliners, A Portrait of the Artist as a Young Man, Ulysses*, and *Finnegans Wake*; according to Vincent Cheng, Joyce has been "essentialized" to the point that he "can be adequately *known* and represented, even successfully marketed,"[7] even to those who have not read his books. And yet one might well argue that the Joyce of academia, having been studied from every conceivable angle and put through every extant theoretical wringer, is by now equally distorted from decades of critical appropriation and application. Every version of Joyce is essentialized to some extent, and each essentialized version of the author belies another version discoverable in the pages of his work. Among those versions, perhaps, is a Joyce who belongs less to academics and authors than to all of us. Declan Kiberd, in *Ulysses and Us*, has argued that the academic and bohemian visions of Joyce are antithetical to the artist's own vision of his work, noting Joyce's markedly democratic notions of literature and readership, as well as his distaste for self-selected and self-segregated artistic communities. In place of a Joyce locked in an ivory tower or seated in some bohemian café, Kiberd, while recognizing the density and difficulty of Joyce's writings, proposes a Joyce accessible to all readers, an author with something broadly relevant to say.[8] Pop music appropriations of Joyce can, in practice, accomplish Kiberd's proposal by pushing Joyce—or at least some version of Joyce—from the margins of intellectualism and bohemianism and into the mainstream.

That these pop-culture appropriations of Joyce and his work are generally, and often profoundly, altered from the text of Joyce's novels raises another question: Are these appropriations misreadings or misprisions? While it may be tempting, particularly for Joycean scholars, to assume the former, the latter raises the more intriguing—and in some ways, Joycean—possibilities. The most interesting appropriations of *Ulysses* and *Finnegans Wake* are those that reimagine the source material in new contexts, much as Joyce reimagined the *Odyssey* and the ballad of Tim Finnegan. By such logic, even an evidently superficial allusion to Joyce can challenge our

140   *Lit-Rock*

preconceptions of the author and force us to reconsider his work. Through these allusions, musicians engage in dialogue with Joyce (or the *idea* of Joyce), just as Joyce had once engaged in dialogue with Homer, Shakespeare, Dante, and countless others. Perhaps that dialogue cannot definitively answer those questions posed above—who is the "real" James Joyce, and to whom does he belong?—but its existence, and our examination of it, makes evident the ways in which Joyce's "meaning" is not unilinear and autonomous, but dynamic, collaborative, and reciprocal; while the author serves as literary capital for bands intent on establishing their intellectual and bohemian credentials, those displays can, in turn, affect our understanding of Joyce and Joyce's fiction.

"Rejoyce": Jefferson Airplane and the Maturing Rock Band

James Joyce did not enter the world of rock and roll until the late 1960s. While allusions to Joyce can be found in folk and avant-garde music well before then, the author and his works likely seemed incongruent with the ethos of early rock and roll, a musical genre that developed far from the academy and had, by the mid-1950s, become largely the province of American teenagers. In its infancy, rock and roll was not considered serious art, a sentiment shared by both its detractors and its most ardent admirers, so early rock and roll singers and lyricists surely felt little need to prove their academic or artistic credibility. That ethos shifted, however, in the mid-1960s with the advent of folk-rock and psychedelia, sub-genres characterized in part by experimental music and self-consciously literary lyrics. By 1965, Bob Dylan was singing of Ezra Pound and T. S. Eliot, so Joyce was surely due to join his fellow modernists.

That happened officially in 1967 with Jefferson Airplane's "Rejoyce," a song from their third album, *After Bathing at Baxter's*. As the follow-up to *Surrealistic Pillow*, the band's most commercially successful and critically acclaimed record, *After Bathing* builds upon the earlier album's experimentation. While this record was something of a commercial flop in comparison with its predecessor, critics offered it considerable praise. *Rolling Stone* declared *After Bathing* "probably the best, considering all the criteria and the exceptions, rock and roll album so far produced by an American group," noting "Rejoyce" in particular as "a good display of [Grace Slick's] amazing vocal control."[9] Bruce Eder, writing for Allmusic, described the song as a "hauntingly beautiful excursion into literary psychedelia, whose James Joyce allusions carry the Lewis Carroll literary allusions of the previous album's 'White Rabbit' into startlingly new and wonderful (if discursive) directions and depths."[10] Airplane's engagement of Joyce, then, not only opened their artistry to a discourse of commercial success vs. critical acclaim but, for Eder, marked a graduation of sorts into more serious material—a narrative of artistic growth substantiated by the songs' contrasting use of direct and discursive lyricism. While Carroll's work, with its bizarre characters and its emphases on illogic and shifting proportion, was an obvious fit for psychedelia, *Ulysses* offered something less immediately adaptable.

And yet the song's punning title, itself a redux of Anthony Burgess's critical work of the same name, suggests a deliberate revision of Joyce's work. Slick, whose allusions take a form more opaque, clumsy even, than those on "White Rabbit," is perhaps more successful in her use of the novel's themes than of its characters or plot. Of particular note is Slick's interrogation of the novel's treatment of female sexuality. According to Nadya Zimmerman, the song is "more than a mere retelling of *Ulysses*"; rather, it "exemplifies the heterogeneous strands that coalesced to form the counterculture's hallucinogenic ethos of 'free love.'"[11] For Zimmerman, "Rejoyce" ultimately rejects both countercultural utopianism and the Joycean affirmation (Molly Bloom's orgasmic "Yes") with a "pessimistic ending," rendering the song "a disjointed tale of desire and consumption that ends in broken pieces."[12]

Zimmerman's interpretation reinforces what the title implies, that the song is more a reimagining than an appropriation, or even an adaptation, of its source text, and that Slick's lyrics, albeit with mixed results, filter Joyce through the ethos of the 1960s counterculture. Included in that ethos is resistance against the Vietnam War, so while Bloom, Molly, and Blazes appear in reference to their sexuality, Stephen Dedalus is introduced as a symbol for the counterculture's pacifism. While Slick's version of Stephen is barely recognizable as Joyce's intellectual and iconoclastic artist, the transformation is not entirely without textual basis. Stephen's pithy phrase in "Circe"—"I say, let my country die for me"[13]—is the novel's most overtly pacifistic statement, a rejection of the violent nationalism endemic throughout Ireland and the rest of Western Europe at the time. In the context of the novel's composition and publication, Stephen's line is a rejection of the rhetoric of patriotic self-sacrifice and the enactment of that rhetoric during both the Easter Rising and the First World War, particularly as Stephen delivers this line to Privates Carr and Compton, British soldiers stationed in Dublin. Slick thereby equates Stephen's *non serviam* with those conscientious objectors who burned their draft cards to protest the Vietnam War: "Stephen won't give his arm," Slick sings, "to no gold star mother's farm."[14] Slick subverts Joyce's version of pacifism, however, by putting his (paraphrased) words into the mouth of a war profiteer: "war's good business so give your son, / and I'd rather have my country die for me."[15] The first line indicates a possible shift in perspective, implying that the speaker is someone from within the military-industrial complex that the song protests, someone growing rich from the self-sacrifice of soldiers in Vietnam. While it's not clear to what the "rather" refers, this speaker's preference is that his country dies for his profit. Slick's rephrasing here is distinct enough that some listeners, perhaps missing the reference to *Ulysses*, hear the line instead as a rebuttal to Kennedy's "ask not what your country can do for you."[16]

Such alterations make for an uneasy relationship between "Rejoyce" and its source material, raising the question of why Slick borrowed from *Ulysses* in the first place. Slick's own account of the song is telling in this regard: "I wrote about what was interesting to me, assuming people had read this stuff. . . . But there's a larger record-buying audience out there that doesn't know shit. '[R]ejoyce' is verse from beginning to end, and it moves around. That's difficult for people. It's almost impossible to dance to and it's difficult to sing along with."[17] Slick uses Joyce, then, as part of a self-conscious

142   *Lit-Rock*

shift away from the more conventional pop and folk structures found on the band's first two albums. This new style is, in Slick's estimation, more akin to literature than it is to rock and roll: she has traded danceable singalongs for poetic verse, a trade that inevitably alienates ignorant listeners with its difficulty and prerequisite knowledge. In such a view, Joyce becomes a sort of bohemian shibboleth, the kind that only equally literate listeners can appreciate. And yet there is a kind of showcased omnivorousness, accentuated by Slick's use of vulgar language in making claims to educated rock music, at play: the so-called "Acid Queen" engages the curriculum of English departments.

Of course, Jefferson Airplane was not unique among rocks bands in appealing to intellectual depth. The ethos of psychedelia was more intricate than mere indulgence in marijuana and LSD, and as its artists increasingly borrowed from modern jazz and avant-garde music in their compositions and recording techniques, a similar attraction to dense literature crept inexorably into the lyrics. Psychedelia would fall largely out of fashion within a few years, but its tacit claims about artistic and literary merit would be adopted by other musicians in the years following the 1960s. For some such artists, Joyce would remain a compelling symbol of artistic ambitiousness.

Revisitations, Rewritings, and Deauthorizations: Kate Bush and Sleepytime Gorilla Museum

While Jefferson Airplane saw Joyce's work as material to be reinvented, some of their contemporaries in psychedelia chose instead to adopt Joyce as their lyricist, setting his writings to music. Such an approach is perhaps less audacious than "Rejoyce," particularly since it has precedent from the author himself, who agreed to let composer G. Molyneaux Palmer write scores for the poems of *Chamber Music*.[18] While Palmer was the first to receive Joyce's authorization, a great many musicians followed suit. In the world of psychedelia, the first of these were Irish band Dr. Strangely Strange, whose "Strings in the Earth and Air," included on their 1969 debut record, takes its lyrics from the first two poems of *Chamber Music*. A year later, Syd Barrett, the original lead singer of Pink Floyd, included an adaptation of Joyce's "Golden Hair" on *The Madcap Laughs*, his solo debut album. Barrett treats Joyce's poem as part of a musical transformation: as Ron Chapman notes, the "plaintive arrangement of the poem indicates a highly developed melodic sensibility, which is completely at odds with the basic musical abilities he displayed in his mid-to-late teens."[19] "Golden Hair," like the rest of *Madcap*, reflects none of the garage rock stylings found on *Piper at the Gates of Dawn* or *A Saucerful of Secrets*, the two albums Barrett recorded while a member of Pink Floyd. If, as Chapman suggests, *Madcap* is more mature and sophisticated than Barrett's earlier work, Joyce is used as evidence of that maturity and sophistication.

Chamber Music lends itself to such projects—compared to his prose, Joyce's verse is relatively straightforward and simple in both structure and diction. Moreover, as Joyce's poetry is less famous than his fiction, adapting it allows artists to claim a relatively obscure work by a major writer, an act of appropriation that confers

A Portrait of the Artist in a Pop Song   143

literariness upon a song without the musicians being wholly eclipsed by Joyce and his reputation, all while demanding less of artist and audience. Both "Strings in the Earth and Air" and "Golden Hair" are adaptations more so than exercises in intertextuality; presented respectively as self-contained nuggets of literary psych-folk, neither presumes nor necessitates extensive engagement with the literature itself.

More daring—and, arguably, more presumptuous—are those artists who pull their lyrics directly from Joyce's fiction. While *Ulysses* and *Finnegans Wake* are oft-quoted and oft-alluded to across a wide variety of media, they are seldom adapted to popular music settings, for obvious reasons. Prose lends itself less readily than verse to such appropriations, and the density and complexity of Joyce's style render it markedly difficult to adapt to anything resembling a conventional pop song. Musical adaptations of *Ulysses* and *Finnegans Wake* have mostly been the province of avant-garde musicians—Luciana Berio's *Thema (Omaggio a Joyce)* or John Cage's *Roartorio, an Irish circus on Finnegans Wake*—rather than popular ones. In more practical terms, the protectiveness of Joyce's estate has made adaptations of *Ulysses* and *Finnegans Wake* all but impossible. Managed for decades by the late Stephen Joyce, Joyce's grandson and last direct descendant, the Estate routinely refused permission for proposed performances or adaptations. This protectiveness, though contrary to the intricately allusive ethos and joyful appropriations of Joyce's own writing, was legendary among Joyce's scholars and fans, its most famous musical casualty being perhaps Kate Bush's "The Sensual World."

Unlike Dr. Strangely Strange or Syd Barrett, Bush was already well established as an art-rock provocateur when she ventured upon Joycean things, an artist who had previously borrowed upon literary capital with her debut single, "Wuthering Heights," over a decade earlier. That track, a number one hit in the UK, found Bush singing from the perspective of Catherine Earnshaw, adopting a famous literary character's voice as material for a pop song. "The Sensual World," the title track of Bush's 1989 album, follows a similar formula to her previous single, albeit exchanging Brontë's gothic Romanticism for Joyce's High Modernism.

In Bush's original conception, the track that became "The Sensual World" was intended to be a direct adaptation of Joyce's prose, setting passages of Molly Bloom's soliloquy to music. The Joyce Estate refused to grant permission for these passages, to which the artist responded by re-writing Joyce's original text. Some two decades later, the Joyce Estate finally relented, allowing Bush the opportunity to re-record the song with the originally intended lyrics. This new version, dubbed "Flower of the Mountain," appeared on Bush's *Director's Cut* (2011), a collection of re-recorded songs from *The Sensual World* and *The Red Shoes*. While "Flower of the Mountain" maintains the same chorus used in "The Sensual World"—"stepping out off the page / into the sensual world"[20]—it replaces Bush's verses with Molly's reminiscences of her husband's marriage proposal, taking its words verbatim from the ending of *Ulysses*.[21] A comparison between these three texts—"The Sensual World," "Flower of the Mountain," and *Ulysses* itself—suggests that the intransigence of the Joyce Estate pushed Bush to reimagine more than just Joyce's language.

The result is a song that blends isolated moments of direct Joycean content with new and imaginative material. Certain elements from Molly's soliloquy—the seedcake, the Howth Head setting—remain in "The Sensual World," as does the line "he said I was a flower of the mountain,"[22] but much of its substance and meaning are otherwise changed. If one takes the speaker of "The Sensual World" to be Molly Bloom, then it is a Molly unbound from Joyce's control, a Molly who has departed the past for the present, the page for the pop environment. The song's chorus makes this clear, as Bush's Molly speaks of "stepping out of the page into the sensual world," the world where (in imagery consistent with the romance of mainstream pop) "you don't need words, just one kiss, then another."[23] The focus of the song, then, is a fictional character's departure from her book to experience real sensual stimulation. Bush subtly construes this departure as rebellion, both against the Joyce Estate and against Molly's male creator. Regarding the former, Bush's invocation of William Blake's "Jerusalem" in the third verse offers her metacommentary upon the song's genesis and composition—"And then our arrows of desire rewrite the speech, mmh, yes"[24]—and hints, in its selection of an author Joyce himself quotes from in *Ulysses*, at the Estate's hypocrisy. As for the latter, Bush's rewrites to the speech are often pointed feminist assertions of autonomy, not just over language, but over the female body itself.

Using "Flower of the Mountain" as a guide, we can reasonably conclude that Bush intended to open her song with Molly's reminiscence of the day Bloom proposed to her at Howth Head. Molly's memory of this event, in *Ulysses*, begins: "first I gave him the bit of seedcake out of my mouth,"[25] an event Bloom remembers wistfully earlier in the novel. Bush reimagines this scene in "The Sensual World," opening instead with Molly having "taken the kiss of seedcake back from his mouth,"[26] an event foreign to Joyce's novel. Where Joyce's Molly remembers herself providing sensual pleasure to a man, Bush's Molly remembers herself reclaiming that sensual pleasure for herself. This act of reclamation grows more profound after Bush's one direct quote from *Ulysses*: "Yes he said I was a flower of the mountain."[27] In both *Ulysses* and "Flower of the Mountain," this phrase is followed by "we are flowers all a woman's body," a sentiment Joyce's Molly regards as the "one true thing [Bloom] said in his life."[28] Bush's Molly, by contrast, omits these increasingly tender thoughts of her husband, replacing them with a claim of physical autonomy: "But now I've powers o'er a woman's body, yes."[29] This assertion imbues Bush's Molly with a feminist and metafictional rebelliousness, and perhaps as a consequence of this newfound autonomy, she qualifies her affirmation, adding "but not yet."[30]

While these changes may have been made out of necessity, they offer intriguing commentary about gender issues in Joyce's novel. "Penelope" has long attracted interest from feminist scholars, but there is no consensus as to how accurately Joyce represents feminine consciousness in his final chapter; indeed, one of Joyce's harshest critics was his wife, Nora, who reportedly felt her husband "[knew] nothing at all about women."[31] *Ulysses* suggests that Joyce may have felt otherwise, as his Molly shows a nostalgic appreciation for Bloom's understanding of women, a sentiment Bush omits from her versions of the soliloquy.

A Portrait of the Artist in a Pop Song

One could, then, plausibly read "The Sensual World," a song far more audacious in its literariness than either "Wuthering Heights" or "Flower of the Mountain," more as a critique than an adaptation of *Ulysses*. However, such audacity, according to Bush's public comments, was not her intent. Upon finally being granted permission to use Joyce's text, Bush admitted that she preferred her original concept of the song to her own rewrite: "well," she said, "I'm not James Joyce, am I?"[32] Her self-effacement, genuine or not, directly acknowledges Joyce as the superior writer, thereby honoring a value distinction between literary music and literature itself. Bush's gender-related challenges to Joyce seem secondary, then, to her deployment of Joyce as literary capital—a selective appropriation of sorts that manifests the aura of *Ulysses* within the contexts of pop song/pop star, and facilitates, as it did for Jefferson Airplane, a narrative of artistic maturity, of mere "literary affiliation" to "avant-garde" credibility.

In 2007, Joyce would be drafted as lyricist for another avant-garde act, when Sleepytime Gorilla Museum, an experimental band from California, took passages from *Finnegans Wake* for "Helpless Corpses Enactment," the second track on their third and final album, *In Glorious Times*. Like most of SGM's work, the song is difficult to categorize musically, a track that, according to Allmusic's Stewart Mason, "is either straight-ahead death metal, complete with Cookie Monster growls, or an utterly straight-faced parody of same; the fact that it's well-nigh impossible to tell one way or the other pretty much sums up Sleepytime Gorilla Museum."[33] Mason fails to mention SGM's illustrious collaborator, perhaps because the lyrics borrowed for "Helpless Corpses Enactment" are as difficult to decipher as they are to interpret—the aforementioned "Cookie Monster growls" render the verses obscure, and the passages selected are not among the *Wake*'s prominently quoted bits. Moreover, these passages are taken from various points within the *Wake*, occurring in seemingly random and disjointed order, linked more by a consistent theme than by speaker, character, or plot.

In some ways, James Joyce seems a suitable collaborator for a band as playfully experimental as SGM, a group of virtuoso musicians armed with homemade instruments and esoteric tastes. Their interest in Joyce fits well with Joyce's longstanding influence on avant-garde music. As Scott Klein notes, despite Joyce's own rather traditional taste in music, the author's influence on avant-garde compositions is "perhaps without precedent" in its scope and cross-genre nature.[34] The esoterica of Joyce's prose seems part of its appeal, both for the band and its fanbase. Patrick Slevin, in a review of SGM's 2007 show at New York's Bowery Ballroom, recounts not only the band's use of Joyce but the audience's response to it:

> Bossi did preface one new song by passing out sing-a-long sheets with a particular passage from James Joyce's *Finnegan's Wake* [*sic*] to deafening applause—I guess incomprehensible prose is a hipster magnet. It was like some bizarrely extroverted bookworm association: "Anybody here like James Joyce?!" Roaring applause. Nothing against Joyce, but usually it's more like "How's everybody doing tonight?!"[35]

The operative word in Slevin's account is "incomprehensible." Slevin assumes, however facetiously, that Joyce appeals to this audience precisely because his prose defies interpretation, rendering *Finnegans Wake* a prop for the pretentious. As such, Slevin presents Joyce as something of a fashion accessory for the so-called hipsters he mocks throughout his review. While it is impossible to judge the sincerity of that crowd's enthusiasm for Joyce, Sleepytime Gorilla Museum themselves have presented literariness as an essential part of a band's ethos, providing an enthusiastic Joycean experience that does not depend upon scholarly expertise. Violinist Carla Kihlstedt, in a 2007 Boston Globe profile, goes so far as to call her various groups, SGM included, "book clubs": "We're such nerds," she says. "But it's really fun to have four or five people all thinking about the same texts and being able to discuss it on tour. We'll be singing passages from *Finnegan's Wake* [*sic*] on the Sleepytime gigs. I just started it, but Nils [Frykdahl] has spent many years with that book."[36]

Frykdahl is formally credited, along with Joyce, as the cocomposer of "Helpless Corpses Enactment," though his role as lyricist appears to have been selecting the various passages from the *Wake* that appear in the song. These passages are nonsequential and largely disconnected from one another: most lyrics are taken either from the final chapter or from Book III, Chapter IV, though the song's opening lines are taken from the book's first chapter. The result is language disconnected from its original context, rendering its meaning even more obscure than in Joyce's original text. Even the title—taken from Shaun's words in Book III, Chapter I, and one of the many epithets Joyce gives to HCE, the book's mercurial protagonist—seems to have been chosen almost at random for its seemingly sinister and morbid effect. In context, however, the Helpless Corpses Enactment refers to a law forbidding Shaun's brother, Shem, from marriage and procreation. In that regard, the title seems unrelated to the rest of the lyrics, which are themselves connected largely through the recurrent theme of death and resurrection. To this theme, SGM attaches a more sinister implication, evident less in the lyrics than in the death-metal-inspired orchestration and, perhaps more pointedly, in the music video released to promote the song. According to Adam Feinstein, the video's director, the aim of the video was "to conjure up images as strange and direct as those in dreams."[37] While readers of the *Wake* may note that nothing about *Finnegans Wake* is particularly direct, the strangeness Feinstein mentions, and the distortion evident in the video, do fit with some of Joyce's literary experiments. However, the darker elements of the video seem less derived from organic implications of Joyce's text than from SGM and Feinstein's own imaginations. The result is a text transformed without revisions to the language, a Joyce who retains his diction without retaining his tone—an approach that, in a sense, *de*-authorizes Joyce, and yet seems in keeping with the highly allusive, bricolage method that characterizes much of literary modernism.

One thing Sleepytime Gorilla Museum and Kate Bush share with Jefferson Airplane, Dr. Strangely Strange, and Syd Barrett is that, however faithful, deferential, or anachronistic their appropriation of Joyce is, they all take the author and his works seriously. Joyce's place as a literary authority is unquestioned, and the value of that authority is held in high esteem. Such esteem, however, is by no means universal.

"Something Called Ulysses": Joyce as Joke

While Joyce may have entered the world of rock and roll courtesy of Jefferson Airplane in 1967, the author's first appearance on the popular music charts came some four years earlier, from a somewhat unlikely source. That summer, comedian and novelty songwriter Allan Sherman's "Hello Muddah, Hello Fadduh (A Letter from Camp)" would rise as high as number two on the Billboard Charts.[38] As the title suggests, Sherman's song is presented as a young boy's letter to his parents, a series of complaints about the fictional Camp Granada. Among these complaints is the camp's use of literature: "And the head coach wants no sissies, / So he reads to us from something called *Ulysses*."[39]

The reference to *Ulysses* elicits a big laugh from Sherman's studio audience, but what, precisely, is the joke? Unlike the camper's other complaints, the self-evident gripes about boredom, disease, and danger that comprise most of the song, the humor here hinges less on recognizing hyperbole than on recognizing a title. From there, the listener need only understand that *Ulysses* is inappropriate reading material for boys at camp, though no more specialized knowledge of the book is required to get the joke. Sherman's phrasing is designed to flatter the listener by highlighting the camper's comparative ignorance: as long as the listener knows that this "something called *Ulysses*" is a famous book ill-suited for young readers, the humor works.

What, then, does this joke say about Joyce's novel? In part, Sherman's phrasing, referring to Joyce's novel as "something called *Ulysses*," emphasizes the book's alienating content, making it clear that the camper fails to connect with or subsume it as his own cultural capital. Perhaps more curiously, the coach at Camp Granada associates *Ulysses* with a brand of masculinity, treating it as a means to cure any "sissies" in his charge. We might well wonder which passages the coach selects, since *Ulysses* is hardly a celebration of conventional manliness, but Sherman is likely playing on perceptions that the novel is obscene, perhaps expecting his audience to remember that *Ulysses* was censored in America until 1933: it resonates generically as a "banned book." One need not know, for example, that the supposed obscenity in question was the masturbation scene in "Nausicaa," but, rather, that the book contains smutty passages that a young boy would find confusing. This vision of *Ulysses* is, of course, a distortion of the book's actual text. As such, Sherman's joke is more about the novel's reputation than it is about the novel itself, though it's unclear to what extent this misconception belongs to Sherman, to his characters, or to his audience; in any case, the reference makes for a fascinating contrast to rock music's soon-to-come Joycean allusions, providing as it does a chummy laugh among adults at a generation that will soon become, largely by way of its music, a formidable challenge to their norms.

For all its pre-rock naivete, we might credit Sherman with establishing a template for jokes about Joyce in popular music. When musicians introduce Joyce as an object of ridicule, rather than as an aspirational peer, the humor tends to revolve around sexuality and incomprehensibility. One such example is Black 47's "I Got Laid on James

148   *Lit-Rock*

Joyce's Grave," a song about a bizarre, drunken quest to have sex in Zurich's Fluntern Cemetary, ostensibly for literary purposes:

> I got laid on James Joyce's grave.
> I was hopin' his genius would rub off on me,
> But all I got was a kick in the head
> From the caretaker who discovered me.[40]

The song says virtually nothing about Joyce or his works, merely acknowledging the author's genius without exploring its nature or its manifestations. The humor comes from contrasting that genius with the drunken illogic and carnality of the song's speaker, whose attempt to "find [his] voice"[41] on Joyce's grave results in a beating at the hands of the Swiss police.[42]

A yet more profane approach can be found on Therapy?'s "Potato Junkie," the closing track on *Pleasure Death* and the band's forceful response to cultural strife in their native Northern Ireland and, as lead singer Andy Cairns put it, "the constant Leprechaunia we were witnessing first hand in Ireland."[43] While the verses angrily dismiss both Unionist romanticism and Nationalist exceptionalism, the opening lines take aim at Joyce: "I'm bitter, I'm twisted, / James Joyce is fucking my sister."[44] These lines, disconnected as they are from the rest of the song, have nonetheless become a focal point of live performances; on 2010s *We're Here to the End*, a live album culled from Therapy?'s three-night residency at the Water Rats in London, Cairns turns the microphone to his audience midway through the song: "you know something," he says, "I only want to hear you people sing this—are you ready to sing really fucking loud?"[45] The band then stops playing altogether, and the crowd enthusiastically complies.

It's hard to say why these fans are so enthusiastic about James Joyce figuratively, or even literally, fucking their sisters, or what these lines mean in the broader context of the song's cultural commentary. According to Cairns, the song's primary target is "the tourist industry" and its vision of Ireland as "the land of the bog fairies and intense, playful literature [that] was nowhere to be seen in our lives."[46] As such, the chant serves as a vulgar takedown of a writer-turned-tourist attraction, emphasizing his petty carnality above his literary genius; others in the crowd, perhaps, simply enjoy juxtaposing a symbol for high culture with vulgarity. Any of these readings, of course, hinge upon misconceptions of Joyce and his texts, ignoring his distaste for the Leprechaunia of his day, his literary interest in petty carnality, and his own use of the word "fuck" in *Ulysses*. If Therapy? means to invoke Joyce as a cliched symbol of Irishness or Irish culture, they lose in the process his identity as an expatriate who wrote all of his major works in continental Europe, saw his flight to artistry as a shedding of the oppressive forces of his native culture, and was every bit as disenchanted as Therapy? in response to nationalism. Such broad, even misdirected, humor returns us to the irony noted by Kiberd, that the Joyce who held such democratic notions of literature has become a symbol of intellectual elitism, a target for those whom Joyce himself may have seen as potential readers. What carries over from SGM's to Therapy?'s performances is the

A Portrait of the Artist in a Pop Song

potential for merely inciting Joyce in the context of a rock performance as a crowd-pleaser—one that prompts audience participation amidst a shared sense of rebellion.

Joyce and the Ideal Reader

In *Finnegans Wake*, during a section devoted to the *Book of Kells*, Joyce posits the notion of "that ideal reader suffering from an ideal insomnia."[47] In such a reader's hands, a book is "sentenced to be nuzzled over a full trillion times for ever and a night."[48] As he does elsewhere in the *Wake*, Joyce here used the *Book of Kells* as a surrogate for his own works, implying that a reader's exertion should aspire to match the creator's own. If that is the standard for Joyce's readers and critics, one might well argue that the musicians referenced in this essay fail to meet this ideal, that their engagement with Joyce is sometimes superficial and their portrait of the artist a distortion. We might well ascribe blame for this distortion to the musicians for failing to "do the reading," or we might blame Joyce himself for demanding more from his readers than can reasonably be expected.

And yet, the continued presence of Joyce in popular music suggests that, to a certain extent, Joyce has, in Tennyson's phrase, "become a name," a figure whose reputation has eclipsed his deeds, or in this case, his fiction. In this, Joyce's lot resembles that of other great minds: one need not read *Hamlet* to recognize Shakespeare's name as synonymous with eloquence and complexity; one need not read *Relativity: The Special and the General Theory* to recognize Einstein's name as synonymous with scientific brilliance. The name of James Joyce, though less ubiquitous than those others, serves a similar function for difficulty and dirtiness, even to those who have yet to (or will never) crack open his books.

Yet another take is to acknowledge that popular music's distortions of Joyce are themselves rather Joycean, echoing the author's own efforts to reimagine great literature, like the *Odyssey*, in new contexts and toward new ends. While it is difficult for any artist to match the depth and sophistication of Joyce's own engagement with Homer, particularly in the three-to-six minute medium of a pop song, the reach of popular music offers a venue wherein Joyce's reputation can be challenged, confirmed, and modified, even if such modifications are, in practice, acts of transfiguration or, to borrow Joyce's term from *A Portrait of the Artist as a Young Man*, transmutations. Part of what should be valued is Joyce's availability to wide-ranging practices and discourses: his work belongs in equal measure to the academy, the avant-garde, and the comedians who mock him. Toward this end, an incident recounted in Richard Ellmann's biography may prove instructive: a young man, having spotted James Joyce in a Zurich café, asked permission to "kiss the hand that wrote *Ulysses*." Joyce declined. "No," he said, "it did lots of other things too."[49]

Notes

1 Patti Smith, "Patti Smith's Favorite Things," *Wall Street Journal Magazine*, August 1, 2016, https://www.wsj.com/articles/patti-smiths-favorite-things-1470069472.

150   *Lit-Rock*

2 Ibid.

3 Sebring's photograph is not the first to feature Patti Smith *not* reading her copy of *Finnegans Wake*. The book had also appeared four years earlier, this time with Smith herself, in Jork Weissman's *Asleep at the Chateau*, a collection of photographs of celebrities sleeping in various places around Los Angeles' Chateau Marmont. In Weissman's photograph, Smith sits sleeping in a red chair, her copy of *Finnegans Wake* resting on her stomach. As in Sebring's photograph, the book is open roughly to the middle, though Weissman has positioned it so that the front cover, the back cover, and the book's spine (and therefore the title and author) are all clearly visible.

4 According to some accounts, Joyce himself appears on the cover of *Sgt. Pepper*, albeit with his face obscured, just below Dylan and just above T. E. Lawrence.

5 While most musicians seem to regard Joyce as a cosmopolitan artist, certain of Joyce's fellow countrymen, particularly Van Morrison and the Pogues, treat him more as a talismanic Irishman. Morrison, on "Too Long in Exile," namechecks Joyce—along with Samuel Beckett, Oscar Wilde, George Best, and Alex Higgins—as a fellow Irishman who has been away from home for too long. For the Pogues, Joyce is a symbol for joyful, boozy affirmation and polyglottic Irishness—see Kevin Farrell, "'If I Should Fall from Grace with God': The Joycean Punk of the Pogues," *New Hibernia Review* 24, no. 2 (2020): 150–60.

6 Derek Pyle, Krzysztof Bartnicki, and Tess Brewer, "The History of James Joyce Music—Adaptations, Interpretations and Inspirations," *Waywords and Meansigns*, October 1, 2019, http://www.waywordsandmeansigns.com/about/james-joyce-music/.

7 Vincent J. Cheng, "The Joycean Unconscious, or Getting Respect in the Real World," in *Joyce and Popular Culture*, ed. Robert Kershner (Gainesville: University Press of Florida, 1996), 181.

8 Declan Kiberd, *Ulysses and Us: The Art of Everyday Living* (London: Faber, 2009), 30.

9 "After Bathing at Baxter's," *Rolling Stone*, January 20, 1968, https://www.rollingstone.com/music/music-album-reviews/after-bathing-at-baxters-179086/.

10 Bruce Eder, "After Bathing at Baxter's," in *All Music Required Listening: Classic Rock*, ed. Christ Woodstra, John Bush, and Stephen Thomas Erlewine (New York: Backbeat, 2007), 98.

11 Nadya Zimmerman, *Counterculture Kaleidoscope: Musical and Cultural Perspectives on Late Sixties San Francisco* (Ann Arbor: University of Michigan Press, 2011), 144.

12 Ibid., 146.

13 James Joyce, *Ulysses*, ed. Hans Walter Gabler (New York: Vintage, 1986), 482.

14 "Rejoyce," track 7 on Jefferson Airplane, *After Bathing at Baxter's*, RCA Victor, 1967.

15 Ibid.

16 Jeff Tamarkin, *Got a Revolution!: The Turbulent Flight of Jefferson Airplane* (New York: Atria, 2003), 170.

17 Grace Slick, quoted in Tamarkin, 153.

18 Richard Ellmann, *James Joyce* (Oxford: Oxford University Press, 1972), 272.

19 Ron Chapman, *A Very Irregular Head: The Life of Syd Barrett* (Cambridge: Da Capo Press, 2010), 56.

20 "Flower of the Mountain," track 1 on Kate Bush, *Director's Cut*, EMI, 2011.

21 "Flower of the Mountain" omits some twenty-five lines of Joyce's text between the end of the first verse and the beginning of the second. Taken together, the second and third verses comprise the last nine lines of the novel.

22 Joyce, *Ulysses*, 643.

23 "The Sensual World," track 1 on Kate Bush, *The Sensual World*, EMI, 1989.

24 Ibid.
25 Joyce, *Ulysses*, 643.
26 Ibid.
27 Ibid.
28 Joyce, *Ulysses*, 643.
29 "The Sensual World," see note 23.
30 Ibid.
31 Ellmann, *James Joyce*, 642. While Nora's pithy phrase is oft-quoted, it is worth noting that Ellmann received it second-hand, from an interview with Samuel Beckett.
32 Sean Michaels, "Kate Bush Reveals Guest Lyricist on New Album—James Joyce," *Guardian*, April 5, 2011, https://www.theguardian.com/music/2011/apr/05/kate-bush -new-album-james-joyce.
33 Stewart Mason, "In Glorious Times: All Music Review," *All Music*, October 1, 2019, https://www.allmusic.com/album/in-glorious-times-mw0000779149/.
34 Scott Klein, "James Joyce and Avant-Garde Music," *Contemporary Music Centre, Ireland*, June 1, 2004, https://www.cmc.ie/features/james-joyce-and-avant-garde -music.
35 Patrick Slevin, "Sleepytime Gorilla Museum @ Bowery Ballroom," *The Aquarian*, April 15, 2007, https://www.theaquarian.com/2007/04/15/sleepytime-gorilla -museum-bowery-ballroom/.
36 Andrew Gilbert, "Has Violin, Will Play Music of All Genres," *The Boston Globe*, March 9, 2007, http://archive.boston.com/news/globe/living/articles/2007/03/09/has _violin_will_play_music_of_all_genres/.
37 "Sleepytime Gorilla Museum: 'Helpless Corpses Enactment' Video Posted Online," *Blabbermouth*, May 22, 2007, https://www.blabbermouth.net/news/sleepytime-gorilla -museum-helpless-corpses-enactment-video-posted-online/.
38 Perhaps coincidentally, Sherman's song takes its melody from Amilcare Ponchielle's "Dance of the Hours," a piece referenced three times in *Ulysses*. Bloom remembers, first in "Calypso" and again in "Nausicaa," that Molly had first met her lover, Blazes Boylan, at a dance where they had heard this work played; the hours themselves later appear to dance at Bella Cohen's brothel, in "Circe."
39 "Hello Muddah, Hello Fadduh! (A Letter from Camp)," track 7 on Allan Sherman, *My Son, the Nut*, Warner Brothers, 1963.
40 "I Got Laid on James Joyce's Grave," track 7 on Black 47, *Trouble in the Land*, Shanachie, 2000.
41 Ibid.
42 The song also hints at the shared experience of an Irishman abroad: like Joyce, the speaker travels to Zurich from Paris; like Joyce, Black 47's lead singer and songwriter, Larry Kirwan, is an Irishman living in self-imposed exile from his homeland.
43 Andy Cairns, "The Best 12 Therapy? Songs, By Andy Cairns," *Louder*, October 26, 2015, https://www.loudersound.com/features/the-best-12-therapy-songs-by-andy -cairns.
44 "Potato Junkie," track 6 on Therapy?, *Pleasure Death*, Wiiija, 1992.
45 "Potato Junkie," track 14 on Therapy?, *We're Here to the End*, Blast, 2010.
46 Cairns, "The Best 12 Therapy? Songs."
47 Joyce, *Finnegans Wake* (New York: Penguin, 1999), 120.
48 Ibid.
49 Ellmann, *James Joyce*, 114.

9

"Hand in Glove"

Punk, Post-punk, and Poetry

Martin Malone

In her 2007 book, *The Importance of Music to Girls,* the poet Lavinia Greenlaw states that "Punk didn't just change what I listened to and how I dressed. It altered my aesthetic sense completely. This is what music could do: change the shape of the world and my shape within it, how I saw, what I liked and what I wanted to look like."[1] Such radical changes brought about by music surely extend, for Greenlaw and others alike, to poetic development, possibility, and attitude: to the fanciful "growth of a poet's mind," as William Wordsworth termed it. Indeed, as the ex-Oxford Professor of Poetry and current UK Laureate, Simon Armitage, notes in his book *Gig: The Life and Times of a Rock-star Fantasist,* "only through the process of failing to become a rock star have I become a writer."[2] And Christopher James, in a 2012 article for the Poetry Society, has quoted my own observation that "Even if you've won the T.S. Eliot Prize, chances are that you've still been to more gigs than poetry readings and bought more records than poetry books."[3] Such sentiments, indicative of the long-sensed relationship between poetry, music, and song, occur frequently enough within casual or autobiographical discourse. Yet there remains relatively little substantive scholarship on the subject, particularly that which traces the influence of this music upon the output of poets coming of age during the punk and post-punk period. I intend to show in this chapter how this music not only provided a deep well of convertible material for writers and poets, but instigated—as a shared history, symbology, and sense of newly granted artistic "permission"—a generational sensibility, and, within it, a uniquely hybridized version of the poet.

The first "New Generation Poets" of 1994 seem particularly suited to such scrutiny. As well as Armitage and Greenlaw, fellow members of this group have acknowledged links to the music which helped form their sensibilities. Don Paterson and Michael Dongahy, for example, are or were accomplished musicians. And other poets, who have made their way into the contemporary scene beyond the marketing construct of the "New Gen" cohort, also testify to the enduring influence of the music culture they grew up around. Indeed, some of them were formerly part of it: the Bloodaxe poet Virginia Astley, for example, was a *doyenne* of the post-punk music scene, whose recent collection *The English River* boasts a foreword by none other than Pete Townshend. Such cross-fertilization shouldn't surprise us—it has always been around—yet, the socio-cultural conditions of the punk and post-punk period provided particularly rich ground. In *Post-Punk Then and Now*, Kodwo Eshun refers to post-punk's "drive towards self-authorization," while his co-editor Gavin Butt points out that "In its restlessness, its allusiveness, its over-reaching, post-punk vigorously affirmed the possibility that culture could be at once popular, experimental and intellectually-driven."[4] The permissions granted by this period of literate and intellectually aspirational music found a natural extension into other areas of creative practice, nowhere more so than in the poetry subsequently written by its fans.

Though no member of the "New Gen" cohort, I do, at least, share their cultural demographic and confess that I've two dogs of my own in this fight. Since the age of sixteen, I've been a songwriter, singer, and guitarist in a succession of punk/post-punk/indie bands, releasing albums and singles along the way, and even working as a sound engineer/producer for several years. No great surprise, therefore, when, between 2008 and 2013, I joined Armitage as a guitarist in his "mid-life crisis" band, the Scaremongers, who would go on to release several singles as well as the album *Born In A Barn*, and appear on BBC Two's *The Culture Show* and at the 2009 Latitude Festival. After a lifetime in bands, I also now publish poetry; indeed, this is how I met Simon Armitage in the first place, having also failed to become a rock star. Such is the personal providence of this discussion, then, though it's also rooted in a generational coincidence that should surprise no one: the "children of punk and post-punk" would naturally filter through into wider culture, just as the hippy generation had done before them, bringing along the formative influences of their pasts. Clearly, there are special conditions facing each generation, though I'd not be alone in arguing that for the one under scrutiny here, there was a particularly marked drift toward synthesizing "low" and "high" cultures, and toward the end of eroding such false distinctions. The time appears right for a proper evaluation of this phenomenon. Like Gavin Butt, I aim to "assess the formative impact of this time upon my political and aesthetic values, as well as upon my mature intellectual and cultural preoccupations."[5]

Academic distinctions are there to be drawn between the terms "punk" and "post-punk," though, to most who lived through the period, their respective sensibilities *felt* much more seamless and in-the-moment than retrospective analysis might suggest. My focus is upon the through-flow of interrelated ideas which conditioned subjective, creative responses to both cultural phenomena as perceived by participants and fans alike. This means painting to some degree with large brush strokes regarding the two terms and their corresponding aesthetics—a discussion that, to be sure, could necessitate a volume of its own. Here, I intend to explore punk and post-punk's hand-in-glove relationship with the poetry it helped spawn—its formative impact and the sense of permission it appeared to grant—as part of a shared cultural moment and by way of exemplars. Central to this will be those acknowledgments made by the poets themselves, in their own writing or comments on the subject. This includes a phone conversation I had with Simon Armitage, during which we addressed the subject of musical influence. I shall, of course, be looking also at the poetry itself and trying to articulate those properties which appear to be the direct product of acquired punk or post-punk sensibilities and vernacular. There are a number of obvious candidates here: Armitage poems like "Clown Punk" and "Don't Sing (*for Paddy MacAloon*)," or Virginia Astley's direct reminiscences of her musical career. However, I hope to also draw out a sense in which the influence of punk and post-punk culture is more substantive than the mere fact of its intuitive license *a la* Greenlaw. I'd like to reflect, too, that this relationship was very much reciprocal, and that musicians were drawing upon resources offered them from the neighboring bank of the creative river: a state of affairs acknowledged and documented at the time and in subsequent memoirs.

Let's start with that phone conversation from a few years back, when the Scaremongers were still a going concern and we'd discussed this topic in passing. It was around the time that I was beginning to assess the formative impact of the punk/post-punk era upon my own "mature intellectual and cultural preoccupations." The questions we considered, therefore, were geared toward drawing out the direct and indirect nature of those links between younger listening habits and "mature" creative practice.

> **Martin Malone:** Can you direct me to any specific instances or lines where you feel you were consciously or subconsciously channeling moments from your record collection?
>
> **Simon Armitage:** This is evident especially in the earlier poems when I thought that they might mean something. Poems like "Eighties/Nineties" in *Zoom*. There are occasions when I've used a song rhythm as a starter; for example, "Killing Time 2" consciously utilizes the rhythm of Bob Dylan's "Subterranean Homesick Blues." And on other occasions, I have chosen a song lyric as a starter, but the song has sort of died away as the writing has thickened itself. "Leaves On The Line," for example, leaned on Nick Cave's song "Into My Arms" but was leached out more and more by the writing. More recently, in *Seeing Stars* the poems: "Bringing It All Back Home," "To The Bridge," and "The Overtones" all have direct echoes but varying distances from sources—if that's what we can call them—in song. Overall, though, I think it would be difficult to look at the style and form of my poems and make a lot of direct traces of lyrics and lines. In terms of actual practice, it's more a question of style than anything else: I've always been drawn to a kitchen-sink style and the bands I like tended to do the same. This is just the sort of thing I like.
>
> **MM:** My focus is—I suppose—those poets whose creative/aesthetic/social sensibilities were at least part-formed by early exposure to punk and then post-punk.
>
> **SA:** The big relationship for me was attitudinal and comes from punk's DIY ethos more than anything else. The musical franchise was extended by punk and I took that to mean the poetry franchise also. But this had sort of been going on since the war and myself and poets like Carol Ann Duffy were inheritors of that drift. Post-punk was even more important because to me that said something about solipsism and internal landscapes. At that time Indie was

a way of being involved musically but without having to participate in easy collectivism; it was still private and cool. You felt as if you were staking a claim in the margins; it was working outside of the mainstream. Attitudinally, that's what I felt I was doing in poetry at the time too. In the early stuff, there were a lot of traditional rhythms and forms working off these attitudes and a lot of American voices. So, I think punk and post-punk *became* democratizing because it was about access to that stuff.

MM: I've certainly found it that way, myself. And the importance cannot be exaggerated, of that permission granted to a working-class boy with no familial academic hinterland and limited access to what might be termed "establishment culture," by people like Morrissey and Paul Weller or (in my case) Richard Jobson of the Skids. Each was intellectually aspirational and suggested the existence of role models from my own class and similar background. How about you?

SA: I'm classic *no-brow*. I think I belong to a generation that feels unembarrassed to talk about the importance of music; to talk about it in terms of high art forms, to feel comfortable with that concept.

MM: I couldn't agree more. Indeed, encouraged by the times and their apparent permission to think of popular music as an art form as worthy of scrutiny as any other, I think we patented this acculturative response; far more than, say, the 1960s generation with their "Dylan-as-poet" tropes. That's not to dismiss them out of hand, I just feel that, perhaps thanks to their groundwork, our generation took it a lot further and, eventually I suppose, into the academy. Whether that's a good or bad thing for poetry *or* rock n' roll, I suppose time, technology, and "leisure opportunity" will tell.

As I write this in 2019, perhaps it is significant that Simon Armitage has gone back for another visit to the musical well: his latest "extracurricular" band project, a loose, ambient alliance called Land Yacht Regatta, is freshly signed to Universal. Introducing the "spoken-word" track "33⅓" on Radio 6's Radcliffe and Maconie Show, Armitage invokes generationally formative moments and memories, such as the death of Joy Division's Ian Curtis and the "redolent" sound of run-out grooves on vinyl.[6] All of which is consistent with the tenor of my conversation with him back in 2013. What both moments reveal is something of Adorno's "element of psychological transfer"[7] between a poet's listening habits around the popular music in whose presence his heart first opened and subsequent acts of self-authorization. Certainly, there appears to be some congruence between Armitage's extension of the musical "franchise" of punk into poetry and Gavin Butt's "vigorously affirmed" possibility, on behalf of post-punk, that culture could be at once popular and intellectually driven—both of which conjure a suggestion of Adorno's image of popular music as "the psychological household of the masses."[8] Where else might we find Armitage's "kitchen-sink" but in just such a household? This phenomenon of psychological transfer is not, after all, unnatural, and has its precursors: for instance, in her book *Stand In The Trench Achilles!*, Elizabeth Vandiver explores the relationship between classical literature and the formative

156   *Lit-Rock*

sensibilities of the Great War poets, describing an awareness of the Classics and their appropriated tropes as part of that generation's "furniture of the mind."[9] As Vandiver reminds us, at the time of the Great War, in the population at large, a "promiscuous" mix of high and low culture was the norm, and this was a historic moment of relatively high levels of literacy among the troops. This somewhat pre-echoes a state of affairs in the 1970s and 1980s, when school English Literature texts such as *Nine Moderns Poets* and *Poets of Our Time* were set before a generation of young minds also exposed to the ubiquitous soundtrack of punk and post-punk. In the UK at least, the same generation was the last to enjoy those egalitarian possibilities offered by fully funded tertiary education, with its lack of tuition fees and full maintenance grants to those poor enough to apply. This was, also, an era when music was a much more pressing cultural imperative than perhaps it is nowadays. Just as the First World War poets went on to "adduce" the Trojan War as a template for their modern conflict, their "New Gen" counterparts went on to adduce the contemporary music scene as part of their own sense of conflict and self-authorization. For each, the language, imagery, and sensibilities culled from such bespoke templates were part of its shared cultural capital. The burden of generational reality is clearly *very* different, but the cultural phenomenology is not. How might this have played out in the poetry which that later—more historically fortunate—generation went on to produce?

"Don't Sing," from Armitage's 1989 debut collection *Zoom!*, is of particular interest here since it clearly involves his poetic reception of a song in which the songwriter is, himself, processing his own reading of a literary work: in this case, Graham Green's novel *The Power and the Glory*. I think we see in the poem an instance of what Armitage described as "forms of working off" post-punk's politically engaged attitudes, an extension of the novel's repressive, South-American state to contemporaneous regimes like that of Augusto Pinochet in 1970s and 1980s Chile. While there are few material echoes, beyond the specific reference of the title, this poem is fascinating in two ways: first, it embodies the notion of rock music's (general) interconnectedness with literary preoccupations and, secondly, it exemplifies how Armitage was, indeed, and early on, developing his poetic voice by working through the cultural capital offered him by his listening. Tropes familiar to Armitage readers are clearly present—the easy conversational style half-masking darker matter—but, significant to my discussion is the fact that they arrive in this particular poem *by way of* his listening to a student playlist staple of the time:

> Any kind of burial was impossible
> so we agreed that the next time a priest was around
> he might say a few words inside the hut, and that
> no one would go singing to the soldiers.[10]

And there are other, more explicit, examples of this transfer of recreational listening into literary contexts to be found elsewhere in Armitage's poetry, both early and more recent. As he was quick to point out, 2010's experimental assemblage of shaggy dog stories, *Seeing Stars*, contains a music-rich work called "The Overtones." This poem archly references ten song titles by Derry punk-pop band the Undertones in a playfully ironic lyric stew that also has Casanova, the Arc de Triomphe, St. Michael's Mount, Don Quixote, and Radio 4 among its ingredients. In the same collection, there are other examples of his echoing of specific songs at varying distances from the source. In "Bringing it All Back Home," for example, as a result of "Googling [his] own name," the Dylan album title eases us into a *picaresque* stroll through the poet's own semi-fictionalized back pages in the company of an "Armitage Trail" guide called "Bob." While the pop references here may reflect more mature listening patterns, they also reflect a habit of mind that has been consistent throughout Armitage's career and which reflects his "classic *no-brow*" comment. Within the same collection, post-punk preoccupations (in this case, the issue of "credibility") are detectable in his light-hearted dismissal of later groups, such as the Manic Street Preachers and Red Hot Chili Peppers, "whereas the Teardrop / Explodes, either by blind accident or through / careful purpose had kept every promise ever made."[11] Such concerns, in whatever spirit they are rendered, remain signifiers of Armitage's cultural vintage. As he points out himself, the big relationship is "attitudinal," but there is more than a hint, also, of that "solipsism and internal landscape" which Armitage identified as having been crucial to both post-punk and his own development. Whatever else is going on here, there is certainly that generational comfort in talking about the importance of music in the context of a high art form.

I suggested earlier that such interdisciplinary relationships were very much two-way. Clearly, "the element of psychological transfer" between post-punk songwriters and their own *reading* habits were similarly cross-fertilized. We witnessed, above, an instance of Paddy McAloon's creative misprision of Graham Greene, for example, and David McComb, chief songwriter with Australian post-punk band the Triffids, provides one of the very many other examples from that period. The reciprocity of this relationship is underscored by *Beautiful Waste,* a collection of McComb's poetry posthumously published by Fremantle Press in 2009. The introduction is provided by John Kinsella, a highly regarded Australian poet, novelist, critic, essayist, and editor, who is also from Perth and a huge fan of the band. In it, Kinsella describes precisely the type of intellectual magpie fit for this discussion: "David did tertiary lit. studies. He was a musician from his early teenage years. This combination makes his position as a writer in Perth different in my era at least."[12] The profile fitted here to Western Australia in the late 1970s and 1980s was nonetheless growing more common throughout the world of popular music thanks, in no small part, to the permissive legacy of punk and post-punk. For example, in a moving memoir of his time with the Go-Betweens, Robert Forster recounts how he met his friend and fellow songwriter, Grant McLennan, at the University of Queensland in EN103, Introduction to Literature B.[13] In a 2016 promotional clip for Penguin Books Australia, Forster goes so far as to observe: "Sometimes I think that writers have been more influential on me than music."[14] I was fortunate enough to chat with him after a recent solo gig in Birmingham, where he kindly agreed to answer questions akin to those put to Armitage. His response serves to elucidate, beautifully, that reciprocity of influence is key to this discussion:

158 *Lit-Rock*

MM: Robert, you touched on this in *Grant & I,* but if you could address it here a bit more directly: Grant and yourself were very young when you started the Go-Betweens so, how much was this a formation which reflected musical and/or cultural inspirations?

Robert Forster: The band at the start was almost all about cultural references. Grant and I weren't whizz musicians or ones that had served any kind of standard rock and roll apprenticeships. That's what punk and post-punk allowed—people with ideas to slip through and gain attention. We looked at what we had to set us apart from normal groups, both inside and outside punk, and our fascination and enthusiasm for things outside of rock culture, be it film, books, and television, we thought offered ideas we could incorporate into the band's aesthetic, without us being too precious or condescending about it. Not be an "art band" but an artful pop band.

MM: Was your drift toward music some reflection of it appearing to grant greater cultural permission than the established literary canon? Or was it purely a reflection of the musical landscape of the times? I've read *Pig City,*[15] and I'm aware that Brisbane under the Bjelke-Petersen regime had its own situation to deal with or react to. People form bands for often complicated reasons, I guess, so could you share some of your thinking back then, some recollections in tranquility perhaps?

RF: I would have to say that under the Bjelke-Peterson government, stifling, as it did, any form of intellectualism or cultural activity or the idea of young people having fun—and given the geographical isolation of Brisbane—there didn't seem to be any kind of "permissions" in Brisbane in the late seventies. Little was on offer. You made your own moves. Not unrelated to this—one of the great things about starting a band at twenty, is that as soon as you start playing gigs in a decent-sized town, three or four hundred know you. If you are writing your own songs with your own words attached, you are reaching audiences. This is a powerful thing at twenty. Also, if you start recording and touring, the audience grows as does your profile. This doesn't happen to a writer or a filmmaker or playwright usually till they're thirty.

MM: My focus is—I suppose—those poets whose creative/aesthetic/social sensibilities were at least part-formed by early exposure to punk and then post-punk. When I put these questions to Simon Armitage he suggested that the big relationship was "attitudinal." Was there a reverse polarity at play in your music: that is, did the "high-brow" culture give you some of your "gut rot rock 'n' roll"?

RF: Grant and I both studied literature at Queensland University. I don't know if this is an answer to your question, but I think what we did was not shy away from, or try to deny, what we had learned at university. That was important, even if it did open us up to the accusation of being pretentious. It was part of our knowledge, why avoid it? And of course, it opened up new ways to say things in a pop lyric. It seemed pointless to copy old world rock and roll language, and attitudes, when I'd just spent a semester studying Doris

Lessing's *The Golden Notebook*. But, at the same time, Grant and I were up for matching high-brow with low-brow—our genuine affection for the music and joy of the Monkees an example. The trick was not to get caught in the middle.

MM: As a songwriter with English degrees, I know, for sure, that I would comb literary references into my own songs. Can you direct me to any specific instances or lines in your songs where you feel you were consciously or subconsciously channeling moments from your library? This doesn't have to be limited to poetry by the way (I recall the reconstructed James Joyce-with-guitar pose of the *Danger In The Past* cover).

RF: Generally, I try and let my admiration for certain writers or books act as an inspiration to my work, flowing into it, without quoting the work or drawing attention to it. When I do reference work from the literary world it tends, to my ear or view, to be quite obscure. For example, in "Head Full Of Steam," there is the lyric—"Her mother works, her father works, in exports but that's of no importance at all." In a favorite novel of mine, Christopher Isherwood's *Mr. Norris Changes Trains*, the central character runs a business from his apartment, with the words "Exports and Imports" on the door—this, I remember, inspired the line. But as you can see, it is very obscure.

MM: As suggested earlier, the Go-Betweens were part of a generation of unusually literate musicians who saw no dissonance between popular music and explicitly "high-brow" cultural signifiers—lots of *Marxism Today* and "Yves Marie-Sainte in *On The Waterfront*," for example—how aware of all this were you at the time? And what other examples of this phenomenon can you think of which, in turn, might have influenced you?

RF: I do think this is a generational phenomenon and it goes back to what I was saying at the start: punk and post-punk was a window that let in a lot of interesting people that normally would not have bothered being in rock bands. Photographers, actors, artists, and graphic designers, jumped into bands because virtuosity on a musical instrument, which had ruled rock music since the mid-1960s, was not of prime importance; it had been replaced by Do You Have Anything To Say? Lloyd Cole crept through. As did Morrissey, Nick Cave, Lydia Lunch, Howard Devoto, Poly Styrene, Ian Curtis, and many more. The window closed, but not entirely. A new lyrical thread, inspired by literature, high-brow and low-brow, had infiltrated the possibilities of the rock lyric.

With Armitage's, Forster's remarks underscore the intricate interdisciplinary dialectic that was taking place at the time and which offered to each of them a cultural resource. They certainly reflect my own motivations when forming the band Innocents Abroad with college friends back in 1984. Clearly, groups like the Go-Betweens and the Triffids belonged to a generation of Australian bands notable, as Forster points out, for their incorporation of "things outside of rock culture." Tellingly, within the context of this discussion, John Kinsella observes of the Triffids' frontman: "As a lyricist, McComb wrote musical metaphors with a strong sense of the literary poetic. His eclectic reading

160 *Lit-Rock*

is evident throughout his poetry, consciously mixing not only 'high' and 'low' cultural registers, but also contemporary and anachronistic forms of expression."[16] It's the word "consciously" here that links songwriters of the period to many of the poets they subsequently helped "grow" from within their fanbase: a phenomenon entirely mutual with Armitage's notion of an extended franchise. Sure enough, this idea found its way into song as well as poetry, and sometimes into both disciplines by the same writer. Kinsella, for instance, goes on to advance his claims for McComb's poetry as much as his songwriting: "It is almost bizarre that David McComb is not yet known as a significant Australian poet. One of the features that should place him in the company of his contemporaries, whether journal or book-published or performing, is his innovative use of form."[17] This may be stretching things a little, given McComb's premature demise and the vagaries of literary reception, but it is interesting that "a significant Australian poet" is claiming some sort of generational and interdisciplinary kinship; that the franchise is, indeed, extended in a way similar to the Nobel Committee's culturally omnivorous, genre-blurring selection of Bob Dylan. And sure enough, when I turn on my second-favorite song of all time, I encounter McComb's beautiful gloss (first excerpt) on a well-known early poem by Les Murray (second excerpt):

I've got a little place to myself up on Stony Ridge
I've got it made in the shade
I sleep in the afternoon
Leave my bed unmade[18]

I'll get up soon, and leave my bed unmade.
I'll go outside and split off kindling wood,
From the yellow-box log that lies beside the gate,
And the sun will be high, for I get up late now.[19]

Of this very track, the poet Matt Merritt recently confided to me: "That one song played a huge part in me getting into poetry in the first place—I loved it and the album so much that as soon as I read McComb saying that it had been inspired by the Les Murray poem, I wanted to read everything Murray had written."[20] Whichever way we cut it, what we're witnessing are compositional methods surely analogous to Armitage's use of song material as stimulus for his own poems, from which direct elements are gradually "leached away" during the writing process. There are of course major departures, in structure and sentiment alike, in McComb's rendition: the willful use of cliché and straight rhyme; the shift in mood from melancholy to contentment; the exchange, by way of verb tense, of the future with the present moment. Metatextually, however, the instance may operate as a kind of mutual lifeline: a tip of the cap on McComb's part back to Murray, whose poetry a listener may now wish to pursue or revisit, and a potential, demonstrated credit for the songwriter as a reader of poetry.

It's a phenomenon with which I am, myself, familiar. Musically, I've recycled my own past reading into subsequent songs, glossing on a 1995 album, for example, the phrase "Though much is taken, much abides" from Tennyson's "Ulysses" in "Holiday Golightly"

"Hand in Glove" 161

(a title itself gleaned from Truman Capote's 1958 novella *Breakfast at Tiffany's*) and, on a different track from the same album, lines from *Macbeth*.[21] Likewise, when it comes to poetry, I've parlayed my years as a sound engineer into poems like "Haas Effect" and "Mic-ing the Kit"[22]; described, in "Waiting for the *Green* World Tour to come to town," the socio-emotional effect of REM fandom; and engaged directly, as in the Smiths-derived "Bigmouth Strikes Again," with post-punk lyrics. The latter example reads as follows:

> I'm afraid I'm an open book, I say stuff,
> confess too readily in my cups and
>
> mess-up in moments like these: you
> with your roman nose held high in disgust
>
> at my latest *faux pas*. And, sweetness,
> I know you are only half-joking when
>
> you say I should be bludgeoned in my bed
> for selling my Smiths ticket so I could
>
> go see The Armoury Show instead
> but, at the time, you were only four
>
> and, having seen them twice before—
> like a Beckett play—I felt I'd got the point.
>
> Besides, liking Jobson longer, there was
> a seniority of quiff thing to be respected.
>
> Connected was my love for McGeogh's guitar
> which I felt would fade out before Marr's.
>
> So, don't give me back those mix tapes, don't melt
> down my old Walkman; consider them my
>
> legacy to this retro age of legacy,
> alongside these inconvenient truths,
>
> my scratched vinyl, your Spotify.com.
> Because here in old Camden Town,
>
> out drinking with the hung-on-too-long
> I sense that I've moved on. Lover, please
>
> stop me if you think you've heard this one before
> and don't make me know how Joan of Arc felt.[23]

Here, the song references are not so much "leached away" as flagrantly interjected—a set of *heteroglossic* utterances through which popular music arrives, as a welcomed "other," into the literary context. The poem's fabric of Smith's allusions invokes, I hope, a broader sense of past-shared culture—a potpourri of media, practices, and proper

162   *Lit-Rock*

names, including, beneath Morrissey's domineering shadow, a sub-strata of the half-forgotten as signified by bands like the Armoury Show. The invoked cultural capital can be seen as an (ongoing) means of negotiating a personal relationship (the poem's "I" and "you"), and performs, like the Murray/McComb pairing above, a mutually constituting function: the invocation and transformation of the Smiths/Morrissey as a meaningful and generationally formative entity, and the interpolation of myself as part of its network—a certain ethos, I suppose, as listener/fan/fellow-songster. And this use of allusion—of textual sign-posting—extends by way of Beckett to Morrissey's own, well-documented reliance on literature. Broadly speaking, then, one can find across the spectrum of the New Gen era poets "And the rest of their generation" (to quote Lloyd Cole)[24] not only a shared musical influence but also a mutual effort, by importing playlists into poetics, to shake up high/low distinctions.

Returning to Greenlaw, whose book *The Importance of Music to Girls* heads this discussion, one finds an interesting deviation from my thesis: despite the revelations of her memoir, direct invocations of music are, in her poetry, hard to find. Declining to be interviewed for this chapter, she offered the view that: "Your questions are good ones, but I've found over the years that the book is the best expression of what I have to say about this."[25] Such understandable reticence does not, however, extend to her 2001 debut novel, *Mary George of Allnorthover*, a *bildungsroman* fizzing with a sense of youthful epiphany, attendant upon her teenage protagonist's exposure to the culturally energizing effect of punk rock:

> They came in from the coast and even from London, drawn by the excitement of a kind of music that had already made its way out of the city and was bubbling up through bedrooms and garages out in the sticks. For the first time, urban boys and girls wished themselves provincial, hopelessly cut off and with an easily shockable audience on hand.[26]

Evoked wonderfully here is that juncture when punk broke out of the metropolitan centers of London and New York to send its wave of cultural possibility and self-authorization crashing over their provincial hinterlands, thereby paving the way for what was to become the less-centralized phenomenon of post-punk. It certainly *feels* akin to Simon Armitage's description of the permission he saw granted by punk and post-punk to stake a claim in the margins. Indeed, Greenlaw depicts the precise moment when those margins became the basis of a new mainstream culture authored by the very youngsters here described. Thus, by the 1990s, *Nine Modern Poets*, *Poets of Our Times*, and the "O"-level qualification they facilitated had been supplanted by the new *GCSE* (General Certificate of Education) qualification and anthologies which featured for the first time a younger generation of punk, post-punk, and dub-influenced poets like Simon Armitage, Carol Ann Duffy, and Benjamin Zephaniah. This was—in many respects—the new order.

Such evolution as I'm describing here was, clearly, a graduated one. The practitioners under scrutiny came up with highly personalized responses to the acculturative possibilities offered by the times. But many approached their core practice in the same intellectually curious spirit of inter-disciplinarity liberated by post-punk. Thus, songwriters were influenced by their reading of literature and authors were, likewise, influenced by their listening. The same could be said of the film and the visual arts, and, as I've already suggested, of other eras. However, there remains a certain *something* afloat here, beyond what I can adequately cover in this chapter. As Simon Reynolds observes in the introduction to his seminal book, *Rip It Up and Start Again*: "Those postpunk years from 1978-1984 saw the systematic ransacking of twentieth-century modernist art and literature. The entire postpunk period looks like an attempt to replay virtually every modernist theme and technique via the medium of pop music."[27] So, it's hardly surprising that music makers of this period modeled and inspired similar levels of reciprocal inquiry among their fans. It is this very quality of interconnectedness generated by an aspirational music culture which was, in turn, reflected by its fans in their own artistic output.

As we've seen, many of the artists even switched practice, at some point, to attempt satisfactory answers in secondary artforms. I've already touched upon Armitage's forays into indie and ambient music, as well as David McComb's more discreet venture into "serious" poetry. This phenomenon might be dismissed as dilettantism were it not for the avowed quality of the results. Virginia Astley is a case in point. To readers of a certain vintage, her eminence in the "pastoral pop" rack of the independent music store of the 1980s might yet be remembered. I first encountered her in 1981 as a headline member of the Ravishing Beauties, who were supporting the Teardrop Explodes in their residency at Liverpool's legendary Club Zoo. I recall her winsomely groomed image staring back at me from the vinyl collection of many a good friend, and recollect her work as the hippest *collaboratrice du jour* with a string of cool post-punk acts, including my own teenage favorites, the Skids, on their ill-fated Stuart-free album, *Joy*. Lately, she has reinvented herself as a talented poet, publishing a couple of collections, the latest of which—2018's *The English River*—I reviewed for *Poetry Ireland*. In that review, I set her work within the canonical context of Thomas Hardy, Edward Thomas, Alice Oswald, et al., and rejoice in how she "takes us on a meditative journey down this most iconic of rivers and, in doing so, evokes a landscape already highly scrutinised and freighted with cultural resonance." I remark too on how "the poet's musical past creeps in with references like 'The white noise flanged / and phased.'"[28] Indeed, a poem such as "How did I ever think this would be OK?" is freighted with lyrical signifiers that sing to readers familiar with the music and personalities of the post-punk era:

> this winter's afternoon they married
> in that same riverside church, your sister
> pale and gorgeous, Russell in his kilt.
> His mothers and sisters are here,
> downing rum punch in the lounge.
> They seem to avoid me, possibly
> because I was the one who slung
> his bass guitar into the Thames.
> That was before you and I were,

164   *Lit-Rock*

before London and Liverpool,
before Oxford and Monmouthshire.
But the last time I was in this house—
I can hardly speak—the last time,
was the day we buried you.
And I remember your father,
Who had never bought your CDs,
Breaking down in Tower Records.
And that day, your poor body,
the only thing the same your hands.[29]

As a fan of the musical era here depicted, I almost feel as if the characters in this otherwise-personal elegy were culled from my very own past. It still feels like an intrusion into private grief to reflect that, unless I'm very much mistaken, "Russell" is here the former Skids bass player, Russell Webb, and the poem's addressee, Pete de Freitas, the drummer for Echo & The Bunnymen, killed in a motorcycle accident in June 1989. Astley is merely adhering to the maxim "write what you know," but what she knows happens to be the post-punk world of which she was once part. I started off by stating a wish to examine those poetic moments which were most clearly the product of acquired punk or post-punk sensibilities and vernacular, and it strikes me that this poem is paradigmatic. Even the places mentioned are locations notable for the studios where many bands of that era recorded: Eden and Trident Studios in London, Amazon in Liverpool, The Manor, just north of Oxford, and Rockfield in Monmouthshire. The resonant context, vital to all successful verse, is here unmistakably specific to the post-punk narrative, just as Wessex might be to a Hardy poem.

As Forster suggested, we are witnessing something of "a generational phenomenon" based upon the widely held feeling that punk and post-punk did, indeed, provide an opportunity to participate in popular music for a range of previously marginalized outsiders from other disciplines. Its mixing-up of "low-" and "high-brow" artforms was not unique to this generation *per se*. However, it was precisely those emblematic notions of "extended franchise," the "open window," and cultural permission, which characterized the era, allowing in Forster's "Photographers, actors, artists, graphic designers" and, as I hope I've adequately demonstrated, nascent poets. Let's not forget, too, that "post-punk" was altogether more protean and multi-layered than being just about "art": the 1980s ska-revival stood, after all, on a ticket of "fuck art let's dance," though this is, in itself, a cultural statement.

In summing up, then, and keenly aware of my many sins of omission, I'll emphasize the expansiveness of the terrain whose surface I've merely scratched: I've not even mentioned the punk poets, themselves, nor the dub poetry of someone like Linton Kwesi Johnson, nor, indeed the crude poetics of John Lydon or the meta-kitsch of bands like the Ramones—all examples of extended poetic franchise beyond those artists discussed here. As for poetry itself, in the final analysis, it is an ever-evolving language machine, constantly rebooting to encompass new registers and speech patterns from the times in which it is written. We are currently witnessing, for example, the linguistic

"Hand in Glove"

adjustment poetry is making to reflect new social sensitivities and digital leisure-time pursuits, as can be seen in Irish poet Stephen Sexton's award-winning debut collection, *If All the World and Love Were Young*, a text dominated by the signifiers of his 16-bit video-game childhood. But this is not my generational reality, nor do I negotiate it with quite the same urgency. What I hope I *have* shown is the cultural heft and seriousness with which punk and post-punk engaged those of its audience members who went on to produce art of their own in the form of poetry, and who enjoyed its hand-in-glove relationship with notions that popular music *was* art, and that art could be made popular under its influence.

Notes

1 Lavinia Greenlaw, *The Importance of Music to Girls* (London: Faber, 2007), 123.
2 Simon Armitage, *Gig: The Life and Times of a Rock-star Fantasist* (London: Penguin, 2009), 3.
3 Christopher James, "Hand in Glove," *Poetry News*, Summer 2012.
4 Gavin Butt, Kodwo Eshun, and Mark Fisher, eds., *Post-Punk Then and Now* (London: Repeater, 2016), 7.
5 Ibid., 8–9.
6 Radcliffe and Maconie, *BBC Radio*, September 29, 2016, https://www.bbc.co.uk/programmes/p049fr52.
7 Theodore Adorno, "Music and Mass Culture," in *Essays on Music*, ed. Richard Leppert, trans. Susan H. Gillespie (London: University of California Press, 2002), 456.
8 Ibid., 458.
9 Elizabeth Vandiver, *Stand In The Trench Achilles!* (Oxford: Oxford University Press, 2013), 39. Vandiver ascribes the phrase to Richard Jenkyns, "The Beginnings of Greats, 1800–1872, I: Classical Studies," in *The History of the University of Oxford, VI: Nineteenth-Century Oxford, Part 1*, ed. M. G. Brock and M. C. Curthoys (Oxford: Clarendon, 1997), 519.
10 Armitage, *"Don't Sing (for Paddy McAloon),"* *Zoom!* (Newcastle: Bloodaxe, 1989), 19.
11 Armitage, "To the Bridge," in *Seeing Stars* (London: Faber, 2010), 45.
12 John Kinsella, introduction to *Beautiful Waste*, David McComb (Fremantle, Western Australia: Fremantle, 2009), 13.
13 Robert Forster, *Grant & I: Inside and Outside the Go-Betweens* (Sydney: Penguin, 2016), 21–2.
14 Ibid., "Grand and I—Robert Forster on Literature," *Penguin Books Australia*, September 27, 2016, https://www.youtube.com/watch?v=TL07zPHq2Ug.
15 Andrew Stafford, *Pig City: From the Saints to Savage Garden* (Brisbane: University of Queensland Press, 2004).
16 Kinsella, *Beautiful Waste*, 11.
17 Ibid., 19.
18 "New Year's Greetings (The Country Widower)," track 8 on the Triffids, *The Black Swan*, Island, 1989.

166   *Lit-Rock*

19   Les Murray, "The Widower in the Country," in *The Ilex Tree* (Canberra: Australian National University Press, 1965), 30.

20   Matt Merrit, email message to author, December 18, 2019.

21   "Holiday Golightly" and "The Land That Time Forgot," on Eskimø Chains, *Nureyev*, Southpaw, 1995.

22   Martin Malone, *The Waiting Hillside* (Matlock: Templar Poetry, 2011), 27–9.

23   Martin Malone, "Bigmouth Strikes Again," in *Cur* (Nottingham: Shoestring Poetry, 2015), 44–5.

24   "Are You Ready To Be Heartbroken?," track 10 on Lloyd Cole and the Commotions, *Rattlesnakes*, Polydor, 1984.

25   Lavinia Greenlaw, email message to author, February 19, 2019.

26   Ibid., *Mary George of Allnorthover* (London: Flamingo, 2001), 270.

27   Simon Reynolds, *Rip It Up and Start Again: Postpunk 1978–1984* (London: Penguin, 2006), 2.

28   Virginia Astley, "The Weir at Benson," in *The English River* (Hexham: Bloodaxe, 2018), 51.

29   Ibid., "How Did I Ever Think This Would Be OK?" in *The English River* (Hexham: Bloodaxe, 2018), 51.

Part V

Nation and Narrative

10

Under an American Spell

U2's *The Joshua Tree* in the Shadow of Flannery O'Connor

Scott Calhoun

As U2's stock rose in the mid-1980s, particularly in the United States, Bono and The Edge read from a curated library of American literature to prepare for recording their next album, *The Joshua Tree* (1987). That album boosted U2 to a height where only rock icons live, such that thirty years later, U2 could successfully stage a global tour of *The Joshua Tree* again. With its prevalent expressions of love for and quarrels with the United States, *The Joshua Tree* remains the bands' most "American" album to date. When the US Library of Congress added it to the National Recording Registry in 2013, Stephen Catanzarite wrote in his essay for the entry:

> Set against the background of an America that is at once awe-inspiring in its expansiveness and beauty, and confounding in its contradictions and distortions, the songs explore both the gleaming heights of the American Idea—President Reagan's "shining city on a hill," where the creative energies of the people are called forth in and through freedom—and the desperation, loneliness, and sorrow found in America's valleys and shadows. This American paradox—a place where love is being both built up and burned down—is plainly laid out in the panoramic opener, "Where the Streets Have No Name." . . . [The album] continues to loom large, enduring not only as a high-water mark in the annals of rock and roll, but as a living artifact from the cultural landscape of late-20th century America.[1]

What has perhaps been overlooked in previous analyses of the album's American imagery and musical heritage is the font of American literature into which Bono and The Edge dipped for developing narrative and tonal signatures. While all four members of the band—Adam Clayton and Larry Mullen, Jr. included—have always had an interest in the arts and their accompanying socio-political milieus, Bono and The Edge's reading histories are better known and have had more influence on U2's lyrics and performative gestures. A closer look at what they were reading, and not just directly witnessing, in the 1980s not only offers further evidence of *The Joshua Tree* as U2's most American album but adds to the notion of "Americanness" as a literary tradition that offers a potential point of entry for "outsiders."

U2's extensive touring through America in the early 1980s piqued their interest in the people, places, and cultures they were experiencing firsthand. When Bono and The Edge sought literature to help familiarize themselves with the creative cultures of America, they did so as receptive readers, critically engaged and attuned, and as artists looking for inspiration and generative capital. What they found turned out to be helpful for the band's creative development at that time and in its future. Bono, especially, was drawn artistically to exploring sources of conflicts in the human experience and promoting efficacious means for resolving them. As teenagers in Dublin in the 1970s, the whole of the band, in fact, well-knew that inner personal conflicts and outer communal tensions could easily turn violent and divisive. Already a Christian reader of William Blake, Bono had penned several songs for U2's first three albums about the duality of the human spirit and would continue drawing upon Blake later in U2's career. Sometime after finishing songs for U2's fourth album, *The Unforgettable Fire* (1984), it's safe to say Bono continued his Blakean-framed interest when he turned his attention to twentieth-century American literature. While *The Unforgettable Fire* offers Bono's inaugural search for American spaces of integration for the self and society, it is— unsurprisingly, as inaugural quests for such ideals go—a "study" couched in Romantic expressions, helped along with the band's music under the direction of Brian Eno and Daniel Lanois. *The Joshua Tree,* however, is a noticeably less-Romanticized portrait of what U2 had already been searching for in previous artistic statements: wholeness and its ensuing peace. This album's shift in tone is attributable, in part, to Bono and The Edge's readings of a kind of American literature that fore-fronted conflicted characters, violence, and uneasy resolutions.

Significantly, in the writings of Flannery O'Connor, Bono found a career-enhancing and artistically liberating source of cultural capital which allowed him to create lyrical spaces and stylized performances. In a more conceptualized way, the rock stars found in work such as O'Connor's, and in Jungian terms that connect back to Blake, portraits of the Self and the Shadow Self. That is, they read depictions of the transcendent human psyche in tension with its own states of desire, deceit, and violence which they could map onto their curious exploration of America as both a physical space and a theorized narrative of the human search for completeness. Bono and The Edge read a handful of American writers known for their unromanticized portraits of personal and societal struggle, but O'Connor, in a peculiar if not totally unsurprising way, seemed an American Blake for Bono, offering in her thematic prose what Blake committed to poetry, and in a form of dramatic characterization that was, perhaps, more readily transferable. And at a time in Bono's development when he was dialed-in to exploring America and why violent and non-violent reactions had equal appeal to the human heart, O'Connor's fiction was a kind of *lingua franca* for him. Bono would come to say about his first encounters with O'Connor's fiction: "I've never felt such sympathy with a writer in America before."[2] While appreciating the power poetic violence has for literature, lyrics, and live performance may very well have been intuitive for Bono in the mid-1980s, the majority of U2's audience was likely less-versed in the literary

Under an American Spell

sources and strategies U2 was accruing. In looking at the material and general tenor of what Bono and The Edge were reading, it becomes evident that O'Connor's fiction granted them license—poetic and mimetic alike, to engage a Self and Shadow Self model of human conflict with greater depth and complexity than they had before.

Readings: Recommended and Realized

Although Bono was not looking for theorists to read in the 1980s, he was asking friends and journalists to send him books they thought would help him build upon interests he already had. As it happened, Bono gravitated toward reading texts which illustrated what the French theorist and sociologist René Girard developed into robust insights into the human proclivity for imitation, desire, violence, and scapegoating, which many literary scholars, such as Susan Srigley, would later apply to their readings of O'Connor:

> Girard's theories relate well to the issue of violence in O'Connor's fiction because Girard recognizes the origins of violence as being rooted in mimetic (imitative) desire, that is, desire in which human beings both seek to imitate and to rival other human beings for their shared objects of desire. Mimetic desire and rivalry inevitably lead to violent opposition, and the source of this violence is directly related to an interior disposition that can either be controlled or allowed free reign. It is this juncture of choice which intrigued Flannery O'Connor. She understood well the connection between human desires and the violence that results in the pursuit of those desires; in this and in many other ways O'Connor and Girard offer similar views.[3]

Bono discovered American voices in conversation with those same questions of the heart he already had an interest in, which aligned likewise with Girard's ideas. Intrigued by the narrative of America as a place of opportunity, Bono's awareness of its exclusionary practices kept him guarded against glorifying it. Speaking in 2020 about Ireland's history of violent uprisings and its future as a better, more inclusive country, Bono expressed what is a now common academic understanding of a narrative theory of identity: "Countries are just the stories we tell ourselves about ourselves. I'm suspicious of nationalism, my father taught me to be suspicious of nationalism. I don't know, was it [John Millington] Synge or [Seán] O'Casey who said, 'What is Ireland but the place that keeps my feet from getting wet?'"[4] His suspicions stretched well back to his formative years as a youth in the 1970s, such that when he did seek "the stories we tell ourselves about ourselves" in the case of America, not Ireland, he was a critically astute reader. As fans of American soul, blues, and gospel music, U2 had an awareness of the diversity of the American experience, which was further informed by the songs of Bob Dylan and Bruce Springsteen. Bono knew the stories of America were stories of oppression, dislocation, and inner turmoil as much as they were stories of freedom and possibility. He said of this time in his life, "I had this love affair with American literature happening at the same time as I became aware of how dangerous American foreign policy could be in the countries around it, with the brutal crushing of the Sandinistas. I started to see two Americas, the mythic America and the real America."[5] In fact, *The Two Americas* was the working title for *The Joshua Tree*.[6] In 1986, as The Edge recounted in *U2 By U2*, "we were still short of a few songs. We spent a lot of time talking about what [*The Joshua Tree*] was going to be. Bono had been reading Flannery O'Connor and Truman Capote,"[7] two writers with strong literary portraits of conflicted selves with violent outcomes. The Edge added that they were also reading Norman Mailer, Raymond Carver, James Baldwin, Ralph Ellison, Allen Ginsberg, Tennessee Williams, and Charles Bukowski,[8] and that the band "had all fallen under the spell of America, not the TV reality but the dream, the version of America that Martin Luther King spoke about. The language of American writers particularly struck Bono, the kind of imagery and cinematic quality of the American landscape became a stepping off point."[9]

What Bono would find in American literature were the notes of disparity, struggle, and perseverance, along with the revolutionary's Romantic tones of hope, all of which he had already encountered in Blake (as well as in W. B. Yeats). Blake's presence during *The Joshua Tree* sessions is made clear with Bono's reciting of "Introduction"—the opening poem for Blake's *Songs of Experience*—on "Beautiful Ghost / Introduction to *Songs of Experience*." If Bono had acted even more on Blake's influence, *The Joshua Tree* might well have been called *The Two Contrary States of America's Soul*. As it happened, though, the more explicit reference to Blake's influence appeared thirty years later with U2's release of the albums *Songs of Innocence* (2014) and *Songs of Experience* (2017), the latter of which includes the song "American Soul."

Bono and The Edge took reading recommendations from those they felt shared their interests in truth-tellers, soul-searchers, fact-facers, and courageous, non-violent protestors. The late Jim Henke, former editor at *Rolling Stone* and vice president at the Rock and Roll Hall of Fame and Museum, for example, use to exchange books with Bono in the early 1980s. Henke sent him Stephen B. Oates's *Let The Trumpet Sound: A Life Of Martin Luther King, Jr.*, which Bono said directly influenced the writing of "Pride: In the Name of Love" for U2's *The Unforgettable Fire*. Bono has publicly thanked Henke many times in concerts when performing the song, one of U2's most popular statements on the power of non-violent protest. More recommendations came directly and indirectly from others in the music industry. In 1984, Bono met Bob Dylan, who encouraged him to know where he came from if he wanted to know where he was going.[10] Dylan was referring to Bono to attend to his own Irish musical traditions, but the advice helped Bono realize his need to learn more about the American roots of rock 'n' roll, as U2 considered themselves as coming from a tradition in rock and popular music, not traditional Irish music. Responding to Dylan's advice with his own sense of direction, Bono looked for works that would help him make more sense of the bifurcated America he came to understand.

It seems Bono didn't start reading O'Connor until about 1985 at the recommendation of music journalist Steve Turner, though it is likely Bruce Springsteen recommended her fiction to Bono when they met in 1981. Springsteen was reading O'Connor then and

Under an American Spell   173

his 1982 album *Nebraska* plays as an homage to O'Connor's storytelling. Springsteen directly credits her influence:

> The really important reading that I did began in my late twenties, with authors like Flannery O'Connor. There was something in those stories of hers that I felt captured a certain part of the American character that I was interested in writing about. They were a big, big revelation. She got to the heart of some part of meanness that she never spelled out because if she spelled it out you wouldn't be getting it. It was always at the core of every one of her stories—the way that she'd left that hole there, that hole that's inside of everybody.[11]

In an excellent analysis of what Springsteen took from O'Connor, Laura Spence-Ash claims his artistic desire was to present America as unsympathetic toward troubled searchers, people who felt out of place, just about out of hope, and physically and existentially exhausted.[12] It would have been natural for Bono to ask Springsteen for reading recommendations, and it would have been natural for Springsteen to direct Bono's attention to a writer who saw the meanness in the American experience and then captured it on the page. But Turner met Bono in 1985 and attests to Bono not having much familiarity with O'Connor's stories. Turner, who would go on to write poetry, biographies, and studies of popular music, also wrote *U2 Rattle & Hum: The Official Book of the U2 Movie* (1988), and began a correspondence with Bono in 1985 that would last for many years. He interviewed the band several times and spoke with Bono and The Edge individually too, gaining more insight into their reading interests. Turner kept diaries of his meetings and interviews, which he shared with me in personal emails I exchanged with him in 2019. In one of these messages, Turner recalls meeting Bono and shopping for books together, noting that, at that time, Bono was hungry for writers who depicted darkness more so than light:

> When we first met in 1985, we went to Foyles on Charing Cross Road in London and that's when I led him to the Flannery O'Connor books. Certainly he picked up the short stories then, and maybe even *Mystery and Manners*. I used to pick up new titles for him. I think Bono had discovered [Raymond] Carver independently and, in fact, introduced me to him. I know that around the time of making *Rattle & Hum* (1988), he was talking about him. He liked the pared down prose and the matter-of-factness. It was when Bono was interested in tough reality. He liked Bukowski as well, for similar reasons. Bono spoke then of "dirty realism"—a term used to describe people like Carver, as well as Bukowski and [William] Burroughs. He was interested in the "whole" truth, which meant to us embracing the fallen as well as the redeemed, the ugly as well as the beautiful, the damned as well as the glorified. . . . I think what he enjoyed most of all about people like Carver and Bukowski was the unflinching look at reality, good and bad, and the use of direct, colloquial language.[13]

Bono and The Edge's readings became valuable resources for helping U2 finish its album and refine it from *The Two Americas* to *The Joshua Tree*. The Edge told Turner:

174   *Lit-Rock*

Bono has been turning me on to Flannery O'Connor. I love people like Truman Capote and Norman Mailer. I don't like a lot of Norman Mailer but I did like *The Executioner's Song*. I thought that was incredible. That started out as a lyrical idea for "Exit." We changed it around a lot. In fact, "Executioner's Song" was its working title, but in the end, we thought it was a bit too direct and a bit too limiting. So we decided to take the lyric in a different direction. I like lyrics that have that openness. My favorite lyrics always do and I think that was a good decision.[14]

Preferring such "openness" in lyrics has helped U2 create songs which resonate with a wide, diverse range of fans. Coming out of this period of reading American authors were several U2 songs that now stand as testaments to how "dirty realism" and dark storylines can be successfully translated into live performances and commercial success by a rock band. The band's efforts to "dislocate" their geographically specific interests by way of a universally appealing theme parallels O'Connor's fiction, as Gary M. Ciuba notes in his Girardian analysis of American Southern writers:

Girard's studies in mimesis and murder point inquiries into southern violence beyond the Mason-Dixon line, beyond even American history. They suggest that such hostility should be understood not only as a problem of a particular region or nation but also as an example of a generative mechanism at work in all culture. . . . Since Girard's theories about violence and culture developed from his study of novels and drama, he regards imaginative writing as playing a critical role in understanding the culture of victimization. Literature can reveal how desire may lead to violence, how violence may climax in scapegoating, and how scapegoating may generate the culture that disguises and deifies its origins in desire.[15]

With the encouragement of Turner, Bono read O'Connor and found direction for acting out his artistic convictions that the whole truth—with both the beautiful and brutal on display—be a part of U2's songs and concerts moving forward.

A Method for the Meanness

The popular level of success U2 achieved in *The Joshua Tree* era is not without debt to Bono's interest in the literary arts. As both a lyricist and performer wanting to deliver U2's songs to greater and greater effect, his literary inspirations fueled what his own instincts were directing him to do in concert. He developed characters for more complex performances communicating the violence borne out of the disintegrated Self on *The Joshua Tree* tour of 1987, and would continue to do so on subsequent tours of albums. As noted above, the song "Exit" was influenced by The Edge's and Bono's reading of Norman Mailer's *The Executioner's Song,* combined with Bono's reading of Truman Capote's *In Cold Blood*. "Exit," Bono said, was his attempt at writing a story in the mind of a killer. It is all very well to address America and the violence that is an aggressive foreign policy, but to really understand that you have to get under the skin of your own darkness, the violence we all contain within us. Violence is something I know quite a bit about. I have a side of me which, in a corner, can be very violent. It's the least attractive thing in anyone and I wanted to own up to that.[16]

Bono's own admission of his violent side suggests he already had some experiential familiarity with a desire for violence, which, it would seem, he was looking to usefully channel as an artist.

Though "Exit" had some of its genesis in Mailer and Capote, when Bono performed the song in concerts he developed a character connected to O'Connor's Hazel Motes in *Wise Blood.* The intensity of the conflicted character found in the lyrics prompted Bono to perform the song with a similar intensity for many years on tour, so much so that when U2 prepared for its 2017 anniversary tour for the album, Bono told *Rolling Stone* that he needed a new way to portray the song without hurting himself:

I had a lot of self-harm over the years playing that song. I was very glad not to play it for many years. I broke my shoulder. I got into some very dark places on the stage. I'd rather not step back into that song, but I found a way by thinking of where it came from and going back to the books I was reading at the time. I realized the real influence was probably Flannery O'Connor, so I developed this character called the Shadow Man and I'm managing to step into the shoes of the Shadow Man without any self-harm.[17]

In O'Connor's *Wise Blood*, the preacher Hazel (Haze) Motes creates the Church of God Without Christ to try to silence the pain in himself. Though disturbed by his chosen vocation, Motes takes up preaching in hopes of catharsis. As Bono wrote "from the mind of a killer" in "Exit," he describes his song's character as a "broken-hearted man" who also wants to "to drive the dreams he had away."[18] O'Connor's Shadow Man follows Motes as he travels the American South, trying to resist what Bono characterizes in "Exit" as the "hands of love."[19] In her own description of such internal struggle O'Connor writes: "Haze's shadow was now behind him and now before him and now and then broken up by other people's shadows, but when it was by itself, stretching behind him, it was a thin nervous shadow walking backward. You were sometimes following him; sometimes leading him; sometimes you went to pieces; alone, you were retreating from him."[20] And it is the fiery, embattled Motes that Bono called upon in his 2017 onstage enactments of the "Shadow Man," quoting the last line from this sermon-passage: "I preach there are all kinds of truth, your truth and somebody else's, but behind all of them, there's only one truth and that is that there's no truth. . . . No truth behind all truths is what I and this church preach! Where you come from is gone, where you thought you were going to never was there, and where you are is no good unless you can get away from it."[21]

O'Connor's language for her troubled, searching Motes, with his equal-parts tone of conviction and desperate defiance, came to Bono at a fortuitous time. After buying

176 *Lit-Rock*

books with Turner in 1985, spending a year or two reading O'Connor and other American authors, and then facing the prospect of needing a few more songs for the album in 1986, Bono was able to draw those songs up from a new well of inspiration. It would seem he was responding to O'Connor's ability to portray both the great violence and the great gentleness of life. The notions informing O'Connor's presentation of violence and gentleness—or grace—came from her Christianity, which also informed her integrity as an artist, prompting her to portray the human condition with honesty—something Bono was likewise attempting to do.

Another song on *The Joshua Tree* revealing Bono's debt to O'Connor is "One Tree Hill," which initiates the album's turn toward a darker mood and, with "Exit," forms a tryptic with the final, elegiac song on the album: "Mothers of the Disappeared." In July 1986, as Bono was writing to finish the album, Greg Carroll, the band's friend and one of their assistants, died in a motorcycle accident. Bono said in *U2 By U2* that "the problem with dealing with death, for me, is that it's always the same death. It's always my mother dying, it's always the center of the universe disappearing and having to find another one."[22] In grief, the band finished and dedicated "One Tree Hill" to Carroll, with Bono referencing in the lyric's first line O'Connor's short story "The Enduring Chill": "We turn away to face the cold, enduring chill / As the day begs the night for mercy."[23] There is an emotional echo in these first lines to U2's earlier song "Sunday Bloody Sunday"—"I can't believe the news today / I can't close my eyes and make it go away"—as both songs are about coming to terms with a life cut short by inexplicable violence.

O'Connor's story is about the artist Asbury, who comes home from New York City to the American South. He falls ill and he thinks he is dying. Asbury feels the effects of what he thinks is his oncoming death and grows increasingly irritable. There's an indication he has always been challenging to live with, perhaps because he's been so full of artistic energy, but now his mother, emotionally obtuse, struggles to show him sympathy because he is both an artist and her (possibly) dying son. O'Connor writes of Asbury's arrival back home:

> The sky was a chill gray and a startling white-gold sun, like some strange potentate from the east, was rising beyond the black woods that surrounded Timberboro. It cast a strange light over the single block of one-story brick and wooden shacks. Asbury felt that he was about to witness a majestic transformation, that the flat of the roofs might at any moment turn into the mounting turrets of some exotic temple of a god he didn't know. The illusion lasted only a moment before his attention was drawn back to his mother. She had given a little cry; she looked aghast. He was pleased that she should see death in his face at once. His mother, at the age of sixty, was going to be introduced to reality and he supposed that if the experience didn't kill her, it would assist her in the process of growing up.[24]

As Asbury grows increasingly ill, the story presents more and more of his awakening consciousness juxtaposed with the confusion of those around him who are living and don't understand either his final requests or the reality of their own lives. O'Connor

Under an American Spell   177

presents death as an oncoming chill, then finishes her story in an evocative, mystical fashion, with Asbury sick in his childhood bed:

> He turned his head. . . . He shuddered and turned his head quickly the other way and stared out the window. A blinding red-gold sun moved serenely from under a purple cloud. . . . His limbs that had been racked for so many weeks by fever and chill were numb now. The old life was exhausted. He awaited the coming of new. It was then that he felt the beginning of a chill, a chill so peculiar, so light, that it was a warm ripple across a deeper sea of cold. . . . He saw that for the rest of his days, frail, racked, but enduring, he would live in the face of a purifying terror. A feeble cry, a last impossible protest escaped him. But the Holy Ghost, emblazoned in ice instead of fire, continued, implacable, to descend.[25]

This point about Asbury going through "a purifying terror" reflects O'Connor's understanding that God will bring someone through the most tragic experiences and use the pain to birth peace. While O'Connor is often described as a Southern Gothic writer and master of the form of the modern grotesque, reading her plots for one or more characters' transformation reveals how the strangeness and violence in her stories yield a kind of peace and spiritual healing.

Soon after she published her most famous—and most famously disturbing—story, "A Good Man is Hard to Find," many readers demanded O'Connor explain her interest in writing about a family dying at the hands of an escaped serial killer. In the early 1960s, the story was read in college classes and a student wrote her asking "just what enlightenment [O'Connor] expected her to get from each of [her] stories."[26] After telling her reader "to forget about enlightenment and just try to enjoy them," O'Connor acquiesced by explaining some of her aesthetic and logic in an essay called "A Reasonable Use of the Unreasonable," which was published posthumously in *Mystery and Manners: Occasional Prose* (the book Turner brought to Bono's attention over lunch in 1985). In the essay, she expressed her artistic *modus operandi* this way:

> I suppose the reasons for the use of so much violence in modern fiction will differ with each writer who uses it, but in my own stories, I have found that violence is strangely capable of returning my characters to reality and preparing them to accept their moment of grace. Their heads are so hard that almost nothing else will do the work. This idea, that reality is something to which we must be returned at considerable cost, is one which is seldom understood by the casual reader, but it is one which is implicit in the Christian view of the world. . . . With the serious writer, violence is never an end in itself. It is the extreme situation that best reveals what we are essentially, and I believe these are times when writers are more interested in what we are essentially than in the tenor of our daily lives. Violence is a force which can be used for good or evil, and among other things taken by it is the kingdom of heaven. . . . The man in the violent situation reveals those qualities least dispensable in his personality, those qualities which are all he will have to take into eternity with him . . . and since the characters in this story are all on the

verge of eternity, it is appropriate to think of what they take with them. . . . In any case, I hope that if you consider these points in connection with the story, you will come to see it as something more than an account of a family murdered on the way to Florida.[27]

In O'Connor's talk about the "serious writer's" interest in violence as a force for redemption as well as her literature, Bono would have discovered a kinship encouraging him to spend more time balancing the dark with the beautiful, as well to reflect on the possibilities for "serious" pop music whose fans operate likewise as "readers." Bono's reading of other American writers would have only strengthened his resolve. In *U2 by U2*, Bono says that as he wrote for *The Joshua Tree*, he began to feel he had not written "real" lyrics for U2's previous albums. After spending a few weeks in July 1986 touring Nicaragua and El Salvador with aid workers, seeing firsthand the effects of US foreign policy and economic support, he returned to Dublin angry at the United States:

> That is when I started to realize that the lyrics on the first four albums were not really lyrics at all, they're sketches. I wasn't a writer, really, I was a painter, or an emoter or a shouter. . . . With *Joshua Tree*, I decided I'd better write some lyrics. I was reading more anyway, so I was more awake to the word. I discovered a love for writers and started to feel like one of them.[28]

Bono's vision of the two Americas was becoming clearer and clearer during the sessions for finishing *The Joshua Tree*. Thirty years later, in 2017, in an interview with Zane Lowe for Beats 1 Radio, Bono described the contrariness of America: "America is a taciturn place . . . it can turn on itself."[29] Taciturn: reluctant to join in conversation; inclined to silence; dour; stern. It's a word O'Connor herself might have used for both America and those she depicted as the spiritually troubled searchers in the American South. The paradox wouldn't have been lost on O'Connor, as it has not been lost on Bono. Hazel Motes becomes fixated on silencing what he found too troubling to hear. He becomes a taciturn man, trying to drown out the voices that talk of God. The competing voices in a robust democratic society such as America can, when fear starts to spread, become rigid and prevent actual conversation with one another. A sternness sets in. A kind of silence takes over where no one else is heard, bringing to mind Bono's lyrics from "Ultraviolet," "There is a silence that comes to a house where no one can sleep,"[30] or from "All Because of You," "It's not the noise / It's the deafening silence / That drowns God out."[31]

In both *Wise Blood* and *The Joshua Tree*, atmospheric darkness and meanness develop as their characters search for peace and love only to be left more distraught than they had been at the outset. *The Joshua Tree* opens with strong evocations of hope, but by the fourth song, "Bullet the Blue Sky," a righteous anger surfaces, and it is this experience of anger that seems to make room later in the album for Bono's Shadow Man to emerge. Drawing upon a recognition of despair, grief, and longing in the soul, the Shadow Man has, by "Exit," grown strong enough to eclipse the innocence of the soul. What's left during this temporary blackout is, in both Jungian and Blakeian senses, the contrary state of the soul: the Shadow Self who traffics in violence. Yet, the Jungian notion—to which O'Connor and Bono both seem to subscribe—is that the Shadow Self has purpose and merit for balancing one's overall psyche.[32] Bono took this approach to internal tension to heart, so to speak, and incorporated it into U2's shows.

Bono's songwriting from 1985–8 produced lyrics for another album, *Rattle and Hum* (1988), which came on the heels of *The Joshua Tree* and offers more themes of human darkness and violence, as in the trio of songs "Desire," "God Part II," and "Hawkmoon 269." In "Desire," Bono is direct in both his acknowledgment and condemnation of the inner state, which he describes as "the candle burnin' in my room" and with reference to illicit drug use: "like the needle, the needle and spoon."[33] Though the topic of desire is quite often presented in popular music as a sexually charged urge, with positive connotations, Bono chooses to present the darker aspects of desire in other arenas of life, specifically in the American economic and political contexts—"Yeah, she's the promise / In the year of election"[34]—as comparable to fraudulent religious evangelists: "Like a preacher stealin' hearts at a travellin' show, / For love or money, money, money . . . ?"[35] "Desire" seems tailor-made in this era of Bono's songwriting as a further articulation of the Girardian expression of "mimetic desire," which rests on the understanding of the human species' proclivity to imitate others in order to learn and assimilate into communities. As humans engage in modeling, they for better and worse imitate other people's desires, leading sometimes to conflicts and rivalries when desiring the same objects.[36] When the person's internal regulations fail and their metaphysical desires increase, especially in proximity to others' desires for the same things, violence in the Self, and outwardly toward others, is a typical result. Often reciprocating acts of violence threaten to destroy an entire community and lead to a decision to select a person or a cause, as a common enemy toward which the entire community can direct their violence in order to save the community—a mechanism which Girard called scapegoating, which he wrote about extensively in terms of its psychological and sociological effects. U2's songs on previous albums addressed national and cultural violence in their Irish-Anglo history, but on *The Joshua Tree* and *Rattle and Hum*, as U2 turned its attention to violence in the Americas, there is also a noticeable pondering of violence in the heart, perhaps offered as a condemnatory corrective to acts of scapegoating the other.

Acting out on stage the more troubling elements of human nature became something of Bono's performative calling-card in the 1990s, as documents of U2's tours can attest. And though there was less play-acting of disturbed characters in the 2000s, many of U2's songs continued to articulate the frustration of living with two contrary states of the soul, right up to "The Troubles," the closing track of *Songs of Innocence*:

Somebody stepped inside your soul
Somebody stepped inside your soul
Little by little they robbed and stole
Till someone else was in control[37]

180   *Lit-Rock*

Bono is fond of quoting another American writer, Sam Shepherd, to explain why he often finds himself between two opposing states: "Right smack in the middle of a contradiction, that's the place to be,"[38]—a sentiment Bono rearticulates as, "There are more contradictions in rock-and-roll than in any other art form and I think that's good."[39] In "The Marriage of Heaven and Hell" William Blake writes, "Without Contraries is no progression. Attraction and Repulsion, Reason and Energy, Love and Hate, are necessary to Human existence. From these contraries spring what the religious call Good & Evil."[40] In Blake, the English Romantic, and O'Connor, the American Southern Gothic, what might seem like contradictions between the two are, for Bono, largely distinctions without a difference in theme or purpose. The split soul in search of integration is on display in both. By portraying the violence that emanates from the rift, inspired by his readings of America, *The Joshua Tree* grew into a landmark, casting a shadowy path toward stardom which U2 smartly followed.

Notes

1 Stephen Catanzarite, "*The Joshua Tree—*U2 (1987)," *US Library of Congress National Recording Registry*, 2013, https://www.loc.gov/static/programs/national-recording -preservation-board/documents/U2JoshuaTree.pdf.

2 Olaf Tyaransen, "Trip through Your Words: Bono and the Books that Became the Seeds for The Joshua Tree," *Hot Press*, March 20, 2017, https://www.hotpress.com/ culture/trip-through-your-words-bono-and-the-books-that-became-the-seeds-for -ithe-joshua-treei-19932902.

3 Susan Srigley, "The Violence of Love: Reflections on Self-Sacrifice through Flannery O'Connor and René Girard," *Religion & Literature* 39, no. 3 (2007): 34.

4 Bono, "Interview with Ryan Tubridy," *The Ryan Tubridy Show RTE 1*, May 8, 2020, https://www.rte.ie/radio/utils/share/radio1/21765308.

5 Bono, The Edge, Adam Clayton, Larry Mullen, Jr., with Neil McCormick, *U2 By U2* (London: HarperCollins, 2006), 177.

6 Graphic designer Stephen Averill and photographer Anton Corbijn talk about deciding on *The Joshua Tree* as the album's final name on "Classic Albums: *The Joshua Tree*," YouTube video, May 24, 2017, https://www.youtube.com/watch?v=hl8HtrD6Kjo.

7 Bono, et al. *U2 by U2*, 177.

8 Ibid.

9 Ibid.

10 Bono, "When Bono Met Bob," *Hot Press*, May 1, 2001, https://www.hotpress.com/ music/when-bono-met-bob-549304.

11 Laura Spence-Ash, "Fiction Responding to Fiction: Flannery O'Connor and Bruce Springsteen," *Ploughshares*, July 1, 2016, http://blog.pshares.org/index.php/fiction -responding-to-fiction-flannery-oconnor-and-bruce-springsteen.

12 Ibid.

13 Steve Turner, email message to author, December 12, 2019.

14 Ibid.

15 Gary M. Ciuba, *Desire, Violence, and Divinity in Modern Southern Fiction* (Baton Rouge: Louisiana State University Press, 2007), 5.

16 Bono, et al. *U2 by U2*, 184.
17 Andy Greene, "Bono Talks 'Joshua Tree' Tour, Trump, Status of U2's Next Album," *Rolling Stone*, May 30, 2017, https://www.rollingstone.com/music/music-features/bono-talks-joshua-tree-tour-trump-status-of-u2s-next-album-121562.
18 Bono, "Exit," *U2.com*, https://www.u2.com/lyrics/45.
19 Ibid.
20 Flannery O'Connor, *Wise Blood* (New York: Farrar, Straus and Giroux, 1949), 33.
21 Ibid., 165. Bono quotes only the last sentence.
22 Bono, et al. *U2 by U2*, 178.
23 Bono, "One Tree Hill," *U2.com*, https://www.u2.com/lyrics/99.
24 Flannery O'Connor, "The Enduring Chill," in *Everything That Rises Must Converge* (New York: Farrar, Straus and Giroux, 1949), 82.
25 Ibid., 114.
26 Flannery O'Connor, "A Reasonable Use of the Unreasonable," in *Mystery and Manners* (New York: Farrar, Straus and Giroux, 1957), 112–14.
27 Ibid.
28 Bono, et al. *U2 by U2*, 179.
29 Zane Lowe, "U2: 'Joshua Tree' 30th Anniversary Interview," *Apple Music*, YouTube video, July 20, 2017, https://www.youtube.com/watch?v=vsKZ3YrF_3Q.
30 Bono, "Ultraviolet (Light My Way)," *U2.com*, https://www.u2.com/lyrics/157.
31 Bono, "All Because of You," *U2.com*, https://www.u2.com/lyrics/11.
32 "The Jungian Model of the Psyche," *Journal Psyche*, May 2, 2020, https://journalpsyche.org/jungian-model-psyche/.
33 Bono, "Desire," *U2.com*, https://www.u2.com/lyrics/33.
34 Ibid.
35 Ibid.
36 Gabriel Andrade, "René Girard," *Internet Encyclopedia of Philosophy*, https://www.iep.utm.edu/girard.
37 Bono, "The Troubles," *U2.com*, https://www.u2.com/lyrics/599.
38 Bert Van De Kamp, *And They Called Him Bono* (Amsterdam, Netherlands: Invy Books, 2010), 86.
39 Ibid.
40 William Blake, "The Marriage of Heaven and Hell," in *The Essential Blake*, ed. Stanley Kunitz (New York: Ecco, 1987), 67.

11

Rock, Hard-Boiled

The Mekons and American Crime Fiction

Peter Hesseldenz

The Mekons, one of rock music's longest-running acts, have throughout their career looked to literature as a contextualizing resource, going so far at times as to include bibliographies in their album liner notes. These bibliographies, which give clues about the books that have influenced or inspired particular songs, betray within their sometimes irreverent exterior an underlying seriousness and depth of intention. As original member Kevin Lycett notes, the titles they list may contain jokes, but also function as "discreet signposts,"[1] working outward from the localized lyrics toward a larger commentary. Though the Mekons have written about many subjects since their formation in 1977, one overarching theme for this Marxist-leaning band has been the way in which individual lives are impacted by history, economics, and politics. To better understand the way these forces interact with each other, they have consistently turned to different types of literature, most notably—during their 1980s output—the hard-boiled detective story of the 1920s through the 1940s. On three successive albums, the Mekons included songs which referred specifically to works by Dashiell Hammett and Raymond Chandler; "Flitcraft" and "If They Hang You" made use of Hammett's *The Maltese Falcon*, while "Big Zombie" borrowed from Chandler's *The Little Sister*.

So how and why did a cultural form so far removed from the bands' roots, and a seemingly unlikely source of literary capital, become so central to their work? The songs referenced above were recorded and released within a relatively short, but highly creative, span following the Mekons' resurrection after a nearly dormant period in the early 1980s. The band had come close to breaking-up, but was reinvigorated in 1984. A once amateurish group—as famous for its musical ineptitude as for its witty and pointed lyrics—had acquired several accomplished musicians who meshed with the steadily improving original core of the band, allowing them to pursue new musical directions. This trend was most obvious in their incorporation of American country music to produce a ragged, punky version of what later became known as Alt-Country. The musical shift was lyrically accompanied, however, by an atmosphere of gloom, world-weariness, and pessimism—an outlook that would pervade one of their best-received albums, *Fear and Whiskey* (1985), and a period of heavy touring

Rock, Hard-Boiled 183

which brought them often to the United States. Guitarist and singer Jon Langford describes this stage of their career as a time when they were readily soaking up new influences:

> When we kind of started up again in the mid-'80s, we were very interested in Dashiell Hammett and Raymond Chandler. We were touring the States a lot and that was our reference for what we thought the States should be like. Dashiell Hammett was our version of San Francisco and Raymond Chandler was our version of L.A. Every time I walked into a room, I'd expect to find a body. Most of the time we didn't.[2]

Langford's statement, though characteristically couched in a joke, indicates that the hard-boiled detective tradition provided a kind of experiential filter, or a sensationalized lens, for taking in and negotiating a foreign culture. Like the band's new country sound, detective fiction pointed away from their native England and toward the United States for inspiration and analogy, providing a form that—in its "lowbrow" status—felt well beyond the literature of "English proper" and more genuinely "of the people." The Mekons' adoption of hard-boiled themes and country music influences were not merely celebrations of the American mystique: in these two uniquely American art forms, they found vehicles more expressive of their ideals than the type of British punk they had been producing. They saw, in the mid-century novels' depictions of alienation, class consciousness, and lack of justice parallels with contemporary developments in Margaret Thatcher's England. Broadly speaking, the language, imagery, and atmosphere of the hard-boiled novels provided them with a transnational political framework and validation of Marxism; more narrowly, it offered a way of commenting on the Thatcherite destruction to human relationships and to art back home.

It would have been hard for someone listening to the Mekons' crude early performances and recordings to predict that they would later adopt either country music or hard-boiled themes. However, it is this beginning part of their career that sets the stage for those changes that would come within just a few years. The Mekons formed in 1977 at the height of the first wave of British punk rock and, like many of the new bands, were consciously trying to differentiate themselves from the pompous, larger-than-life rock bands that dominated the airwaves. Although the Mekons embraced the democratic ideals and the disdain for the excesses of past bands espoused by punk musicians and their followers, they seemed to be most drawn to punk rock's sense of freedom. For Langford and the other Mekons, this freedom manifested itself in an atmosphere that "let you do anything you want."[3] The original sense of exuberance and unlimited possibility which had been a part of rock at its beginnings in the 1950s had, by the mid-1970s, been replaced by an uninspired set of clichéd lyrical topics and an over-reliance on technical skills which took the music out of the hands of the average fan. The Mekons, as mostly non-musicians, were inspired by the idea that anyone could play music and were drawn to the idea that there was little differentiating punk performers from their audiences.

The original band members—Jon Langford on drums (and eventually guitar), Tom Greenhalgh and Kevin Lycett on guitars, Ros Allen on bass, and Mark White and Andy Corrigan as singers—met as fine arts students at the University of Leeds, where they were exposed to the leftist theories that would inform many of their early lyrics.[4] The Marxist philosophy that the Mekons absorbed was expressed in lyrics that were harshly critical of capitalist society. Politics was, from the beginning, an integral part of the band. Langford says "we always thought music and politics go together, and it would be a cop-out not to keep addressing political and social issues."[5] But, though their lyrics were political, they were not manifested as a series of slogans like those written by the Clash. Instead, as Greil Marcus notes, they wrote about politics in the context of ordinary life: "drinking, all-night arguments, wage labor, jealousy, political dread, sloth, blocked desires, consumerism, friendship, fatigue, love, good times."[6] For the Mekons, these everyday human experiences did not occur in a vacuum, but were the product of broader forces; they sought in their art not simply to convey local experiences but to unmask the "impact of history on people's lives."[7]

The original punk era's atmosphere of unlimited possibility soon began to dim as a series of setbacks and disappointments lead to the band's disillusionment and near break-up. Within a few short months, they experienced a dizzying series of changes, taking them from a small independent label, Fast Product, for which they had recorded only two singles, to a contract with Virgin. For Virgin—a label whose "major" status perhaps felt at odds with the bands' aesthetic from the outset—they managed to record one album, which they did not feel accurately represented their artistic vision.[8] It received in the end little promotional support, resulting in poor sales and the band quickly being dropped. In addition to this brief and disheartening relationship with the corporate music industry, the band began to feel less connected to the punk rock movement. The freedom that had so inspired them began to give way to a set of rigid strictures, which Langford termed "the politics of punk rock."[9] Punk audiences were coming to expect an increasingly finite set of musical and fashion styles, which the band was not willing to accommodate: "It was the dog-end days of punk. We wanted to do something different, and people would just come in spitting at you, 'Play louder, play faster.' It got kind of dull. We were never a leather-jacket shaven-head punk band."[10] This souring is evidenced in the change in style that occurs on the second album, which briefly saw their guitar-based punk sound replaced with keyboards.

These difficulties played out against of backdrop of turmoil in Great Britain. The mid- to late 1970s, labeled "one long crisis"[11] by Simon Reynolds, included power cuts, inflation, rising racial and class divisions, gender inequalities, and the highest levels of unemployment in the post–Second World War era. The period culminated in the election of Margaret Thatcher as Prime Minister in 1979, which, for many, only exacerbated the problems. Under the policies she enacted, "poverty and income and wealth inequality increased dramatically,"[12] and the resulting frustration and anxieties became palpable at live music performances. A growing number of disaffected working-class youth in Britain found an outlet in violent, neo-fascist organizations, whose "skinheads" started appearing in Leeds at punk rock shows by the Mekons and other bands. What had at first been joyous events, filled, according to Gang of

Four's Hugo Burnham, with "complete art noise chaos,"[13] became marked with an escalating level of violence. The racist skinhead coalition joined an already volatile mix of college students and locals, resulting in an increasing number of fights in the audience and objects thrown at the band. These disillusioning factors led the Mekons to stop performing around 1981.

Although the band did not formally break-up at this point and, in fact, sporadically released material on small independent labels, they did go through a transformational period with several original members leaving to return to school and new members joining. When they decided to resume as an active performing and recording band in 1984, it was in response to Thatcher's battle with the striking British miners, part of a larger assault by her administration on trade unions.[14] The government's threat to close mines prompted the miners—in a conflict that would famously inspire many songs and literary works alike—to strike. Langford, who grew up near Welsh mining country, and the rest of the Mekons saw the moment as a call to action and decided to resume active performing again in order to, as Langford says, "get out there and make some money for the miners"[15] by participating in benefit concerts.

The miners' strike, considered "one of the most bloody and tragic industrial disputes of modern times,"[16] followed the strikes of 1972 and 1974, which had ended, despite formidable opposition from Edward Heath's conservative government, in wage increases. When Thatcher regained control of the government for the Tories, she was determined not to repeat Heath's failings. Unlike the case in the earlier strikes, Thatcher and her government were well prepared with large stockpiles of coal and a willingness to use riot-gear-equipped police to violently put down protest. She and the miners' charismatic leader, Arthur Scargill, were to face-off numerous times during the year-long strike, with Thatcher proving to be the more disciplined and, ultimately, stronger combatant. Her government was able to cripple the National Union of Mineworkers which, in the end, resulted "in the total defeat of the miners followed by the virtual end of deep coal-mining in Britain."[17] The crushing defeat of the miners, symbolic, perhaps, as a defeat of leftist ideals in Britain, ushered in the period in which the band explicitly turned to hard-boiled literature.

The "hard-boiled" Mekons period brought, in addition to its country-inspired sound, a new mood. Where the early records were brash, exuberant, and filled with energy, the new records were downcast, anxious, and suffused with a sense of dread. As Marcus notes, the Mekons of this period are "like casualties of a defeated revolution— nervous, on good terms with oblivion, filled with rage and guilt."[18] Part of the reason for this new feeling, first evident on *Fear and Whiskey*, was that the songs were written in direct response to the mirrored political situations in England and America. As Langford explains, the record "is basically about Thatcher and Reagan, that sort of right-wing agenda which put all the lefties on the [defensive] for quite a long time."[19] Punning, perhaps, on their newly adapted musical influence, the Mekons renounce their homeland as such in "Country": "we know that for many years there's been no country here / Nothing here but the war."[20]

The same might be said of the cultural and political upheaval in the United States of the 1920s and 1930s—the period that produced the hard-boiled story, whose authors were, among other things, responding to a prohibition war fought between organized crime and the authorities. That crimewave, part of what George Grella calls "the disorder that accompanies explosive social change,"[21] was compounded by the rapid and disorienting urbanization and industrialization of what was once an agrarian nation. Those issues, in turn, were aggravated by racial tensions in the overcrowded cities after the arrival of a large influx of ethnically diverse immigrants and recently migrated African Americans. The rise of the bureaucratic government, combined with rampant political corruption, added to a deeply unsettled atmosphere, creating what Peter Messent calls "a world that seems out of joint—where anxieties about crime, capitalism, and the conditions of urban life were increasingly and urgently pressing."[22]

The Mekons were encountering a parallel situation in Great Britain in the 1970s and 1980s. Mark White points out that Leeds was a troubled place when he and the rest of the group arrived for college in the mid-1970s, describing it as "economically deprived, dirty, run-down, and extremely violent."[23] Thatcher's election, according to White, had heightened divisions and turned Britain into "a politicized, intolerant and repressive place."[24] Large, non-white communities made up of immigrants who had come to Great Britain in the 1950s and 1960s from former British colonies in Asia, Africa, and the Caribbean led to tensions in the larger cities where they settled, and their long-simmering resentments—from years of living in sub-standard housing, suffering from poverty, high levels of crime, and unfair policing[25]—clashed with disaffected neo-fascist skinhead groups looking for scapegoats.

The Mekons were observing these street-level tensions firsthand, but they were also cognizant of the dramatic changes in the political philosophy that was steering the British government. As students of political history and theory, the Mekons would have understood that Reagan's and Thatcher's ascent to power represented a return to the classical liberal ideas of the late nineteenth and early twentieth century, now labeled "neoliberalism." Thatcher's agenda of aggressive de-regulation, privatization, and reduced taxation lends credence to Milton Freidman's description of her as a "nineteenth-century liberal."[26]

Such anachronistic politics bear connection to the cultural context of 1920s detective literature. Golden Age, or classical, mysteries—the genteel, mostly British detective stories descended from Conan Doyle's Sherlock Holmes stories and typified by authors like Agatha Christie and Dorothy L. Sayers—were the dominant form in the United States at that time. Hard-boiled literature, in its initial appearance, can been viewed partly as a reaction against that popularized style. The Golden Age novels saw the world as ultimately a good place and considered the isolated crimes that occurred in them to be aberrations that were soon healed by the genius detective. Sean McCann sees this type of story as deeply rooted in the older nineteenth-century values of classical liberalism, in which free individuals mutually accept a minimum of rules in order to achieve the greater good. The Golden Age detective story, he finds, usually centers on upper-class characters and portrays a flourishing society, unconcerned with the living conditions of the poor. The crimes, though they are solved, do hint, however, at the fragility of the system, providing a glimpse at what would happen if it were to break down.[27]

Hard-boiled novels show a society in which that breakdown is complete. The world they portray is beyond fixing by the detective or anyone else. It is a chaotic and violent urban landscape so filled with crime and corruption that the police have no chance of controlling it. In fact, rather than actually solve the crimes, the authorities produce an "official" solution that benefits the rich and powerful. The best, then, that the private detectives, the novels' heroes, can hope for is to temporally halt the chaos in the limited area in which they work.

Though the hard-boiled writers completely rejected the vision of the Golden Age detective story and its classical liberal underpinnings, they did not, for the most part, see Franklin Roosevelt's revision of nineteenth-century liberalism, his New Deal, as a solution for society's ills. Their stories, at times, reflect on New Deal ideas, but usually as a way of pointing out their shortcomings. The pessimistic authors could not imagine a world in which the wildly diverse and incohesive communities in the United States could coalesce behind a government in order to stem social and political decay.[28] The resulting literature depicted a sullied world, devoid of hope, in which women and minorities were often scapegoated as villains or otherwise undesirable characters. Even in the more prosperous post-war years, hard-boiled writers depicted a world in which mass communication and mass consumerism created a society dulled in its sensibilities, and susceptible to new forms of exploitation and corruption.[29]

The Mekons, by the time they came to America, possessed an equally hard-boiled pessimism (though without the fictions writers' misogynistic and racist tendencies), stemming in part from their experiences in the world of rock music. Mark White characterizes his early approach to lyric writing, for example, as an eschewal of "all the appalling sexism and macho strut that so characterized songs of the period that we all hated."[30] Since their earliest days, the band have been outspokenly dedicated to gender and racial equality, as their mixed-gender lineup and participation in the early Rock Against Racism concerts reflect.[31] Their use of hard-boiled imagery, in this regard, is less a tribute than it is a repurposing, in keeping with feminist revisions to the hard-boiled genre as carried out by novelists like Sue Grafton and Sara Paretsky.

Yet even while actively resisting the genre's disconcerting elements, the Mekons maintain a certain faith in its potential as an effective vehicle for exposing socio-political issues. In this way they put into practice the views of critics such as Lee Horsley, who, while finding such potential in *all* types of crime writing, singles out the hard-boiled school in particular—its attention to the exploitation of the working class, racial prejudice, and rampant consumerism—as one that "addressed the problems of [its] society explicitly."[32] Messent builds on this idea, asserting that hard-boiled fictions can be read as critiques of capitalism that raise "direct and challenging questions about the values of the dominant social order and our status both as individuals and community members within it."[33]

Dashiell Hammett, widely considered to be the first great hard-boiled writer, certainly wrote novels that critiqued modern society. His works portray a world that is, as J.A. Zumoff describes, "fundamentally and irredeemably corrupt, violent, and irrational."[34] Hammett's dark vision, coupled with his communist sympathies and pro-labor stances, made him an obvious subject choice for the left-leaning Mekons.

188   *Lit-Rock*

That he did not publicly embrace these beliefs during his active writing career and, in fact, worked in the 1910s as an anti-labor Pinkerton strikebreaker, has not prevented readers from locating in his works early expressions of the radical ideas he would later support. It wasn't until after he completed his last novel in 1934, and while working in Hollywood as a highly paid, though fairly unproductive, screenwriter, that Hammett began attaching his famous name to radical causes, serving, for instance, as chairman of the anti-fascist Motion Picture Artists Committee. Such activities would later draw the attention of anti-communist governmental bodies, such as the House Un-American Activities Committee.

"If They Hang You"—which weaves together elements from Hammett's life with allusions to his most famous work, *The Maltese Falcon*—addresses that negative attention, while also providing insight into how the Mekons see their world reflected in Hammett's work. In the first verse, singer Sally Timms assumes the voice of Lillian Hellman, Hammett's longtime companion, quoting lines from her introduction to *The Big Knockover*, a collection of Hammett's short stories and other writings that she compiled after his death. The bouncy, jaunty tune then touches on Hammett's steadfast defiance of the red-baiting authorities in the 1950s. The Mekons seem intent, however, on not simplistically lionizing Hammett: they touch, for example, on his alcoholism, womanizing, and lack of late-career production. Rising above these flaws, however, is the author's fierce dedication to certain principles and to those who fight for them; in the line "at the witch-trial you would not reveal the names of comrades that you never knew,"[35] the Mekons take note of Hammett's refusal to betray in court those who contributed to the Civil Rights Congress—an organization that fought to support Communist Party members and against the mistreatment of African Americans.

The song's title comes directly from the last chapter of *The Maltese Falcon*. Sam Spade, the book's detective hero, speaks the line to Brigid O'Shaunessy, a woman he may or may not have fallen in love with, as he decides whether or not to turn her over to the authorities to be tried, and possibly executed, for her crimes. He recounts the many lies, deceptions, and violent acts that Brigid has committed, concluding finally that he "won't play the sap"[36] and must turn her in. Sam provides several reasons for his actions, but a basic lack of trust—the fact that she "never played square"[37]—is chief among them. For Sam, "the whole fabric of society is based on trust,"[38] making any relationship with Brigid, who is firmly entrenched in the violent criminal world and supremely untrustworthy, doomed from the start. If Sam cannot trust Brigid, then he cannot give in to any feelings of love or affection because they would "deny reason"[39] and make him vulnerable to violent attacks. The hard-boiled world they mutually inhabit, then, renders void the prospects of a true and lasting attachment.

Sam's decision would have resonated with the Mekons. Langford says of this period, "a lot of the songs sound like love songs, but they're also about something else."[40] That something else might be the looming presence of the violent, corrupt society which seems to thwart many of the songs' characters as they attempt to find love, or even simply to connect. As Marcus puts it, they are left with "loneliness, alienation, and a fantasy of comradeship."[41] A good example of this theme is found in "Hard to be Human." Though the song's imagery is fragmented, the singers (Langford and

Greenhalgh, alternately and together at different points) seem to be describing a scene that occurs outside of a public bathroom, possibly in a train or bus station prior to a trip to Sheffield. The world as depicted is violent ("I've been punched and beaten") and its singer, "looking for a friend," is in the end swindled or in some way betrayed ("He shaved me dry").[42] Like *The Maltese Falcon*, the song depicts a world where the basics of humanity—including friendships and trust—are in desperately short supply.

A second song coming directly from Hammett is "Flitcraft," whose title is taken from a short section in Chapter Seven of *The Maltese Falcon*, and which appears as a parable, unrelated to the main plot, shared by Sam with Brigid O'Shaughnessy. In it, Sam describes a time when he was hired by a woman in Tacoma to find her husband, Flitcraft, who had disappeared about five years earlier. After Sam tracks him down, he learns that Flitcraft was a real estate agent leading an uneventful suburban life with his family. One day, while walking to lunch, Flitcraft is nearly hit by a falling beam from a construction site, which would surely have killed him. Badly shaken by this event, Flitcraft resolves to leave his comfortable life. He feels that this near-death experience had made him privy to the inner workings of the universe and, to his horror, he realizes that it is not the sane, orderly place he had thought it to be. In order to ensure his survival, he feels he must step outside of his pattern. So he leaves town without a word to anyone and travels the world. Eventually, he ends up back in the United States where he acquires a new name, Charles Pierce, and settles into a new domestic life with a wife and family very similar to the one he had left. Sam explains that, in leaving his old, ordered life, Flitcraft "adjusted himself to beams falling, and then no more of them fell, and he adjusted himself to them not falling."[43]

This mysterious addition to the novel is generally viewed by scholars as a meditation on uncertainty and the randomness of the universe. This seems to be what Hammett had in mind, since the name he gives to Flitcraft after he establishes his new identity, Charles Pierce, is similar to that of the nineteenth-century American philosopher who wrote extensively about the chance nature of the universe. Some critics see this section as "the cipher to Hammett's oeuvre, and perhaps hard-boiled fiction in general."[44] Hammett, himself, was especially proud of this passage, which, according to his daughter Jo, he considered an "ultimate truth."[45] Sam persists in telling the story to a distracted and uninterested Brigid because he considers it an essential warning to her about the dangers of complacency in the uncertain world in which they operate. He tries to impress on Brigid the need for constant vigilance—something that William Nolan sees as protecting Sam in his dangerous line of work: he lives "longer," Nolan observes, "because he knows the beams are falling, and is watching for them."[46]

Langford and Greenhalgh, who sing "Flitcraft" in alternating verses, would seem to agree. But, whereas Sam Spade's vigilance relates to physical violence or death, the Mekons warn about the dangers of artistic complacency and political apathy. Their interpretation of the story connects to the reasons for their earlier break with the punk rock community. As the Mekons recognized that the music was becoming restrictive and unimaginative, they were able to avoid artistic death by changing styles, or, in a manner of speaking, by stepping out of the pattern. This idea is reinforced by the ominous reference to "Flitcraft" in the liner notes: "destroy your safe and happy lives

190   *Lit-Rock*

before it is too late."[47] This mantra became the opening line for the Mekons' later song, "Memphis, Egypt," which addresses the ways in which the forces of capitalism have co-opted the original sense of freedom in rock and roll. The exuberance with which they approach this country-punk song, made up mostly of lines taken directly from the novel, indicates that they are singing about an idea that they, like Hammett, understand to be an ultimate truth, and a truth that has been a hallmark of their long career. Unlike many other long-lived bands, the Mekons have continually strived to reach a punk-inspired goal identified by Marcus early on as an "unfinished utopia in which the freedom to say everything would lead to the freedom to do everything."[48] It was a utopian vision that, given the twinned, disillusioning struggles of the United States and the United Kingdom, was not to be found in national borders, but, rather, in the over-branching, artistic space of music and literature.

Given the consistency between Hammett's and the Mekons' political beliefs, Raymond Chandler seems a less likely influence on their music. Chandler, in fact, did not articulate any coherent political ideology, having seemingly equal contempt for politicians of all persuasions.[49] Educated in England before moving to the United States in 1912, Chandler's feeling of being an exile in America was tied to his nostalgia for an imperial era to which he was "born a half century too late."[50] And yet the Mekons would find inspiration not only in Chandler's defection, as a fellow Brit, to the United States, but also in his damning portraits of economic injustice perpetuated by the decadent rich, and his harsh criticisms of the crass, greed-filled, commercial culture he found in California.

Chandler's disdain for Los Angeles, the setting of all seven of his novels, is hard to ignore. In Chandler's hands, "Los Angeles is a baroque landscape of corruption and perversity,"[51] rife with unscrupulous politicians and ruthless gangsters. Chandler's disparaging interpretation presents Los Angeles as a temple to superficiality with a bright, neon-lit façade hiding a rotten core. The popularized view of California as Promised Land is supplanted in his fiction by a dystopian land of deceit,[52] a characterization made explicit by the many charlatans passing through his narratives, as well as many other characters hiding their true identities. Often these characters are from other places but have come to California to create a new life, hiding unsavory pasts or problems.

Private Investigator Philip Marlowe, the protagonist in all of Chandler's novels, is acutely aware of these cultural failings, but, for the most part, remains undistracted by them in his work. Occasionally, however, Marlowe's frustrations get the better of him, as they do in Chapter Thirteen of *The Little Sister*—a travelogue in which Marlowe drives in a loop around Southern California, starting in Hollywood, then heading west to the Pacific Ocean, before ending up back in downtown L.A., and venting all the while about the city's vapid, disposable culture. Marlowe's disgust ranges across varied observations of L.A. life, from its ubiquitous false illusions, to its cheaply produced commodities, to the soulless lives of the inhabitants. As he drives, Marlowe punctuates his thoughts, as a kind of mantra, with the phrase "you're not human tonight."

The song "Big Zombie" is made up mostly of lines from this particular passage. But, whereas Marlowe's account is somber and bitter, Langford, who sings, seems to

Rock, Hard-Boiled 191

be exhilarated by the road trip, which he and the Mekons present as an upbeat, Cajun-influenced stomp. One of the song's only parts that does not come directly from the novel is its singalong chorus—"pardon merci, je suis le grand zombie."[53] It is in the use of the word "zombie" that the Mekons' intentions become clear: whereas Chandler seems to be concerned, for the most part, with the tawdriness and lowbrow nature of California's mass-produced culture—his disgust and disenchantment at being part of it—Langford and the Mekons use this textual moment as a jumping-off point, from crass Americanism and dystopian city-scape to European industrialism and Marxist ideology. They are not only cleverly using the term "zombie" to play on Marlowe's "not human," but also deploying its neo-Marxist use as a way of characterizing victims who, as products of "enslavement, colonialization, and proletarianization," are "dehumanized and left only with the ability to work."[54] In offering this (Europeanized, via French) addition to the song, the Mekons bring Chandler's latent critiques of capitalism to the forefront. Although Chandler would dismiss Marlowe as having "as much social conscience as a horse,"[55] his choice to insert such an isolated rant within the novel's narrative structure suggests, much like Hammett's short existential detour in *The Maltese Falcon*, an understanding of larger, soul-stifling forces at work.[56]

The Marlowe persona, for all of its affiliation with the autonomous masculinity of the hard-boiled protagonist, bears much in common with the Mekons. Both, that is to say, operate to some extent as revisions to, or critics of, the very genres in which they participate. Just as the Mekons' first single, "Never Been in a Riot," creates a critical distance from anticipated, hyper-masculine punk imagery—contrasting itself specifically to the Clash's "White Riot" and songs like it—Chandler challenges, by way of his protagonist, the "tough guy" image often associated with hard-boiled writing. Marlowe, like the Mekons, is chiefly defined by his wit, and, on the occasion when he does get into physical altercations, finds himself typically on the receiving end.

But Marlow also shares with the Mekons a certain persistence—an enduring work ethic despite any tangible reward or clear evidence of success. Marlowe's honesty and idealism often hinder him as he works to rid Los Angeles of crime, knowing that his efforts hardly make a dent in the systemic corruption that pervades his society. This typical reality of hard-boiled literature, in which the detectives "may solve a particular crime, but they do not change society at all,"[57] parallels the Mekons' own sense of "powerlessness"[58] in the face of the Reagan and Thatcher administrations. Yet, like Marlowe, as Langford points out, they persist in fighting the good fight, even if it is only "a noble rear-guard action."[59]

Interestingly, it is the imagery of the medieval romance that serves both Chandler and the Mekons in the face of seeming hopelessness, and as a means of showing the impossibility of intimacy within the "fallen" world. Chandler often presents Marlowe as a knight, as when he refers to him, in *The High Window*, as "the shop-soiled Galahad,"[60] or, in *The Big Sleep*, when Marlowe identifies with a knight on a stained glass window.[61] These medieval mirrorings seem to position Marlowe as, in Sean McCann's words, "struggling desperately to hold the grail of justice and love above the seas of corruption that surround him."[62] The honor is clearly present, yet lacks usefulness in the modern context; as Kevin O'Reilly observes, having knight-like qualities would in fact put a private detective at a "severe disadvantage" in 1940s America, leaving him vulnerable to dishonest police or unscrupulous clients.[63] And so Marlowe becomes the anachronistic loner, playing both sides of a chessboard in between his equally isolating assignments. Unlike Sam Spade, whose isolation is self-imposed and protective in nature, Marlowe seems always to be pursuing friendship only to have it "undermined by the various evils of the modern world."[64]

In two songs from the mid-1980s period, both with specifically medieval titles, the Mekons present similar images of isolation and loneliness.[65] While set in the modern day and lacking in their lyrics any direct references to knighthood, both "Chivalry" and "King Arthur" point, like Chandler, to a lack of nobility in current times. "Chivalry," according to the liner notes, is, for example, "an apology from a comrade for his unspeakable behavior."[66] The listener can only guess at what this unnamed comrade (a word reflecting, of course, the band's leftist ideology and its discourse of a political "brotherhood") has done to lose "his honor and our respect,"[67] as he can't seem to clearly remember what happened the drunken night before. He expresses his regret, however, for his unchivalrous actions, and—feeling "just a disgrace"[68]—walks off alone under the rain, as if into one of Chandler's novels. "King Arthur" is set in a fragmented, nearly empty urban landscape with people "scattered all over" and "divided and lonely."[69] This song—as we have seen with the Mekons' aesthetic in general—moves out from under the world of personal relationships into a more politicized realm. The first verse describes someone hiding in an abandoned rail yard, possibly being chased by the police. The image is generic enough to cover a century's worth of related instances: an immigrant, perhaps, pursued as a result of the Thatcher government's aggressive policing policies or seeking refuge within the equally oppressive context of Chandler's L.A. This is not, the setting makes clear, the noble and prosperous England of Arthurian legend, though its title seems to beckon the unifying return of the mythical king.

While the Sex Pistols and many of the other early punk bands burned out quickly, the Mekons are—some forty years later—still around, waiting, it would seem, for that mythic return. Though things have changed since the days of Reagan and Thatcher, the current situation—"the assault," as Langford has recently put it, "on consensus democracy and the brutal consolidation of wealth and powers"—has gotten visibly worse.[70] Perhaps frustratingly, then, social and political criticism remains a point of continuity for the Mekons, whose sound—though it retains some vestiges of that mid-1980s style—continues to evolve and to absorb other genres. Also remaining constant in the face of change is the band's lack of commercial success: an enduring "failure" that, coupled with the Mekons' continued reliance on literature as template, lends a kind of ironic validation to their political representation of the defeated.

Notes

1   Mike Boehm, "The Mekons Mix Music Styles and Politics," *Los Angeles Times*, July 21, 1988, https://www.latimes.com/archives/la-xpm-1988-07-21-ca-9358-story.html.

Rock, Hard-Boiled   193

2 Emily Ryan, "The Mekons: Paul McCartney Should Be Punished," *L.A. Record*, July 24, 2009, https://larecord.com/interviews/2009/07/24/the-mekons-jon-langford -interview-paul-mccartney-should-be-taken-out-and-punished.

3 Joshua Klein, "Mekons Reissue *Fear and Whiskey*," *Chicago Tribune*, January 29, 2002, http://www.chicagotribune.com/news/ct-xpm-2002-01-29-0201290008-story .html.

4 Jon King of Gang of Four, also a Fine Arts student at the University of Leeds, says that the department, at that time, was "the most radical—politically radical—art department in Western Europe, probably the world." Jim Dooley, *Red Set: A History of Gang of Four* (London: Repeater Books, 2018), 61.

5 Russ Bestley, "Still Fighting the Cuts: An Interview with Mekons 77," *Punk and Post Punk* 7, no. 1 (March 2018): 112, https://ualresearchonline.arts.ac.uk/id/eprint/12599 /1/P%26PP_7.1_Mekons_77_interview.pdf.

6 Greil Marcus, *Ranters and Crowd Pleasers: Punk in Pop Music, 1977–92* (New York: Doubleday, 1993), 245.

7 Jon Pareles, "Adding Melody to Noise, Mekons Remain a Force," *New York Times*, November 06, 1990, https://www.nytimes.com/1990/11/06/arts/reviews-music -adding-melody-to-noise-mekons-remain-a-force.html.

8 This album was *The Quality of Mercy Is Not Strnen* (1979), which the band, according to Kevin Lycett, dismissed at the time as a "disappointment; overproduced and directionless." Bestley, "Still Fighting the Cuts," 114.

9 Klein, "Mekons Reissue *Fear and Whiskey*."

10 Bill Wyman, "The Mekons Love You," *Chicago Reader*, September 30, 1993, https:// www.chicagoreader.com/chicago/the-mekons-love-you/Content?oid=882876.

11 Simon Reynolds, *Rip It Up and Start Again: Postpunk 1978–1984* (New York: Penguin Books, 2006), 54.

12 Pat Thane, *Divided Kingdom: A History of Britain, 1900 to the Present* (New York: Cambridge University Press, 2018), 346.

13 Reynolds, *Rip It Up and Start Again*, 58.

14 Although the Mekons chose to write songs about Dashiell Hammett's *The Maltese Falcon*, perhaps a more likely choice would have been *Red Harvest*, an earlier novel which is set in a western town following the violent suppression of a miner's strike. Judging from their interest in Hammett, it is almost certain that the Mekons would have been familiar with *Red Harvest*, though they never directly refer to it. Its subject matter would have resonance for them considering their interest in and empathy for the striking British miners. Several songs from this period—"Abernant 84/85," "Coal Hole," and their version of "The Trimdon Grange Explosion"—directly address miners or the mining strike. A version of Ed Pickford's "Johnny Miner" appears a short while later.

15 Bestley, "Still Fighting the Cuts," 106.

16 Andrew Marr, *A History of Modern Britain* (London: Pan, 2008), 411.

17 Ibid.

18 Marcus, *Ranters and Crowd Pleasers*, 331.

19 Klein, "Mekons Reissue *Fear and Whiskey*."

20 Mekons, *Hello Cruel World: Selected Lyrics* (Portland: Verse Chorus, 2002), 42. The song "Country" quotes from Michael Herr's book *Dispatches* where it refers to war-torn Vietnam.

21 George Grella, "The Hard-Boiled Detective Novel," in *Detective Fiction: A Collection of Critical Essays*, ed. Robin W. Winks (Englewood Cliffs: Prentice Hall, 1980), 105.

22 Peter Messent, *The Crime Fiction Handbook* (Malden: Wiley-Blackwell, 2013), 35.

23 Bestley, "Still Fighting the Cuts," 105.

24 Ibid.

25 Anthony Mark Messina, "United Kingdom: The Making of British Race Relations," in *Encyclopedia of Modern Ethnic Conflicts*, ed. Joseph R. Rudolph, Jr., vol. 2, 2nd ed. (Santa Barbara: ABC-CLIO, 2016), 627–39.

26 Robert Leach, "What is Thatcherism?," in *British Politics: A Reader*, ed. Martin Burch and Michael Moran (Manchester: Manchester University Press, 1987), 157.

27 Sean McCann, *Gumshoe America: Hard-Boiled Crime Fiction and the Rise and Fall of New Deal Liberalism* (Durham: Duke University Press, 2000), 7–8.

28 Ibid., 5.

29 Ibid., 173–4.

30 Bestley, "Still Fighting the Cuts," 105.

31 Langford notes that "the Mekons have always been a mixed band, with men and women in prominent roles. I think there was some kind of barrier that got kicked down with punk rock around that time. It was very unusual for women to be in rock music, other than being the lead singer or backing vocalist. While it's not commented on that much now, that was something that was kind of fundamental [then]. It's not such a big novelty. Yet, having said that, I still think there's so much further to go in all stratas of society. As a male feminist, I think it's kind of scary how society reverts to its stereotypical posturing." "Extended Interview: Jon Langford of the Mekons Talks Activism, Gender Politics, Punk, and Country," *The Local Voice*, September 9, 2015, https://www.thelocalvoice.net/oxford/extended-interview-jon-langford-of-the-mekons-talks-activism-gender-politics-punk-and-country/.

32 Lee Horsley, *Twentieth-Century Crime Fiction* (New York: Oxford University Press, 2005), 68.

33 Messent, *The Crime Fiction Handbook*, 21–2.

34 J. A. Zumoff, "Politics and the 1920s Writings of Dashiell Hammett," *American Studies* 52, no. 1 (2012): 78–9.

35 Mekons, *Hello Cruel World*, 81.

36 Dashiell Hammett, *The Maltese Falcon* (New York: Vintage, 1984), 250.

37 Ibid., 251.

38 Dennis Dooley, *Dashiell Hammett* (New York: F. Ungar, 1984), 106.

39 Peter Wolfe, *Beams Falling: The Art of Dashiell Hammett* (Bowling Green: Bowling Green University Popular Press, 1980), 124.

40 Klein, "Mekons Reissue *Fear and Whiskey*."

41 Greil Marcus, *Conversations with Greil Marcus*, ed. Joe Bonomo (Jackson: University Press of Mississippi, 2012), 166.

42 Mekons, *Hello Cruel World*, 77.

43 Hammett, *The Maltese Falcon*, 72.

44 Dean DeFino, "Lead Birds and Falling Beams," *Journal of Modern Literature* 27, no. 4 (2004): 76.

45 Jo Hammett, Richard Layman, and Julie M. Rivett, *Dashiell Hammett: A Daughter Remembers* (New York: Carroll and Graf, 2001), 101.

46 William F. Nolan, *Dashiell Hammett: A Casebook* (Santa Barbara: McNally and Loftin, 1969), 62.

47 Mekons, liner notes for *Fear and Whiskey*, Quarterstick Records, 1985.

48 Marcus, *Ranters and Crowd Pleasers*, 332.

49 A statement from one of his letters seems to sum up Chandler's views on politics: "P. Marlowe doesn't give a damn who is President; neither do I, because I know he will be a politician." *Raymond Chandler Speaking*, ed. Dorothy Gardiner and Kathrine Sorely Walker (Berkeley: University of California Press), 214–15.

50 Frank MacShane, *The Life of Raymond Chandler* (Boston: G.K. Hall and Co., 1986), 76.

51 Sean McCann, "The Hard-boiled Novel," in *The Cambridge Companion to American Crime Fiction*, ed. Catherine Ross Nickerson (New York: Cambridge University Press, 2010), 53.

52 A comparable vision of Los Angeles, updated for the 1960s, can be found in Gram Parsons's "Sin City," a song recorded by the Mekons on *Honky Tonkin'*.

53 French for "I am the big zombie." As a tribute and/or musical joke, the Mekons borrow that line from Dr. John's "I Walk on Gilded Splinters."

54 "Zombies," in *International Encyclopedia of the Social Sciences*, ed. William A. Darity, Jr., vol. 9, 2nd ed. (Detroit: Macmillan Reference USA, 2008), 180–1.

55 Raymond Chandler, *Raymond Chandler Speaking*, 214. See note 49.

56 McCann sees in Chandler "a kind of pseudo-Marxism" which "paints capital as a vampiric force driven to steal the labor power of honest working men." *Gumshoe America*, 167.

57 Messent, *The Crime Fiction Handbook*, 39.

58 Marcus, *Ranters and Crowd Pleasers*, 333.

59 Bestley, "Still Fighting the Cuts," 112.

60 Raymond Chandler, *The High Window* (New York: Ballantine, 1973), 161.

61 Raymond Chandler, *The Big Sleep* (New York: Vintage Crime/Black Lizard, 1992), 3–4.

62 McCann, "The Hard-boiled Novel," 53.

63 Kevin O'Reilly, "The Shop-Soiled Galahad: Raymond Chandler's Knight," *AJAS* 1, no. 2 (1981): 49.

64 McCann, *Gumshoe America*, 140–1.

65 In addition to the songs with medieval titles, the Mekons have several others from their early years—including "Where Were You," "Last Dance," and "Country"—which depict the difficulty of making intimate connections with other people.

66 Mekons, *Hello Cruel World*.

67 Ibid.

68 Mekons, *Hello Cruel World*, 33.

69 Ibid., 105.

70 Bestley, "Still Fighting the Cuts," 113.

12

When Poetry Meets Popular Music

The Case of Polish Rock Artists in the Late Twentieth Century

Marek Jeziński

In this chapter, I discuss the use of poems as song lyrics by Polish rock musicians in the period from 1967 to 1980—a period in which Poland was ruled by the Polish United Worker's Party.[1] This was a time of rapid and vivid development in Polish popular music, during which many newly established artists used the poetry of the nineteenth and twentieth centuries, along with other literary inspirations, as their artistic trademarks. I concentrate on a certain kind of dialectic in which parallel cultural circuits, namely those of high and low culture, are interlinked. Popular music performers who used poetry in their songs revealed their aspirations toward high culture; and simultaneously, sophisticated poetry was promoted as a part of popular culture. Both cultural systems and circuits overlapped with each other and formed a symbiotic relationship, as the advantages of their coexistence were visible for both. It seems that such a symbiosis was most effective in the 1970s when numerous artists intensively used poetry as lyrics. However, the specific dialectics of popular music in contemporary social systems is always related to political power. Popular culture in general was/is entangled by some means in the balance of power and serves as an instrument of values reproduction. Thus, popular culture in the discussed period was an ideological battleground, as the pro-democratic ideas were expressed by some performers, while the mainstream artists who published non-politically involved songs were aired on the official media.[2] Interestingly, both groups of musicians employed poetry (either of the Romantic or contemporary periods) in their songs. This chapter, in introducing readers to a uniquely intensified moment of lit-rock production and consumption, and by showing a "transmedia" phenomenon whose many examples and collaborations might best be termed a "movement," will challenge the notions of such practices as inherently marginal or antithetical to mass reception; of the "rock star poet" as an (legendarily) isolated and rarefied figure; and—by teasing apart a variety of methods and forms by which poems are inculcated as song lyrics—of "poetry-as-lyrics" as a uniform application. Additionally, this chapter will reveal the potential for localized political contexts, including the contentious space of national identity amidst a changing guard, to complicate, intensify, or reshape the high/low binary itself.

The Polish Political Context

As noted, the dialectics related to the use of poetry as lyrics were manifested as a kind of systemic tension between high and popular culture. This juxtaposition was also related to another type of conflict: the class and ideological differences regarding the prevailing values in Poland's post-war society. After the Second World War, Poland's leaders were perceived by the majority of citizens as an externally imposed class: they were Polish communists and socialists nominated or approved by the Soviet Union political authorities in order to form the "new elites" for the "new Polish state." In order to offset this sense of imposition—of an authentic elite displace by outsiders—the newly instated communist elites sought to establish an alliance with the underprivileged and the poor. This entailed establishing hegemony not just politically, but culturally—influencing the patterns of social behavior in the long term, both in terms of consumption and shared practices. As Henryk Domański argues, the government's wide-reaching and diverse means of power were viewed by many as a basic source of social inequality.[3] Hence, in the PRL (Polska Rzeczpospolita Ludowa, or Polish People's Republic), a division between "society" and the "authorities" was keenly felt, and perceived by average citizens as unjustified.

Unsurprisingly, class tastes evolved within and were complicated by such power struggles with high culture serving the educated classes rather than the politically privileged classes (in Pierre Bourdieu's framework, *cultural* capital contended with other forms, such as political and economic capital). Education itself, in turn, became a battlefield for defining values that were important for the identity of individuals, and a space of conflict regarding who had the right to define these values, whose stakeholders included the conservative intelligentsia (privileged symbolically but not materially), the mass media, and—less expectedly—the new music idols whose activities were considered part of an urban folk culture. The latter enjoyed popularity, and contemporary rock and roll music was fashionable among the youth; however, this form of art was devalued by labels like "commercial" and "folk," and consequently gained the (classist) stigma of "light mass entertainment."

The authorities in Poland tried to use rock and roll music to channel the youth's attitudes. Western popular music (exemplified with the popularity of the Beatles and the Rolling Stones) was permitted in the media and the concert halls as part of a system fully controlled by the political powers of the 1960s. Artists had to be led by the official managerial offices, for example, Polskie Stowarzyszenie Jazzowe, PAGART, or Estrada Bałtycka. At the same time, amateur bands were allowed to hold their rehearsals in officially led cultural centers in which rehearsal rooms, instruments, and the media were supplied and controlled by certified managers. Moreover, musicians playing at state-run official festivals had to behave according to politicians' expectations. For instance, Tadeusz Nalepa claimed that the record company encouraged him to include an anti-American protest song about the Vietnam War ("Te bomby lecą na nasz dom" / "These bombs are falling upon our house"[4]) on the band's first LP. Also, during a performance with his next band Breakout at the 1969 Opole Festival (1969), the musicians were required to wear "proper" non-hippie clothes. As Nalepa recalls: "We faced some troubles with hair in Opole. We had to put the hair behind our ears."[5] There was, in other words, a cultural paradox at work: the music of youthful rebellion and liberation was subjected to political regulation and censorship, as communism—a notoriously "intellectual" movement associated with high art—struggled to position itself in relation to the Rock Revolution.

Rock music was not initially a part of the state's ideologically oriented, official cultural policy at the time: rather, it was treated primarily as an American fashion that would likely pass quickly. When rock groups gained enormous popularity, however, the ruling party activists tried to channel listeners' attitudes and responses, promoting this popular, imported genre as "youth music," and as part of an ideological game in which the entire system's institutionalization was at stake. As a result, the youth artists were allowed to be aired on the radio or TV, and to participate in song festivals. Rock seemed relatively harmless and useful in political terms, and the activities of the bands were initially effectively controlled. At the end of the 1960s, however, a second-circuit scene independent of the authorities was created; it functioned semi-officially, next to, but not fully merged with, the mainstream. The ruling party was likely taken by surprise at the themes this new generation of artists took up, and (while encouraging such groups to position or refer to their work as part of a "rural folk" or "folklore" tradition) certainly were not expecting them to pillage the storehouse of "legitimate" high art—that is, Polish poetry, new and old—for their lyrics.

The PRL Music Scene

Though, in the communist-governed period between 1967 and 1980, popular music in Poland underwent several significant changes, it was a phenomenon subjugated mainly to the rules of the entertainment business typical for the state-controlled music industry.[6] In 1967, Czesław Niemen performed his protest song "Dziwny jest ten świat" ("Strange is the World") at the Festival of Polish Song in Opole (also referred to as the Opole Festival), which gave a new value to popular music in Poland. Although there were numerous youth "big-beat" bands active in the late 1950s and early 1960s,[7] this particular performance is perceived as the first manifestation of "mature" rock music in Poland due to both Niemen's song's originality and his unprecedented (in official media), highly expressive onstage performance. In 1980, during the Opole Festival and shortly after, a new wave of Polish bands (e.g., Maanam, Perfect, Bajm, TSA, and Lombard) achieved access to the radio, TV, and the press, and introduced to mainstream media a variety of rock sub-genres. This period is now referred to as the "boom of Polish rock," the music of which has become extremely popular among youthful listeners.

Rock performers may use poetry as lyrics to broaden their art and stress their professional status as literary, educated, and mature artists, thus dispelling the adolescent or immature rock musicians' image. The image of a sensitive rock artist implies creating an individual who, through the use of poetry, demonstrates the signs of high culture and can therefore aspire to elitist cultural circuits usually not accessible to the masses. Additionally, the attractiveness of poetry results from the fact that poems chosen as lyrics are written in a rhythmically regular way, using a sophisticated artistic technique visibly distinct from language as used in everyday practice. Traditional poetry based on metrical patterns can in fact be easily combined with music, as the formally arranged rhythms and sentence cadences bring "ready-made" elements to songwriting. For example, in his interpretation of the early nineteenth-century poem "Niepewność"/"Uncertainty" by Adam Mickiewicz, Marek Grechuta suggests that melodic harmony, as associated with song, is established purely by way of poetic meter. This is also true for the poems of contemporary authors cooperating with songwriters, such as Leszek A. Moczulski, who penned lyrics for Andrzej Zieliński and Marek Grechuta; Bogdan Chorążuk, who worked with Tadeusz Woźniak; Bogdan Loebl, writing for Tadeusz Nalepa; and Julian Matej, working with Józef Skrzek and the SBB group.

In the case of Polish rock performers in general, however, the use of poetry as song lyrics was not a common practice. As with other countries, rock in the PRL was an aesthetic challenge made by young artists toward the older generation and thus needed to be treated as a generational choice: young rebels vs. conservative parents. Prior to rock, the prevailing patterns of songwriting reflected the poetic, Interwar period practices of cabaret and (in the French tradition) "chanson." In this context, poetry was in fact an essential source of reference; the authors of the lyrics—such as Julian Tuwim, Tadeusz Żeleński, Konstanty Ildefons Gałczyński, Jerzy Jurandot, Marian Hemar, Kazimierz Wierzyński, Jan Lechoń, and Antoni Słonimski—enjoyed literary careers and were recognized as poets.[8] Popular singers of the 1960s and 1970s cultivated these traditions as an expression of mainstream entertainment: the poems of Wojciech Młynarski, Jonasz Kofta, and Agnieszka Osiecka were a significant part of the Polish mass entertainment and, importantly, were also recognized by literary critics.[9] Their songs were performed by mainstream-oriented singers and targeted middle-aged and older listeners. Thus, they were, to some extent, "stage products" designed to show that the Polish audience did not fully accept the new Western fashion in popular music (i.e., rock and roll).

Rock artists rarely referred to such predecessors. Indeed, if rock musicians employed literary texts in their songs, they did it primarily to broaden the audience of their works by grabbing the attention of older listeners in addition to their music's "regular" recipients. Epitomizing this strategy is one of Czesław Niemen's most successful hits during the early period of his career, "Wspomnienie": the artist sings Julian Tuwim's poem which was (and still is) present in school textbooks as an example of contemporary poetry. This period's popular mainstream rock groups often used verses written by contemporary poets who willingly collaborated with musicians, including Jan Wołek, Krzysztof Dzikowski, Janusz Kondratowicz, Kazimierz Winkler,

Jan Zych, Ernest Bryll, Andrzej Bianusz, and the above-mentioned Osiecka, Kofta, and Młynarski. The reference to renowned names active in the Polish entertainment industry of the era guaranteed media exposure and, in turn, improved the commercial circulation of the songs in question.

Polish rock artists who employ poems and literary motifs in their art may be divided into four broad categories: (1) those who use or adapt external poems—texts not planned initially as song lyrics or written in song-friendly form—to their music; (2) those who use, as song lyrics, poems intended by their authors for that purpose; (3) those who incorporate poetry specifically on stage, that is, as a performative, blended experience rather than as a static artifact; and (4) those who employ poetry as part of a larger, more ambitious project such as a concept album focused on a particular author or a separate, prevailing motif or idea in art. Bands incorporated poetry across a wide and proliferating range of music genres, including the ballad, chanson, pop-rock, folk-rock, fusion, experimental, progressive rock, and avant-garde. Though the examples focused on in this chapter tend to fall within the first two categories, it is worthwhile to elaborate on each.

The first category includes performers who intentionally employ poetic verses as words for their songs, as a part of a planned artistic program. The poems are taken either from the past or are specially delivered by poets collaborating with particular performers, but not initially composed or conceived of as rock lyrics—they are written by artists not assimilated to the popular music scene. The list of poets used in this manner is sprawling, and includes Adam Mickiewicz, Sergiusz Jesienin, Julian Tuwim, Konstanty Ildefons Gałczyński, Adam Asnyk, Tadeusz Kubiak, Jarosław Iwaszkiewicz, Bolesław Leśmian, Stanisław Ignacy Witkiewicz, Edward Stachura, Ryszard Krynicki, Ryszard Milczewski-Bruno, Julian Przyboś, Józed Czechowicz, Maria Pawlikowska-Jasnorzewska, Ernest Bryll, Jan Zych, Ewa Lipska, Tadeusz Śliwiak, Jonasz Kofta, Zbigniew Herbert, Mieczysław Jastrun, Tadeusz Nowak, and Wisława Szymborska. In such collaborations, the listener encounters a combination of two types of media—a "transmedia" effect through which, in the language of structuralism, one particular system of signs is transposed into another. In the cases discussed in this chapter, it mainly means the music's functional primacy over the lyrics, which are adjusted to the aural composition.

The second category contains those poems that originated as poetry but were declared song lyrics by the authors or with their agreement. This was the case for contemporary poets who collaborated directly with rock artists, as happened in the PRL period from time to time. Some poets formed a kind of authors' company with musicians, as the examples of Leszek Aleksander Moczulski, Bogdan Chorążuk, Julian Matej, Andrzej Kuryło, and Bogdan Loebl (writing for Skaldowie, Tadeusz Woźniak, SBB, Romuald & Roman, and Breakout, respectively) indicate. Of the four defined categories, this one is perhaps the most vast; it is represented, among others, by such names as Krzysztof Dzikowski, Janusz Kondratowicz, Kazimierz Winkler, Andrzej Kuryło, Stanisław Halny, Grzegorz Walczak, or Małgorzata Maliszewska.

The third category includes poems sung onstage by their authors-turned-rock-musicians, who performed their own poetry backed by instrumentalists. In Polish popular music, a poet singing his/her verses is a phenomenon that does not occur very often, but—as an example in which the dual roles of author and performing artist most fully merge—is worth accounting for. Singing poets of this sort are not just reproducers of someone else's verses by way of their own voices, but are, simultaneously, the authors and interpreters of their own words. This category includes such names as Kora Jackowska of Maanam, Lech Janerka, Grzegorz Ciechowski of Republika, Tomasz Budzyński of Armia, Tomasz Adamski of Siekiera, and Grzegorz Kaźmierczak of Variete.

Finally, I distinguish as a separate class the conceptual albums created around a particular poet's poems. The performers who belong to this category occasionally use poetry in their music or sometimes record songs and anniversary concept albums devoted to particular artists. It includes such artists and albums/projects as Dwa Plus Jeden and Ernest Bryll (*Irlandzki Tancerz*); Marek Grechuta (*Jastrun, Szalona Lokomotywa* and *Pieśni do słów Tadeusza Nowaka*); Ernest Bryll and Katarzyna Gaertner (*Na szkle malowane* and *Zagrajcie nam dzisiaj wszystkie srebrne dzwony*); and Adam Kreczmar, Jacek Hohensee, and Marek Sewen (*To pejzaż mojej ziemi—Beat oratorio*).

As one can gather from these lists, the uses of poetry in Polish rock from this period is far from an oddity, and quite diverse in strategy and application. One thing all of the musician-composers discussed in this chapter do have in common is their explicit emphasis, in interviews and LP/CD liner notes, on the importance of their lyrics. The decision to use poetry as a literary program for musical works was not accidental, even if it happened spontaneously during informal meetings (as was the case for Romuald & Roman as well as for Breakout) or as a result of loose cooperation (e.g., Dżamble). Regardless of the context in which the relationship was established, song lyrics written by the poets lent to the music a sense of thoughtfulness, education, and craft. Andrzej Zieliński and Adam Pawlik—sounding like early-century, literary Modernists—thus describe the role of Leszek A. Moczulski as a sensitive songwriting partner. According to the former, "Leszek and I knew each other before the band Skaldowie started. While in college, I wrote music to his poems . . . [and] we had some spiritual and artistic contact with each other. . . . I wrote songs and arranged them in an exact thoughtful way, there were no accidents, everything was mathematically arranged, everyone knew what to play."[10] Pawlik similarly notes: "We attached great importance while working on these songs not only to music but also to the textual layer. We wanted our music to express something [important] in every aspect. Ambitious music had to go hand in hand with ambitious lyrics."[11] Moczulski, meanwhile, who contributed poetry for Skaldowie, Grechuta, and Dżamble, as well as Bogdan Loebel (writing for Breakout) verifies from the poets' end of such collaborations a kindred seriousness. "I am trying," Moczulski comments, "to look at a song from a literary position. I would like to perceive poetic text written for the song as not one of the 'second sort'. . . . The song has its poetics. Song lyrics should be poetic, yet at the same time, they must be communicative, they must 'adhere' to the mood of the melody."[12] Loebl, for his part, touches specifically on honesty: "When we started doing this, I wasn't preparing myself specifically, I didn't have any books with the original blues lyrics. I thought I would write the lyrics in the usual way I write my poems because it was to be honest writing."[13]

The importance of lyrical values represented in the song texts was a significant part of the creative process for numerous artists with high cultural aspirations—namely, those who aimed their art at the intelligentsia circles of students, people educated in the humanities and social sciences, or to middle and high levels of management. The words of Jan Kanty Pawluśkiewicz, who was the musical leader of Anawa and a distinguished composer who blended classical, experimental, and traditional forms in his music, are significant here. After his split with Marek Grechuta, the first vocalist and co-leader of Anawa, Pawluśkiewicz tried to educate (with regard to lyrics) a new singer in his band—Andrzej Zaucha. This educational program was taken seriously by Pawluśkiewicz because Anawa was a group that aspired to the classical art canon on the one hand, and, on the other, the avant-garde experiments in the nineteenth- and twentieth-century music.[14] Pawluśkiewicz comments on the collaboration:

> Preparing the album, we spent lots of time together and I had a certain tendency to shape him in an intellectual way. As it turned out—I was wrong. He was a very simple man, with no erudite background. . . . I dreamt that Andrzej, while singing the lyrics, would be a competent partner to understand the words. When I asked him to study the *Bhagavad-Gita* and other readings he accepted my point, but later on it turned out that he was so tired of the readings that after the recording of the album he approached me saying: "Well, listen, I'm out of it." It was my fault, I wanted to form him too much.[15]

One can see in Pawluśkiewicz's recollection both a determination that the vocalist should absorb and appreciate the lyrics, and a trust in the context of the band as a site in which such educational processes may be instituted. For all his humility and self-blame, there is the conclusion that Zaucha is the wrong *kind* of person—that is, "too simplistic"—for such undertakings.

Interestingly, determinedly poetic approaches to music such as Anawa's— bands who deliberately envisioned or targeted a finite audience with the necessary intellectual background for lyrical exegesis—did not preclude commercial success. The band Skaldowie, for example, gained nationwide popularity even while addressing their music to specially prepared listeners. The members of the group knew that cooperating with an artist who had a distinct poetic profile might prevent them from reaching a mass audience; and yet the popularity they had already accrued by that point seemed to have been sufficient for audiences to accept such a move generally. Jacek Zieliński, whose songs were performed by Skaldowie, describes his audience as exclusively academic: "Our audience was the students, mainly students. In general, you can say that it was a sophisticated audience. The more literary-oriented or more poetic lyrics of our songs reached it. [. . .] Leszek Moczulski wrote poems for us."[16] Elsewhere, Zieliński stresses his personal attitude while writing music: the compositions had to be supplemented by a specific lyrical program; hence, there could be no randomness in the selection of texts for his songs—a role which was to be performed by poems.[17] This

When Poetry Meets Popular Music 203

was an extremely important assumption, which determined firstly the whole approach to music and the working process, and secondly, approaches to the music market as such. In a sense, the recipient, in seeking an attractive piece of music, had to accept the conditions imposed by the artist.

Marek Grechuta offers another interesting case study of an artist employing poetry in his music. Each of the artist's LPs contains poetry, emphasizing the works of the nineteenth-century Romantic period and—as if to bind the present to Poland's deeper poetic history—contemporary twentieth-century poets as well. Grechuta was familiar with both worldwide and Polish literature; he was interested in literary work as a reader and, later, as an author.[18] Polish literature became for Grechuta a primary and noticeable resource for recognition among the Polish intelligentsia at that time. His works combined such disparate forms and sources as subtle ballads; cabaret songs; tunes inspired by existential philosophy (which was truly popular, particularly in students' circles, at the beginning of the 1960s); jazz; improvised music; and—as was characteristic of most of his 1970s work—progressive rock and fusion. Notable within this context are three LP/CDs dedicated entirely to the authors of poems: specifically, Grechuta's music written for the words of Stanisław Ignacy Witkiewicz on *Szalona lokomotywa* (1977), Tadeusz Nowak on *Pieśni do słów Tadeusza Nowaka* (1979), and Bolesław Leśmian on the *W malinowym chruśniaku* (1984). On other albums, he presented poems by Stanisław Wyspiański, Adam Mickiewicz, Julian Tuwim, Tadeusz Śliwiak, Jan Zych, Jan Przyboś, Leszek Aleksander Moczulski, Ryszard Krynicki, Tadeusz Jastrun, Ryszard Milczewski-Bruno, Józef Czechowicz, and Ewa Lipska. Given the extensiveness of such a list, one might say that listeners receive, by way of Grechuta's albums, a tailored anthology of contemporary Polish poetry (with Grechuta's own poetic lyrics in the mix)—an ongoing collection of poems backed with sophisticated music of varied expression. And the exclusively Polish texts point to a potential marriage of national identity with literary sophistication—an indication that, amidst the changing political climate, poetry was seen as a genuinely revolutionary, galvanizing, and transmedia resource. Grechuta was in many respects enabled and inspired by Moczulski. As the artist himself recollects:

I had long conversations with Leszek Aleksander Moczulski, who urged me to "demolish the chapel" which I had been building since 1967. At the end of the '60s, many young poets debuted, and Leszek, very active in this milieu, facilitated my contacts with them, he "fished out" interesting, freshly written texts. We all felt the rebellious attitude against [the system], disagreement with the events of 1970, but nothing had changed. I was looking for poems that would reflect our frustration—I found them in [the verses of] Faber, Lipska, Śliwiak, Milczewski-Bruno, Krynicki and others.[19]

Poetic music, in the vein of Grechuta and the many others here cited, finds in its adoption of poems an indirect rather than overt response to their politically charged, present moment; like much of the literary tradition, that is, they seek commentary by way of ontological investigation and archetypal imagery rather than a journalistic didacticism, and show

204   *Lit-Rock*

a mutual preoccupation with themes and imagery of psychological deprivation: moral dilemmas, emotional unsteadiness, nostalgic longings, atrophy in human relationships, feelings of "otherness," nervous breakdowns, maladjustment, madness, and so on. There is little room here, it seems, for the "upbeat" or light-hearted sensibilities often associated with pop music, though that is not to say these dark investigations are without hope.

I will conclude this section, then, by introducing small samples from two different poets, each exemplifying, within this shared tradition and with these shared concerns, a unique aesthetic. The poetry of Julian Matej and Bogdan Chorążuk appeared on the very popular LPs of the progressive fusion trio SBB and in the Donovan-style folk-rock performed by Tadeusz Woźniak, respectively. In the following example from Matej, whose writing SBB leader Józef Skrzek used also for his solo albums, the biblical "fall" is vividly reconstituted in terms of creative potential and curiosity: "Actually, there is nothing extraordinary about eating fruit and in a fruit itself / An apple—the little planet of the omni-garden, you lift it and shake off water and fire."[20] Elsewhere, Matej showcases the nostalgic language and imagery of the (specifically Polish) pastoral hymn: "The wind sings the song of the willows, the rough bread smells like the sun, / the Vistula is rolling golden sand."[21] Chorążuk, in turn, is more impressionistic and aesthetically consistent with rock psychedelia, including his 1972 hit collaboration with Woźniak, "The Watchmaker of the Light"—a folk-rock tune played with a jazzy feeling, enthusiastically received at Polish music festivals and in the media; undoubtedly, the song has become one of the most popular hits not only of the 1970s but throughout the entire history of Polish popular music, and despite being notoriously identified as an LSD trip report: a "daringly performed . . . journey to the other side of the rainbow," as Kamil Sipowicz puts it in his "Encyclopedia of Polish Psychedelia."[22] This approach places Chorążuk among contemporary Polish poets associated with the psychedelic hippie movement, such as Ryszard Krynicki, Wiesław Sadurski, Jarosław Markiewicz, Ryszard Kozłowski, and Krzysztof Karasek. In "The Watchmaker of the Light," something of Chorążuk's apocalyptic vision remains, though not without a sense of the contemporary psychedelic journey, and luringly reminiscent of Dylan's tambourine man: "And when the purple Watchmaker of the Light will come for me too, / To stir the blue in my head—I'll be bright and ready."[23] And, finally, in "A Shade of Silence," one finds surrealistic and pastoral/romantic imagery curiously intertwined:

> The cloud of violin flew up extremely high,
> And its hair-strings are woven into the wind into the softest sighs
> And the hair-strings are like the night when the moon is like an evening in the
> night-scented stocks."[24]

Czesław Niemen: Romanticism Revisited

Among Polish performers, Czesław Niemen undoubtedly represents the most successful effort to merge poetry and music. Unlike Zieliński or Grechuta, Niemen focused centrally (though without shunning other authors) on the poems of Cyprian Kamil Norwid, a major Polish poet of the Romantic era. His *Niemen Enigmatic* album (1970), recognized as one of the most important Polish rock recordings of all time, contains, in addition to Norwid's lyrics, the poetry of Adam Asnyk ("Jednego serca"), Tadeusz Kubiak ("Kwiaty ojczyste"), and Kazimierz Przerwa-Tetmajer ("Mów do mnie jeszcze"). Similarly, the artist's later recordings are lyrically built around poetry by Norwid (e.g., "Katharsis") in addition to a long list of contemporary Polish poets.[25]

Norwid's poetry is an example of hermetic art: depressive in mood, difficult to understand, devoid of the easily interpreted motifs typical of commercially oriented art. But Niemen also gains, by self-affiliation, something of Norwid's *generational* aesthetics—an artistic approach that, for all its Romantic heritage, is self-consciously attuned to and representative of its time and place. Norwid seems, in this respect, to enable Niemen's negotiation of high literary culture with the emergent European phenomenon of progressive rock, of which "Bema pamięci żałobny rapsod" (from the 1970 LP *Enigmatic*) is a mature manifestation. This sixteen-plus-minute composition, divided into three parts and performed by a rock band with a choir, is a testament not only to Niemen's extraordinary creativity but his familiarity with contemporary directions in pop culture. Within its rock foundation, the piece presents elements of concrete and experimental music, chorale, funeral mass, and funeral march. All these elements are subordinated, however, to the content of the poem: an elegy in honor of an outstanding general, whose military glory is celebrated by the poet.

Norwid conceived his verses in the form of a rhapsody, that is, a solemn song on a serious subject imbued with funeral imagery. The burial procession carrying the general's body is slowly heading to the place where the deceased leader will be entombed; almost the entire world soberly watches general Józef Bem's last farewell. The funeral is attended not only by human beings (funeral maids, young men, and soldiers in the procession) but also by real and symbolic animals (falcons, horses, lizards, prehistoric reptiles, and dragons), as well as inanimate forms of nature such as the sky and the wind. The war hero is wept for by the whole community, which pays him the great tribute he has earned. In a magazine interview, Niemen recalls his efforts to musically complement such motifs: "I knew it had to be a big form, monumental, maybe with a symphony orchestra, certainly with a large choir. . . . After all, it's a rhapsody: a heroic, historical event, and thus the sublime, festive style. Written with a 15-digit hexagon, it contains very dynamic images."[26]

Norwid's poem is written in difficult language, marked by many metaphors, highlighting Bem's merits and emphasizing the extraordinary character of the great leader's funeral: people, nature, and objects alike experience this historic moment. In the last stanza, Norwid draws a parallel between the mourners' retinue and the fate of the whole world: the march of the conduct becomes the march of humanity into the future: "On—on—till it's time to roll into the grave: / We shall behold a black chasm lurking beyond the road."[27]

Despite its artistic ambitiousness and experimentation, the work was commercially successful: the album became a bestseller (confirmed by its Gold Record status) and was even used in schools as a didactic tool for teachers of Polish. Concert performances,

206   *Lit-Rock*

too, were popular and left a powerful impression on their audiences. Niemen recollects an early performance of the work in a "hall filled to the brim," at whose conclusion "silence reigned" over an awestruck audience.[28] Subsequent performances were applauded with great, long-lasting ovations, as can be heard on *Enigmatic Live*'s 1971 Opole festival recordings.

Some journalists, however, accused Niemen of "tarnishing national saints." This allegation meant that, for part of the journalistic and political milieu, a rock artist crossing genre borders was carrying out an unauthorized activity. Mixing the orders of high ("serious poetry") and low (pop music targeting a mass audience) culture—domains that, like the sacred and the profane, should be kept separate—was considered devastating for cultural heritage. This strategy is particularly visible in the case of Romantic-period poetry (e.g., Mickiewicz, Norwid), which had played a significant role in shaping national identity under the partitions of Poland in the nineteenth century: the objective of poetry then went far beyond the aesthetic function; it acquired, as an aspect of cultural resistance to foreign powers, the features of a political manifesto. Niemen, however, because he had established himself as Poland's most popular rock performer, was in a position to challenge such cultural authorities, and to experiment with form and substance in his songs in otherwise taboo ways: he published music that went far beyond the popular culture genre as previously understood. He touches, in a press interview, on the resistance with which his efforts met, complaining that, although he wanted to bring Polish poetry and high culture closer to the masses, the decision-making spheres were less than enthusiastic:

> The political situation in the last year of Gomułka's decade was not optimistic. I felt the need to continue singing important poetic texts. "Italiam, Italiam" and "Aerumnarum Plenus" by Cyprian Kamil Norwid, by analogy with the sign of the times, was apt but an inconvenient move for so-called factors [i.e., political decision-makers]. It was too much for socialist propaganda. Ideologically right poets still tried to suggest that I do not understand what I am singing, and obedient journalists accused that I behave unkindly.[29]

One can see in this quotation Niemen pushing against some familiar, anti-pop biases, namely the assumption that the form of rock music (including instrumentation and stage performance, but also its unrivaled aura of stardom) means a cheapening or adulteration of the "high art" it attempts to engage or incorporate. Niemen's determined complexity, demanding professional standards, and unprecedented popularity push likewise against the trope of mass audiences as resistant to demanding and experimental forms.

Conclusion

During the 1960s and 1970s, the use of poetry as lyrics was practiced by multiple Polish artists who gained both commercial success and artistic recognition. The examples they provide demonstrate how artistically significant was the conjunction of literature and music not only as two kinds of media, but amidst a contentious and shifting political climate in which the high/low binary was visibly amplified and played a role in negotiations of national identity. Although in the late 1970s music critics and journalists disfavored the combination of poetry and rock music, over time the works of the performers discussed in the chapter became critically acclaimed and accrued the potential to be embraced as part of Poland's canonical poetic tradition. In the cases observed in this chapter, a dialectic of the two aesthetical orders—that is, high- and low-culture circuits—was manifested in the form of popular songs. Poetry used in popular music reflected the tension between elitist and populist cultures, and as represented in the mass media and political ideologies. Moreover, the references to high culture served as a means for shaping and reproducing, at least to some extent, socially accepted standards of musical taste.

The use of a transmedia conceptual approach in the field of popular music—whereby well-recognized poets wrote their poems as rock lyrics for popular Polish bands—marked an unanticipated shift, as well as reception, within the rock milieu. Rather than flopping commercially or succumbing to populist accusations of elitism, such works often gained broad interest and airplay, prompting a wealth of magazine write-ups and artist interviews. Finally, the socialists' promotion, as a marketing and political strategy, of rock music as "youth culture" and as an imported fad set the stage for this generation of transmedia rock performers to challenge the assumptions of rock as an inherently "low" form, and to assume within their artistry the function of cultural education.

Notes

1 The socialist regime in Poland extended from 1945 to 1989.

2 Polish politically oriented cabaret groups or singers include Przemysław Gintrowski, Kabaret Tey, Kabaret Elita, Salon Niezależnych, Jacek Kleyff, 74 Grupa Biednych (and its leader Jerzy Izdebski). Mainstream performers include, among others, artists such as Zdzisława Sośnicka, Zbigniew Wodecki, Edward Hulewicz, Teresa Tutinas, and Hanna Banaszak.

3 Henryk Domański, *Czy w Polsce są Klasy Społeczne?* (Warszawa: Wydawnictwo Krytyki Politycznej, 2015).

4 "Te bomby lecą na nasz dom," track 5 on Blackout, *Blackout*, Polskie Nagrania / Muza, 1967.

5 Wiesław Królikowski, *Tadeusz Nalepa: Breakout Absolutnie* (Warszawa: Wydawnictwo Iskry, 2008), 52, 72.

6 For more details concerning the music scene in Poland, see Marek Jeziński, "The Perimeter Walk: The 1960s/1970s Psychedelic Music Movement in Poland," *Rock Music Studies* 5, no. 3 (2018): 238–56; Renata Pasternak-Mazur, "No Country for Sheer Entertainment: Cultural Politics of Socialist Poland, its Conceptual Scheme, and Vision of Popular Music," in *Made in Poland: Studies in Popular Music*, ed. Patryk Gałuszka (New York: Routledge, 2020), 17–36; Raymond A. Patton,

Screamed Poetry: Rock in Poland's Last Decade of Communism (doctoral dissertation, University of Michigan, 2011); Raymond A. Patton, "The Communist Culture Industry: The Music Business in 1980s Poland," *Journal of Contemporary History* 47, no. 2 (2012): 427–49.

7   Their music was called "big-beat" to avoid unfavorable ideological connotations with the American "rock and roll" name. Among the many bands and artists falling under this label are: Polanie, Rhythm and Blues, Chochoły, Dzikusy, Niebiesko-Czarni, Czerwono-Czarni, Czerwone-Gitary, Bogusław Wyrobek, Michaj Burano, Stan Borys, Bizony, and Tarpany. Musically, their songs, known for amateurish lyrics and youthful emotions, were modeled on the Western popular music heard on Radio Luxembourg or from the Western discs (illegally copied in Poland).

8   For more details on cabaret in Poland (and in the post-war, socialist era), see: Izolda Kiec, *Historia Polskiego Kabaretu* (Poznań: Poznańskie, 2014); Janusz R. Kowalczyk, "Polish Cabaret under the Communist Regime," *Culture.PL*, September 27, 2019, https://culture.pl/en/article/polish-cabaret-under-the-communist-regime.

9   This trend is evidenced by the careers of Łucja Prus, Halina Żytkowiak, Maryla Rodowicz, Irena Jarocka, Mieczysław Wojnicki, Danuta Rinn, Zbigniew Kurtycz, Halina Kunicka, Piotr Szczepanik, Bogdan Czyżewski, the Kramers, Dwa Plus Jeden, and Roman Gerczak, who sometimes sung poems written by contemporary Polish poets.

10   Andrzej Icha, *Skaldowie: Historia i Muzyka Zespołu* (Gdynia: Professional Music, 2004), 47–8.

11   P. Chlebowski, "Dżamble: Wołanie o słońce nad światem," *Lizard* 34 (2019): 33.

12   Icha, *Skaldowie*, 48.

13   Królikowski, *Tadeusz Nalepa*, 57.

14   Jan Kanty Pawluśkiewicz, "Anawa: Jak Linoskoczek," interview by Jarosław Sawic, *Lizard* 10 (2013): 33–4.

15   Ibid.

16   Icha, *Skaldowie*, 48.

17   Ibid., 219.

18   Wojciech Majewski, *Marek Grechuta: Portret Artysty* (Kraków: Wydawnictwo Znak, 2006).

19   Ibid., 74. "[T]he events of 1970" (known as "Grudzień 1970" or "December 1970" in Polish history) refers to the social and political turmoil that took place in several Polish cities, mainly at the Baltic seaside. The citizens were disappointed by and rebelled against the general shortages in the market, particularly by planned price increases for daily goods (including meat, fish, flour, butter, and sugar) announced by the communist authorities. The mass demonstrations, a general strike in some factories, and fights of the workers' unorganized groups against the state militia corps and the army took place in Gdańsk, Gdynia, Elbląg, and Szczecin. As a result, more than forty people were killed, and over 1,100 were injured. Grudzień 1970 was a literal shock for the whole society; it resulted in the growing disappointment of Polish society with the socialist system's inefficiencies and political leadership. Moreover, it led to a deep political crisis at the top of the Polish United Workers' Party which ruled the state: at the beginning of 1971, the leader of the party, Wiesław Gomułka, was dismissed and replaced by Edward Gierek (who in turn was discharged from political leadership during the workers' strikes in August of 1980 at the break of the "Solidarity" social movement). For more details, see Jerzy Eisler,

Grudzień 1970 (Warszawa: IPN, 2012), and Piotr Jegliński, ed., *Grudzień 1970* (Paris: Editions Spotkania, 1986).

20 "Memento Z Banalnym Tryptykiem," track 4 on SBB, *Memento Z Banalnym Tryptykiem*, Polskie Nagrania / Muza, 1981.

21 "Pamięć w kamień wrasta," track 3 on SBB, *Pamięć*, Polskie Nagrania / Muza, 1976.

22 Kamil Sipowicz, *Encyklopedia Polskiej Psychodelii* (Warszawa: Wydawnictwo Krytyki Politycznej, 2013), 167.

23 "Zegarmistrz Światła," track 13 on Tadeusz Woźniak, *Tadeusz Woźniak*, Polskie Nagrania / Muza, 1972.

24 "Odcień Ciszy," track 7 on Tadeusz Woźniak, *Odcień Ciszy*, Polskie Nagrania / Muza, 1974.

25 For instance, the album *Człowiek jam niewdzięczny* (1971, released by Polskie Nagrania / Muza) contains poems by Wojciech Młynarski, Jarosław Iwaszkiewicz, Maria Pawlikowska-Jasnorzewska, Bolesław Leśmian, and Leszek Aleksander Moczulski. *Aerolit* (1974, Polskie Nagrania / Muza) uses the words of Jonasz Kofta, Maria Pawlikowska-Jasnorzewska, and Zbigniew Herbert. In the later part of his music career, Niemen used his own poetry as the primary source of lyrics (*Postscriptum*, 1980, Polskie Nagrania / Muza) and focused on recording instrumental music (*Katharsis*, 1976, Polskie Nagrania / Muza; *Przeprowadzka*, 1982, Rogot; *Terra Defolrata*, 1989, Veriton).

26 Czesław Niemen, "Czesław Niemen: To Przecież Rapsod," *Lizard* 20 (2016): 28.

27 "Bema Pamięci Żałobny—Rapsod," track 1 on Niemen, *Enigmatic*, Polskie Nagrania / Muza, 1970.

28 Niemen, "Czesław Niemen," 28.

29 Czesław Niemen, qt. in Grzegorz Hajduk, "Under the shadow of the Lazio sails . . .," in Czesław Niemen, *Człowiek Jam Niewdzięczny*, Polskie Nagrania / Muza, CD booklet, 15.

Part VI

Identity and Discourse

13

"It's Our Version of *Almost Famous*"

Toward a Reimagined Canon of Rock Criticism[1]

Kimberly Mack

When most people envision an American rock music critic—particularly one from the early era: 1964–80—they imagine someone white and male. And, certainly, the writers at the forefront of the new rock critical establishment were, at least initially, white men. But there is a different and much more compelling story to tell. In teen magazines, Black and brown newspapers, regional dailies and weeklies, and corporate rock publications, BIPOC and white women rock writers were also there at the beginning, and they played a crucial role in developing American rock criticism during the 1960s and 1970s. These writers contributed groundbreaking works to establishment[2] rock music magazines such as *Rolling Stone, Creem, Hit Parader*, and *Trouser Press*, as well as underground music magazines and zines such as *Cheetah, Mojo-Navigator Rock and Roll News, Rock Scene, Star*, and *Punk*. Writers from diverse backgrounds also wrote for monthlies, weeklies, and dailies that were not necessarily focused on music but offered reviews or occasional features about the famous rockers of the day. Such writers included Earl Calloway, a Black critic at *The Chicago Defender* who wrote about rock during the 1970s; Judith Smith, a Black teen writer also at *The Chicago Defender*, who, while still a college student, offered an impassioned defense of the Beatles in a May 1964 article at a time when other journalists did not take the four young men from Liverpool seriously;[3] Jane Scott, a white woman writer at the *Plain Dealer* in Cleveland, Ohio; and Edna Gunderson, another white female writer who wrote about rock for the *El Paso Times* during the 1970s, and was eventually a music critic for *USA Today*.

Their works, and lives, are important because they offer an alternative narrative of rock writing, rock music, and rock (and rock and roll) history writ large. In this new story, writers who are not white men subvert, reshape, and expand the rock canon. In some cases, they disrupt white masculinist approaches to rock criticism from publication venues (teen magazines or regional dailies, for instance) outside of rock criticism's hegemonic norms. And sometimes they operate subversively from within, in a Muñozian disidentification that works both "on and against dominant ideology,"[4] as, for example, fashion or food columns in the pages of *Creem*. As Lisa Robinson shares in *In Their Own Write: Adventures in the Music Press*, "Barry Kramer and Dave

214 *Lit-Rock*

Marsh loved my style column in *Creem*, 'Eleganza,' but people like Robert Christgau didn't like it and threatened to quit *Creem* unless they dropped my column. He'll say it never happened, but I've got the letters to prove it."[5] Through her column in *Creem* and as an editor for *Rock Scene*—"by the winter of 1974 we were at [legendary NYC music club] CBGB every night, so *Rock Scene* became a shameless promotional vehicle for that scene and me as well. There'd be thousands of pictures of me grinning with people backstage"—Robinson rejects the precious seriousness of rock criticism and rock music in general at that time.[6] Though she and others, in myriad ways, resist white male critical dominance through their very existence as rock writers, as well as the form, style, and content of their output, their historical significance remains, for the most part, obscured.[7]

Bearing in mind philosopher Kristie Dotson's concept of the "culture of justification," which she defines as "a culture that privileges legitimation according to presumed commonly-held, univocally relevant justifying norms," one can ascertain how BIPOC and white women's voices have been delegitimized as rock journalists because of their perceived raced and gendered "otherness."[8] Though people of color and women worked side by side with white male writers at *Creem* and *Rolling Stone* during the 1960s and 1970s, endeavoring to fit within these publications' "justifying norms," their acceptance was provisional at best.[9] As music critic Gina Arnold, who began her career at the start of the 1980s, suggests in her August 2020 interview with me, the parameters of an admissible writerly approach are gendered. About her own first-person writing style in which, influenced by the New Journalism she grew up admiring, she situates herself within the story, she states, "Yeah, I totally did that. And it was taken extremely poorly by a lot of people. Yeah, I don't know why it was okay for Lester Bangs to do it but not me. But that's very much the sense that I got from readers."[10] While some non-white men who wrote about rock, such as Geoffrey Jacques, likely encountered barriers, women—particularly women of color—had to navigate racism and sexism both inside and outside of the rock world. Cynthia Dagnal-Myron and Ellen Sander are two groundbreaking rock journalists whose works effectively reshape and expand the canon of rock criticism. Using examples from their early writing, I argue that as a response to rock's "culture of justification,"[11] Dagnal-Myron's and Sander's presence in the early rock scene, and their unconventional and innovative writing approaches, serve as resistive practices. Furthermore, rather than allowing men the final written word on the nexus of art and women's sexuality, both writers, in different ways, engage the subject of sex unflinchingly and with empathy and humor, reclaiming their narrative power along the way.

* * *

Rock criticism was, at first, an attempt to legitimize rock music as something worthy of serious study, as with Western art music. At the beginning of 1966, at seventeen years old, Paul Williams launched *Crawdaddy!*, the first rock music publication that included articles and record reviews geared toward other young fans of this burgeoning musical genre. As Williams states in his "Crawdaddy! Credo," "You are looking at the first issue of a magazine of rock and roll criticism. *Crawdaddy* will feature neither pin-ups nor news-briefs; the specialty of this magazine is intelligent writing about pop music. . . . *Crawdaddy* believes that someone in the United States might be interested in what others have to say about the music they like."[12] A few months later, Richard Goldstein's "Pop Eye" column first appeared in New York's *Village Voice*, covering as its first subject the NYC girl group, the Shangri-Las.[13] Almost two years later, *Rolling Stone* followed suit. Before Williams, if mainstream publications like the *New York Times* covered rock and roll at all, the writer's tone was most likely bemused or condescending. In a February 8, 1964 *Times* article with the headline "The Beatles Invade, Complete With Long Hair and Screaming Fans," writer Paul Gardner sniffs, "The Beatles, who popularized rock 'n' roll in Britain, have added new gimmicks: tight pants, boots, and hair that never seems to be cut."[14] Music industry trade publications and teen-oriented fan magazines covered rock and roll music with more enthusiasm; however, *Billboard*, *Cashbox*, and other trades discussed rock and roll in financial terms, with music reviews focusing on the commercial viability of a song or album instead of the music's artistic merits. And teen magazines such as *16*, *Teen*, and *Tiger Beat*, which appeared on the scene as early as the mid-1950s, almost exclusively approached rock and roll as a vehicle for female, teen-aged romantic fantasies. These magazines, it should be noted, featured some of the earliest women rock writers—such as Ann Moses at *Tiger Beat* and Gloria Stavers at *16*—whose contributions, necessarily different in their approach from Williams, remain a vital but generally overlooked component of early rock criticism in the United States. Similarly, Black publications, such as *Ebony* and *The Chicago Defender*, covered rock and roll artists like LaVern Baker and Little Richard during the 1950s and early 1960s.

Through *Crawdaddy!*, Williams inspired other young people who shared a love of rock (and rock and roll) to start publications of their own and write articles, reviews, and books about this music with critical reverence, and toward the end of collapsing the relationship between rock and literature as examples of low and high culture. Despite such lofty goals, and due to what music journalist Evelyn McDonnell, in a 2019 article about the lack of non-white male representation among the Rock and Roll Hall of Fame inductees, describes as "manhandling," rock criticism's purported democratizing aims have fallen short.[15] As McDonnell explains:

> Manhandling is akin to, and often—as with the Rock Hall—intersects with, whitewashing. Manhandling pushes women out of the frame just as whitewashing covers up black bodies. People of color account for 32 percent of Rock Hall inductees, a far better figure than for women, but still not representative of the enormous role African Americans and Latinx people have played in American popular music. Manhandling is standard practice on country radio; there were no women in the Top 20 of Billboard's country airplay chart for two weeks in December. Manhandling is standard practice on classic rock radio, where women are relegated to token spots on playlists, and are never played back-to-back. It's standard in histories of music; there are no women featured in Greil Marcus's seminal book *Mystery Train: Images of Rock 'n' Roll in America*.[16]

In the latter part of the 1960s, and well into the 1970s, as white men such as *Creem*'s Barry Kramer and *Rolling Stone*'s Jann Wenner created the ground rules for what counts as legitimate rock expression (and, by extension, rock criticism), women and people of color were largely pushed to the margins.

That does not mean that all publication venues replicated this exclusionary structure, and certainly, there were BIPOC and white women who thrived and paved the way for later generations. Ellen Willis was a founding writer for the short-lived *Cheetah* and the first critic to write about popular music for the *New Yorker* between 1968 and 1975. Despite Willis's considerable public platform, and the many contemporary rock critics—Ann Powers, Evelyn McDonnell, Joe Levy, and Robert Christgau, to name a few—who have cited her as an influence, her book of collected rock music reviews and essays, *Out of the Vinyl Deeps: Ellen Willis on Rock Music*, was not published until 2011. And during the 1960s, Carman Moore, an African American, male classical composer and conductor, was the first Black music critic for the *Village Voice*, where he had a new column focusing on classical, jazz, and popular music, including rock. Yet he is almost never included in rock writing compilations or discussions about the early rock critics.[17]

In her 2008 article, "The Write to Rock: Racial Mythologies, Feminist Theory, and the Pleasures of Rock Music Criticism," Daphne Brooks addresses

> the role that rock music criticism has played in shaping contemporary cultural fetishizations of white male performative virtuosity and latent black male innovations—at the expense of producing more nuanced, heterogeneous tales of racial and gender collaborations and (dis)identifications in popular music culture. What are the ways that rock music criticism has shaped and continues to shape our understandings of racialized musical encounters, and what are the alternative stories that we might tell?[18]

Brooks's question is crucial, and the continued expansion of the canon of rock criticism, with a revisitation of the many lost and forgotten rock voices, is an important next step in response to what Kembrew McLeod deems "a specific 'ideology of rock criticism,' one that . . . valorizes serious, masculine 'authentic' rock and dismisses trivial, feminine 'prefabricated' pop music."[19] And this approach to writing about rock music is replicated in the industry's gatekeeping practices: "The way business is done within the rock critic establishment resembles the classic 'old boy network' more so than most types of contemporary businesses, and the music industry as a whole also runs by these 'who knows who' networking rules."[20] Thus, rock criticism in the twenty-first century continues to be viewed as a white male enterprise despite efforts by women and non-white rock writers to change this perception through important recovery projects such as the publication of Ellen Willis's *Out of the Vinyl Deeps: Ellen Willis on Rock Music* in 2011; the release of Jessica Hopper's *The First Collection of Criticism by a Living Female Rock Critic* in 2015, as well as her efforts to amplify some of the women who worked for *Rolling Stone* in a 2018 *Vanity Fair* article, "'It Was Us Against Those Guys': The Women Who Transformed *Rolling Stone* in the Mid-70s"; and the 1995 publication of *Rock She*

Wrote: Women Write about Rock, Pop, and Rap edited by Evelyn McDonnell and Ann Powers. All of these publications have served to highlight the contributions of a diverse group of rock writers, while also offering them much overdue recognition. As Dagnal-Myron suggested about my larger book project (of which this essay is a part), at the start of our July 2020 interview, "It's our version of *Almost Famous*, huh?"[21]

In the early 1970s, Dagnal-Myron (then simply Dagnal) was a bold young Black woman from Chicago's South Side, who had decided at a very young age that rock was her life—"I had fallen in love . . . with four long haired, wise cracking white guys when I was about ten years old. They were the Beatles, and after them, there would be the Who and many, many more."[22] She later wrote stories about and, in her role as a journalist, spent time with legendary rock stars such as Steven Tyler and Roger Daltrey. She was the first Black woman to write about rock for a major metropolitan daily newspaper—the *Chicago Sun Times*—where renowned film critic Roger Ebert served as her mentor. Over a seven-year span, she interviewed or reviewed the work of Rod Stewart, Kiss, Queen, Todd Rundgren, Traffic, Cheap Trick, Brian Eno, Led Zeppelin, and Peter Frampton. As she states in her book based on her Open Salon blog, *The Keka Collection: Soul Food for Lone Wolves and Wild Women*, "I was living a fantasy life, traveling with bands I'd once idolized, interviewing movie and TV stars, going to parties and red carpet affairs most people only see on TV. I was *on* TV, and radio, often. My life was the stuff of dreams and diary entries."[23] Yet in the twenty-first century, her rock criticism is largely unknown.

In Dagnal-Myron's first article for *Rolling Stone*, "Eno and the Jets: Controlled Chaos," published in 1974, she focuses her attention on Brian Eno. Not the version of Eno that is familiar to most music fans today—the iconic record producer whose credits include highly acclaimed works by U2, Devo, the Talking Heads, and Coldplay, and a founding father of ambient music—but the Eno who, immediately post-Roxy Music, had become a solo artist with a record of his own to promote: *Here Come the Warm Jets*.

Dagnal-Myron adopts a wry tone in her profile, poking fun at the hyperbolic proclamations of Eno's promotional team, who apparently boasted about his sexual prowess in a press release. As Dagnal-Myron puts it:

> His sexual exploits, we were also told, would apparently make both Don Juan and de Sade seem grossly overrated, and promotion women called ahead with breathless descriptions of his magnetism and his "intellect." He was purportedly beautiful hermaphroditic, sensual and seductive. "The man that groupies of three continents have come to know as The Refreshing Experience" was coming to devastate our town with his presence and we were never to be the same again.[24]

It is difficult to know how seriously anyone was supposed to take the words in the press packet, but given the era, where sex, drugs, and rock and roll was a popular ethos rather than a well-worn cliché, it is quite possible that the press release and the publicists' "breathless descriptions"[25] were delivered in earnest. After all, in this phase of his career, Eno was toying with rock stardom.[26] Dagnal-Myron's article is as notable for its formidable critical voice as for the heralding of Eno's solo career: While she allows Eno to speak at length about his music, his lack of musicianship, and his failing health, she lends a satirical skepticism to the proceedings:

> However, arriving in Chicago during a relentless heat and humidity spell, The Refreshing Experience was reduced to a somewhat limp and miserable little stringbean. He was pallid, what there is left of his thinning hair clinging to his neck: and a half-hearted smudge of rouge on either cheek only made his pallor more alarming. Any emotions on my part at that time would have to be classified as strictly maternal.[27]

It is striking that Dagnal-Myron uses self-feminizing language to describe her relationality to Eno, fully embracing her womanness in the male-dominated rock space. In her discussion about the gendered discourse in rock criticism by men, Holly Kruse suggests that "the frequency of generalizing, patronizing, objectifying terminology points to an underlying supposition in most popular criticism that rock is fundamentally rooted in male experience and governed by an aesthetic that only a man can understand. Because most rock criticism is anchored in male experience, critics tend to see rock as essentially male."[28] This sense of rock being by and for men often permeates discussions about women artists in particular, as well as the lyrical content in rock songs. It is hardly unheard of for male rock journalists to pen sexist, leering descriptions of female musicians' bodies. In her engagement with Eno, however, Dagnal-Myron upends the usual male rock critic/female artist power imbalance, commenting on his "pallid skin," "thinning hair," and "limp" body.[29] Rather than accepting the words of his PR people, and allowing them to dictate her sexual desires or gendered positionality, Dagnal-Myron transforms the prescriptive lust into a motherly protectiveness.[30]

This was Dagnal-Myron's first major byline. She was already writing for local Chicago publications such as WXFM's *Triad*, but it was the *Rolling Stone* clip that set her on a path to writing for *Creem*, and later for the *Chicago Sun Times*. Lester Bangs was an early mentor. As Dagnal-Myron told me, "I wrote for *Creem* a lot. And it's because of Lester Bangs. That's why I mentioned *Almost Famous*. He was like my dad. And anything I wanted to do, he was willing to help me do."[31] Dagnal-Myron wrote the Brian Eno story on spec after writing to *Rolling Stone* and suggesting that she was the right person for the job. As she explains:

> Somebody sent me a packet about him coming to Chicago, and I wrote to *Rolling Stone*. . . . I just said, "You know, I think I can do this." . . . I had a lot of nerve. I was the nerviest kid alive. I just believed I was good, and I could do this. And I said, here's what I'm gonna do. And I think I had already done some things in Chicago and sent copies of that. And they said, "Well, you know, take a shot," so I sat down with Brian Eno for an afternoon. Hilarious. And wrote . . . I can't remember it, "Eno and the Jets" or something like that. . . . And I was stunned, you know, when they bought it. It was ridiculous. But that was one, and that helped me to, again, get

other things. And then Lester would, anytime somebody was gonna be in Chicago and maybe not where he was, or just 'cause he wanted me to, he would say, "You know, Stevie Winwood is here, or Queen is coming," or whoever, you know, "You want to do that?" And I would do it.[32]

As Dagnal-Myron reflects on her first major rock article, she self-deprecatingly downplays her strong voice and impressive comedic skills. In reality, her first serious effort was anything but "ridiculous." Nervy and unconventional? Absolutely, though her style melds such moments with conventional content rather than completely usurping it. Sometimes she engages Eno more passively, commenting on his music and stepping out the way while allowing him to speak on the page uninterrupted and at great length, while at other times she cracks jokes at his expense: "His health had been described as chronically perilous in all of the articles supplied. One physical breakdown had reportedly occurred after some 30 hours of sexual activities involving no fewer than six women. It seemed, therefore, that he should be quite accustomed to performing in mid-collapse."[33] Eno, as Dagnal-Myron reports, would seem to agree with this assessment:

My health has always been bad. But you see, usually it doesn't affect my brain. In fact usually I find it quite stimulating. When I'm really physically inoperative I think very fast. I'll give you an example. Yesterday I was in San Francisco and I was working on this new project which is a piece of music called "Taking Tiger Mountain by Strategy." It's a revoluionary [sic]/military battle seen as a form of contemporary dance. And I was really getting along very well with it, thinking *very* clean. And as soon as I got here I picked up my notebook and I thought, Great! I'll get back to "Tiger Mountain!" But I started looking at my notes and I said,

he continued, running a hand through his receding hair,

"What does this mean?" I realized that my IQ has dropped 60 points since I've been here in Chicago! I tell you . . . God! I so much want to get out of this town. I mean we got off this lovely air-conditioned plane and into a car and I rolled down the window and this great rush of humidity came in. I thought there was a vapor leakage or something. I could not imagine that this was a condition people actually live in![34]

Not only does Eno provide a (very likely unwitting) comic foil in this narrative, but Dagnal-Myron once again disparages his physical appearance, as she focuses on his "receding hair," and expresses skepticism about the outlandish claims regarding his sexual prowess.[35] But most importantly, she disrupts the conversation that Eno's team expected to have with a man, even doing so directly on the page, and in a way that refuses the position of spellbound audience. The expectation is that he would encounter a male critic who would be more thoroughly impressed and aligned with his exploits. Instead, he meets a Black woman who does not find him attractive and has the confidence and narrative agency to say so in a hilarious way in print for all to see. This is significant. After all, as Ann Powers notes in the Outro to *Rock She Wrote*:

Women in pop have been denied authority, even as they've been welcomed as desiring subjects and fantasy objects. If they claim that authority, develop it, the man at the center may lose his place. Everything—from the metaphor for phallic prowess that is the extended guitar solo, to the industrywide silence that, in 1992, allowed a half-dozen record executives separately accused of sexual harassment to retain employment in the field—might shatter. Then we'd have to put it back together, and the women might be in charge. So in many subtle ways, women are still encouraged to stay under those covers, keep their quiet, gaze adoringly, and dream alone.[36]

Dagnal-Myron is extraordinary because she is resisting this. She knows the contradictions, but she pushes against, and past them, at least on the page. As part of this strategy, she evinces a humorous and sarcastic critical writing persona that fits well within the style of circa 1970s *Rolling Stone* and *Creem*, yet her substantial body of work cannot be found in Rock's Backpages, or in print rock criticism histories. It is fair to suggest that Dagnal-Myron, despite her substantial and unique output—her ability to claim and reclaim narrative power within a discourse meant to suppress it— has been "denied authority" in terms of the prestige and name recognition history has afforded other, typically white and male, critics.[37]

The same might be said for Dagnal-Myron's fellow rock critic Ellen Sander, whose groundbreaking 1968 story on the Plaster Casters, "The Case of the Cock-Sure Groupies,"[38] likewise challenges the gender dynamics of rock. Whereas Dagnal-Myron uses humor to subvert the gendered power differential, Sander disrupts it by way of subject matter, bypassing the male artist for two very young (one underage) female groupies, and establishing (in the vein of the New Journalism writers that influenced her), a first-person, participatory approach.

Beginning in the mid-1960s, Sander wrote about rock music for *Saturday Review*, *Vogue*, the *L.A. Free Press*, and the Sunday *New York Times* Arts & Leisure section. In her journalistic memoir, *Trips: Rock Life in the Sixties*, a groundbreaking and unflinching look at the era's rock scene, she includes a now-classic story about her experiences traveling with Led Zeppelin for a *Life* magazine article, during which she had to fend off the sexual advances of their "greasy road manager" and endure a physical assault by two unnamed "members of the group" who tore her dress[39] (she has since revealed that the late drummer John Bonham was the band member, while the other assailant was someone in Zeppelin's entourage[40]). *Trips*, published in 1973 by Charles Scribner's Sons, a major New York publisher, was out of print a few years later and was finally re-released in May 2019. It is reasonable to imagine that Sander's book would have been received differently if she had been a white, male rock critic.

Sander's story about the Plaster Casters—a group of young female fans known for creating plaster casts of rock stars' penises—features distinct writerly approaches: straight journalism, reportage, and even letters to rock stars from the young women themselves. While Sander inserts herself into the narrative, she does so in a way that does not feel voyeuristic or exploitative:

It is now Saturday early evening and we are in Lisa's house in a flouncy girl's bedroom, all pink and white and precious. And there are posters and popstars' pictures and hundreds of albums—Traffic, Procol Harum, Rhinoceros, the Beatles, the Stones—pretty good taste, I must confess, not a chickenshit album in the bunch. And Rennie is assembling the plaster kit, putting all the paraphernalia in a little briefcase with a sign on it, "The Plaster Casters of Chicago." That briefcase has become their trademark, and a well-respected one at that. The underground radio station knows about them and so do all the club owners who let them into the clubs for free now. After all, they're celebrities in their own right. They lovingly show me the casts and allow me to photograph them and other mementos, the signs, the apparatus in the plaster casting kit and all. And I read their letters and they proudly show me their clipping file.[41]

As the story unfolds, Sander is very clear with Rennie and Lisa (pseudonyms for Cynthia and Dianne, respectively), and her readers, that she is hoping to witness a casting, but it does not ultimately transpire because Cynthia becomes distracted on the night blues-rock guitarist and singer-songwriter Steve Miller is willing (and a little too eager) to have a cast made. It turns out that Cynthia had long had her eye on Lonnie, Steve's bass player, but Dianne started talking to him first. Consumed with anger and jealousy, Cynthia ignores Steve and ends up with Lonnie at the end of the evening. Sander writes:

I close the door behind me and across the hall Tim's door is opening. Steve Miller is gone. The guests and friends are leaving. Rennie, I correctly surmise, is with Lonnie. Lisa was with the road manager. And I'm standing here in the hall with my face hanging out. It's the middle of the night and I'm not even sure where the hell I am, what does "Elk Grove" mean to me? I don't know what cab company to call, the desk is closed and I forget the address of the place I'm staying and whatthefuckamigonnado? I stand there, that's what I do. I am hoping that Tim is, um, a gentleman. . . . (n.b. he was). The morning after. The boys in the band are checking out of the hotel and everybody is saying good-bye and Steve Miller is really irritable. He's looking at me, half surprised to see me there. He knows Rennie was with Lonnie and Lisa was with the road manager and he's figuring I was with Tim, and boy, he's pretty crabby 'cause *he* spent the night alone. And in my mind I'm going hahahahah, eat your *heart* out you stupid garbagemouth, bugging the Plaster Casters like that, hahahahah.[42]

Even though Sander is just twenty-four, she is still three years older than Cynthia and seven years older than Dianne. Yet she does not talk down to the young women or judge them in any way. Her tone suggests a woman-loving camaraderie, a subversion of rock criticism's typical, if not disapproving then certainly condescending, male response to the groupie phenomenon. Tom Nolan's 1967 *Cheetah* article, "Groupies: A Story Of Our Times," for instance, adopts a melancholy tone, reading as a cautionary tale for what can happen to nice young female rock and roll fans who become groupies. When discussing *"known"* nineteen-year-old groupie Sherry Sklar, he mentions that

> her old friend and sometime-companion Karen is beginning to wonder about it all, or at least certain parts of it, like the way she will ask strangers do they think she looks—well, *used . . .* and it is true that her fragile blonde prettiness is beginning to harden around the edges, and though she isn't quite as hard-looking as Sherry, maybe she has gotten to the point where the faces are all beginning to blur together in a hazy kind of fog.[43]

A few months after Sander's story was published to great fanfare and predictable moral panics, *Rolling Stone* ran their first groupie piece. Sander was quite aware of the contrast between her treatment of this subject and that of other, male writers. As Sander shared with me in a June 2020 interview:

> You know, I didn't know what to think, but the minute I met those young ladies, I just knew they were phenomenal. Fantastic. Wonderful. They were really a story, not so much what they were doing but who they were and how they went about what they were doing. So it was, you know, it was really wonderful. *Rolling Stone* did an issue on groupies, which came out the following week[44] after the Plaster Caster story broke. . . . It was just, you know, people were just shocked. It just blew them away, and then a week later *Rolling Stone* came out with a groupie issue and they had a piece on the Plaster Casters, and Cynthia Plaster Caster told me that she never met anybody from *Rolling Stone*, it was all done by phone, and you know, [famed *Rolling Stone* photographer] Baron Wolman came out and took a picture and left an hour later and everything else was by phone. Nobody, nobody came and hung out with them. . . . I think there is a tendency to see groupies as either immoral or victims. And I didn't get that at all.[45]

Sander's comfort with both telling, and including herself, in this particular tale, in spite of the respectability politics around the flourishing groupie scene, speaks to her sense of connectedness to other women and their stories. Sander's feature suggests an intimate bonding with the young casters; her prose reads as if she and the women are friends who enjoy each other's company, while the *Rolling Stone* groupie story, written by three men, quite predictably has a sensationalistic tinge. In the preface to the 2019 reissue of *Trips*, Sander pulls the curtain back on the editorial process, mentioning her desire to not revise too much: "It was especially important to retain the exuberant feminine *esprit*."[46] When I asked Sander to define "feminine *esprit*," she did so as follows:

> Looking back on it now, now that there has been so much rock journalism, ad infinitum, and you would see that the men took a more analytical approach, where mine was very emotional, and just kind of full of the excitement of being there. And so I did, after a while, not while I was doing it, see a difference in the way most men covered rock and roll and the way I did. And it occurred to me that that

"It's Our Version of Almost Famous"   223

was because I was a young woman, and that I responded to it a little bit differently. And that also, I didn't know a lot about journalism. I didn't know a lot about music theory. I didn't know a lot about the genealogy of rock and roll. I mean, I learned, but so I would just be very much in the present experiencing things. And that's, I believe, what I call the feminine *esprit*. In the, I don't know which version of the introduction it is, but it's about, you know, that I say that rock and roll was *for* women. It was *about* women. It was directed at women, at first.[47]

Sander's commitment to staying true to the youthful enthusiasm she experienced as a rock journalist during the heyday of rock music is reflected in her rendering of the Plaster Casters adventures, and makes a political statement echoing McDonnell's point that "women journalists have used the power of their difference not simply to address that difference, but to write differently, to exploit their advantage as outsiders."[48] Sander's positionality is what allowed her to gain the Plaster Casters's trust. It is what elevated their story from something that, in the wrong hands, could be framed as banal and sordid to a serious conversation about the intersections of art and sex against the backdrop of free love and rock. Strikingly, Sander told me that some readers of the Plaster Casters piece assumed the author was male: "I was told by a couple of people that they knew people who didn't believe that the Plastic Castor story could have been written by a woman."[49] While astonishing to me, my only guess as to why is because of Sander's bold treatment of free love, including detailed descriptions of some encounters; a liberal use of cuss words; and her sincere desire to see a casting up close. Given Sander's gender, there were (as there still are) notions and expectations regarding white middle-class female respectability that Sander does not even attempt to engage.

The canon of rock criticism, over time, has been formed and dominated by white men. As McDonnell suggests, rock criticism that is deemed acceptable is the kind that supports rock music that passes through the highly subjective filter of rock authenticity.[50] For BIPOC and white women rock writers, choosing the right sorts of bands to write about, and doing so in ways that are sanctioned by the rock critical establishment, as coalesced around a handful of influential American rock publications, does not guarantee full or enduring inclusion in the canon; non-white male journalists must find their own ways to redefine and reshape it. As Gina Arnold reminded me directly, after a successful freelance career in which she contributed hundreds of rock articles to elite publications including *Rolling Stone*, *Spin*, and *Entertainment Weekly*, she was never on the masthead at any of the magazines for which she freelanced.[51] What is clear is that many writers have accepted the canon as it was shaped by others, but find that they are not ultimately welcomed inside. My book project takes up Daphne Brooks's challenge and reimagines the genealogies of rock criticism. From teen magazines to Black and brown newspapers, to regional dailies and weeklies, and finally to mainstream rock publications such as *Rolling Stone* and *Creem*, BIPOC and white women writers have been, and continue to be, vital contributors to rock criticism. Through their narrative disruptions (via form, style, and content) from inside and outside of establishment rock publications, these writers actively resist their marginalization within, and potential erasure from, the canon of rock criticism. And through their works they forcefully reclaim their power, allowing for an important reconsideration of their rightful place in rock history.

Notes

1   While the title of this essay suggests an exclusive focus on rock criticism, this work allows for a capacious definition of rock music writing that includes criticism and journalism.
2   My use of the term "establishment" throughout this essay to describe rock publications like *Rolling Stone* and *Creem* refers to their positionality within the realms of rock criticism and rock journalism. While these magazines were largely viewed as countercultural in the early years and stood in stark contrast with mainstream publications such as the *New York Times*, they very quickly became the shapers and creators of a canon of rock music and writing.
3   Judith Smith, "'Beatles Forever,' Says Collegian Judith Smith," *Chicago Defender* (National edition), May 9, 1964, 16.
4   As José Muñoz explains, "Disidentification is the third mode of dealing with dominant ideology, one that neither opts to assimilate within such a structure nor strictly opposes it; rather, disidentification is a strategy that works on and against dominant ideology. Instead of buckling under the pressures of dominant ideology (identification, assimilation) or attempting to break free of its inescapable sphere (counteridentification, utopianism), this 'working on and against' is a strategy that tries to transform a cultural logic from within, always laboring to enact permanent structural change while at the same time valuing the importance of local or everyday struggles of resistance." *Disidentifications: Queers of Color and the Performance of Politics* (Minneapolis: University of Minnesota Press, 1999), 11–12.
5   Paul Gorman, *In Their Own Write: Adventures in the Music Press* (London: Sanctuary, 2001), 124.
6   Ibid., 142.
7   The degree of, and reasons for, such erasures differ considerably among rock writers active during the 1960s and 1970s. Some white women writers, such as Ellen Willis and Ellen Sander, were quite successful in their era, but their notoriety in subsequent generations has waxed and waned. Others, like Black scribes Richard Pinkston IV, Carman Moore, and Cynthia Dagnal-Myron, who all wrote for establishment rock magazines and prominent regional weeklies such as *Rolling Stone*, *Creem*, and the *Village Voice*, have, inexplicably, been largely forgotten. And then there are writers who published in teen magazines, zines, Black and brown newspapers, and regional and local publications based in smaller cities, whose works have been obscured for more obvious reasons: While rock music and rock criticism canonicity, as developed largely by white men, has played a significant part in the erasure of the legacies of BIPOC and white women rock writers, it is also true that certain publications were viewed as more legitimate than others, negating and marginalizing the important works of many writers of color and women.
8   Kristie Dotson, "How is This Paper Philosophy?" *Comparative Philosophy* 3, no. 1 (2012): 6.

9 Ibid.
10 Gina Arnold, in discussion with author, August 2020.
11 Dotson, "How is This Paper Philosophy?"
12 Paul Williams, "*Crawdaddy*: Get Off Of My Cloud!," *Crawdaddy!*, 1966. Rock's Backpages, http://www.rocksbackpages.com/Library/Article/icrawdaddyi-get-off-of-my-cloud.
13 Darren Reidy, "Sex, Drugs & Rock Criticism: Richard Goldstein on the Sixties," *Rolling Stone*, May 29, 2015, https://www.rollingstone.com/music/music-news/sex-drugs-rock-criticism-richard-goldstein-on-the-sixties-177734/.
14 Paul Gardner, "The Beatles Invade, Complete with Long Hair and Screaming Fans," *New York Times*, February 8, 1964, https://www.nytimes.com/1964/02/08/the-beatles-invade-complete-with-long-hair-and-screaming-fans.html.
15 Evelyn McDonnell, "The Manhandling of Rock 'N' Roll History," *Longreads*, March 2019, https://longreads.com/2019/03/29/the-manhandling-of-rock-n-roll-history/.
16 Ibid.
17 My book, tentatively titled *The Untold History of American Rock Criticism*, is under contract with Bloomsbury Academic. In addition to the writers I discussed earlier, my book will also include Robin Green, Ben Fong-Torres, Patricia Kennealy-Morrison, Gerri Hirshey, Carol Cooper, Jaan Uhelszki, Roberta Cruger, Susan Whitall, Sandra Carroll, Carola Dibbell, Richard Pinkston IV, Vernon Gibbs, and writers who emerged later in the twentieth and twenty-first centuries, including Ann Powers, Greg Tate, Jessica Hopper, Lisa Jones, and more.
18 Daphne A. Brooks, "The Write to Rock: Racial Mythologies, Feminist Theory, and the Pleasures of Rock Music Criticism," *Women and Music: A Journal of Gender and Culture* 12 (2008): 55–6.
19 Kembrew McLeod, "A Critique of Rock Criticism in North America," *Popular Music* 20, no. 1 (2001): 47.
20 Ibid., 57.
21 Cynthia Dagnal-Myron, in discussion with author, July 2020.
22 Cynthia Dagnal-Myron, *The Keka Collection: Soul Food for Lone Wolves and Wild Women from Keka's Blog on Open Salon* (CreateSpace, 2011), 94.
23 Ibid., 103.
24 Cynthia Dagnal, "Eno and the Jets: Controlled Chaos," *Rolling Stone*, September 12, 1974, Jeffrey Morgan Archive, http://music.hyperreal.org/artists/brian_eno/interviews/rs74c.html.
25 Ibid.
26 Tyler Wilcox, "When Brian Eno Was a Rock Star: Live Highlights from His Early Days," *Pitchfork*, May 15, 2018, https://pitchfork.com/thepitch/when-brian-eno-was-a-rock-star-live-highlights-from-his-early-days/.
27 Dagnal, "Eno and the Jets."
28 Holly Kruse, "Abandoning the Absolute: Transcendence and Gender on Popular Music Discourse," in *Pop Music and the Press*, ed. Steve Jones (Philadelphia: Temple University Press, 2002), 136.
29 Dagnal, "Eno and the Jets."
30 Ibid.
31 Dagnal-Myron, in discussion with author.
32 Ibid.
33 Dagnal, "Eno and the Jets."

34 Ibid.

35 Ibid.

36 Ann Powers, "Outro: Who's That Girl?" in *Rock She Wrote: Women Write about Rock, Pop, and Rap*, ed. Evelyn McDonnell and Ann Powers (New York: Cooper Square Press, 1999), 466.

37 Ibid.

38 "The Case of the Cock-Sure Groupies" was published in November 1968 in *The Realist*, and later re-titled "The Plaster Casters of Chicago" in *Trips*.

39 Ellen Sander, *Trips: Rock Life in the Sixties* (Mineola: Dover, 2019), 135, Kindle.

40 Hank Shteamer, "Pioneering Rock Writer Ellen Sander on the Joy and Terror of the Sixties Scene," *Rolling Stone*, May 1, 2019, https://www.rollingstone.com/music/music-features/ellen-sander-rock-author-trips-interview-816210/.

41 Sander, *Trips*, 151–2.

42 Ibid., 155.

43 Tom Nolan, "Groupies: A Story of Our Times," *Cheetah*, 1967. Rock's Backpages, https://www.rocksbackpages.com/Library/Article/groupies-a-story-of-our-times.

44 "The Groupies and Other Girls" was published in the February 15, 1969 issue of *Rolling Stone*.

45 Sander, in discussion with author, June 2020.

46 *Trips*, "Preface."

47 Ibid., in discussion with author.

48 Evelyn McDonnell, "The Feminine Critique: The Secret History of Women and Rock Journalism," in *Rock She Wrote: Women Write about Rock, Pop, and Rap*, ed. Evelyn McDonnell and Ann Powers (New York: Cooper Square Press, 1999), 15.

49 Sander, in discussion with author.

50 McDonnell, "The Manhandling of Rock 'N' Roll History."

51 Arnold, in discussion with author.

14

Limits of the Literary

Rethinking Allusions in Pop Music

Pat O'Grady

"Islands in the Stream" is a popular country song that contains a striking connection to the literary world. Written by the Bee Gees (comprising Barry, Robin, and Maurice Gibb), and recorded as a duet between Kenny Rogers and Dolly Parton, the lyrics of the song make reference to a novel of the same title by Pulitzer Prize winner Ernest Hemingway.[1] In one of the most prominent television documentaries of their career, the Bee Gees state that they were inspired by Hemingway's title. Maurice Gibb notes:

> *Islands in the Stream* was an Ernest Hemingway book, not that I've ever read them. I must admit I'm not a big reader of Ernest Hemingway. But the titles stick out at you and you say "wouldn't that make a great song?" Being islands in the stream, or being islands away from everyone else and just being the two of us.[2]

One of the more curious elements of this song/literature connection lies in how it is represented—or perhaps more accurately, how it is *not* represented—within the pop music world. The relationships between the literary and pop music worlds are frequently heralded and discussed within music and literary domains, the preeminent example being that of Bob Dylan, whose frequently noted literary references—it is safe to assume—played a role in his receiving the Nobel Prize in Literature in 2016. Conversely, the literary allusion within "Islands in the Stream" has barely received any acknowledgment at all—a response that appears justified, or even furthered, by Gibbs's own self-distancing and casual recollection of the matter. For him, a connection to the author is less important than is the songwriter's recognition of a phrase/title readily transferable (as, his comment suggests, a simple, relatable, and romantic metaphor) to the domain of pop.

This chapter critically examines the socially driven relationships between pop music and the literary world. What I am *not* trying to argue here is that the Bee Gees' invocation of Hemingway was an effort to demonstrate sophistication or depth, or even that they necessarily deserve to be celebrated as "serious" artists; what I *am* asserting, however, is that "Islands in the Stream" suggests there are unconscious boundaries to what constitutes a meaningful relationship between literature and pop music. In making such boundaries more visible, I aim to expose the lingering dominance of rockism and canon-formation within the broader domain of popular music and its corresponding social divisions. Using Pierre Bourdieu's notions of field and capital—and in keeping with the aims of this book—I will explore how representations of literature in pop music reveal or operate as "literary capital." This discussion, I hope, will make apparent what I will call the "influence potential" of literature (when does a literary reference "work," and what factors prevent it from "working"?) referenced in pop music, and the ways in which some musicians accrue "literary capital" from it. With this in mind, I ask whether the example of "Islands in the Stream" suggests that a more complex understanding of how literary capital is acquired is needed, one which understands how it can be used to influence the status of musicians and songs in pop music, where its boundaries preside, and what variables or contexts cause it to succeed or fail.

Bourdieu's well-established ideas on class and taste remain instrumental in connecting the status of objects and artistic practices—the values and preferences of individuals—to the organization of class systems. In particular, his term "field" helps to conceptualize distinct social spaces in which individuals apply their acquired knowledge, or "cultural capital," to achieve or to maintain a position therein.[3] Within Bourdieu's model, the literary and pop music worlds can be understood as two distinct fields. Nevertheless, as both simply observation and ongoing scholarship make evident, the two field have established clear lines of dialogue and interchange: some artists practice both songwriting and poetry,[4] rock music is often represented in literary texts,[5] and literature is sometimes referenced in pop music.[6] The two fields, that is to say, clearly have use for one another even as they attempt to showcase autonomy or invoke, by way of such references, a high/low binary. Indeed, this very collection is a demonstration of the permeable boundaries within which these fields operate, as well as the potential for capital associated with one "field" to serve as a currency within the other. As an extension of "cultural capital," "literary capital" refers specifically to a knowledge of the literary world—an awareness, one may presume, of (mostly) canonical literary texts and methods for their interpretation. And a chief form of demonstrating this knowledge—signifying, potentially, one's depth of artistry or character—is the literary allusion, though the precarious nature of such demonstrations—the space they open for potential accusations of naivete, for example—is also a potential outcome.

Crucially, Bourdieu's works show how demonstrations of cultural capital are linked more broadly to one's economic circumstances and educational resources. Despite emanating from 1960s and 1970s France, Bourdieu's paradigm remains instructive in cross-cultural applications, with scholarship showing the continued importance of "the literary" in relation to class formations. David Wright, for example, demonstrates how cultural capital associated with book culture is embedded—in the form of restricted access to literary material—into social constructions of class and—in the form of distinct genre tastes—gender.[7] For Wright, the conflation of book ownership and the literary field obscures other reading practices: "Whilst participation in book culture is largely concentrated into a significant minority, reading practices in themselves are more diverse when magazine and newspaper reading is taken into account."[8] Bourdieu, I'd like to add, broached the literary field directly in his work *Rules of Art*.[9] Although his work has often been viewed as an attack on "high" culture, here he offers a defense of the value of the literary field. This defense coincides with a distinct increase in his engagement in politics at the time, where he advocated for the arts broadly, and in spite of his earlier critiques of "high art" sections of the cultural industries.[10] This should give pause to dismissals of Bourdieu's project as anti-art, pointing instead to the potential for cultural or literary capital to functionally shift depending on its current and political contexts.

The cultural context of pop music, in relation to that of the literary world, is more vastly decentralized and hard to locate. The social status of pop music has trended upward significantly since the time of Bourdieu's early work, and despite an originally shared skepticism toward it—as a form compromised by market objectives and high-volume production—among intellectuals. Some have argued that pop music has since developed a high/low art divide of its own, with distinct forms of cultural capital,[11] while others have argued that assumptions about what constitutes cultural capital have evolved. For Taylor, such evolution "has destabilized the position of the fine arts at the top of the hierarchy of cultural production."[12] The question for this study is whether demonstrations, as well as receptions, of literary capital within the (seemingly antithetical) field of pop further our sense of a "rock canon."

Neglected Islands: Production, Performance, and Literary Capital

In searching for a literary presence, or value, within "Islands in the Stream," one must account for the song's multi-dimensionality in terms of production. As mentioned previously, the Bee Gees-to-Hemingway connection hinges tenuously on the borrowed title phrase, which likewise supplies the repeated, first line of the song's chorus. The surrounding lyrical content describes a romantic relationship where two people meet, develop intense feelings for each other, lament the prospect of being apart, and proclaim a mutual desire to nurture their love in isolation from society—standard fair, essentially, for a mainstream pop tune. Hemingway's book, by contrast, is centered around themes of isolation and death. The posthumously published story follows an American painter, Thomas Hudson, who moves to the Bahamas to work. It covers three periods in his life, during which he must deal with the death of his sons. The story ends following a "search and find" mission for a sunken boat, during which Hudson presumably dies in a battle. Before his own looming death, the character reflects on those of his sons.

Given the thematic disconnect between the two texts, coupled with Gibbs's recollections, it is safe to say that the allusion is both finite and borderline incidental: it entails the extraction of a particular and isolated "nugget," with which the reader/

writer runs in an entirely different, self-serving direction: quite the opposite of exegesis, and an approach to literature typically associated with the naïve rather than the learned reader. But should the songwriter's sheer love of the phrase be so easily discounted? And does affiliation with Hemingway, despite Gibbs's humble disclaimer, offer anything beneficial? The contact, between a (relatively obscure) Hemingway book and the Bee Gees' singer *did* occur; and it *was* a canonical, "highbrow" author, not a writer of popular westerns, for example, whose title was chosen. Hemingway's reputation is not one I wish to comment on uncritically. Having said that, he is one of the most celebrated literary writers of the twentieth century, who has received both a Nobel Prize and Pulitzer Prize for his accomplishments. He of course has major name recognition, and the familiar, suicide-cemented persona of the troubled artist. All of this is to say that his work and name fall securely into the realm of "consecrated" or "legitimate" culture.

The significance of this connection is treated differently by the various people associated with its production—in this case, a "tin pan alley" approach, in which the songwriting (the Bee Gees) and vocal performance (Kenny Rogers and Dolly Parton) are contributed separately, and necessitating a genre-hop from disco to country. Accounts of the song by Kenny Rogers disregard its links to the novel altogether. Instead, he focuses on his idea, having been initially frustrated with the song, to bring Parton into the mix,[13] and the duo's subsequent, performative "chemistry."[14] For Rogers, in other words, the song's association with literature or with Hemingway is immaterial and inconsequential—something he is either unaware of, doesn't value, or doesn't find relevant within the context and community of his interviews. While certainly it makes sense that Rogers would not comment on those aspects of the song for which he is not directly instrumental, his role in its production brings to light the conflicted criteria— "chemistry," for example, or other performative elements that do not resonate within the singer-songwriter tradition—of pop song success.

The song's connection to Hemingway has, however, remained a standard part of its narrative as reproduced by biographers and within distribution blurbs. Jeff Apter confirms, for example, Gibbs's earlier narrative in his Bee Gees biography: "The name was borrowed from a novel by Ernest Hemingway—[Maurice Gibb] had chanced upon it and mentioned that it would make a great song title."[15] Not unlike Gibbs's own remarks, Apter's use of "chanced" seems to distance the connection from any potential claim to literariness, or act of pretentiousness, on the part of the songwriters, almost underscoring the notion of two incompatible worlds randomly brushing shoulders. The literary inspiration for "Islands in the Stream" also remains present in popular media blurbs. Following suit, Tom Eames writes for *Smooth Radio*: "The love song was named after the novel of the same name by Ernest Hemingway,"[16] and the song's biographic entry on the music blog *Genius* states: "'Islands in the Stream' was a Bee Gees-authored mega hit named after an Ernest Hemingway novel and performed by country superstars Kenny Rogers and Dolly Parton."[17]

It is fair to say, then, that the song's connection to its literary source remains, however tenuously, a part of its story and framing. Even as one blows it off, this connection seems to play a role in value production and social distinction, and reflects

Limits of the Literary 231

something of an invisible wall when it comes to literary capital—a boundary-line that, when flirted with, may in fact amplify distinctions between taste and ignorance, the authentic and the superficial. Unsurprisingly, some critics (prompted, perhaps, by the very audacity of connecting one's pop tune to Hemingway) find the lyrics an opportunity for caustic and indignant sneering; a review in *People*, for example, describes the lyrical content of *Eyes that See in the Dark* (the album on which the song appears) as "sequiturs, clichés and subliterate blathering" that is "not English."[18] The song, in such instances, is positioned as the embarrassing, polar opposite of the literary world from which its title sprang. Harder to come by is commentary, such as a blog entry on Medium.com, which finds in the Hemingway allusion evidence of the song's depth. Presented as a tribute to Rogers after his death, the piece refers to the song's title as a "great metaphor," adding "boy, did Ernest Hemingway know how to write."[19] The author quotes and analyzes part of the song's lyrics, and notes the Bee Gees' longevity and success in producing chart-topping singles as second only to Lennon and McCartney. In the author's unpacking of the metaphor, one can find the use of clichés and sentimental wisdom that would, from the perspective of legitimized literary discourse, be likely perceived as evidence of naïve or subjective misreading. It is with these kinds of textual tensions in mind that I am interested in pop music's uncelebrated literary allusions. Why are some texts revered for their use of literary allusions? Why do they accrue literary capital while others do not? "Islands in the Stream" offers an example of an allusion that is neither revered nor celebrated, and therefore—while showing that the ghost of high art resides even in very unexpected places—raises questions about the limitations and functions of cultural capital within popular music. While such limitations have largely eluded debate so far, they offer a fascinating insight into the sociological dimensions of the field and its hegemonic forms of value.

Literary Allusion and Status: The Case of Bob Dylan

Although the literary connection to "Islands in the Stream" has been largely ignored, industry domains often focus on and celebrate other literary allusions in songs, or songs that are deemed to have achieved literary status. A figure such as Bob Dylan— who occupies, as Ryan Hibbett argues in this book's introduction, a Shakespearean position within the hierarchical structure of pop prestige—perhaps epitomizes the "successful" (i.e., instrumental in accruing prestige) importation of literature into popular song. Dylan's elevated status reveals, however, something of a "chicken or egg" conundrum regarding the relationship between persona/ethos/reputation and actual lyrics; the latter was deemed brilliant and tagged as "literary" by critics early on, thus establishing a persona—an aura of authenticity and musical genius—that would in turn lend status ongoingly to future compositions. Elissa Blake examines several literary critiques of Dylan from the 1960s, which describe him as someone who in "every sense revolutionized modern poetry, American folk music, popular music and the whole of modern-day thought."[20] From this perspective, Dylan's literariness emanates from his

1960s work—itself a key intrusion into a relationship between literature and popular music that had in fact preceded him by at least two decades.

But many discussions, of this broader relationship or of Dylan's literariness specifically, come on the heels of his 2016 Nobel Prize. Caroline Crosson Gilpin and Katherine Schulten ask, for example, in the *New York Times*, "Can song lyrics be literature?,"[21] noting that Dylan's prize was the "same award previously given to literary greats like T. S. Eliot, Gabriel García Márquez, Toni Morrison and Samuel Beckett." The positioning of Dylan's work as literature likewise appears in articles published in the *Independent,* the *Los Angeles Daily News,* and the *Conversation.*[22] Brian Wheeler, reporting for the BBC, comments on this spiked interest in aesthetic judgments: "Bob Dylan's Nobel Prize has reignited the debate about whether song lyrics can ever be considered literature. Is it time to finally tear down these cultural barriers?"[23] Wheeler then quotes UK Poet Laureate (and rock composer[24]) Simon Armitage as a representative "no": "[S]ongs are often bad poems. Take the music away and what you're left with is often an awkward piece of creative writing full of lumpy syllables, cheesy rhymes, exhausted clichés and mixed metaphors."[25] In response, Wheeler argues that rap has literary roots and that Bob Dylan's music is "poetic and highly literary."[26] Such debates prompted Mark Ferdinand Canoy and Vida Lacano from the *Pop Inquirer* to present numerous lyrical phrases—from pop artists such as Air Supply, U2, Roxette, Hozier, and Jennifer Paige—as inherently and structurally poetic.[27] So the debate itself—with Dylan almost always as a respected point of reference and a central means to positioning popular music as high art—continues to flourish, but potentially, as with Armitage's comment, toward the end of reinforcing rather than relaxing boundaries.

Are pop songs, then, except for those owned by a handful of fully consecrated, Dylanesque auteurs, to be understood as "lowbrow" poetry? A poorly executed form of literature? Many scholars say no, citing the presence, in terms of both craft and convention, of poetry within a popular song. Dai Griffiths, for example, transcribes "The Boy With a Moon and Star on His Head" by Cat Stevens to showcase the song's various poetic conventions. For Griffiths, "[i]n defining songs where music and words were invented by the one person, and often sung by the same, the prevailing approach is to understand them in the close relationship in subject matter suggested by authorship (songwriter), performance (the singer's voice) and biography (proximity to life often termed authenticity)."[28]

While Griffith's work helps to contextualize the above discussions, questions about the politics of such classifications remain. Such discussions risk constructing a social hierarchy where the lyrics of some songs, based on a finite and academically biased set of criteria, achieve literary status. In a Bourdieusian sense, literary practices and their symbolic meanings become currency within the social spaces of both academic and fan-based discourse. The narratives that dominate these spaces tend to preserve, I would argue, a largely exclusionary hierarchy, in which figures like Dylan (who possesses, it should not be overlooked, the privileged traits of being white, male, heterosexual, and rock-affiliated) are more readily accepted as "literary." It is hard to imagine, for example, the "Harvard Professor" who takes on Taylor Swift elsewhere in this collection feeling equally authorized to assess Dylan,[29] or that a comparable

Limits of the Literary

assessment—of where and how Dylan's lyrics lack depth or craft, employ thin and fleeting allusions, or are found to constitute, without the music, "bad poetry,"—would be a likely or well-received undertaking. There is when it comes to criticizing certain, monolithic pop artists, far more so than with literary figures, an element of taboo. This brings into question the distinct political implications for other pop practitioners, specifically those who are left out of such narratives and analyses altogether, and which surely may include those associated with queer culture as are the Bee Gees.

As an observable technique, the literary allusion occupies a central and precarious place within judgments of literary value: it is, by definition, isolated, and therefore highly susceptible to accusations of pretense and superficiality (i.e., the allusion as name-dropping). It also has the flexibility to be either overt or subtle, to cite plainly a universally recognized author or title, or provide an "insider moment" whose meaning is, for others, obscured. Literary allusions in pop music are extensively published on, with both a Wikipedia page[30] and a blog entitled *From Novels to Notes*[31] dedicated to the practice. The music and cultural press, as well as various fansites, typically generate similar lists in connection to particular artists. A basic interest in connecting pop stars to books, then, remains a fairly common practice and a way in which fans engage their idols, as highlighted by mainstream news presses like the *Guardian*, culture magazines such as *Flavourwire*, and literary blogs such as *Hazlit*.[32] Some artists and songs, of course, more frequently enter this discourse than do others. Among these oft-cited examples are: David Bowie's reference to *1984* by George Orwell in "We are the Dead"; Patti Smith's references to the work of Rimbaud; the Doors' references to the work of Rimbaud, William Blake, Jack Kerouac, and Bertolt Brecht; Nick Cave's references to the work of John Milton; Kate Bush's references to the work of Wilhelm Reich; the Velvet Underground's references to work by Dylan Thomas and Edgar Allan Poe; and Bob Dylan's references to the work of Ezra Pound and T. S. Eliot.

One can see in this list a general connection in terms of white rock artists, though it is beyond the scope of this study to ascertain the extent to which other genres and artists are less prone to using literary allusions, come from backgrounds in which such capital remains unavailable, or simply go unrecognized as literary despite their use of allusions. Surely all of these elements remain in play. Bob Dylan, however, seems to preside larger than life among pop music's literary elite—a status perhaps justified by the sheer extensiveness with which he employs the literary allusion within his titles and lyrics, and which has led to a more exhaustive exploration of his literary connections and influences. Writing for the aptly titled *Highbrow* magazine, Benjamin Wright observes: "Dylan was significantly touched by the American Beats—by Kerouac's *On the Road*, and also by the poetry of Allen Ginsberg and Lawrence Ferlinghetti—and by French symbolists like Paul Verlaine and Arthur Rimbaud. Both Verlaine and Rimbaud are mentioned specifically in the *Blood on the Tracks* song 'You're Gonna Make Me Lonesome When You Go.'"[33] And, following Dylan's (awkwardly delayed) Nobel Prize speech, Mac Cameron revisits more closely Dylan's references to *Moby-Dick*, *All Quiet on the Western Front*, and *The Odyssey*.[34] Critics like Ben Child further Dylan's position from one of scattered connection to affiliation with an entire literary aesthetic—Dylan, that is, as the inheritor of literary modernism. *Love and Theft*, Child writes, "zeroes in on a certain kind of literary modernism with unprecedented panache, allowing the techniques and concerns of modernism to shape both the record's aesthetics and its potential meanings." In Child's analysis, Dylan takes his place among a network of major authors both contemporary and old: regarding "Moonlight," he finds that "Hemingway's take on Donne is refracted back again in an elegantly wheezy song of seduction—'whom does the bell toll for, love? It tolls for you and me.'"[35] At the very least, and even without disputing Dylan's considerable talent or accomplishments, it can be observed that entry into these kinds of discussions—given the wide and diverse range of musicians dealing in literary sources—is disproportionately selective. Indeed, Dylan's relationship to the literary establishment seems to have become its own reciprocal phenomenon, with the songwriter, as Hibbett points out, amplifying his literary allusions and persona in 2020's *Rough and Rowdy Ways*.

Literature and the Rock Canon

The exclusion of "Islands in the Stream" from the hegemonic discourse of literary allusions prompts questions about what constitutes literary capital, and how one acquires it. One of the ways that this form of capital can be understood is by analyzing how the group of artists who are frequently heralded for their literary allusions fit within the "rock canon"—a frequently celebrated cohort of artists who align with dominant values regarding authenticity, politics, race, and gender, and which is comprised mostly of artists from the 1960s through the 1990s. While the rock canon is textually present in pop music discourse, it hasn't received much critical interrogation. Carys Wyn Jones, for one, critiques this canon in terms of a loose set of aesthetic values, noting that "[r]ock music has been, from the beginning, a recorded medium"—a feature crucial, he argues, to the genre's authenticity[36]—and observing that "[t]he appeal of the rebellious, charismatic, maverick artists is enduring in the reception of albums."[37] The artists who contribute to this canon are, as a whole, difficult to produce as a finalized list, though Jones's focus on artists such as Bob Dylan, the Beach Boys, the Beatles, the Velvet Underground, Van Morrison, Marvin Gaye, the Rolling Stones, Patti Smith, the Sex Pistols, and Nirvana—most of whom deploy literary capital in some way, shape, or form—is telling. Jones's work, furthermore, helps to show how this canon functions as cultural currency: "The canon defines the boundaries of the field that both rock music writers and collectors work with, and deep knowledge of this field bestows a form of cultural capital."[38] Through their connection to the rock canon, figures such as Bob Dylan are posited as geniuses who resisted the commercial pressures of the world through an authentic approach to music, with literary capital serving as key evidence. Questions that might be asked in light of such observations are: If Bob Dylan, who is rich in cultural capital, were to have written "Islands in the Stream," would it have been more celebrated for its literary allusions than it currently is? Would listeners and critics be more likely to position the song as a thoughtful adaptation rather than as a throwaway allusion? And, in Dylan's vast repertoire, are there not lyrics invoking, as

Limits of the Literary 235

the Rogers/Parton duet does, a simple romance, but held thanks to his reputation in much higher esteem?

The Bee Gees not only lie somewhere outside of the rock canon but they also have often been considered a threat to its central values. At the time when "Islands in the Stream" was released, the Bee Gees—part of a mainstream disco culture that followed a "predominantly male gay subculture"[39]—were in the midst of a significant backlash to their music following the success they had experienced with disco music in the 1970s. As Gillian Frank writes, "The violent backlash against disco in 1979 transformed disco from a socially acceptable form of music and culture to one that was highly stigmatized."[40] This backlash, however, was complex. On the one hand, "the Bee Gees and [John] Travolta made disco safe for white, straight, male, young, and middle-Americans." Yet, on the other hand, "the commercial success of disco music triggered a fearful and homophobic reaction from rock fans because it was considered to be a quintessentially gay genre of music."[41] In the same documentary in which "Islands in the Stream" is discussed, Maurice Gibbs describes the backlash, which included "Bee Gees free weekends" on American radio, as "scary." While the band partially recovered in the late 1990s with some success, they were the subject of ridicule for many years; in 1980 a parody group, the Hee Bee Gee Bees, released songs such as "Meaningless Songs in Very High Voices," ridiculing both the Bee Gees' fashion and musical style, and appealing (as with the word "meaningless") to a sense of disco as a comparatively vapid and silly pop genre. I believe that this gendered history contributes to the Bee Gees' incompatibility with normative ideas regarding legitimate artistry, as well as the formulae by which literary references are deemed legitimate. Disco's connections to dancing and to the body itself, it might be added, are likely deterrents from the "cerebral" prerequisites of the genuinely literary rock star.[42] By contrast, rock music, in its privileged manifestations, carries an aura of rebelliousness and an expectation of social commentary; within its confines, literary allusion is more likely to signify refined sensibilities and a genuine connection to high art.

The distinction between meaningful and superficial allusions largely melts away as one attempts to fix its criteria. Does a song like "Islands in the Stream," whose lyrics do not, beyond the title phrase, engage the literary source; whose authors (at least one of them, anyway) have not read the book; and whose singers do not bother to acknowledge the connection, qualify as a meaningful intersection of the literary and pop music fields? Is the songwriter's fondness for Hemingway's phrase, or recognition of it as a "good title," sufficient to qualify the moment as a meaningful allusion? The kinds of literary lists referenced above rarely account for the quality of, or make distinctions between, particular allusions. While *Flavourwire* pronounces Dylan "perhaps the ultimate troubadour of our time," citing his "devotion to poetry as much as to music" along with his lyrical references (in "Desolation Row") to Ezra Pound and T. S. Eliot, there is nothing to indicate why his allusions are deep or meaningful as opposed to isolated name-drops. Certainly, Dylan's approach to literary allusion values quantity and consistency over the development of extended interaction with the source material; his sprawling, cataloging approach to literary references is strikingly different from adaptations such as Iron Maidan's "Rime of the Ancient Mariner" or

236 *Lit-Rock*

the Alan Parsons Project's Poe-inspired *Tales of Mystery and Imagination*. The kind of Dylan-centric presumptions guiding lists like *Flavourwire*'s inevitably narrows the possibilities of what constitutes a literary allusion worthy of celebration. I would suggest that, within such discourses, what does consistently surface as a meaningful and substantial allusion to literature is one that circulates as secret or "insider" knowledge, prompting perhaps a bit of Googling on the listener's part even as it implies that someone else, somewhere, "doesn't get it."

Dylan's actual reference to Pound and Eliot consists of one, concise mention within the eleven-verse, sixty-six line "Desolation Row": "And Ezra Pound and T. S. Eliot fighting in the captain's tower." Though the song's subsequent "where lovely mermaids flow" appears to echo Eliot's imagery at the conclusion of "The Love Song of J. Alfred Prufrock," the two Modernists are ushered offstage, as just two of the song's large and fleeting cast, just as soon as they appear. And yet the reference has been hugely impactful: Pound and Eliot, names signifying profound education, literary genius, artistic refinement, and avant-garde experimentation and abstruseness (and who, at the time of the song's composition in 1965, were a hip if not-quite-contemporary cultural import), carried with them a great deal of prestige. As a "sign-post," the isolated reference shifts the network in which the song may be located, opening up possibilities for academic analysis and categorical praise, oftentimes by way of linking it with additional names and modes of artistry. For Andy Gill, the song is

> an 11-minute epic of entropy, which takes the form of a Fellini-esque parade of grotesques and oddities featuring a huge cast of iconic characters, some historical (Albert Einstein, Nero), some biblical (Noah, Cain and Abel), some fictional (Ophelia, Romeo, Cinderella), some literary (T.S. Eliot and Ezra Pound), and some who fit into none of the above categories, notably Dr. Filth and his dubious nurse.[43]

While this would seem to align Dylan with Eliot's own, allusion-heavy and fragmented methodology, it also functions as a kind of reading resume, positing Dylan's credentials as a cultural authority. Josh Jones is likewise able to find substance in the Eliot/Pound reference:

> As with every other line in the song, this could mean just about anything. But given Dylan's admiration for *The Waste Land*, it could easily refer to the editorial tug-of-war between the two poets, as it was Pound who shaped Eliot's poem into the work we have today. And then there's the tower image so prominent in Eliot's great poem, an occult motif Dylan returned to.[44]

What matters, in other words, is not Dylan's direct or extended engagement with a particular literary work, but his scattered distribution of what are clearly literary borrowings, as well as his presumed admiration for the works thus referenced. The connection to Eliot specifically becomes, for Chris Mugan, a key piece to Dylan's own cultural status:

Limits of the Literary 237

Eliot remains the number one poet for musicians seeking to deliver something more original or meaningful than just another girl-meets-boy scenario. It is an accolade that you can trace all the way back to the artist who has done more than anyone to ensure we take rock and pop seriously, Bob Dylan. It was not long after the poet's death in 1965 that Dylan wrote him into his epic "Desolation Row."[45]

In terms of Bourdieu's division of "restrictive" (not driven by economic capital and having a specialized audience, i.e., "high art") versus "non-restrictive" (driven by economic capital and having a mass audience, i.e., "popular culture") fields,[46] one may argue that linking to Eliot helps to distance Dylan from the latter, positing him instead as an artist not driven by profit or the conventions of pop production. Whatever the case, Dylan's literary allusions clearly function as cultural capital, and do so in the manner of a long-term, interest-accruing investment.

It is not my expectation that anyone would depart this chapter thinking that "Islands in the Stream" is a substantially literary song, or that the Bee Gees have been unfairly excluded from the elite ranks of literary rock stars. What I *do* hope this study does is expose the extent to which complicating biases and predispositions are at work when we enter the discourse of "lit-rock." Which artists, for example, possess the authority to position themselves in relation to literature in the first place? Secondarily, I hope that this chapter makes clear that strategies such as literary allusions are subject to failure— that is, they don't necessarily convert to cultural capital or increased prestige, and may in fact provide evidence of naivete in a way that further solidifies the binary of serious versus silly artists. In terms of the Bee Gees specifically, their brand is not compatible with an appreciation for the literary world, and their allusions to it are not considered legitimate enough for inclusion within it. Though the Bee Gees are not attempting to demonstrate literariness or sophistication, we can see how their use of literature both emanated from and is swept into this larger structure or process.

It is, finally, my hope that this analysis helps import to the realm of pop music questions more typically encountered within the isolated study of literature. How, for example, are canons created and reproduced? Why are some artists excluded, and what is at risk when we do so? Regardless of our aesthetic judgments, we should continue to thoughtfully seek out and tend to these "other" voices, and to question the extent to which they are excluded from pre-established and largely unquestioned hierarchies. While popular music criticism cautions about the perils of canon-formation, it tends to concentrate nonetheless on the work of a small and specific group of representatives, whose work can be deemed compatible with "high art" by way of aged criteria. Indeed, the idea of "literary pop music" remains, at least in terms of scholarly discourse, narrowing and predictable, with the Cambridge Companion music series including only Dylan, the Beatles, and the Rolling Stones as its single-volume pop representatives among a wealth of classical composers. There is something to Simon Frith's observation that, despite the pretense of objectivity, popular music scholars tend to write about what they like: "How often," he wonders, "do populist cultural theorists celebrate popular cultural forms which they themselves soon find boring? How are their own feelings for the good and the bad coded into their own analyses?"[47] Even in purely literary analyses, the fan within the critic is usually present, and there remain thresholds—some, I'm sure, still quite invisible—that go uncrossed.

Notes

1   Ernest Hemingway, *Islands in the Stream* (New York: Charles Scribner's Sons, 1970).
2   *Keppel Road: The Life and Music of the Bee Gees* (Polygram Video, 1997).
3   Pierre Bourdieu, *The Field of Cultural Production: Essays on Art and Literature* (New York: Columbia University Press, 1993); Pierre Bourdieu, *Distinction* (London: Routledge, 1984); Pierre Bourdieu, "The Forms of Capital," in *Handbook of Theory and Research for the Sociology of Education*, ed. J. Richardson (Westport: Greenwood, 1986), 241–58.
4   Andrew Hurley, "'Jack of All Trades' or 'Double Agent?': The German Popular Musician as Novelist," *Journal of Popular Music Studies* 25, no. 2 (2013): 127–53; Peter Mills, "Into the Mystic: The Aural Poetry of Van Morrison," *Popular Music* 13, no. 1 (1994): 91–103.
5   Thomas Swiss, "Representing Rock: Poetry and Popular Music," *Popular Music and Society* 18, no. 2 (1994): 1–12.
6   Ben Child, "Raised in the Country, Working in the Town: Temporal and Spatial Modernisms in Bob Dylan's *Love and Theft*," *Popular Music and Society* 32, no. 2 (2009): 199–210.
7   David Wright, "Cultural Capital and the Literary Field," *Cultural Trends* 15, no. 2 (2006): 123–39.
8   Ibid., 137.
9   Pierre Bourdieu, *The Rules of Art: Genesis and Structure of the Literary Field* (Palo Alto: Stanford University Press, 1996).
10 Jeremy Ahearne and John Speller, "Introduction: Bourdieu and the Literary Field," *Paragraph* 35, no. 1 (2012): 1–9.
11 Simon Frith, *Performing Rites: On the Value of Popular Music* (Cambridge, MA: Harvard University Press, 1996); Ryan Hibbett, "What is Indie Rock?" *Popular Music and Society* 28, no. 1 (2005): 55–77.
12 Timothy Taylor, "Advertising and the Conquest of Culture," *Social Semiotics* 19, no. 4 (2009): 406.
13 Rob Rauffer, "How Kenny Rogers Got Dolly Parton to Sing 'Islands in the Stream,'" *Blackbird Presents*, 2017, https://blackbirdpresents.com/kenny-rogers-shares-story-islands-stream/.
14 Kenny Rogers "Kenny Rogers; Dolly Parton—Island In The Stream [#1 Duet, 15 Years Later] [2005]," 6:26, YouTube video, August 19, 2012, November 30, 2020, https://www.youtube.com/watch?v=0V-LGVKOHgU.
15 Jeff Apter, *Tragedy: The Sad Ballard of the Gibb Brothers* (Sydney: Echo, 2018), 223.
16 Tom Eames, "The Story of . . . 'Islands in the Stream' by Dolly Parton and Kenny Rogers," *Smooth Radio*, September 4, 2019, https://www.smoothradio.com/features/the-story-of/islands-in-the-stream-dolly-kenny-lyrics-meaning/.
17 "Islands in the Stream," *Genius*, https://genius.com/Kenny-rogers-islands-in-the-stream-lyrics.

18 "Picks and Pan Review: Eyes that See in the Dark," *People*, October 10, 1983, https://people.com/archive/picks-and-pans-review-eyes-that-see-in-the-dark-vol-20-no-15/.

19 "'Islands in the Stream': Kenny Rogers and Dolly Parton," No Words, No Song, Medium.com, https://nowordsnosong.medium.com/islands-in-the-stream-kenny-rogers-and-dolly-parton-a092eede746b.

20 Elissa Blake, "The Poetry of Pop," *Sydney Morning Herald*, May 19, 2010, https://amp.smh.com.au/entertainment/music/the-poetry-of-pop-20100514-v3kr.html.

21 Crosson Gilpin and Caroline and Katherine Schulten, "What Song Lyrics Do You Consider Literature?" *New York Times*, June 7, 2017, https://www.nytimes.com/2017/06/07/learning/what-song-lyrics-do-you-consider-literature.html.

22 Respectively: Andy Gill and Jack Shepherd, "70 Reasons Why Bob Dylan is the Most Important Figure in Pop-Culture History," *Independent*, October 13, 2016, http://www.independent.co.uk/arts-entertainment/music/features/70-reasons-why-bob-dylan-is-the-most-important-figure-in-pop-culture-history-2286368.html; Peter Larsen, "How Dylan, Pop's First Singer-songwriter, Turned Folk-rock Songs into Nobel-winning Literature," *Los Angeles Daily News*, October 13, 2016, http://www.dailynews.com/arts-and-entertainment/20161013/how-dylan-pops-first-singer-songwriter-turned-folk-rock-songs-into-nobel-winning-literature; Alex Lubet, "No, Bob Dylan Isn't the First Lyricist to Win the Nobel," *Conversation*, October 14, 2016, https://theconversation.com/amp/no-bob-dylan-isnt-the-first-lyricist-to-win-the-nobel-67023.

23 Brain Wheeler, "Can Song Lyrics Ever Be Poetry," *BBC*, October 14, 2016, https://www.bbc.com/news/magazine-37637797.

24 See Martin Malone's chapter in this book.

25 Wheeler, "Can Song Lyrics Ever Be Poetry."

26 Ibid.

27 Mark Ferdinand Canoy, "16 Pop Songs with Lyrics that Work as Poetry," *Pop Inquirer*, April 17, 2016, https://pop.inquirer.net/22678/16-pop-songs-with-lyrics-that-work-as-poetry.

28 Dai Griffiths, "Internal Rhyme in 'The Boy with a Moon and Star on His Head,' Cat Stevens 1972," *Popular Music* 31, no. 3 (2012): 396.

29 See Weishun Lu's chapter, "Pop Star vs. Harvard Professor: The 'Amateur' Poetry of Taylor Swift."

30 "List of Songs that Retell a Work of Literature," *Wikipedia*, https://en.wikipedia.org/w/index.php?title=List_of_songs_that_retell_a_work_of_literature&oldid=923578416.

31 "Lana Del Rey's 'Ultraviolence' Inspiration from Burgess' *A Clockwork Orange*," From Novels to Notes, May 7, 201, https://fromnovelstonotes.wordpress.com.

32 Respectively: Kuba Shand-Baptiste, "10 Songs Inspired by Literature," *Guardian*, May 20, 2016, https://amp.theguardian.com/childrens-books-site/2016/may/20/10-songs-inspired-by-literature; "10 of Music's Most Literature-Obsessed Songwriters," *Flavourwire*, October 11, 2012, https://www.flavorwire.com/335531/10-of-musics-most-literature-obsessed-songwriters; Tobias Carroll, "Pop Lit: When Books and Music Meet, Flawlessly and Otherwise," *Hazlitt*, March 12, 2014, https://hazlitt.net/feature/pop-lit-when-books-and-music-meet-flawlessly-and-otherwise.

33 Benjamin Wright, "The Weird and Wonderful Literary World of Bob Dylan," *Highbrow Magazine*, October 5, 2012, http://www.highbrowmagazine.com/1640-weird-and-wonderful-literary-world-bob-dylan.

34 Mac Cameron, "3 Classic Novels that Inspired Nobel Prize Winner Bob Dylan," *CBC*, June 12, 2017, https://www.cbc.ca/books/3-classic-novels-that-inspired-nobel-prize-winner-bob-dylan-1.4156324.

35 Ibid.

36 Carys Wyn Jones, *The Rock Canon: Canonical Values in the Reception of Rock Albums* (Aldershot and Burlington: Ashgate, 2008), 79.

37 Ibid., 84.

38 Ibid., 125.

39 Tim Lawrence, "Disco and the Queering of the Dance Floor," *Cultural Studies* 25, no. 2 (2011): 230–43.

40 Gillian Frank, "Discophobia: Antigay Prejudice and the 1979 Backlash against Disco," *Journal of the History of Sexuality* 16, no. 2 (2007): 278.

41 Ibid., 288.

42 Wyn Jones, *The Rock Canon*; Frank, "Discophobia."

43 Andy Gill, *Classic Bob Dylan: My Back Pages* (New York: Carlton, 1999), 89.

44 Josh Jones, "Bob Dylan Reads from T.S. Eliot's Great Modernist Poem 'The Waste Land,'" *Open Culture*, December 5, 2013, http://www.openculture.com/2013/12/bob-dylan-reads-from-t-s-eliots-the-waste-land.html.

45 Chris Mugan, "T.S. Eliot: The Pop Star's Poet," *Independent*, September 1, 2013, https://www.independent.co.uk/arts-entertainment/music/news/ts-eliot-the-pop-stars-poet-8802532.html.

46 Randal Johnson, Introduction to *The Field of Cultural Production: Essays on Art and Literature* by Pierre Bourdieu, ed. Randal Johnson (New York: Columbia University Press, 1993), 15.

47 Simon Frith, *Performing Rites: On the Value of Popular Music* (Cambridge, MA: Harvard University Press, 1998), 16.

Acknowledgments

I'd like to thank the entire English Department faculty and staff at Northern Illinois University for their support, and all of my wonderful students, whose insights, anecdotes, and classroom conversations no doubt feed and further my intellectual pursuits. Thank you to the editors at Bloomsbury—Leah Babb-Rosenfeld, Rachel Moore, and Amy Martin—for making this book possible and for all of their assistance in seeing it through, and to my amazing wife Jessica, whose endless hard work and accomplishments have opened up time and space for my own research and writing. And, of course, I wish to thank each of this collection's contributing authors, who remained dedicated and a pleasure to work with despite the intrusion of a pandemic; the many external reviewers for their gracious, timely, and helpful feedback; and all of those writers whose exciting submissions I was unable to accommodate.

Contributors

Tymon Adamczewski is Assistant Professor in the Department of Anglophone Literatures of Kazimierz Wielki University in Bydgoszcz, Poland, where he teaches literary and cultural studies. His academic interests include critical discourses of contemporary humanities, music, and ecocriticism. He is the editor of *All Along Bob Dylan: America and the World* (2020) and the author of *Following the Textual Revolution: The Standardization of Radical Critical Theories of the 1960s* (2016) and related articles.

Scott Calhoun directs the U2 Conference (U2conference.com) and has edited three volumes of critical essays about U2: *Exploring U2: Is This Rock and Roll?*; *U2 Above, Across, and Beyond: Interdisciplinary Assessments*; and *U2 and the Religious Impulse: Take Me Higher.* He is a curator for U2: Made in Dublin, a permanent exhibit at The Little Museum of Dublin, and is a professor of English at Cedarville University, USA.

Kevin Farrell is Associate Professor of English at Radford University, USA. His research interests include James Joyce, Irish literature, modernism, and popular music, and his work has appeared in *The James Joyce Quarterly*, *The Journal of Popular Music Studies*, and *New Hibernia Review*.

Barry J. Faulk is Professor of English at Florida State University, USA. His books include *British Rock Modernism* and *Punk Rock Warlord: The Life and Work of Joe Strummer,* co-edited with Brady Harrison. Recent publications include an essay on Bob Dylan and studio recording included in *Sound and Literature* (Cambridge Critical Concepts, 2020), edited by Anna Snaith.

Peter Hesseldenz is the Academic Liaison for Literature and Humanities at the University of Kentucky Libraries in Lexington, Kentucky, USA. In addition to his interests in library-related research areas such as humanities librarianship, information literacy, and reference services, he is also interested in the study of popular music and crime fiction.

Ryan Hibbett is Associate Professor of English at Northern Illinois University, USA, whose research focuses on the high-art/pop-culture spectrum in literature and music alike. He is the author of *Philip Larkin, Popular Culture, and the English Individual* (2019), "Wilde's Side: Morrissey and the Culture of Queer Distinction" (2021), "What is Indie Rock?" (2005), and several other articles. His poetry has appeared in journals including *Atlanta Review, Willow Springs, I-70 Review,* and *Codex,* and he enjoys collaborating on experimental, electro-acoustic sound recordings under the monikers

Midwest Sound Museum and, formerly, Gutta Percha. His next project is a book on poetry and poets as mediated through popular culture.

Marek Jeziński is Professor of Media, Communication, and Journalism at Nicolaus Copernicus University, Poland, whose research examines contemporary popular culture, media and journalism, social anthropology, and political communication. He is the author of *The Quest for Political Myth and Symbol* (2003), *Muzyka popularna jako wehikuł ideologiczny* (2011), and *Muzyka popularna i jej odbiorcy w poszukiwaniu autorytetu* (2017), and his articles have appeared in *Rock Music Studies, Riffs, M/C Journal, Medien und Zeit, AVANT*, and *Kultura Współczesna*.

John Kimsey is an Associate Professor at DePaul University, USA, whose resumé includes numerous Popular Music Studies publications and projects, including the concluding chapter in *The Cambridge Companion to the Beatles* and the song cycle (supported by a DePaul Humanities Center fellowship), *Twisted Roots: Music, Politics and the American Dream Blues*. The latter has been described by jazz composer/historian Ben Sidran as "an ingenious way to integrate political and social commentary into a musical architecture."

Weishun Lu is a PhD candidate in literary studies at the University of Wisconsin-Madison, USA. Her research focuses on contemporary poetry, affect theory, and the development of Ethnic Literature in the United States.

Kimberly Mack is Associate Professor of African American literature and culture at the University of Toledo, USA. She's the author of *Fictional Blues: Narrative Self-Invention from Bessie Smith to Jack White* (2020), and her forthcoming book projects, *The Untold History of American Rock Criticism* and *Living Colour's Time's Up* (33 1/3 book series), are under contract with Bloomsbury Academic. Her scholarly and public-facing articles have appeared in *Popular Music and Society, Journal of Popular Music Studies, Longreads, No Depression*, and elsewhere.

Martin Malone is Honorary Research Fellow at the University of Aberdeen, UK, and a widely published poet and critic. He's published four poetry collections and has a PhD from the University of Sheffield. His research examines the high-art/pop-culture relation in literature and music, as well as Great War and contemporary poetry. Before all this, he was a guitarist, singer, songwriter, and sound engineer/producer in a variety of rock bands from the age of sixteen. Website: https://www.martinmalonepoetry .com/.

Patricia Malone is an Early Career Research and Teaching Fellow in English at the University of Edinburgh, UK. She is writing a book, *Reality Hunger: Image and Appetite in Twenty-First-Century Literature*, that offers an account of the contemporary through the modalities of the "age of image." Essays arising from this work have been published in *Textual Practice, Contemporary Women's Writing, C21*, and elsewhere.

244   *Contributors*

Chris Mustazza is Co-Director of the PennSound archive and Director of Academic Computing for Penn's School of Arts and Sciences, USA. He teaches in Penn's English department, where he also earned his PhD. His research focuses on poetry performance, and he has edited previously unreleased collections of sound recordings of modernist poets including Gertrude Stein, T. S. Eliot, Robert Frost, and James Weldon Johnson. His book manuscript, *Speech Labs*, examines the world's first poetry audio archives, assembled in the early days of sound recording.

Pat O'Grady is a popular music scholar based in Sydney, Australia. He holds a PhD for his thesis on music production from Macquarie University. His research is published in *Popular Music and Society*, *Popular Music*, *Journal of Popular Music Studies*, *Creative Industries Journal*, *Convergence*, *Continuum*, and *Perfect Beat*. Pat teaches at Macquarie University in media and music. He is currently serving as Treasurer of the International Association for the Study of Popular Music (Australia and New Zealand branch).

David R. Shumway is Professor of English, Director of Literary and Cultural Studies, and the founding Director of the Humanities Center at Carnegie Mellon University, USA. His most recent book is *Rock Star: The Making of Musical Icons from Elvis to Springsteen* (2014), and he has published numerous articles on popular music. Some of his other books include *Michel Foucault* (1989), *Modern Love: Romance, Intimacy, and the Marriage Crisis* (2003), and *John Sayles* (2012).

Index

"4'33" (Cage)   111
12 Songs (1970s)   95
13th Floor Elevators   122
16   215
"19" (song)   109, 110, 114–16
"33⅓" (song)   155
1984 (Orwell)   43, 44, 233

Abrams, M. H.   92
academic culture   79
acid   128–31
"Acid Queen" (song)   142
Acid Tests   129
Acker, Kathy   12, 50–3, 55–8
Adamski, Tomasz   201
Adkins, N. King   112
Adorno, Theodore   155
Advertisements for Myself (Mailer)   66
"aesthetic of disgust"   53, 54
aesthetic populism   81
African Americans   186, 188, 215
After Bathing at Baxter's (1967)   140
Air Supply   232
Aladdin Sane (1973)   35
Allen, Ros   184
Allen, Woody   66, 67
Allison, Mose   93
"All I Want" (song)   72, 74
Allmusic   140, 145
All Quiet on the Western Front
      (Remarque)   233
All Them Witches   130
"All the Young Dudes" (song)   42
Alt-Country   182
altered experiences   121, 125
Alterman, Loraine   75
Althusser, Louis   85
amateur bands   197
amateur poets   79, 88
Amazon   164
ambient music   118, 163

Amboy Dukes   122
America   171–3, 175, 178, 179, 182,
      185–7, 190, 215
American Family, The (TV show)   49
Americanness   170
Anawa   202
Anderson, Chester   43
Anderson, Joan   73
"Andy Warhol" (song)   40
Angelou, Maya   80
Anglophone culture   123
Annie Hall (1977)   67, 75
anti-Semitism   69
anti-Vietnam-War protest   66, 141
Apter, Jeff   230
Armia   201
*Armies of the Night: History as a Novel/The
      Novel as History, The* (Mailer)   66,
      67
Armitage, Simon   11, 152–5, 156–60,
      162, 163, 232
Armitage Trail   157
Armoury Show   162
Arnold, Gina   214, 223
"Arnold Lane" (song)   126
art form   38
artistic practice   37, 57, 58
Art of Noise (band)   109, 110, 112–14,
      117
"The Art of Noise" (Russolo)   111
art-pop   95
art-rock   38
Asnyk, Adam   200, 205
Astley, Virginia   152, 154, 163, 164
Atrocity Exhibition, The (Ballard)   53
audio deformations   110
audio technology   115
Austerlitz, Saul   6–7
authenticity   40, 49–51, 82, 92, 101, 102,
      223, 231
autobiography   53, 75

246   *Index*

avant-garde   35, 110, 116, 128, 132, 145, 149
    compositions   145
    experiments and experimentation   202, 236
    music   140, 142, 145
    poetics   127
avant-gardism   11–12, 138
Awful Truth, The (1937)   67

"Back to December" (song)   84
Bahktin, Mikhail   55
Bajm   198
Baker, LaVern   215
Bakhtin, Mikhail   80
Balch, Antony   42
Baldwin, James   172
Ball, Hugo   110, 115, 116, 118
"The Ballad of Frankie Lee and Judas Priest" (song)   39
ballads   84, 203
Ballard, J. G.   43, 46, 53, 57
Bandcamp   138
Bangs, Lester   214, 218
Bare, Bobby   93
Barrett, Syd   12, 121, 126–8, 130, 132, 139, 142, 143, 146
Barry, John   100
Barthes, Roland   101
Bartnicki, Krzysztof   138
Basement Tapes, The (1975)   39
Bataille, George   55
Baudelaire, Charles   4, 123, 137
Bauhaus   117
BBC Two   153
Beach Boys   9, 38, 234
Beat Happening   50
Beatles   1, 4, 8–10, 18, 25, 36, 38, 40, 93, 95, 120, 122, 126, 128, 137, 197, 213, 215, 217, 221, 234, 237
"The Beatles Invade, Complete With Long Hair and Screaming Fans" (Gardner)   215
Beats   53
Beats 1 Radio   178
Beautiful Waste (McComb)   157
Beckett, Samuel   162, 232

Bee Gees   7, 227, 230, 231, 233, 235, 237
"Bee Gees free weekends"   235
Bem, Józef   205
"Bema pamięci żałobny rapsod" (song)   205
Berio, Luciana   143
Berlant, Lauren   87
Berman, David   6
Bernstein, Leonard   7–9
Berryman, John   68
"The Bewlay Brothers" (song)   40
Bianusz, Andrzej   200
bibliographies   182
Bieber, Justin   6
big-beat bands   198
Big Knockover, The (Hammett)   188
"Bigmouth Strikes Again" (poem)   161
Big Sleep, The (Chandler)   191
"Big Yellow Taxi" (song)   71
"Big Zombie" (song)   182, 190–1
Bikceem, Ramdasha   57
"Bike" (song)   125, 126
bike rides   128, 129
Billboard   215
Bill Haley and His Comets   4
BIPOC and white women rock writers   213, 214, 216, 223
Bjelke-Petersen regime   158
Black 47   139, 147
Black Sabbath   130, 131
Blake, Elissa   231
Blake, William   22, 123, 144, 170, 172, 180, 233
"Blonde in the Bleachers" (song)   73, 75
Blonde on Blonde (1966)   38, 39
Blondie   117
Blood and Guts in High School (Acker)   55
Blood on the Tracks (1975)   233
Blue (1971)   40, 71–5
Blume in Love (1973)   67
BMI   101
Bogel, Frederic   102
bohemianism   139
Bonham, John   220
Bono   169–80
Book of Kells (Joyce)   149
Born Again (1979)   95

Born In A Barn (2009)   153
Bourdieu, Pierre   12–14, 16, 21, 23, 80, 197, 228, 229, 237
Boutté, John   100
Bowery Ballroom, New York   145
Bowie, David   7, 12, 35–46, 233
Boyd, Joe   125
"The Boy With a Moon and Star on His Head" (song)   232
Bradley, Adam   11, 15–26, 80, 85
Braudy, Leo   21
Breakfast at Tiffany's (Capote)   161
Breakout   198, 200, 201
Brecht, Bertolt   45, 233
Brewer, Tess   138
Bridge, Frank   138
Brill Building   114
Bringing it All Back Home (album, 1965)   38, 137
"Bringing It All Back Home" (poem)   154, 157
Britain   12, 13, 184–6, 190
British punk rock   182
Brontë, Charlotte   69, 143
Brooks, Daphne   216, 223
Brooks, Gwendolyn   3
Brown, Jackson   65
Browne, David   3, 10
Browning, Robert   91, 98, 100, 102
Bruce, Jeff   114
Bryll, Ernest   200, 201
Buckley, Jeff   10
Budzyński, Tomasz   201
Bukowski, Charles   172
"Bullet the Blue Sky" (song)   178
bureaucratic government   186
Burgess, Anthony   43, 44, 141
Burnham, Hugo   185
"Burn On" (song)   95
Burroughs, William S.   5, 12, 35–8, 41–3, 45, 46, 50–5, 57, 58
Burt, Stephanie   78, 79, 81–3
Bush, Kate   138–9, 142–6, 233
Butler, Judith   56
Butt, Gavin   153, 154
Byrds   125
Byrne, David   117
Byron, Glennis   92

cabaret   199, 203
Cabaret Voltaire   45, 110, 115, 118
Cage, John   111, 143
Cairns, Andy   148
California   190, 191
"California" (song)   74
Calloway, Earl   213
Cameron, Mac   233
cannabis   130–2
canonization   130
Canoy, Mark Ferdinand   232
capitalism   187, 190, 191
capitalist society   184
Capote, Truman   67, 161, 172, 174, 175
"Carey" (song)   74
"Car on a Hill" (song)   75
Carroll, Greg   176
Carroll, Lewis   5, 126, 127, 140
Carver, Raymond   172
"The Case of the Cock-Sure Groupies" (Sander)   220
"A Case of You" (song)   24, 72
Cashbox   215
Catanzarite, Stephen   169
Cave, Nick   154, 159, 233
censorship   55
Chamber Music (1907)   142
Chandler, Raymond   182, 183, 190–2
"Changes" (song)   40
chanson   199
Chapman, Rob   128
Chapman, Ron   142
Charles Dickens Museum   137
Charles Scribner's Sons   220
Charleston Bay   96–8
Cheap Trick   217
Cheetah   213, 216, 221
Cheng, Vincent   139
Chicago Defender, The   213, 215
Chicago Sun Times   217, 218
Child, Ben   233, 234
"Chivalry" (song)   192
Chorążuk, Bogdan   199, 200, 204
Christgau, Robert   3, 9, 10, 94, 95, 214, 216
Christie, Agatha   186
Christopher, Roy   3
Ciechowski, Grzegorz   201

248   Index

cinema 67
"Circle Game" (song) 71
Ciuba, Gary M. 174
Civil Rights Congress 188
Clash 184, 191
class 13, 14, 100–1, 197, 228
classical liberalism 186, 187
classical music 1, 13
classic rock 46
Clayton, Adam 169
Clement, Jack 93
Clemons, Clarence 102
Clockwork Orange, A (Burgess) 43, 44
"Clown Punk" (poem) 154
Cobain, Kurt 12, 49–58
Cocker, Joe 95, 99
Cohen, Debra Rae 39
Cohen, Leonard 70, 98
Colby, Georgina 51
Coldplay 217
Cole, Lloyd 159, 162
Coleridge, Samuel Taylor 113
collage aesthetics 112
collage technique 50–3, 55
Collins, Judy 95
commercial genres 80
"commodification of crazy" 57
Communist Party 188
conceptual albums 201
concrete music 128, 205
confessional albums 71, 72
confessional art 66
confessionalism 24, 65, 67, 68, 70, 71,
      75, 83, 84, 86, 88
confessionalist poetics 83, 84
confessional prose 68, 69
confessional songwriting 93
Confidence Man, The (Melville) 92
contemporary music 156
Conversation 232
Cooder, Ry 95
"Cookie Monster growls" 145
Cool Characters (Konstantinou) 52
Copetas, Craig 35, 36
Copland, Aaron 100
corporate music industry 184
Corrigan, Andy 184
corruption 51, 186, 187, 190, 191

Cosmopolitan 78, 82
country music 13, 182, 183
Courrier, Kevin 92, 98
Court and Spark (1974) 74, 75
Coval, Kevin 3
Coyle, Michael 39
Cracked Actor (1974) 41
craft 79–82
craft criticism 81–2
Crane, Stephen 5
Crash (Ballard) 43
Crawdaddy! 214–15
creation 13, 109
creative process 128, 202
creative writing 81, 232
Creem 213, 214, 216, 218, 220, 223, 224 n.2
crimes 186, 187
Crosby, David 93
Crosby, Stills, Nash & Young 93
Cross, Charles 56
Cubism 43
Cubist painting 43
cultural activity 158
cultural capital 13, 16, 23, 80, 147, 156,
      162, 170, 197, 228, 229, 231, 234,
      237
cultural confessionalism 65
cultural developments 66–7
cultural form 182
cultural production 43, 80, 88, 123, 229
cultural stereotypes 40
cultural studies 80
"culture of justification" 214
Culture of Narcissism, The (Lasch) 66, 67
Culture Show, The (TV show) 153
Curtis, Ian 45, 46, 155
cutting edge culture 39
cut-up technique 12, 36–8, 41–6, 50,
      52–3, 55, 57, 58
Czechowicz, Józed 200
Czechowicz, Józef 203
Człowiek jam niewdzięczny
      (1971) 209 n.25

Dada aesthetics 109, 115
Dada/Dadaists 37, 110, 114, 115–17
"Daddy" (song) 127
"Da Doo Ron Ron" (song) 114

Dagnal-Myron, Cynthia   214, 217–20
Daltrey, Roger   217
Damon, Maria   80
Danger In The Past (1990)   159
Dante   140
"David Bowie Is" (exhibit)   35
"Davy the Fat Boy" (song)   101
Dead Meadow   130
"Dear John" (song)   84
deconstructive practices   56
DeCurtis, Anthony   38
Dedalus, Stephen   21
defamiliarization   113
"Definizione di Futurismo" (song)   113
de Freitas, Pete   164
degradation   55
Deities and Demigods (1980)   131
Depeche Mode   118
depoliticized speech   101
DeRogatis, Jim   125
Derrida, Jacques   56, 127
"Desire" (song)   179
"Desolation Row" (song)   18, 21, 38, 43,
      235, 236
De Stijl   115
detective fiction   182
détournement   112, 113
Devo   118, 217
Devoto, Howard   159
dialectics   196, 197
Diamond Dogs (1974)   36, 37, 41–6
Didion, Joan   66, 67
Dill Pickle Club   118
Director's Cut (2011)   143
Dischord   50
disco culture   235
disco music   235
DIY artists   138
DIY community   50–3
DIY ethos   50–2, 154
Domański, Henryk   197
Dongahy, Michael   152
"Do Nothing Till You Hear From Me"
      (song)   93
Donovan   122
Don't Read Poetry (Burt)   81
"Don't Sing (*for Paddy MacAloon*)"
      (poem)   154, 156

Doors of Perception, The (Huxley)   123
Dopesmoker (2003)   131, 132
Dos Passos, John Roderigo   52
Doyle, Conan   186
Doyle, Tad   54
"Dragonaut" (song)   131
Dramatic Monologue (Byron)   92
dramatic monologues   91–7, 99, 100
Dream Songs (Berryman)   68
Dr. Strangely Strange   142, 143, 146
"Druid" (song)   131
Dubliners (Joyce)   138, 139
Dudley, Anne   109
Duffy, Carol Ann   99, 154, 162
Dunbar, Paul Laurence   98
Dunne, Sara   91–2
Duran Duran   117
Dwa Plus Jeden   201
Dylan, Bob   1, 8–10, 14, 15–26, 37–41,
      43, 46, 70, 75, 93, 99, 120, 124, 137,
      140, 154, 157, 160, 171, 172, 204,
      227, 231–7
Dylancentrism   15–26
Dżamble   201
Dzikowski, Krzysztof   199, 200
"Dziwny jest ten świat" ("Strange is the
      World," song)   198

Eames, Tom   230
Earnshaw, Catherine   143
Ebert, Roger   217
Ebony   215
Echo & The Bunnymen   164
eclecticism   37
Eden and Trident Studios   164
Eder, Bruce   140
The Edge   169–74
education   197
"Eighties/Nineties" (poem)   154
"Eight Miles High" (song)   122, 125
Electric Kool-Aid Acid Test, The
      (Wolfe)   67
Electric Wizard   130
electronic revolution   42, 43
Eliot, George   69
Eliot, T. S.   22, 26, 36, 43, 52, 68, 83, 127,
      140, 232, 233, 236, 237
elitism   81, 124, 130, 132, 148, 207

Ellington, Duke   93
Ellison, Ralph   172
Ellmann, Richard   149
El Paso Times   213
embodied grotesque   54
"Encyclopedia of Polish Psychedelia"
      (Sipowicz)   204
"The Enduring Chill" (O'Connor)   176–7
England   182, 185, 190
English River, The (Astley)   153, 163
Enigmatic Live (1971)   206
Eno, Brian   11, 170, 217–19
"Eno and the Jets: Controlled Chaos"
      (Dagnal-Myron)   217
Entertainment Weekly   223
epic theater   45
Eshun, Kodwo   153
establishment culture   155
Estrada Bałtycka   197
Evermore (2020)   23, 24
"Evil Gypsy/Solomon's Theme"
      (song)   131
Executioner's Song, The (Mailer)   174
Exiles (Joyce)   138
"Exit" (song)   174–6, 178
experimental art   118
experimental artists   37
experimental music   110, 140, 205
experimentation   120, 121, 127–9, 131,
      140, 205
extended franchise   160
Eyes that See in the Dark (1983)   231
E-Z Listening (1987)   118

The Fab Four   126
"The Farmer's Bride" (poem)   99
fascism   69, 110, 113
Fast Product   184
faux-naïve aesthetic   51, 55
Fear and Whiskey (1985)   182, 185
Feinstein, Adam   146
female sexuality   51
"feminized" rock culture   40
Ferlinghetti, Lawrence   233
"Fill Your Heart" (song)   40
Finnegan, Tim   139
Finnegans Wake (Joyce)   137–9, 143, 145,
      146, 149, 150 n.3

"Fire and Rain" (song)   70, 74
*First Collection of Criticism by a
      Living Female Rock Critic, The*
      (Hopper)   216
Fish, Duane   56
Fisher, Mark   49
Fisher, Robert   55
Fitzgerald, F. Scott   66
Flavourwire   233, 235, 236
"Flitcraft" (song)   182, 189
"Flower of the Mountain" (song)   143–5
fluid poetics   121
folklore   198
Folklore (2020)   23–5
folk music   23, 38, 65, 71, 140
folk revolution   46
folk-rock   140, 204
folk singers   38
folk virus   52
foreign policy   172, 175, 178
Forster, Robert   157, 158–9, 164
For the Roses (1972)   73–5
Foster, Stephen   96
Four Way Street (1971)   93
Frampton, Peter   217
Frank, Anne   22
Frank, Gillian   235
Frankie Goes to Hollywood   113
"Free Man in Paris" (song)   74
Freidman, Milton   186
Fremantle Press   157
Fripp, Robert   122
Frith, Simon   1, 6, 14, 101, 102, 237
From Novels to Notes (blog)   233
Frykdahl, Nils   146
Fu Manchu   130
fusion   203
Futurist aesthetics   115
Futurist art   109
"Futurist Manifesto" (Marinetti)   109,
      113
Futurist poetics   110
Futurists   109, 110, 112, 114, 115, 117–18

"Gadji Beri Bimba" (poem)   110, 115,
      116
Gaertner, Katarzyna   201
Gałczyński, Konstanty Ildefons   199, 200

Gamble, Kenny   44
Gang of Four   184–5
Gardner, Paul   215
Gaye, Marvin   234
gay genre   235
Geffen, David   74
gender   14, 98–100, 187, 228
  discourse   218
  dynamics   220
  equality   75
  issues   144, 145
Gender Trouble (Butler)   56
General Certificate of Education
  (GCSE)   162
generational aesthetics   205
Genius (music blog)   230
Gen Xers   56
Gibb, Maurice   227, 229, 230, 235
*Gig: The Life and Times of a Rock-star
  Fantasist* (Armitage)   152
Gill, Andy   236
Gill, Jo   83
Gilpin, Caroline Crosson   232
Ginsberg, Allen   172, 233
Girard, René   171, 179
glam-rock   43, 45
Go-Betweens   157–9
"God Part II" (song)   179
Goines, Donald   3
Golden Age novels   186, 187
"Golden Gridiron Boy" (song)   95
"Golden Hair" (song)   138, 142, 143
Golden Notebook, The (Lessing)   158–9
Goldschmidt, Jessica   24, 25
Goldstein, Richard   215
"A Good Man is Hard to Find"
  (O'Connor)   177
Good Old Boys (1974)   95, 96, 100
Grafton, Sue   187
Grahame, Kenneth   126
Great War   114, 116, 156
Grechuta, Marek   199, 201–4
Green, Graham   156, 157
Greenhalgh, Tom   184, 189
Greenhaus, Rachel   83
Greenlaw, Lavinia   152, 154, 162
Greenwich, Ellie   114
Grella, George   186

Grier, Miles Parks   5
Griffiths, Dai   232
Grossberg, Lawrence   3
groupies   217, 220–2
"Groupies: A Story Of Our Times"
  (Nolan)   221
"Grudzień 1970" ("December
  1970")   208 n.19
grunge   130
Guardian   233
"Guilty" (song)   95
Gunderson, Edna   213
GUNK   57
Gysin, Brion   52–3

"Haas Effect" (poem)   161
Halliwell, Martin   121
Halny, Stanisław   200
Hammett, Dashiell   182, 183, 187–91,
  193 n.14
"handholding"   110, 117, 118
Handholding: 5 Kinds (Morris)   117
Hanna, Kathleen   50, 51, 56, 58
Hanover Dada   110
hard-boiled genre   182, 187
hard-boiled novels   187, 189
Hardcastle, Paul   109, 110, 114,
  115, 117
hard rock   39, 44
"Hard to be Human" (song)   188
Hardy, Thomas   163, 164
Harker, Dave   18
Harris, Oliver   53
"Have You Seen My Baby" (song)   95
"Hawkmoon 269" (song)   179
Hazlit (blog)   233
"Head Full Of Steam" (song)   159
Heartfield, John   118
"Heart Shaped Box" (song)   54
Heath, Edward   185
Heavier Than Heaven (Cross)   56
Hee Bee Gee Bees   235
Hegarty, Paul   121
hegemony   3, 13, 197, 213, 231, 234
Hellman, Lillian   188
"Hello Muddah, Hello Fadduh (A Letter
  from Camp)" (song)   147
Hell's Angels (Thompson)   67

"Helpless Corpses Enactment"
(song) 145, 146
"Help Me" (song) 75
Hemar, Marian 199
Hemingway, Ernest 66, 227, 229–31, 235
Hendrix, Jimi 4
Henke, Jim 172
Herbert, Zbigniew 200
Here Come the Warm Jets (1974) 217
hermetic art 205
Hibbett, Ryan 231, 234
high art 22, 110, 138, 155, 157, 198, 206,
229, 232
Highbrow 233
high-brow culture 158, 159
high-brow genres 80
high culture 23, 81, 148, 153, 156, 160,
196, 197, 199, 206, 207, 215, 229
High Fidelity (2000) 67
high modernism 68, 132, 143
Highway 61 Revisited (1965) 18, 22, 38
High Window, The (Chandler) 191
hip-hop 3, 22
Hit Parader 213
Hofmann, Albert 125
Hohensee, Jacek 201
Holden, Stephen 70
Hollywood 22, 129, 188
Holocaust 69, 70
Holt, Douglas 14
Homer 140, 149
homophonic translation 116
Hopper, Jessica 216
Horn, Howard 1
Horn, Trevor 109, 112, 117
Horsley, Lee 187
House Un-American Activities
Committee 188
How the Beatles Destroyed Rock 'n' Roll
(Wald) 4
Hozier 232
Huff, Leon 44
Human League 45
Hunky Dory (1971) 39–41
"Hurrah, die butter ist Allah!"
(Heartfield) 118
Huxley, Aldous 12, 123
Huyssen, Andreas 40

"I" (song) 74
identity 36, 38, 56, 73, 148, 171
If All the World and Love Were Young
(Sexton) 165
"If They Hang You" (song) 182, 188
"If You're Anything Like Me" (song) 78,
84
"I Got Laid on James Joyce's Grave"
(song) 147–8
"I Just Dropped in (To See What My
Condition was In)" (song) 122
"I Knew You Were Trouble" (song) 84
il duce dei Futuristi 113
Il Futurismo 109, 110, 113, 114
"I'll Be Your Baby Tonight" (song) 39
image culture 52
Importance of Music to Girls, The
(Greenlaw) 152, 162
improvised music 203
In Cold Blood (Capote) 67, 174
Independent 83, 232
independent artists 138
independent music 163
Indie 154, 163
industrialization 186
industrial music 111, 113, 118
In Glorious Times (2007) 145
Innocents Abroad 159
insanity 91, 92
Inside Pop: The Rock Revolution (TV
show) 7, 9
intellectualism 115, 137–9, 158
intelligentsia 197, 202, 203
internal landscapes 154, 157
International Times 36
"Interstellar Overdrive" (song) 126
intertextuality 112, 120, 139, 143
*In Their Own Write: Adventures in the
Music Press* (Gorman) 213
"Into My Arms" (song) 154
In Utero (1993) 50, 51, 54–6
"The Invisible Generation"
(Burroughs) 36
Irlandzki Tancerz (1979) 201
Iron Maidan 235
Isherwood, Christopher 159
"Islands in the Stream" (song) 7, 227–31,
234, 235, 237

Italian Futurism and Futurists   109, 110, 118

"I Think It's Going to Rain Today" (song)   95

"'It Was Us Against Those Guys': The Women Who Transformed *Rolling Stone* in the Mid-70s"   216

Iwaszkiewicz, Jarosław   200

"I Zimbra" (song)   110, 115

Jackowska, Kora   201

Jackson, Michael   4

Jacques, Geoffrey   214

Jakobson, Roman   80

Jamaican Rasta culture   130

James, Christopher   152

Jameson, Fredric   81

Janerka, Lech   201

Jastrun, Mieczysław   200

Jastrun, Tadeusz   203

Jastrun (1974)   201

jazz   203

Jeczalik, J. J.   109, 110, 112

"Jednego serca" (song)   205

Jefferson Airplane   139, 140–2, 145–7

Jerusalem. See Dopesmoker (2003)

"Jerusalem" (song)   144

Jesienin, Sergiusz   200

Jobson, Richard   155

Joel, Billy   85

Johnson, Calvin   50

Johnson, Linton Kwesi   164

John Wesley Harding (1967)   39

Jones, Carys Wyn   234

Jones, Josh   236

Jones, Tom   95, 99

Jong, Erica   66

Joplin, Janice   4

Joshua Tree, The (1987)   169–70, 172–4, 176, 178–80

Journals (Cobain)   52, 54

Joyce, James   5, 11, 21, 55, 127, 137–49, 159

Joyce, Stephen   143

Joyce Estate   143, 144

Joy Division   45, 117, 155

Joy (1981)   163

JSTOR Daily   83

"Jugband Blues" (song)   127

Jung, Carl   98

Junky (Burroughs)   53

Jurandot, Jerzy   199

"Just One Fix" (1992)   35

Juvenalian satire (poem)   118

Kadavar   130

Kael, Pauline   67

Kahn, Seth   57

Karasek, Krzysztof   204

"Katharsis" (song)   205

Kathy Acker: Writing the Impossible (Colby)   51

Kaźmierczak, Grzegorz   201

Keightley, Keir   102

Keka Collection: Soul Food for Lone Wolves and Wild Women, The (Dagnal-Myron)   217

Kerouac, Jack   36, 233

Kesey, Ken   12, 123, 128

Khlebnikov, Velimir   115

Kiberd, Declan   139, 148

Kihlstedt, Carla   146

"Killing Time 2" (poem)   154

King, Carole   40, 65

King, Martin Luther   172

"King Arthur" (song)   192

Kinks   93

Kinsella, John   157, 159, 160

Kiss (band)   217

"Kiss" (song)   110

Klein, Scott   145

Kmart   55

"Knocking Around the Zoo" (song)   70

Kofta, Jonasz   199, 200

Kondratowicz, Janusz   199, 200

Konstantinou, Lee   51–3

"Kooks" (song)   40

Kornhaber, Spencer   24

Kozłowski, Ryszard   204

Kramer, Barry   213, 216

K Records   50

Kreczmar, Adam   201

Kristeva, Julia   80

Kruse, Holly   218

Krynicki, Ryszard   200, 203, 204

Kubiak, Tadeusz   200, 205

"Kubla Kahn" (poem) 113
Kubrick, Stanley 44
Kureishi, Hanif 3
Kuryło, Andrzej 200
"Kwiaty ojczyste" (song) 205
Kyuss 130, 131

Lacano, Vida 232
LaConte, Stephen 80
Ladies of the Canyon (1970) 70–1
"Lady Lazarus" (song) 70
L.A. Free Press 220
Laing, Dave 98
Lamar, Kendrick 3
Landau, Jon 70
Land Yacht Regatta 155
Langan, Gary 109
Langbaum, Robert 91, 92
Langford, Jon 183–5, 188–92, 194 n.31
Lanois, Daniel 170
Larkin, Philip 10
Lasch, Christopher 66, 67, 69, 72
"The Last Time I Saw Richard" 72
Latham, Rob 50, 51
Latitude Festival (2009) 153
Lautner, Taylor 84
Leary, Timothy 123, 127
"Leaves On The Line" (song) 154
Lechoń, Jan 199
Led Zeppelin 217, 220
Le Figaro 109
Lennon, John 17, 93, 231
Lerner, Laurence 83
Leśmian, Bolesław 200, 203
Lessing, Doris 69, 158–9
Let The Trumpet Sound: A Life Of Martin Luther King, Jr. (Oates) 172
Levy, Joe 216
liberalism 187
Lieber, Jerry 114
Life 220
Life Studies (Lowell) 68, 69, 72, 83, 86
lifestyle TV 49
linguistic deformations 110
Lipska, Ewa 200, 203
literariness 124, 130–2, 143, 231, 237
literary allusions 7, 18, 43, 125, 140, 231–5, 237

literary capital 117, 140, 143, 145, 182, 228–31, 234
literary confessionalism 65
literary critic 65, 78, 79, 82, 199
literary culture 5, 11, 23, 205
literary modernism 127, 146, 233–4
literary poetics 121, 159
literary pop music 237
literary psychedelia 140
literary rock music 1, 13, 26
literary status 231–4
literary texts 36, 120, 127, 199, 228
literary tradition 58, 81, 82, 88, 170, 203
literature 5, 37, 43, 182
    American 81, 169, 170–2
    detective 186
    hard-boiled 185, 186, 191
    Polish 203
    pop music and 227, 228, 233
    and popular music 232
    postmodern 39
    and rock canon 234–8
Little Criminals (1977) 95
"Little Green" (song) 73
Little Sister, The (Chandler) 182, 190
live performances 45, 50, 148, 174, 184
Loebel, Bogdan 199–201
Lombard 198
London 162
"Lonely at the Top" (song) 95
Long, Huey P. 95, 100
"Look What You Made Me Do" (song) 78
Los Angeles 190, 191
Los Angeles Daily News 232
"Louisiana 1927" (song) 100–1
Love, Courtney 49
Love and Theft (Child) 233
Lovecraft, H. P. 130
Lover (2019) 23
"The Love Song of J. Alfred Prufrock" (Eliot) 236
low-brow culture 159
low culture 23, 75, 156, 160, 196, 206, 207, 215
Lowe, Zane 178
Lowell, Robert 65, 68, 69, 72, 83, 84, 86

"Lower Nine" (song) 101
LPs 124, 137, 198, 203, 204
LSD 121–3, 125, 129, 130, 142, 204
Lunch, Lydia 159
Lycett, Kevin 182, 184
Lydon, John 164

M8N 138
Maanam 198, 201
McAloon, Paddy 157
MacArthur, Marit 115
Macbeth (Shakespeare play) 161
McCann, Sean 186, 191
McCarey, Leo 67
McCartney, Paul 17, 20, 93, 231
McComb, David 157, 159, 160, 162, 163
McDonnell, Evelyn 215–17, 223
McGann, Jerome 114
McGurl, Mark 81
McHale, Brian 39
machine-centric process 109
machinic sounds 111–17
McKaye, Ian 50
McLennan, Grant 157–9
McLeod, Kembrew 216
McLuhan, Marshall 42, 43
Madcap Laughs, The (1970) 142
Mailer, Norman 66, 67, 172, 174, 175
Malcolm X 97
male fetishism 99
Maliszewska, Małgorzata 200
Malone, Martin 154–9
Maltese Falcon, The (Hammett) 182, 188, 189, 191, 193 n.14
"Mama Told Me Not Come" (song) 95
"manhandling" 215
Manic Street Preachers 157
The Manor 164
Man Who Sold the World, The (1970) 40
Marcus, Greil 51, 52, 69, 99, 109, 110, 116, 184, 185, 188, 190, 215
Marcus, Jane 69
marginal body 54
Marie-Sainte, Yves 159
Marinetti, F. T. 109, 110, 112–15, 117, 118
Markiewicz, Jarosław 204
Márquez, Gabriel García 232

"The Marriage of Heaven and Hell" (Blake) 180
Marsh, Dave 213–14
Marxism 182, 184
Marxism Today 159
Mary George of Allnorthover (Greenlaw) 162
masculinity 114, 147
Mason, Stewart 145
mass entertainment 197, 199
mass media 53, 197, 207
Matej, Julian 199, 200, 204
"Mathilda Mother" (song) 126, 127
Matos, Michaelangelo 4
Mayer, John 84
Mayers, Tim 81
Mazursky, Paul 66, 67
"Meaningless Songs in Very High Voices" (song) 235
meanness 173–80
media revolution 42–3
media theory 42
The Mekons 12, 182–92, 193 n.14, 194 n.31
"Melanctha" (Stein) 117
Melville, Herman 92
"Memphis, Egypt" (song) 190
Merritt, Matt 160
Messent, Peter 186
metrical patterns 199
Metric Music 95
"Mic-ing the Kit" (poem) 161
Mickiewicz, Adam 199, 200, 203
micropoetry 80
micropolitics 6
Mid-Life Crisis 153
Milczewski-Bruno, Ryszard 200, 203
Miller, Steve 221
"Miller's Cave" (song) 93
"Million Dollar Bash" (song) 39
Milton, John 233
mimetic desire 171, 179
miners' strike 185
Mitchell, Chuck 73
Mitchell, Joni 6, 24–5, 40, 65–7, 70–5, 93
"Mittageisen" (song) 118
Młynarski, Wojciech 199, 200
Moby-Dick (Melville) 233

256   *Index*

Moczulski, Leszek A. 199–203
modernism 125–8, 132
modern jazz 142
Modern Poets, The (Rosenthal) 68
Mojo-Navigator Rock and Roll News 213
Monster Magnet 130
Montgomery, Scott B. 120
"Moonlight" (song) 234
Moore, Carman 216
Morely, Paul 109
Morgan, Monique 92
Morris, Tracie 110, 116, 117
Morrison, Jim 10, 123
Morrison, Toni 232
Morrison, Van 234
Morrissey 6, 155, 159, 162
Moses, Ann 215
"Mothers of the Disappeared"
    (song) 176
Motion Picture Artists Committee 188
"Mów do mnie jeszcze" (song) 205
Mr. Norris Changes Trains
    (Isherwood) 159
"Mr. Tambourine Man" (song) 124
MTV 49
Mugan, Chris 236
Mullen, Larry, Jr. 169
Munch, Edvard 118
Murray, Les 160, 162
musical composition 80, 87, 95, 111,
    114, 116, 121, 122, 126, 130–2,
    144, 160
musical franchise 154, 155
musical poetics 122
Mussolini, Benito 113
"My Last Duchess" (poem) 91, 98–9
"My Life Is Good" (song) 102
"My Old Man" (song) 72, 74
Mystery and Manners: Occasional Prose
    (O'Connor) 173, 177
Mystery Train: Images of Rock 'n' Roll in
    America (Marcus) 215
mythic America 172
"My White Bicycle" (song) 125

Nalepa, Tadeusz 197–9
narcissism 69, 75, 83
Nash, Graham 71, 72

Na szkle malowane (1971) 201
national identity 12, 197, 203–7
National Recording Registry 169
National Union of Mineworkers 185
Nebraska (1982) 173
Nelson, Jeff 50
neoliberalism 186
"Never Been in a Riot" (song) 191
New Deal 187
"New Gen" cohort 152, 153, 156, 162
new journalism 66, 67
Newman, Alfred 94
Newman, Emil 94
Newman, Lionel 94
Newman, Randy 12, 91–102
New Wave 11, 109, 112, 113, 115, 117,
    118
    aesthetics 110
    artists 110
New York 162
New Yorker 216
New York Times 5, 215, 220, 224 n.2,
    232
Nguyen, Mimi Thi 57, 58
Niemen, Czesław 198, 199, 204–6
Niemen Enigmatic (1970) 205
"Niepewność"/"Uncertainty"
    (poem) 199
Nine Modern Poets 15, 162
Nirvana 46, 50, 234
Nobel Committee 160
noise-sound dichotomy 111, 112, 116
Nolan, Tom 221
Nolan, William 189
Noname (Fatimah Warner) 3
nonfiction novel 67
non-violent protest 172
non-Western cultures 131
Nordlund, Marcus 86
Norwid, Kamil 205, 206
Nova Express (Burroughs) 36
Nowak, Tadeusz 200, 203

Oates, Joyce Carol 17
Oates, Stephen B. 172
O'Connor, Flannery 12, 170–80
"Odds and Ends" (song) 39
Odyssey (poem) 139, 149, 233

O'Grady, Pat 7
"Oh! You Pretty Things" (song) 40
Olympia 50
Omi, Michael 97
One Flew Over the Cuckoo's Nest
(Pranksters) 92, 129
O'Neill, Terry 35
"one long crisis" (Reynolds) 184
"One Tree Hill" (song) 176
On the Road (Kerouac) 233
On The Waterfront (1954) 159
Opole Festival (Festival of Polish Song in
Opole, 1969) 198
Oppenheim, David 7
O'Reilly, Kevin 191
organized crime 186
Orwell, George 43, 233
Osiecka, Agnieszka 199, 200
Ostriker, Alicia 54
Oswald, Alice 163
Otiono, Nduka 37
Ouellette, Laurie 49
*Out of the Vinyl Deeps: Ellen Willis on
Rock Music* (Willis) 216
"The Overtones" (poem) 154, 156–7

pacifism 141
PAGART 197
Paige, Jennifer 232
Palmer, G. Molyneaux 142
"Parchman Farm" (song) 93
Paretsky, Sara 187
Paris Review 52
Parks, Van Dyke 9, 95
Parsons, Alan 236
Parton, Dolly 227, 230
Pastels 50
Paterson, Don 152
Pawlik, Adam 201
Pawlikowska-Jasnorzewska, Maria 200
Pawluśkiewicz, Jan Kanty 202
Pearson, Gabriel 86
"Penelope" (Joyce) 144
Penguin Books Australia 157
"Penny Lane" (song) 126
"Pennyroyal Tea" (song) 56
people of color 215, 216
"People's Parties" (song) 75

Perfect 198
Perloff, Marjorie 80, 84
"The Pernicious Rise of Poptimism"
(Austerlitz) 6
Perry, Katie 6
persona poems and songs 91–3, 95, 102
pervasive theory 56
"Peter Gunn" (song) 110, 112
Phelan, James 92
"Philly Soul" (song) 44
Pieśni do słów Tadeusza Nowaka
(1979) 201, 203
Pig City (Stafford) 158
Pink Floyd 121, 125–7, 129, 130, 132,
142
Pinochet, Augusto 156
Piper at the Gates of Dawn, The
(1967) 126–8, 132, 142
Pixar 94
Plain Dealer 213
Plaster Casters 220–3
Plath, Sylvia 65, 68–70, 73, 75, 83, 86,
127
Please Please Me (1963) 4
Pleasure Death (1992) 148
Poe, Edgar Allan 5, 22, 123, 125, 126,
233, 236
poems/poetry
amateur 78–82
confessional 65–70, 72–4, 82–4, 86
contemporary 199
experimental 80
franchise 154
popular 78, 79
studies 80
poetic discourse 79–82
poetic franchise 164
poetic identity 79, 86
poeticity 79, 81
poetic meter 199
poetic music 203
poetry-as-lyrics 196–207
Poetry Ireland 163
Poetry of Pop, The (Bradley) 11, 80
Poetry of Rock, The 10
Poetry Society 152
Poets of Our Times (1968) 162
Poland 196

Polish politics 197–8
polish rock artists 199, 200
Polish United Worker's Party 196
political radicalism 127
"Political Science" (song) 95
politics 184. *See also* Polish politics
Polska Rzeczpospolita Ludowa (PRL/
  Polish People's Republic) 197–204
Polskie Stowarzyszenie Jazzowe 197
Pop, Iggy 91
pop culture 22, 139, 205
pop-feminism 56
Pop Group 46
Pop Inquirer 232
pop music 91, 94, 95, 112, 139, 163, 178,
  216, 229, 231, 234, 237
pop psychedelia 129
pop-rock 92
pop song 99, 120, 143, 149
"Pop Star Poetics" (Browne) 10
poptimism 5, 6
popular culture 22, 137, 196, 197, 206
popular music 1–3, 65, 70, 80, 92, 93,
  101, 110, 118, 137–9, 147, 149,
  155, 157, 159, 161, 164, 172, 179,
  196–201, 204, 207, 215, 228,
  231, 237
popular song 23, 70, 74, 92–6
"Porphyria's Lover" (poem) 91, 93
Portnoy's Complaint (Roth) 66
Portrait of the Artist as a Young Man, A
  (Joyce) 21, 138, 139, 149
postmodernism 52, 56
postmodernity 56, 112
post-punk 11, 152–9, 161–5
Post-Punk Then and Now (Eshun) 153
Post Traumatic Stress Disorder
  (PTSD) 114
"Potato Junkie" (song) 148
Pound, Ezra 43, 55, 68, 69, 140, 233,
  235, 236
Pounds, Wayne 53, 54
Power and the Glory, The (Green) 156
Powers, Ann 216, 217, 219
Pranksters, Merry 129
Pratella, Francesco Balilla 111
precorporation 49
pre-traumatic stress disorder 118

Price, Alan 95
"Pride: In the Name of Love" (song) 172
Procol Harum 221
Program Era, The (McGurl) 81
progressive rock 130, 203, 205
proto-deconstructionism 51
Przerwa-Tetmajer, Kazimierz 205
Przyboś, Jan 203
Przyboś, Julian 200
psychedelia 120–1, 129, 130, 132,
  140, 142
  modernism 125–8
  reading 121–5
psychedelic art 122, 123
psychedelic coding 121, 122, 125,
  126, 130
psychedelic experience 123, 128,
  131, 132
psychedelic hippie movement 204
psychedelic music 121, 128, 132
psychedelic poetics 129
psychedelic pop 132
psychedelic rock 122, 132, 204
psychedelic songs 125
psychological transfer 155, 157
public discourse 51, 57
Punk 213
punk rock 11, 49, 50, 57, 130, 152–9,
  162, 164–5, 184
  community 189
  movement 53, 184
pure sounds 110, 111
Pyle, Derek 138
"Pyschopath" (poem) 99

Queen 217
"Queen Bitch" (song) 39, 40
Queensland University 158
Queens of the Stone Age 130
queer culture 233
"Quicksand" (song) 40

race 14, 96–8, 101
racial equality 187
racial tensions 186
racism 97, 214
Radcliffe and Maconie Show (radio
  show) 155

Radio 6 155
Rae, Casey 36 41
Ragtime (1981) 94
"Rainy Day Women #12 and 35"
    (song) 124
"Raised on Robbery" (song) 74
Raitt, Bonnie 95
Ramones 164
"Randy Newman and the
    Extraordinary Moral Position"
    (Dunne) 91
*Randy Newman Creates Something New
    Under the Sun* (1968) 95
"The Rap Against Rockism" (Sanneh) 5
"Rape Me" (song) 55, 58
Rattle and Hum (1988) 179
Ravishing Beauties 163
Reagan, Ronald 51, 185, 186, 191, 192
real America 172
"Real Emotional Girl" (song) 98
reality genre 57
Real World, The (TV show) 49
"A Reasonable Use of the Unreasonable"
    (O'Connor) 177
"Rebel Rebel" (song) 44, 45
Reckless Daughter (Yaffe) 71
recreational listening 156
Red Harvest (Hammett) 193 n.14
Red Hot Chili Peppers 157
"Rednecks" (song) 96–7, 99
Red Shoes, The (1993) 143
Reich, Wilhelm 233
Reising, Russel 122
"Rejoyce" (song) 140–2
relationship story 67
"Relax" (song) 113
Republika 201
Reputation (2017) 23, 78, 86
revolutionary approach 37
revolutions per minute (RPM) 124
Reynolds, Simon 46, 163, 184
Rhinoceros 221
rhythm-and-blues 95
Richard, Little 215
Rimbaud, Arthur 233
"Rime of the Ancient Mariner"
    (song) 235
riot grrrl 50–3, 55–8

Rip It Up and Start Again
    (Reynolds) 163
Rise and Fall of Ziggy Stardust, The
    (1972) 41
rivalry 171, 179
"River" (song) 71, 72, 74
*Roartorio, an Irish circus on Finnegans
    Wake* (Cage) 143
Robinson, Lisa 213, 214
Rock Against Racism 187
Rock and Roll Hall of Fame 3, 138, 172,
    215
rock canon 213, 214, 216, 223, 229,
    234–8
rock counterculture 40, 41
rock culture 40, 101, 158, 159
Rockfield 164
rockism 5, 7
rock lyrics 10, 37, 159, 200, 207
"Rock Lyrics are Poetry (Maybe)"
    (Christgau) 9
rock music 37–9, 44, 45, 112, 120,
    142, 147, 156, 159, 172, 182,
    187, 198, 200, 206, 207, 223,
    228, 235
    criticism 213–16, 218, 220, 221, 223,
        224, 224 nn.2, 7
    journalism 7, 213, 222, 224 nn.2, 7
    literary structuring 15–26
rock musicians 35, 38, 199
rock 'n' roll 38, 43, 45, 65, 74, 95, 110,
    118, 140, 142, 147, 158, 172, 180,
    190, 197, 199, 214, 215
Rock Scene 213, 214
*Rock She Wrote: Women Write about Rock,
    Pop, and Rap* (McDonnell and
    Powers) 216–17, 219
*Rock Star: The Making of Cultural
    Icons from Elvis to Springsteen*
    (Shumway) 66
Rogers, Kenny 227, 230, 231
Rolling Stone (magazine) 35, 36, 42, 70,
    140, 172, 175, 213–18, 220, 222,
    223, 224 n.2
Rolling Stones (band) 128, 197, 237
Romanticism 204–6
Romeo Void 117
Romuald & Roman 200, 201

Ronstadt, Linda 99
Roosevelt, Franklin 187
Rose, Biff 40
Rosenthal, M. L. 65, 68, 69, 83, 86
Roth, Phillip 66, 67
Rotten, Johnny 91
Rough and Rowdy Ways (2020) 25, 234
Roxette 232
Royle, Nicholas 120, 124, 132
Rules of Art (Bourdieu) 229
Rundgren, Todd 217
rural folk 198
Russell, Bob 93
Russian Futurism and Futurists 110, 113
Russolo, Luigi 109–12, 116, 118

"Sad Eyed Lady of the Lowlands"
    (song) 39
Sadurski, Wiesław 204
Sagan, Carl 7
Sail Away (album, 1972) 95, 96
"Sail Away" (song) 96, 97, 99, 100
Saint-Amour, Paul 118
Saint Vitus 131
"The Same Situation" (song) 75
sampling 112, 113
Samuels, Lisa 114
Sandburg, Carl 3
Sander, Ellen 214, 220–3, 224 n.7
San Francisco Digger 43
Sanneh, Kelefa 5, 6
satire 100, 102
Saturday Review 220
Saucerful of Secrets, A (1968) 142
Sayers, Dorothy L. 186
SBB 199, 200, 204
scapegoating 171, 174, 179
Scaremongers 153, 154
Scargill, Arthur 185
Schulten, Katherine 232
Schwitters, Kurt 110, 115, 116, 118
Schwitters school of Dada 110
Scott, Jane 213
Scott, Michael 12
Scream, The (Munch) 118
Sebring, Steven 137
second-wave feminism 51, 69, 75
"See Emily Play" (song) 126

Seeing Stars (2010) 154, 156
Segal, George 67
self-analysis 71, 72, 74
Self and Shadow Self model 170, 171,
    178–9
self and society 170
self-authorization 153, 155, 156, 162
self-feminizing language 218
self-identification 139
self-promotion 68
self-reflexivity 56
sensory synaesthesia 122
Sensual World, The (album, 1989) 143
"The Sensual World" (song) 143–5
Sewen, Marek 201
sexism 214
Sex Pistols 192, 234
Sexton, Anne 68–70, 73, 75, 83, 84
Sexton, Stephen 165
SGM 145, 146, 148
Sgt. Pepper's Lonely Hearts Club Band
    (1967) 4, 95
"A Shade of Silence" (song) 204
Shakespeare, William 18–19, 140
Shakur, Tupac 3, 16
Shangri-La 215
"Shapes of Things" (song) 125
Shepherd, Sam 180
Sherlock Holmes stories 186
Sherman, Allan 139, 147
Sherwin, Miranda 83, 84
"Short People" (song) 99
Showalter, Elaine 69
Shumway, David 12
Siekiera 201
sign-posting 162, 236
Signs 69
Simon, Carly 65
Simon, Paul 9, 10, 26
"Simon Smith and the Amazing Dancing
    Bear" (song) 95
Sinatra, Frank 95
Siouxsie and the Banshees 118
Sipowicz, Kamil 204
Situationists 110, 112, 116
Skaldowie 200–2
Skids 155, 163, 164
Sklar, Sherry 222

Skrzek, Józef   199, 204
slave trade   96
Sleep   121, 130–2
Sleep's Holy Mountain (1992)   131
Sleepytime Gorilla Museum   139, 142–6
Slevin, Patrick   145, 146
Śliwiak, Tadeusz   200, 203
Słonimski, Antoni   199
Slouching Toward Bethlehem (Didion)   67
Smith, Judith   213
Smith, Patti   137, 233, 234
Smiths   161, 162
Smooth Radio   230
Snodgrass, W. D.   68
social media   49
social pathology   92, 96–101
Sol   3
soliloquy   143, 144
solipsism   154, 157
Sommerville, Ian   42
"Song for Bob Dylan" (song)   37, 40
song production   229–31
Songs of Experience (album, 2017)   172
Songs of Experience (book, Blake)   172
Songs of Innocence (2014)   172, 179
Songs of Leonard Cohen (1967)   10
songwriting process   37, 38, 40, 41,
      199, 228
sonic frequencies   111
sonic manipulation   114
sonic transliteration   116
soul music   45
sound engineers   112, 113
sound machines   110
Southern, Terry   5
Soviet Union   197
Spector, Phil   112
speech sounds   116
Spence-Ash, Laura   173
Spencer-Regan, Eleanor   83
Spiers, Emily   56, 57
Spin   223
spontaneity   53, 57
Springsteen, Bruce   17, 102, 171–3
Srigley, Susan   171
Stachura, Edward   200
Stand In The Trench Achilles!
      (Vandiver)   155

Star   213
stardom   4, 78, 102, 180, 206, 217
Starr, Ringo   95
Stavers, Gloria   215
Stein, Gertrude   117
Stevens, Cat   232
Stevenson, Robert Louis   80
Stewart, Mark   45, 46
Stewart, Rod   217
Stoll, Werner   125
Stoller, Mike   114
stoner rock   12, 129–32
Stones   221
"Strawberry Fields Forever" (song)   126
"Strings in the Earth and Air"
      (song)   142, 143
"Stuck Inside of Mobile" (Dylan)   39
studio recording   38, 242
Styrene, Poly   159
"Subterranean Homesick Blues"
      (song)   154
"Sunday Bloody Sunday" (song)   176
"Sunny Afternoon" (song)   93
Surrealism   110, 118
Surrealistic Pillow (1967)   140
"Suzanne" (song)   98
Sweet Baby James (1970)   70
"Sweet Thing-Reprise" (song)   44, 45
Swift, Taylor   23–6, 78, 79, 88, 232
      appraisals   79–82
      as confessionalist   82–7
Swinging London   126, 128
synesthetic stylistics   124
synthesizer   110, 112
Szalona lokomotywa (1977)   201, 203
Szymborska, Wisława   200

Tales of Mystery and Imagination
      (Poe)   236
Talking Heads   110, 115, 117, 217
tape loops   44
Tapestry (1971)   40
tastes   13, 36, 84, 145, 197, 207, 228, 231
Taylor, James   65, 70
Teardrop Explodes   163
technological processes   114
techno-martial poetics   114
Teen   215

262 *Index*

Television 117
televisual culture 49
televisual imaginations 52–3
"Tell Her About It" (song) 85
Terada, Rei 80
tertiary education 156
textual assemblage 55
Thatcher, Margaret 182, 184–6,
191, 192
"The Gnome" (song) 126
Thema (*Omaggio a Joyce*, 1958) 143
therapeutic prose 69
Therapy? 139, 148
Third Mind, The (Burroughs) 52
Thomas, Dylan 4, 5, 233
Thomas, Edward 163
Thomas, Peter 114, 115
Thompson, Hunter 66, 67
Three Dog Night 95
Three Lives (Stein) 117
Throbbing Gristle 44
Tibetan Book of the Dead 123
Tiger Beat 215
Times 215
Timms, Sally 188
"tin pan alley" approach 230
Tolkien, J. R. R. 126
Tomorrow 125
"Tomorrow Never Knows" (song) 122
To pejzaż mojej ziemi-Beat oratorio
(1973) 201
Toth, Josh 37
"To The Bridge" (poem) 154
Townshend, Pete 153
Toy Story (1995) 91, 94
trade unions 185
Traffic 217, 221
transmedia phenomenon 196, 200,
207
Transparent Anatomical Mannikin 55
Travolta, John 235
Triad 218
"Triad" (song) 93
Triffids 157, 159
Trips: Rock Life in the Sixties
(Sander) 220, 222
Trouble in Paradise (1983) 95
"The Troubles" (song) 179

Trouser Press 213
TSA 198
Turner, Lonnie 221
Turner, Steve 172, 173, 176, 177
Tuwim, Julian 199, 200, 203
Tyler, Steven 217
Tzara, Tristan 37, 52

U2 12, 169–75, 179, 180, 217, 232
U2 By U2 (Bone, The Edge, Clayton and
Mullen, Jr.) 172, 176, 178
*U2 Rattle & Hum: The Official Book of the
U2 Movie* (Turner) 173
UCLA 95
ULSSS, The (2018) 138
"Ultraviolet" (song) 178
Ulysses (Joyce) 11, 21, 138–41, 143–5,
147–9
"Ulysses" (Tennyson) 161
Ulysses and Us (Kiberd) 139
Uncle Acid 130
Understanding Media (McLuhan) 42
Undertones 157
Unforgettable Fire (1984), *The* 170, 172
United Kingdom. *See* Britain
United States. *See* America
Universal 155
Universal Amphitheater 41
University of Leeds 184, 186
University of Queensland 157
urban folk culture 197
urbanization 186
Ursonate (Schwitters) 116
USA Today 213
US Library of Congress 169

Vandiver, Elizabeth 155, 156
Vanity Fair 216
Variete 201
Vaselines 50
veering effect 39, 120, 123, 124, 131
Velvet Underground 39, 233, 234
verbal artifice 94
Verlaine, Paul 233
Verne, Jules 126
Vietnam Requiem (1982) 114
Vietnam War 114, 141, 198
Vig, Butch 112

Index

Village Voice 215, 216
violence 171, 174–80, 185
Virgin 184
visual art 52, 53, 130, 163
visual culture 42
vocal performance 53, 230
Vogue 220
Vogue UK 84

Walczak, Grzegorz 200
Wald, Elijah 4
Waldrep, Shelton 43, 44
Wall of Sound 112
Wall Street Journal, The 137
Walmart 55
Warde, Alan 12
Waronker, Lenny 94
"The Waste Land" (poem) 22, 26, 52, 236
"The Watchmaker of the Light" (song) 204
Watkins, Evan 85
"Waywords and Meansigns" 138
"We Are the Dead" (song) 44, 233
Webb, Russell 164
"Welcome to the Pleasuredome" (song) 113
Weller, Paul 155
Wells, H. G. 5
Wenner, Jann 216
We're Here to the End (2010s) 148
Western counterculture 41, 42
"We Wear the Mask" (poem) 98
Wham! 117
Wheeler, Brian 232
When Harry Met Sally (1989) 67
"When the Words that once Liberated You" (song) 56
White, Clarence 95
White, Mark 184, 186, 187
White Album, The (Didion) 67
Whitely, Sheila 121
"White Rabbit" (song) 140, 141
"White Riot" (song) 191
white rock artists 233
white supremacy 97
"Why She Disappeared" (song) 78, 82, 86–7

Wierzyński, Kazimierz 199
Wild Boys, The (Burroughs) 43, 44
Wilde, Oscar 5
William Burroughs and the Cult of Rock 'n' Roll (Rae) 36
Williams, Paul 214, 215
Williams, Tennessee 172
Williams, William Carlos 127
Williamson, Alan 83
Willis, Ellen 74, 216, 224 n.7
"Willy" (song) 71
Wilson, Brian 9, 95
Wilson, Ric 3
Wilson, Steven 122
Winant, Howard 97
Wind in the Willows (Grahame) 126
Winkler, Kazimierz 199, 200
Winkler, Peter 100
Winwood, Stevie 219
Wise Blood (O'Connor) 175, 178
Witkiewicz, Stanisław Ignacy 200, 203
W malinowym chruśniaku (1984) 203
Wołek, Jan 199
Wolfe, Tom 66, 67
Wolman, Baron 222
women
  of color 214
  in pop 220
  rock writers 215
Wood, Jessica L. 53, 54, 56, 57
"Woodstock" (song) 71
Woolf, Virginia 69, 127
Wordsworth, William 152
World War I 156
World War II 114, 197
Woźniak, Tadeusz 199, 200, 204
Wright, Benjamin 233
Wright, David 228
"The Write to Rock: Racial Mythologies, Feminist Theory, and the Pleasures of Rock Music Criticism" (Brooks) 216
"Wspomnienie" (song) 199
"Wuthering Heights" (song) 143, 145
Wyspiański, Stanisław 203

Yaffe, David 71, 73
Yardbirds 122, 125

Index

Yeats, W. B. 68, 69, 83, 122
"Yellow Submarine" (song) 36
Yentob, Alan 41
"You Can Leave Your Hat On" (song) 95, 99, 101
Young Americans (1975) 45
"A Young Woman, A Tree" (Ostriker) 54
"You're Gonna Make Me Lonesome When You Go" (song) 233
youth culture 207
youth music 198
"You Turn Me On I'm a Radio" (song) 74
Yu, Timothy 81
Yusuf, Naimo 3

Zagrajcie nam dzisiaj wszystkie srebrne dzwony (1975) 201
"Zang Tumb Tumb" (poem) 113, 116
Zang Tumb Tumb (ZTT) records 109, 110, 112, 113, 117
Zappa, Frank 122
Zaucha, Andrzej 202
Żeleński, Tadeusz 199
Zephaniah, Benjamin 162
Zieliński, Andrzej 199, 201, 204
Zieliński, Jacek 202
Zimmerman, Nadya 141
Zoom! (1989) 154, 156
Zumoff, J. A. 187
Zurich Dada 110, 118
Zych, Jan 200, 203

Printed in the USA
CPSIA information can be obtained
at www.ICGtesting.com
LVHW022254120424
777218LV00001B/153